Using Land
to Save Energy

Using Land to Save Energy

Corbin Crews Harwood

Environmental Law Institute State and Local Energy
Conservation Project

Ballinger Publishing Company • Cambridge, Massachusetts
A Subsidiary of J.B. Lippincott Company

This book is printed on recycled paper.

"This book was prepared with the support of NSF Grant APR7504814. However, any opinions, findings, conclusions, or recommendations herein are those of the author and do not necessarily reflect the views of NSF."

International Standard Book Number: 0-88410-061-8

Library of Congress Catalog Card Number: 77-739

Printed in the United States of America

Library of Congress Cataloging in Publication Data

Harwood, Corbin Crews.
   Environmental Law Institute state and local energy conservation project.

   1. Land use—Planning—United States.   2. Energy conservation—United States.   I. Title.   II. Title: Using land to save energy.
HD205 1977.H37   333.7'0973   77-739
ISBN 0-88410-061-8

Dedication

To: John

Contents

List of Figures and Tables

Preface

Energy conservation has suddenly become fashionable.
Where once it was the province of the environmentalist,
the enthusiast, or the follower of apparently lost causes, it
now commands the attention of Congress, the president, and ordinary
citizens. Much of the action that has been taken in the past months
in the name of energy conservation has actually been energy curtail-
ment. True conservation actions—better insulation, smaller cars, more
efficient industries—will be slower in coming.

Beyond the technological solutions to using less energy to live
comfortably and happily lie larger questions about the way we design
our communities for efficiency. Intuitively, we all know that a link
exists between energy demand and the layout of housing, employment, and transportation systems. Recently, efforts to quantify that
relationship have verified our intuitive feelings. The present volume
by Corbin Crews Harwood, research attorney on the staff of the
Environmental Law Institute, reviews the findings of those quantita-
tive studies and, based on their results, identifies energy-saving land
development options available to state and local governments.

The book focuses on energy-efficient design strategies ("Is it better to build single family or multifamily housing?") and location
strategies ("Where should the new municipal auditorium be built?").
The emphasis here—and in other books in this series—is on implementation strategies: zoning, subdivision, capital facility expansion
policies, and other land management tools. The reader of this book
will find no simple solutions to energy waste, but rather a series of

carefully crafted tools for carrying us toward communities designed for energy efficiency.

The book is a part of a larger series, the Environmental Law Institute State and Local Energy Conservation Project, that examines legal and administrative strategies that can be used by states and localities to promote energy conservation. Funded by a grant from the National Science Foundation, the series offers a range of approaches to eliminate energy waste in homes, industries, farms, governments, and commercial establishments. The recommendations are based on an examination of existing laws and regulations that affect energy demand and experience with conservation programs that have already been adopted. Although the core of the analysis is legal, the series takes into account the views of a number of other disciplines relevant to energy conservation and notes the social need for some energy-intensive activities, despite the overall objective of fuel conservation.

Energy shortfalls will be with us for a long time. The legal and administrative arrangements put into effect now will have a substantial influence on energy consumption well into the next decades. The crisis that is now perceived to exist must be used to develop a sound approach to energy use. This series offers a starting point for development of those policies.

Grant P. Thompson
Institute Fellow
Principal Investigator
Energy Conservation Project

Acknowledgments

It is no small irony that my name alone appears on the cover of this book, for it was written not only by me, but by an enormous team of willing and unwilling but generous recruits. It would require another book the size of this one simply to recount the tremendous efforts of my co-authors, their patience, their skills and insights. And such a book would pose the most difficult of organization problems, for there are too many logical places to start in thanking everyone:

Professor Norman Williams, Jr., Edward J. Sullivan, Daniel W. O'Connell, Dale L. Keyes, Kim Gillan, and Randall W. Scott, whose analysis and criticisms made the good parts of the book possible;

Mark Hennigh, Jocelyn Karp, and Christine Lipaj, whose research assistance deserves credit for the substance of the book;

Barbara Shaw and Pat Sagurton, assisted by Janet Coffin, Stephanie Nagata, Tina Luebke, Anne Lucas Falk, Karla Heimann, Pat Hayden, and Bernadette Nowicki, whose typing, patience, typing, and oh thank you for your patience and de facto editing, put me, the book, and our collective lives through so many drafts;

Gail Hayes, Juliet Pierson, and Kathy Courrier, who transformed my thoughts into intelligible prose and resisted the impulse to question my literacy;

and Grant Thompson, director of the Energy Conservation Project, who buoyed my spirits when they were down.

Part I

An Overview

Chapter 1

Land Use—Another Tool
for Energy Conservation

Although the winter of 1973 was comparatively mild, the oil embargo forced Americans to face cold reality. Realizing that the years of feasting upon cheap energy were over, citizens across the country rallied to slogans of energy conservation. They turned down thermostats, turned off lights, replaced stop signs with yield signs, and observed lower speed limits. During the "crisis," belt tightening was accompanied by only rare complaints, most often heard in patience-wearing gas lines. But as the Arab oil embargo ended and the "crisis" receded, most Americans returned to their energy-wasteful habits. In spite of continued warnings that an energy shortage remains one of our most pressing problems, consumer demand for energy continues to rise.

Nevertheless, efforts to make this country "energy independent" have gained momentum and, along with concern for developing energy sources, there has been a growing recognition that efforts to supply energy must be supplemented by efforts to conserve it. Although the federal government has partly led the way, state and local governments have also committed themselves to energy conservation. Promises by governors, mayors, and county officials to save energy have been backed up by tangible conservation programs. Virtually every state has created a state energy office [1]; state and local governments have introduced and adopted thousands of energy conservation proposals; and they have initiated innumerable conservation research, education, and assistance programs.

Several explanations account for the keen state and local interest in energy conservation. The first stems from the responsibility of government to provide for the welfare of its citizens. Although an energy shortage may be a national and international problem, its impact is nevertheless felt and observed at the state and local levels. Some states have seen their industries, jolted by the energy crisis, pack their bags and move to "sunbelt" states; longer unemployment lines and grumbling by constitutuents about frequent utility rate increases remind others of the energy shortage. State and local governments have recognized that through energy conservation programs, they can help combat citizen hardships caused by the energy shortage. They are well-equipped to handle the job, for their direct contact with citizens often makes them better able than the large federal bureaucracy to make rapid and refined assessments of politically acceptable ways to shape energy conservation programs with large payoffs.

But the motivation for state and local initiation of conservation efforts is not simply one of fulfilling governmental obligations; numerous benefits accrue directly to those governments that push for conservation.

The 1973 energy crisis put an enormous strain on local resources, as communities unprepared for sudden, dramatic shifts in consumer needs found their buses overloaded, their police and fire services overtaxed, their public employees demanding pay increases to cover higher commuting costs, and their officials overworked as they strained to alleviate the problems arising from the oil embargo. By enacting conservation measures, state and local governments hope to avoid the reoccurrence of sudden inflationary burdens on municipal, county, and state services should there be another oil cut-off. In any event, they recognize that conservation programs undertaken now can prepare consumers for the changes that fuel shortages and the inevitable increases in energy prices will prompt, whether or not there is another embargo.

The federal government has already determined that energy conservation must be pursued and has authorized appropriation of $255 million as an incentive to state governments to implement conservation programs [2]. As long as that money is available and can be used to serve their constituents, state governments (and localities working through the states) would be foolish should they fail to take advantage of the federal largesse: in addition to saving energy, programs created with federal funds will help preserve state and local autonomy. Unless state and local governments voluntarily buckle down and use federal funds to devise energy conservation programs that reflect their own preferences, they may be inviting future federal intervention and control of yet another matter with significant state and local impacts.

PURPOSE AND SCOPE OF BOOK

Because transportation uses 25 percent of the nation's energy, while space heating and cooling accounts for an additional 20 percent, most energy conservation work by governments at all levels has focused on short term methods to reduce the energy requirements of vehicles and buildings. Thus consumers have been urged to buy smaller cars that require less gas per mile, to use public transportation, to buy houses with proper insulation, and to install storm windows. These strategies promote energy efficiency in the short run and usually involve only minor personal sacrifices.

This book looks at another energy conservation strategy—alteration of land development patterns—and attempts to identify, insofar as possible, energy-efficient land development patterns that our land use policies should promote. Studies show that by modifying the way we use land, we can not only reduce the claims of transportation and of space heating and cooling on our energy supply, but also cut back the amount of energy used to install and to maintain public and private facilities. Unlike buying smaller cars, however, influencing land development patterns to save energy is a strategy that will bear fruit only over the long run. But the potential savings associated with careful land development are so great that state and local governments serious about energy conservation cannot afford to ignore land use strategies. This book is designed to help governments review existing land use options by suggesting modifications in state and local regulations, spending, and taxing policies to promote energy-efficient land use. The goal is to stimulate everyone—from consumers, developers, builders, and lending institutions to state and local politicians and officials, planning departments, zoning commissions, and transportation and environmental experts—to consider the energy impacts of their actions.

CONTENTS OF THE BOOK

Chapter 2 examines reasons for using land use policies as energy conservation tools and scans land use policies that can help reduce energy demand. Chapter 3 calls for state and local comprehensive planning that uses energy conservation as a touchstone. Part II covers the conservation strategies in more detail. Chapter 4 reviews relatively easy to implement strategies for conserving energy through site-specific development designs. It assesses strategies for making the density, uses, layout, orientation, and landscaping of new developments energy-efficient. Miscellaneous design strategies, use of energy efficiency standards in reviewing development permit applications, and zoning for planned unit developments are also covered in Chapter 4. Chapter 5 tackles the somewhat harder question of how to attract developers and settlers to energy-efficient locations. Capital facilities programming, open space zoning, land acquisition programs, and the transfer of development rights are all examined. Chapter 6 looks at energy impact statements as a device for assessing the desirability of proposed developments.

Although Part II discusses briefly the legal issues raised by each strategy, Appendix I provides further information on general legal issues that states and localities may enounter in adopting and implementing the strategies recommended in this book. The book concludes with an examination of the importance of citizen participation and government leadership in devising land use policies that contribute to energy conservation.

LIMITS TO STRATEGIES

This book does not advocate radical changes in lifestyles, even though such changes would be necessary if energy conservation were our only goal. It also attempts to weed out "pie in the sky" approaches that disregard the limited financial or technical abilities of state and local governments. Most energy-conserving land use strategies discussed here have been considered or tried by various states and localities, although often for purposes other than energy conservation.

Practicality justifies this rather moderate approach. Though land use decisions directly affect our energy demands, the data on how much energy can be saved by the application of land planning techniques is incomplete. Hence, to recommend sweeping land use and lifestyle changes before more conclusive evidence is available, would be foolish. Even if conclusive evidence were available, energy considerations alone do not, and should not, govern land use decisions; other compelling social, environmental, and economic factors also must be weighed. Nevertheless, energy conservation through proper land use should become a routine concern of public officials and of the citizens they serve, so that it may be factored into the decision-making process. For this approach to work, citizens must understand the energy costs of land use habits.

This book emphasizes measures to save energy in new developments, rather than in existing urban centers. The two are closely tied, however, and failure to scrutinize energy conservation in developed urban areas simply reflects the more narrow focus of this book, not the relative importance of energy-efficient land use in developing and developed areas. Cities must be rehabilitated and made attractive for living as well as for working if energy conservation is to succeed. Urban homesteading [3], tax increment financing [4], curbing redlining [5], and other measures to stimulate rehabilitation and adaptive reuse of existing structures should be explored. Moreover, these fiscal land-planning measures must be supplemented by programs that treat the social ills of urban areas, ills that the energy crisis may provide a fresh impetus for tackling.

Other land use considerations are also beyond the book's present scope. For instance, maximizing energy-efficient land development might require channeling population movements within and among the states. One study found that individuals in cities over one million have an average commute to work of 14.1 miles, compared to 7.8 miles in cities under 100,000 [6]. These statistics suggest that once an urban area has reached its optimal size for energy efficiency, states should consider constructing government buildings, roads, and other growth-inducing facilities in designated growth centers outside metropolitan areas. The federal government has taken this approach, although not for purposes of energy conservation, by relocating entire agencies outside the District of Columbia. Unless a new growth center can satisfy the employment, recreational, shopping, and other requirements of the people who live there, however, its residents may use more energy per capita than those of an oversized city, as long commutes will be made to larger urban areas for entertainment, supplies, services, and jobs. However, much additional scholarly research must be done before populations can be shunted about solely for the sake of energy conservation.

Another subject only touched upon in this book is the impact of new technology on land use and energy demand. Solar, wind, total energy [7], and telecommunication systems may significantly alter patterns of land development and may even make some strategies discussed later in this book inappropriate or obsolete. But many years will intervene before these technologies are refined enough to permit widespread adoption. Meanwhile, hundreds of thousands of acres will be permanently lost to energy-wasteful subdivisions and developments unless efforts begin immediately to save energy through land development practices that are efficient in light of present technology.

The strategies recommended in this book are far from comprehensive. Neither are they equally effective, simple to use, or economically, socially, and environmentally desirable. They are merely suggestions; to satisfy local needs and laws, modifications and different combinations of strategies will be necessary. Since the companion books in this series cover building design and transportation strategies that are inextricably entwined with land use strategies [8], the reader should consult all three books to get a broader and deeper view of the subject.

NOTES TO CHAPTER 1

1. The Council of State Governments, *State Growth Management*, prepared for the Office of Community Planning and Development, United States Department of Housing and Urban Development (Washington, D.C.: U.S. Government Printing Office, May 1976), pp. 17—19.

2. This money has been authorized under the Energy Policy and Conservation Act (EPCA) §§361—66, Pub. L. No. 94—163, 42 U.S.C. §§6321—26 (Dec. 22, 1975); and the Energy Conservation and Production Act (ECPA) §§431—32, Pub. L. No. 94—385, 42 U.S.C. §§6326—27 (August 14, 1976). EPCA authorizes appropriation of $50 million per year for fiscal years 1976—1978 to be used by states to produce state energy conservation plans. ECPA authorizes additional appropriations of $25 million in fiscal year 1977 and $40 million each in fiscal years 1978—1979 for supplemental state energy conservation plans. In fact, only $5 million was appropriated for FY 1976 under EPCA; $25 million was appropriated for FY 1977.

3. "Urban homesteading" is a process whereby a local government acquires abandoned property and transfers such property through sale or otherwise to individuals who agree to rehabilitate and occupy the property.

4. "Tax increment financing," a technique to stimulate redevelopment of urban areas, freezes the general revenue property taxes in the redevelopment district at their existing level at the time tax increment financing is adopted. Although taxes will increase as a result of future increases in assessed valuation, taxes above the frozen level are reinvested in the redevelopment district to rehabilitate that district. An example of a tax increment financing provision may be found in Or. Rev. Stat. §§457.410—457.450 (1975).

5. "Redlining" is the process characterized by the failure of financial institutions to make mortgage loans in certain geographically defined "high risk" areas—those areas associated with high unemployment and crime rates and with a history of property damage and decay.

6. Thomas Muller, "The Cost of Public Service Provision," Land Use Center Working Paper No. 9—5031—10 (draft), (Washington, D.C.: The Urban Institute, June 1975, revised August 1975), pp. 11—12, citing U.S. Department of Transportation National Highway Needs Report, Part II (Washington, D.C.: U.S. Government Printing Office, April 1972).

7. A "total energy system" typically collects waste heat cast off in the generation of electricity and uses it to heat or cool buildings within the community.

8. Grant P. Thompson, *Building to Save Energy: Legal and Regulatory Approaches* (Cambridge, Massachusetts: Ballinger Publishing Co., 1977); Durwood J. Zaelke, *Saving Energy in Urban Transportation* (Cambridge, Massachusetts: Ballinger Publishing Co., 1977). Thompson's book concentrates on improving thermal efficiency of the building envelope, reducing lighting demands, lowering air infiltration, improving the efficiency of building equipment, reducing energy demands through proper building operation and maintenance, and using design features, shading, and orientation to cut energy costs. Zaelke's book examines energy-efficient alternatives to the automobile and strategies for discouraging use of the automobile.

Chapter 2

Promises and Problems
of Regulating Land Use
to Save Energy

Research on the energy demands of alternative land use patterns has proliferated over the past two years. Although such studies merely whet our appetites for more empirical data, researchers agree that land development patterns clearly affect the amount of energy we consume, particularly for transportation and for space heating and cooling [1].

What remains fuzzy is the extent to which changes in land use can reduce our general level of energy consumption. One early, highly optimistic study, *The Costs of Sprawl* [2], found that "high-density planned" communities use 44 percent less energy than unplanned sprawling communities [3]. Later, a similar study estimated additional energy demands attributed to new growth between 1976 and 1992 in the Washington, D.C., metropolitan area. It concluded that one-half the additional transportation energy and one-quarter the space heating and cooling energy could be saved by avoiding low density, noncontiguous development [4]. Other studies, some simulated and some based on empirical data, have looked at the impacts of land use and building design in Wisconsin and in the New York, Trenton, and Baltimore-Washington metropolitan areas [5]. All have reported that large-scale energy savings would flow from changes in land development patterns.

These studies and their projections for energy savings have not, however, been wholeheartedly endorsed. Critics charge that several studies postulate unrealistic development scenarios and base their conclusions on highly questionable assumptions backed by little empirical data [6]. Yet even the Urban Institute, which has been one of the severest critics of the earlier studies, agrees that land development patterns significantly affect energy demands. The institute estimates that the thermal efficiency of low-rise and small high-rise multifamily units (up to about ten stories in height) is 30 percent greater on a square foot basis than in single family detached units [7]; and it projects that "acceptable levels" of land use control can produce a 15 percent savings in transportation energy demands by 1985 [8].

Because experts disagree on the overall amount of energy that can be saved by comprehensively altering land development patterns, it should come as no surprise that they also dispute the amount of savings that can be attributed to the adoption of strategies aimed at modifying energy-wasteful land use habits. Yet, in spite of their divergent findings, the studies do identify energy-conserving goals that land use decisions can promote and they do give us a rough idea of the savings that are possible if each goal is achieved [9].

CHANGES IN LAND DEVELOPMENT PATTERNS CAN SAVE ENERGY

Transportation Goals and Strategies

Land use policies can cut transportation energy demands in four primary ways. We must pry people out of their inefficient automobiles and cajole them into more efficient modes of transportation like buses, subways, or bicycles. We must increase passenger loads in vehicles that currently operate at less than full capacity. We must reduce the length of necessary trips. And we must reduce the number of unnecessary trips.

Our reliance on private automobiles is startlingly complete. A survey conducted in 1969–1970 found that only 4 percent of all trips by people five years old and over involved the use of public transportation [10]. Automobile trips from home to work accounted for 36 percent of all trips, and for 42 percent of all vehicle miles traveled [11]. Yet only 10.2 percent of home-to-work miles traveled were logged by public transportation [12], and, even more telling, almost three out of four automobiles used for work trips carried only the driver [13].

Cars with cold engines operate less efficiently than cars that have been warmed up. Thus it takes more gas per mile to go short distances than to make long trips. Still, the average length of over three-fifths of our auto trips is five miles or less [14]. The use of cars with cold engines plus the frequent starts and stops involved in a two mile trip within an urban area results in consumption of 80 percent more fuel than for a trip of comparable length between cities [15]. This is not to suggest that we should lengthen the distances we drive, but rather that we should look for more efficient transportation modes when making short urban trips. Consummately inefficient, urban driving consumes 63 percent of all the fuel used by automobiles, yet accounts for only 55 percent of vehicle miles traveled [16].

Unlike automobiles, public transportation offers an energy-efficient means of getting around. The most conservative estimates show that buses are at least twice as energy-efficient as cars, while trolleys and subways are three times as efficient [17]. Bus efficiency during traffic's peak periods ranges even higher. The American Public Transit Association found that buses with seventy-five passengers get 307 passenger-miles per gallon of fuel while the average commuter automobile, assuming a passenger load of 1.4, gets only nineteen passenger-miles per gallon [18]. Others estimate that using fully loaded city buses is ten times as efficient as using cars of average weight that carry 1.4 passengers [19]. Of course, walking or using bicycles instead of motorized transportation is ideal from a conservationist's viewpoint, but even carpooling that raises commuter occupancy from 1.2 to 1.6 passengers per car would save 440,000 barrels of oil a day by 1980 [20].

Using Sioux Falls, South Dakota, as a model, one study concludes that by increasing the density of development, which brings homes and jobs closer together and thus permits use of efficient public transportation systems, a city would need one-tenth the transportation energy required by more dispersed developments [21]. Other studies have helped strengthen the contention that considerable transportation savings can be achieved by locating employment closer to residential areas. For example, one that assumed that residential development would be scattered, found that transportation energy savings would result when two-thirds of the total industrial employment of a hypothetical metropolitan area was dispersed within a seven mile radius of the area's center. Such communities would be from 10 to 20 percent more energy-efficient than those in which 90 percent of the employment was concentrated within a one mile radius of the center (again, assuming a dispersed residential pattern) [22]. Another study that arranged a few large employment centers in clusters throughout a simulated metropolitan area and created low density residential villages around the centers concluded that transportation energy savings of 20 and 35 percent over the most energy-intensive development pattern would be possible by the years 1985 and 2000, respectively. Twenty-five and 30 percent savings by 1985 and 2000, respectively, were also deemed possible with high density residential patterns and scattered employment opportunities [23]. Indeed, one research team concludes that even though concentrating jobs in the central business district can save significant amounts of energy, almost as much energy can probably be saved by dispersing employment opportunities throughout regions with moderately high density residential development [24].

As these studies imply, the land use policies best able to reduce transportation energy demand have several features: they would promote moderately high density, contiguous development, would mix residential and employment opportunities, and would be served by adequate public transportation lines. When moderately high density residential growth cannot be concentrated near the urban center, employment opportunities would be distributed throughout whole regions rather than being concentrated in one central business district. Although most studies dwell on the energy costs of work-related trips, land development strategies that distribute shopping, entertainment, recreational, medical, educational, religious, and civic facilities within residential areas also quite clearly would promote energy efficiency by reducing trip lengths. Yet, even when traffic-generating facilities and jobs are dispersed throughout a region, it may be desirable to create small clusters of them at many locations. Thus people could accomplish in one trip the errands that might otherwise take several in unplanned development. These clusters, as well as high density residential development, should facilitate design and use of public transportation systems that can give individuals quick and easy access to job, shopping, and other destinations. One exception to this rule is that, when possible, facilities serving small communities, such as a convenience store or dry cleaning outlet, should be dispersed at a neighborhood level so that people may walk to those facilities, thereby achieving additional energy savings.

Whether or not trip origins and destinations are evenly distributed throughout a region, compact (or moderately high density), contiguous development clustered around transit stations remains essential to transportation energy savings. And when concentric growth is not possible, linear growth along transportation corridors or polynucleated development consisting of several outlying high density clusters connected to urban centers by adequate public transportation lines can also be more energy-efficient than unplanned, low-density, non-contiguous growth [25].

Strategies reviewed in this book that are relatively easy to implement and that make large transportation energy savings possible include

- Zoning for higher density development, especially in areas close to existing or proposed transportation lines and activity centers (pp. 69−76)
  - zoning for more multifamily development
  - reducing lot requirements
  - reducing building height restrictions
  - increasing building floor-to-area ratios
  - allowing conversion of single family homes into multifamily homes
- Providing adequate sewer, water, and utility lines and transportation networks to accommodate increased density in energy-efficient locations (pp. 136−138)
- Zoning for mixed used of land (pp. 76−85)
  - mixing buildings that have different uses
  - mixing uses within buildings
  - permitting occupations in homes
  - zoning for planned unit developments with a mixture of uses
- Locating those public facilities that generate traffic in clusters near high density areas and along transportation lines (pp. 136−138).

Strategies aimed at preventing noncontiguous growth may be more difficult to implement than those just mentioned, but they can nevertheless offer large transportation energy savings. Those strategies include

- Clustering growth-inducing capital facilities near existing activity centers rather than on the urban fringe (pp. 136−154)
- Extending public services and facilities (roads and water, sewer, and utility lines) into areas on the urban fringe only when previously serviced land has been developed (pp. 136−154)
- Adopting zoning ordinances that condition development approval on the availability of adequate public facilities (pp. 136−154)
- Preventing premature annexation (pp. 143−145)
- Using open space zoning to prevent development on the urban fringe and to guide new development into areas contiguous to existing development (pp. 154−164).

Two additional strategies that may offer significant transportation energy savings by discouraging noncontiguous development are (1) land banking of fringe land subject to premature growth pressures (pp. 164−172), and (2) transfer of development rights (pp. 172−180). Of increasing interest as general land management tools, these two techniques face economic and political obstacles and are thus unlikely candidates for widespread state and local use.

Other strategies that can contribute to transportation energy savings on a lesser scale include

- Zoning for clustered developments in which the length of streets can be reduced (pp. 85–87)
- Creating neighborhood parks (p. 93)
- Requiring developers to dedicate conveniently located land for recreational use (pp. 93–97)
- Constructing bicycle and pedestrian paths to activity centers (pp. 97–98)
- Requiring developers of large planned unit developments to locate activity centers so they are conveniently accessible to the maximum numbers of residents (pp. 100, 111–112).

Strategies that can promote small transportation energy savings include

- Shading streets to make them more inviting to pedestrians and bicyclists (p. 98)
- Reducing the width of streets and the number of "through" streets to discourage automobile traffic and to encourage use by pedestrians and bicyclists (p. 88).

Space Heating and Cooling Goals and Strategies
A second goal of those attempting to manipulate land use to save energy—increasing the thermal efficiency of new construction [26]—is best served by legislation that permits or encourages us to build more low-rise and small high-rise, multifamily structures. Maximizing the energy-saving features of the natural environment can also reduce the energy requirements of space heating and cooling.

Constructing Multiunit Structures. Because multiunit structures have fewer surfaces exposed to outside weather extremes, less air infiltrates and less heated or cooled air is conducted through their walls, ceilings, floors, windows, and doors.

Many different variables—climate, the number of windows and storm windows in a building, the amount of insulation used, the number of square feet of floor space, and so on—can influence the energy demands made by space heating and cooling. Nevertheless, studies show that we can expect to consume about 30 percent less energy per square foot in medium-sized multifamily structures (ranging from apartment buildings with as few as twenty units up to small high rises of ten stories or less) than in detached single family homes. And, because they are typically smaller than single family houses, units in multifamily buildings will use 60 percent less energy for space heating and cooling on a per unit basis than will single family detached homes [27]. The actual energy savings can, therefore, be far greater than the 30 percent figure if people switch from single family to multifamily housing.

Buildings over about fifty stories tall appear to be energy-inefficient; they require large amounts of energy to move elevators, to heat common spaces, and to provide general services. Indeed, the breaking point for thermal efficiencies seems to lie somewhere between ten and fifty stories, but experts are not sure just where. If, therefore, we build only low-rise and small high-rise buildings, we can expect thermal energy savings of about 60 percent on a per unit basis [28]. It is essential to note, however, that the location of the thermal-efficient building remains crucial. Unless it is placed near adequate transportation lines and close to employment and shopping centers, the savings on heating and cooling may be outweighed by transportation energy requirements. On the other hand, a fifty story building located near an adequate public transportation line may offer transportation energy savings that compensate in part for its thermal inefficiencies.

Relatively easy to implement strategies that can have large energy-saving impacts by promoting the construction of low-rise and small high-rise multifamily buildings include

- Zoning for low-rise and small high-rise multifamily housing (pp. 67–76. Pertinent elements of this strategy are listed in connection with transportation strategies on page 15)
- Permitting or requiring planned unit developments and developments over a certain size to include a specified percentage of low-rise and small high-rise buildings (pp. 111–112, 116–122)
- Providing adequate sewer, water, utility, and transportation lines to accommodate increased density arising from increased multi-family housing (pp. 136–138)
- Providing density bonuses to developers that propose to build at energy-efficient densities (pp. 111–112, 116–122).

Constructing single family attached housing—duplexes, townhouses, and multifamily structures with two or more units—will probably also save considerable space heating and cooling energy since such units share common walls, but the extent of savings has not been ascertained. The same strategies for promoting construction of low-rise and small high-rise buildings are also applicable to encourage construction of small multifamily structures.

Taking Advantage of the Natural Environment. Another way to increase the thermal efficiency of buildings, one not covered in most studies of land use and energy conservation, is to use the natural environment to shelter buildings from temperature extremes.

As Victor Olgyay points out in his book *Design With Climate* [29], human beings have tried to control their environment to maximize their comfort as long as they have been on this earth. This concern has often produced distinctive architectural modes that reflect a region's climate. In the Arctic, Eskimo igloos deflect the wind and take advantage of the insulating effect of snow. By contrast, in hot, arid zones, some Indians built "multifamily" homes that shared thick adobe walls to protect the desert dwellers from extreme heat and from the glaring sun; adobes were usually oriented on an east-west axis that minimized the direct rays of sun in summer while maximizing them in winter [30]. Although the igloo and the adobe pueblo are perhaps ill-suited to modern life, the principle of designing buildings to take advantage of our natural environment and climate still rings perfectly true.

The development site and building orientation must be selected carefully if buildings are to be spared a never-ending argument with the land and the weather. Hills, for example, can buffer harsh winds in cold climates; or they can form a "pedestal" on which to place buildings in hot climates where cool breezes are welcome. The natural terrain may also contain slopes on which buildings can be placed to receive maximum sunlight during the winter and minimum solar radiation during the summer. Generally, in cool zones, sites halfway up a slope facing south-southeast will offer the most protection from the wind and exposure to the sun. In temperature zones without blasting winds, both the lower and upper portions of a slope facing in a southeasterly direction are desirable. In hot-arid zones, buildings should have east-southeast exposures and be sited on the lower portions of hills in order to take advantage of cool air flows and the afternoon shade. In hot-humid zones that depend on cooling breezes, sites with a windward exposure near the top of hills and, where possible, with a more north-south orientation are best [31].

The layout or arrangement of buildings on the land also matters, since buildings may protect each other by deflecting harsh winds in cold climates or channeling cooling breezes toward other structures in hot zones. Figures 2—1 and 2—2 illustrate how arranging buildings

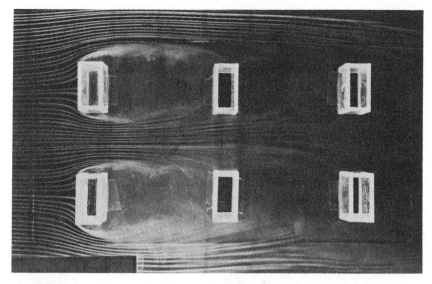

Figure 2–1.   Linear Building Arrangement Provides Protection From the Wind.

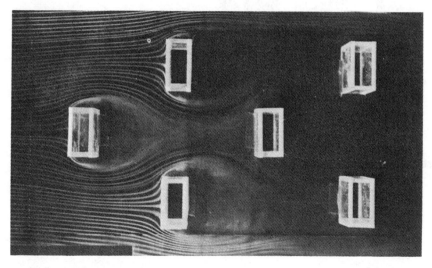

Figure 2–2.   Staggered Building Arrangement Takes Advantage of Cool Breezes in Warm Climates.

in rows protects them from strong wind while staggering buildings permits cool breezes to flow among them.

Landscaping, too, must be considered as more than an ornamental nicety. For example, deciduous trees that shade homes in the summer while allowing in solar rays in the winter cut down on the energy homes require in temperate climates. Evergreens that are strategically located to deflect harsh winter winds also conserve energy (Figure 2−3). And hedges and trees may direct cool breezes into a house that would otherwise be bypassed (Figure 2−4).

Finally, building shape must be considered. Cool zones call for the construction of compact or square buildings that are grouped closely enough to provide natural shelter from the wind, but not so close that sunlight is blocked. Such buildings may be connected to reduce

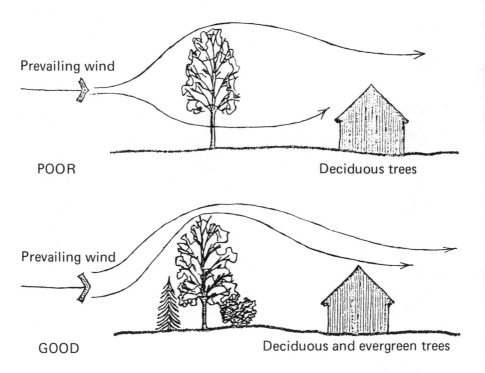

Figure 2−3. Strategically Located Evergreens Help Deflect Harsh Winds.

Reprinted from:
   "State of Vermont Energy Conservation Guidelines," prepared by the Vermont Public Service Board and the Agency of Environmental Conservation (Montpelier, April 1974).

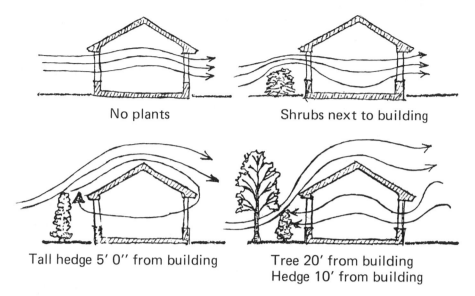

No plants   Shrubs next to building

Tall hedge 5' 0" from building   Tree 20' from building
Hedge 10' from building

Figure 2—4. Strategically Located Plants Can Direct Breezes Into Buildings in Warm Seasons and also Act as Windbreaks in Cold Seasons.

Reprinted from:
 "State of Vermont Energy Conservation Guidelines," prepared by the Vermont Public Service Board and the Agency of Environmental Conservation (Montpelier, April 1974).

heat losses from exposed surfaces. Temperate climates permit more flexibility, but elongated buildings placed on an east-west axis work out best. In hot, arid climates, massive, high structures with shady inner courts are most comfortable and efficient; the bulky walls and close grouping of the buildings shut out some of the sun's heat and rays. In hot, humid climates, on the other hand, free-standing houses best utilize air movements; buildings in these climates should be elongated in an east-west direction, and should be surrounded by shade trees [32].

A study of typical residences by a Princeton, New Jersey, research team confirms the principles outlined by Olgyay. The researchers found that one-fifth of the energy (heat) added to the interior of a house in the Princeton area during the winter comes from the sun, but two-thirds of all heat is lost by conduction through closed windows and opaque surfaces, and another one-third through air infiltration [33]. Townhouses on Princeton's windward side needed 5 percent more natural gas than did houses on the leeward side, as the latter were sheltered by the windward buildings [34]. And townhouses at the end of a row, with an exposed wall, used an additional 10 percent more gas [35].

A project carried out by a Philadelphia firm demonstrates the energy and money that can be saved by taking advantage of natural conditions rather than by expending energy to change them. The firm reports:

> ... [I]t was found that prevailing summer winds flow up the valleys. In the winter, the major wind pattern shifts 90 degrees. It was recommended that by not building in the valley or on the moraine, and by using the valley as a natural watering system, the natural growth of trees could be encouraged in these areas. Since the trees would be parallel to the summer breezes, air flow was permitted providing cooling in the summer. In the winter, the trees would provide shelter belts serving as wind buffers. The result is a general reduction in heating and cooling costs [36].

Another firm examined unoccupied buildings in Davis, California, and found that in that climate, on several sunny days, apartments facing south registered internal temperatures seventeen degrees above apartments facing north, east, and west [37].

Quite apparently, the proper siting, arrangement, orientation, landscaping, and design of buildings has a quantifiable impact on energy use, although exact numbers vary according to the climate. Working with instead of against the natural environment to reduce the energy demands associated with space heating and cooling will not achieve energy savings as large as those made possible through the construction of multifamily homes. But proper use of the natural environment will contribute to energy conservation. And, fortuitously, the design principles involved apply to single family as well as to multifamily structures.

Strategies for maximizing energy-saving elements of the natural environment include

- Zoning for flexible yard and setback standards that permit energy-efficient orientation and optimal building shapes for the pertinent climate (pp. 85−89)
  −encouraging cluster zoning
  −issuing special permits to allow optimal orientation
- Using site plan review to enforce requirements that new developments maximize energy-saving features of the natural environment and design developments to minimize effects of temperature extremes (pp. 99−106)
- Requiring roads and lots to be laid out to permit energy-efficient building orientation and design (p. 88)

- Requiring preservation of natural vegetation to the greatest extent practicable (pp. 89−90)
- Requiring planting of vegetation appropriate to the climate in locations where it will shelter buildings from temperature extremes (pp. 89−90).

One additional factor affecting the relationship between the energy demands of space heating and cooling and land use should be noted: the arrangement and density of buildings determine whether efficient heating systems can be used. Since about two-thirds of the fossil fuel energy used by power plants to make electricity is lost during the generation and transmission process [38], much energy could be saved if this waste heat were captured and used for space heating and cooling. To achieve such savings, plants would have to be close to the final energy consumers, and the community would have to be densely populated. The technology needed to capture waste heat already exists; in Jersey City, New Jersey, the U.S. Department of Housing and Urban Development has set up a demonstration project that uses waste heat [39]. The next step is to modify land use arrangements so that the technology can be broadly applied. Those strategies listed on page 15 for increasing density of development would pave the way for sustained waste heat recapture as well as for reducing transportation energy demand.

Construction Goals and Strategies

The first two goals, reducing energy needs for transportation and space heating and cooling, can help cut back on the amount of energy we consume directly to provide intangible services such as heating our homes and moving ourselves from one place to another. In contrast, the construction goal involves the examination of methods for reducing indirect energy costs, or the amount of energy consumed in producing a tangible product, such as a road or sewer line. The size of these indirect energy expenditures is determined in some instances by how we use land.

Energy can be saved by eliminating wasteful construction practices associated with haphazard growth—unnecessarily wide streets, excessive grading, and leapfrog, or noncontiguous, development. If development were to occur only on small lots adjacent to existing communities, we could save the energy now used to extend and to maintain the additional miles of roads, sewers, and water and utility lines needed to serve scattered, low density growth. These indirect energy costs consist not only of the cost of fuel for operating and maintaining construction equipment, but also the cost of the materials from which public utilities and facilities are constructed.

Streets and roads are particularly notorious energy consumers. In addition to encouraging automobile use, asphalt streets use petroleum as a base; pound for pound, the concrete in concrete streets requires even more energy to manufacture than aluminum does. In spite of the hidden high energy costs of road building, however, streets not only are extended to serve developments prematurely located on the urban fringe, but are also often made far wider than they need be to bear the traffic they were designed to serve. Consequently, streets intended for residential use have become major thoroughfares, thus adding to unnecessary energy expenditures for construction and making walking and bicycling unpleasant and even unsafe. Where possible, clustered development should replace grid patterns, since clusters require fewer linear feet of street and have the additional energy benefits of helping to preserve the natural landscape and of permitting flexible orientation. One study recommends that collector and subcollector streets should be reduced to twenty-six feet in width and streets in cul-de-sacs should be reduced to sixteen to eighteen feet [40].

One firm has reported energy savings in construction by using natural drainage swales instead of manmade curbs and gutters and by clustering structures to reduce the length of streets:

At Flying Hills, no curb or gutters are used. By allowing water to run into grassed swales, a natural watering system is utilized and natural replenishment of the water supply is obtained with considerable cost and energy savings. At a cost of approximately $5.50 per linear foot for 6" × 18" concrete curb, the savings to the developer was nearly $174,800, about 50% of which is materials. Not only is energy saved through reduced need for materials, but also the water velocity is controlled. . . .

Housing units were run along the contours of the land, molding construction into the site. By bending a linear cluster of buildings parallel to the typographic contours, cut and fill as well as end wall construction is minimized. The result is considerable energy savings through both reduced grading activity and material requirements. The concept of contour clustering also permits a major reduction in road lengths, . . . with a significant saving in the amount of energy intensive paving materials. A linear road length comparison study between the site designed as a single family layout and as an open space [planned unit development] resulted in a 300% reduction in roads required and a cost saving of $720,720 [41].

Although these energy benefits are minor when compared with possibilities for reducing transportation and space heating and cooling costs, they nevertheless are genuine energy savings. And, as the example discussed above demonstrates, these techniques for conserving fuel can also save money for the developer and the home buyer.

Strategies noted earlier for encouraging contiguous, moderately high density development and for protecting the natural landscape are equally effective in reducing the indirect energy costs of construction [42]. Other possible strategies are

- Reducing street width requirements (pp. 98–99)
- Including in the site plan specific review requirements for reducing the length of streets and curbs and gutters unless environmental or other constraints make shorter systems undesirable (pp. 99–106)

Several more general techniques can be used to complement each of the strategies listed here to promote savings in specific areas. One is to require preparation of comprehensive state and local land use plans that incorporate energy conservation considerations (Chapter 3). Another technique, preparation of energy impact statements, can help land use officials review whether or not a project has been designed and located for maximum practicable energy efficiency (Chapter 4). Providing incentives to developers through density bonuses in exchange for energy-efficient designs and conditioning annexation on the energy efficiency of proposed projects are still additional ways to encourage energy conservation through land use (pp. 116–123).

HUMAN NATURE VERSUS THE LAWS OF NATURE

Although we know that land development patterns significantly affect energy consumption, not everyone is enthusiastic about controlling or influencing land development to curb energy demands. Humans are less noted for their willingness to relinquish small luxuries and conveniences than for their ability to procrastinate.

One common argument against consuming energy by altering land development patterns is that new technology, in the form of more energy-efficient automobiles, solar energy, and telecommunications, will soon offer far greater energy savings and entail far less sacrifice than the technology now at our disposal. Although golden opportunities for savings may indeed materialize, their pursuit should not preclude the use of available land use techniques to conserve energy. New technology can produce more energy-efficient automobiles, but even less gas will be used when land has been developed to reduce the need for automobiles. Solar energy may be "free energy," but solar systems work best on houses that are already energy-efficient [43]. Moreover, though most solar energy systems we now have can be used most effectively in low density developments, that may not be true for long. Large scale, centralized solar facilities to serve dense developments are now on the drawing boards.

Similarly, the energy impacts of scattered, low density growth will not be so severe if people use telephones and television rather than the "business trip" to further communication. But even if telecommunications drastically reduces the need for job-related trips, it is unlikely to replace household, recreational, or social travel any more than the telephone has. Since many automobile trips are not work-related, the impact of land use planning on the number of miles traveled for shopping, pursuing entertainment, visiting friends, and so on will remain important.

Another commonly raised argument against saving energy through land use is that we don't know enough about the relationship between land use and energy demand to act constructively. Unlike those two extra inches of insulation, the transportation energy that a conveniently located neighborhood grocery saves its patrons cannot be calculated with certainty. But lack of exact measurements has not halted action in other areas once problems and potential solutions have been identified. Prime examples are environmental and toxic substances controls that have been imposed before the precise implications of a problem are known.

At any rate, as desirable as additional information would be, we already have concrete data, both from empirical research and simulated studies, that show that the potential for energy conservation through alternative development patterns is significant. Common sense also tells us that when other variables are constant, more compact, mixed use land development can help us break the automotive habit. Nevertheless, critics are correct in believing that it is the "other variables" that present the major questions and that require us to be prudent when adopting new land controls [44]. Consequently, while it would be foolish to continue our wasteful habits when conservation techniques have been developed, it would be just as foolish to change our lifestyles radically on the sole basis of the information we have now.

Difficult as the data problem may seem, human nature and economics present more serious obstacles. A response to saving energy in one area may mean an unexpected increase in consumption in another. If, for example, we move closer to our jobs, and thereby reduce commuting time, will we spend the extra minutes by driving to friends' homes after work? And if we settle in a multifamily development, will we flee each weekend to the countryside by automobile? [45].

Some aspects of human nature are predictably energy-inefficient. Studies show that income, age, and family makeup all determine individual energy demands. Wealthier people commute farther and own larger houses that are expensive to heat and cool; families with children make more automobile trips. For many families, living close to an elementary school is more important than proximity to both a job and downtown destinations [46]. A North Carolina study shows that even though residents of planned communities tend to use facilities close to their homes, they choose their golf courses and doctors without thinking much about distances [47]. Hence, even the most energy-efficient community will be full of human beings with ingrained habits and unpredictable whims.

In addition to other obstacles, energy conservation through land use will require our nation to revamp land use plans, enact new legislation, make changes in old legislation, provide technical and economic assistance to state and local governments, create massive public education programs, and, perhaps, completely restructure the tax system. With so many barriers to impede energy-conserving land development, one may ask why the effort is worth pursuing. But in today's economic, political, and social milieu, one would not have to wait long for an answer.

ENERGY-EFFICIENT LAND DEVELOPMENT IS WORTH A MAJOR EFFORT

First, as noted earlier, land use tools can help us realize the full potential of our ability to conserve energy. Although technological changes may offer greater overall savings than are possible simply through changes in land use, the fact remains that even more savings are possible when technological and nontechnological strategies are coordinated. And, although some may argue that changing land development patterns by altering lifestyles rather than technologies is too complicated and too politically objectionable to work, the answer is that states and localities may pick among strategies to achieve the greatest level of conservation consistent with their social, economic, environmental, and other goals. Energy-efficient land use policies are, therefore, a useful supplement to other energy conservation strategies.

Second, many land use techniques can offer significant energy savings with little effort. Minor changes in layout, design, and landscaping can have major conserving effects. Other more dramatic changes, with more dramatic results (such as discouraging noncontiguous development), are already being pursued for reasons independent of energy conservation. Energy impact statements, development permit systems based on energy efficiency, and many other energy-saving techniques discussed in this book are modeled after techniques already used to protect the environment or the local pocketbook.

Third, energy-saving land use policies can have beneficial economic, social, and environmental side effects. Clustering housing to preserve natural vegetation saves the developer money on clearing land, reduces the homeowner's heating and cooling bills by permitting energy-efficient orientation and landscaping, and relieves the local government and developers of the financial burden of building unnecessarily long and redundant road and sewer systems [48]. Building higher density, multiunit housing may enable individuals with a range of income levels to find housing in suburban developments, thereby cutting energy waste and commuting expenses (by insuring that people of all incomes can live close to their jobs) as well as protecting communities from charges of illegal exclusionary zoning. Preventing leapfrog or noncontiguous development on large lots can help preserve open space and agricultural land near urban areas. Bringing people and their destinations closer together can save time and money spent on frequent automobile trips. Landscaping can both save energy and please the eye.

Typically, the economic, environmental, and social benefits reported in *The Costs of Sprawl* and that study's progeny are cited as evidence that energy-efficient land use policies parallel and complement other important societal goals. Critics have, however, argued that some of the savings reported in such studies may be unrealistically high and even erroneous [49]. Between the extremes is the quite reasonable position that holds that significant benefits are possible but will not accrue in all circumstances. In some instances, particularly when policies require increases in density, undesirable side effects may require that the energy-efficient land use policy be modified or abandoned or that mitigation measures be taken. For example, although high density developments contiguous to urban areas may permit shorter road and utility networks, the operating and maintenance costs may outweigh capital cost savings [50]. Studies also show that high density development will reduce the overall air pollution emission levels but may increase atmospheric concentrations in areas where people live and work [51]. Hence, high density development must be complemented with "clean" public transportation systems if air pollution concentration is to be minimized. Communities must also recognize that efficient building forms may be unsuited to certain groups of persons. Ten-story apartment buildings, for example, may be undesirable for large families. Yet some problems associated with high density living—noise, loss of privacy, and a sense of overcrowding—that deter families without children from living in multifamily housing may be combatted by the use of open space, good design, and good construction [52].

The point is that energy-efficient land development offers opportunities for beneficial economic, environmental, and social side effects. But any community adopting energy efficiency as a land use goal must expect some detrimental side effects as well and must take steps to avoid or to mitigate those effects.

HOW A FREE MARKET LIMITS
FREEDOM OF CHOICE

Even if we have been convinced that energy-efficient land use is a desirable goal, one nagging question may still remain: Why not let the free market guide us into energy-saving development patterns? Must state and local governments be involved? After all, we saw that at the height of the Arab oil embargo, when gasoline prices soared, developers temporarily halted speculation in land on the fringes of metropolitan areas, and interest in homes near the urban center rekindled. Doesn't that swift public reaction to high energy prices prove that the marketplace, and not government regulation, is the ultimate fuel conservation tool?

The answer, of course, does not have the simplicity of extremes. Although the concept that the marketplace should govern is basically sound, and although the market will, for the most part, be the ultimate determinant of our land use choices, we should not—for several reasons—rely on economics as proof that our current land development policies are sound.

First, the market reflects land use biases that arise from existing regulations and incentives that encourage energy waste. To avoid large lot zoning in developing areas, for example, developers of low or moderately priced housing are often forced to leapfrog the large lot zone, sticking new homes farther away from employment centers. To pay high property taxes, those who hold agricultural land may be compelled to subdivide and to develop their rural land prematurely. Or, to keep local property taxes at a minimum, communities may find themselves competing for "good" tax ratables and thus interfering with plans that would allow industries and moderate-income workers to settle close to each other. Economics may impel individuals to purchase the most energy-efficient house available within their price range. But an inflexible zoning or subdivision ordinance may prevent builders from orienting buildings to capture the natural heating and cooling benefits of the sun and wind or from clustering buildings to preserve natural vegetation. A restrictive zoning ordinance may prohibit construction of multifamily housing even though proximity to a transportation corridor would seem to justify higher density living. Economic incentives for energy conservation must be set free of these institutional obstacles.

In other instances, public ignorance may skew economic values. Common sense may tell people that moving closer to their jobs would save them money on gasoline costs. But when making these mental calculations—and a surprising number of people fail to do so [53]— few factor in the additional savings from reduced car maintenance bills, a reduced need for cars, and reduced insurance and license fees. Even fewer translate these rather subtle savings into the additional money they could then afford to spend on more efficient housing. Similarly, only a wise few realize how quickly the extra costs for a well-landscaped and designed house can be recouped through lower fuel bills. At present, most consumers are interested only in "first" costs of buying a house, not the costs of operating it. As a result, although the marketplace will be the final arbiter, state and local government action is needed to insure that consumers are aware of the true costs of their decisions.

Another reason for not relying solely on the market is that it fails to reflect that the time is ripe for building energy efficiencies into land development patterns. It fails to reflect that hundreds of communities are currently using billions of federal dollars to construct waste water treatment facilities that will be major determinants of where and how our new growth will be accommodated [54]. It fails to reflect that decisions are being made now that will affect the housing choices for the additional forty-seven million people who will need shelter in this country by the end of this century, and that, for example, by 1990 close to one-half of the dwelling units in the Washington, D.C., metropolitan area will have been built after 1974 if housing starts continue to increase by 2 percent annually [55]. Development is inevitable, but energy-efficient development is not. Unlike automobiles, which have short lives so that their average efficiency can be greatly improved over a few years, land development patterns can hold for decades or even centuries. Consequently, energy-conserving policies adopted now, while the framework for housing and serving future generations is being designed, is crucial.

Finally, since the marketplace cannot anticipate a crisis in time to take prophylactic action and occasionally relies upon the government to bail it out of emergencies, the marketplace cannot adequately protect us from another sudden, dramatic increase in energy prices. Planning for such contingencies can give us options that might otherwise be nonexistent when an emergency exists. Governments have traditionally been responsible for anticipating crises and taking steps to avoid public discomfort or harm. The same principle applies to regulating land use to save energy. Although the marketplace should and will continue to dominate our land use decisions, it is necessary to alter our land use policies so that the marketplace accurately reflects the current and future need for energy conservation.

NOTES TO CHAPTER 2

1. For a review of land use/energy conservation studies and issues, *see* Dale L. Keyes and George E. Peterson, "Metropolitan Development and Energy Consumption," Land Use Center Working Paper (draft), (Washington, D.C.: The Urban Institute, September 1976); W. Curtiss Priest et al., "An Overview and Critical Evaluation of the Relationship Between Land Use and Energy Conservation," FEA Contract No. CO−04−50250−00, (Cambridge, Massachusetts: Technology + Economics, March 2, 1976); and W. Curtiss Priest et al., "The Energy Vista: Policy Perspectives on Energy Conservation Through Land Use Management," prepared for the U.S. Federal Energy Administration, (Cambridge, Massachusetts: Technology + Economics, June 22, 1976). In addition, the Urban Institute in Washington, D.C., has received a large grant from several federal agencies to look at, among other things, the impact of land development patterns on energy consumption in metropolitan areas, and James S. Roberts of the Real Estate Research Corporation is preparing for the U.S. Council on Environmental Quality a report summarizing land use/energy conservation studies and their policy implications.

2. Real Estate Research Corporation, *The Costs of Sprawl: Detailed Cost Analysis* and *Literature Review and Bibliography*, prepared for the U.S. Council on Environmental Quality, the U.S. Department of Housing and Urban Development, and the U.S. Environmental Protection Agency (Washington, D.C.: U.S. Government Printing Office, April 1974).

3. Real Estate Research Corporation, *supra* note 2, *Detailed Cost Analysis* at 21. In the study, which simulates communities and neighborhoods, the sprawling community consists entirely of single family homes, with 75 percent in a conventional grid pattern and 25 percent in clusters. Such neighborhoods are developed in a "leapfrog" pattern. A "high-density planned" community has 40

percent high-rise apartments, 30 percent walk-up apartments, 20 percent town-houses and 10 percent clustered single family homes. Housing types in the high density community are mixed in contiguous neighborhoods with a great deal of remaining open space. *Id.* at 90.

4. James S. Roberts, *Energy, Land Use, and Growth Policy: Implications for Metropolitan Washington* (Washington, D.C.: Metropolitan Washington Council of Governments, June 1975).

5. Robert S. DeVoy et al., "The Public Service Costs of Alternative Development Patterns (Chicago: Real Estate Research Corporation, December 1974); Regional Plan Association, Inc. and Resources for the Future, Inc., "Regional Energy Consumption/Second Interim Report," (New York: Regional Plan Association, 1974). (The final results of the regional energy consumption study are published in Joel Darmstadter, *Conserving Energy/Prospects and Opportunities in the New York Region* [Baltimore: Johns Hopkins University Press, 1975]); Margaret F. Fels and Michael J. Munson, "Energy Thrift in Urban Transportation: Options for the Future," in Robert H. Williams, ed., *The Energy Conservation Papers*, Reports prepared for the Energy Policy Project of the Ford Foundation (Cambridge, Massachusetts: Ballinger Publishing Company, 1975), p. 7; Hittman Associates, *Residential Energy Consumption/Single-Family Housing* (Washington, D.C.: U.S. Government Printing Office, 1973); and *id.*, *Residential Energy Consumption/Multi-Family Housing, Final Report* (Washington, D.C.: U.S. Government Printing Office, 1974). *See also* Booz, Allen & Hamilton, Inc., "Interaction of Land Use Patterns and Residential Energy Consumption," draft report prepared for the U.S. Federal Energy Administration (Bethesda, Maryland: Booz, Allen & Hamilton, Inc., October 20, 1976).

6. For example, the studies do not account for the fact that easy access to destinations may encourage people to make more automobile trips. *See* Keyes and Peterson, *supra* note 1 at 26.

7. *Id.* at 69.

8. *Id.* at 79.

9. Readers are cautioned that statistics used in this chapter may be disputed and, in any case, will be refined as energy conservation/land use work progresses.

10. Nationwide Personal Transportation Study, "Mode of Transportation and Personal Characteristics of Tripmakers," Report no. 9 (Washington, D.C.: U.S. Department of Transportation, Federal Highway Administration, November 1973), p. 4. Public transportation includes taxicabs, buses, subways, trains, and airplanes. Trips not made by automobile or public transportation include 6 percent by truck and motorcycle and 5 percent by schoolbus. *Id.*

11. Nationwide Personal Transportation Study, "Household Travel in the United States," Report no. 7 (Washington, D.C.: U.S. Department of Transportation, Federal Highway Administration, December 1972), p. 4.

12. Nationwide Personal Transportation Study, "Home-to-Work Trips and Travel," Report no. 8 (Washington, D.C.: U.S. Department of Transportation, Federal Highway Administration, August 1973), p. 23.

13. *Id.* at 45. Significantly, workers' perceptions of accessibility to public transportation had a large impact on its use. A study of commuters several years

ago showed that 58.1 percent of workers who used private cars for commuting thought public transportation was not available to them. *Id.* at 36.

14. Nationwide Personal Transportation Study, "Purposes of Automobile Trips and Travel," Report no. 10 (Washington, D.C.: U.S. Department of Transportation, Federal Highway Administration, May 1974), p. 16.

15. Eric Hirst, "Direct and Indirect Energy Requirements for Automobiles," (Oak Ridge, Tennessee: Oak Ridge National Laboratory, February 1974), p. 7.

16. *Id.*

17. Mayo S. Stuntz and Eric Hirst, "Energy Conservation Potential of Urban Mass Transit," Energy Conservation Paper Number 34 (Washington, D.C.: Office of Transportation Programs, U.S. Federal Energy Administration, n.d.), p. 8.

18. American Public Transit Association, " '76 Fact Book," (Washington, D.C.: March 1976), p. 46.

19. Fels and Munson, *supra* note 5 at 56.

20. Stuntz and Hirst, *supra* note 17 at 24.

21. Jerry L. Edwards and Joseph L. Schofer, *Relationships Between Transportation Energy Consumption and Urban Structure: Results of Simulation Studies* (Evanston, Illinois: Department of Civil Engineering, Northwestern University, January 1975).

22. T.O. Carroll, A.S. Kydes, and J.B. Sanborn, "A Regional Land Use and Energy Modelling System," Brookhaven National Laboratory, presented at the Seventh Annual Pittsburgh Conference on Modelling and Simulation (April 1976).

23. Fels and Munson, *supra* note 5. It should be noted, however, that although the authors of this study used the population, employment, transportation network, and transportation behavior characteristics of Trenton, New Jersey, as the basis for their simulations, thus lending credibility to their assumptions, one critic has cautioned that the estimated savings may be unreliable since "the degree to which travel patterns change under the various development options rests clearly on the authors' collective (and largely intuitive) judgment." (Keyes and Peterson, *supra* note 1 at 23–24.)

24. Keyes and Peterson, *supra* note 1. The conclusions are based on an analysis of existing land use/energy consumption studies and on ongoing research conducted by the Urban Institute.

25. *See* Roberts, *supra* note 4.

26. The following discussion reviews energy savings that are possible in residential buildings, but presumably some of the concepts, if not the exact figures discussed here, are transferable to commercial buildings.

27. Keyes and Peterson, *supra* note 1. *See also* Hittman Associates, *Single-Family Housing* and *Multi-Family Housing*, *supra* note 5; and A.D. Little, Inc., *Residential and Commercial Energy Use Patterns, 1970–90*, Project Independence (Washington, D.C.: U.S. Federal Energy Administration, November 1974).

28. It should be noted that the studies contributing to this conclusion all examined multifamily units in which the occupying families were much smaller than those in single family detached houses. The living space per occupant in the apartments was, however, much higher. This suggests that large families cannot

be accommodated in multifamily units as they are now built, or that multifamily units may have to be increased in size to accommodate those larger families, in which case the per unit energy savings will be less than 60 percent. Keyes and Peterson, *supra* note 1 at 65.

29. Victor Olgyay, *Design With Climate: Bioclimatic Approach to Architectural Regionalism* (Princeton, New Jersey: Princeton University Press, 1963). *See also* Ralph L. Knowles, *Energy and Form: An Ecological Approach to Urban Growth* (Cambridge, Massachusetts: MIT Press, 1974); and Raymond D. Reed et al., "The Impact of and the Potential for Energy Conservation Practices in Residential and Commercial Buildings in Texas," prepared for the Governor's Energy Advisory Council, (Texas A & M University, College of Architecture and Environmental Design, October 15, 1974).

30. Olgyay, *supra* note 29 at 4−5.

31. *Id.* at 52.

32. *Id.* at 90−91.

33. Robert H. Socolow, "Energy Conservation in Housing: Concepts and Options," in Robert W. Burchell and David Listokin, eds., *Future Land Use/ Energy, Environmental*, and *Legal Constraints* (New Brunswick, New Jersey: Rutgers University Press, 1975), p. 316.

34. *Id.* at 319.

35. *Id.* at 320.

36. Philip Goldberg, "Planning with Energy" (Philadelphia: Rahenkamp, Sachs, Wells & Associates, Inc., January 31, 1975) (Pine Hills Project, Brookhaven, Suffolk County, New York).

37. Jonathan Hammond et al., "A Strategy for Energy Conservation: Proposed Energy Conservation and Solar Utilization Ordinance for the City of Davis, California," (Davis, California, 1974), p. 14.

38. Roberts, *supra* note 4 at 3−4.

39. The technology used is known as a Modular Integrated Utility System.

40. Urban Land Institute et al., *Residential Streets: Objectives, Principles, and Design Considerations* (Washington, D.C., 1974), pp. 32−33.

41. Goldberg, *supra* note 36 (Flying Hills Project, Cumru Township, Berks County, Pennsylvania).

42. *See* pages 15 through 23, *infra.*

43. "Professional Builder's Report on Solar Energy," *Professional Builder*, June 1976, pp. 105−106; American Institute of Architects Research Corporation, "Early Use of Solar Energy in Buildings," Technical Report to the National Science Foundation (Washington, D.C., August 1976), p. 47.

44. *See* Dale L. Keyes, "Energy and Land Use: An Instrument of US Conservation Policy?" *Energy Policy*, September 1976, pp. 225−36; and Phyllis Myers, "Land-Use Policies and Energy Conservation," *Energy Conservation Training Institute* (Washington, D.C.: The Conservation Foundation, 1976), pp. III−73 to III−106.

45. *See* Bruce Hannon, "Energy Conservation and the Consumer," *Science* 189, no. 4197 (July 11, 1975): 95−102, for a discussion of the problem that saving energy in one area may lead to increased consumption in another.

46. Kathleen Christensen, "Social Justice and Patterns of City Growth," Land Use Center Working Paper (Washington, D.C.: The Urban Institute, October 1975), p. 19.

47. Raymond J. Burby, III, and Shirley F. Weiss, *New Communities U.S.A.* (Lexington, Massachusetts: D.C. Heath and Co., 1976), pp. 322–24.

48. As noted on page 24, *supra*, one firm recorded a 300 percent reduction in roads required, at a cost saving of $720,720, when it built a large planned unit development with clustered housing instead of a conventional single family housing development in a grid pattern. By using grassed swales rather than curbs and gutters for drainage, the developer saved nearly $174,800.

49. *See* Thomas Muller, *Fiscal Impacts of Land Development* (Washington, D.C.: The Urban Institute, 1975); and *id.*, *Economic Impacts of Land Development: Employment, Housing, and Property Values* (Washington, D.C.: The Urban Institute, 1976); Kathleen Christensen, *Social Impacts of Land Development* (Washington, D.C.: The Urban Institute, 1976); and Dale L. Keyes, *Land Development and the Natural Environment: Estimating Impacts* (Washington, D.C.: The Urban Institute, 1976).

50. *See* Muller, *supra* note 49 at 21–23.

51. Dale L. Keyes, "Metropolitan Development and Air Quality," The Land Use Center Working Paper No. 5049–16 (Washington, D.C.: The Urban Institute, November 1976). Interestingly, Keyes asserts that high versus low density development patterns appear to have little effect on the overall level of water pollution.

52. Christensen, *supra* note 49.

53. Myers, *supra* note 44 at III–98.

54. The funds have been appropriated pursuant to the Federal Water Pollution Control Act Amendments of 1972, 33 U.S.C. §1251 et seq. (Supp. 1973). *See* Richard D. Tabors et al., *Land Use and the Pipe* (Lexington, Massachusetts: D.C. Heath and Co., 1976), p. 4, for a succinct overview of the federal sewerage grants program.

55. Roberts, *supra* note 4 at 8–3.

Chapter 3

Planning for Energy Conservation

Energy conservation issues transcend jurisdictional boundaries and resist compartmentalization within one administrative agency or legislative committee. Growth that does not stop at city, county, or even state lines establishes the level of our energy demand. Decisions by transportation agencies, planning commissions, public utility boards, and many other governmental bodies shape our land development, thereby directly influencing our energy needs. Local governments have the advantage of close contact with citizens and can thus design energy conservation programs that reflect localized problems and needs. But the increasing number and size of standard metropolitan statistical areas (SMSAs) that result in amoebalike patterns of energy use and the simultaneous increase in interaction among local governments within a metropolis [1] highlight the importance of regional and state as well as local land use and energy conservation planning.

Comprehensive planning for energy conservation that is coordinated at all levels of government and injected into all agency decisions can promote energy-saving land development most effectively. A comprehensive plan is a long range policy guide for future development. Based on a thorough examination of community [2] characteristics and a careful balancing of community goals, comprehensive plans outline actions for implementing the policies they endorse.

Comprehensive land use plans are a prerequisite to good land development since they force communities to take stock of their resources and to project their demands. They show where the coordination of land use activities is needed to meet goals, and they provide a standard for review so that proposed activities can be evaluated with regard to goals. Plans allow comparisons between projected and actual development patterns and reflect, if they are kept up to date, the desires and activities of the community [3]. More importantly, comprehensive plans can be the primary working document for developing energy-efficient land use.

The need to make energy conservation a policy goal for all governmental actions and the role of regional land use planning in promoting that goal are discussed in the first part of this chapter. The necessity for local comprehensive land use planning, coordinated on a statewide basis and reflecting the goal of energy-efficient land use, is then taken up.

ESTABLISHING AN ENERGY CONSERVATION POLICY

One of the most important steps that state and even regional and local governments can take to promote energy-efficient land development is to amend their general comprehensive planning acts to require that energy conservation be factored into all agency decisions and actions.

General comprehensive planning acts cover more than land use planning; planning in broad policy areas such as the economy, employment, education, industrial development, transportation, and the environment are also included. Decisions in many of these areas directly affect the amount of energy we consume through our land use practices. Consequently, if a legislature adopts energy conservation as a goal in the planning process, comprehensive planning will offer tremendous leverage for promoting energy-efficient land development; all agency actions and budgets must conform to that energy policy guideline. Thereafter, for example, a state transportation department will have to consider the energy impacts of extending a superhighway into an undeveloped region. Or, the state parks commission must incorporate energy conservation considerations in deciding where to locate a new regional park.

This strategy of establishing energy conservation as a planning policy is particularly appealing because it is easy to implement. By simply adding the phrase "energy conservation" to the list of planning goals, state, regional, and local governments can, with relatively little effort, create a framework for saving significant amounts of energy. Just such a framework was developed in Eugene, Oregon, during the unexpected energy crisis of 1973. Eugene supplemented its previously adopted metropolitan area plan with a "Goals and Policies Document" that includes a chapter on energy [4]. Similarly, the "Albuquerque/Bernalillo County [New Mexico] Comprehensive Plan/Policies Plan" for 1975 includes a statement that the "City and County shall pursue land use planning that will maximize potential for energy conservation" [5].

Naturally, word changes will mean little or nothing unless the goal of energy conservation and methods for accomplishing that goal are set forth in detail by the governing body or administrative agency. Regional and local governments may find an example to follow in the broad energy conservation goals and guidelines adopted by the governing bodies of the city of Lincoln and Lancaster County, Nebraska, for use in updating their comprehensive regional plan [6]. Selected portions of those goals and guidelines, which spell out the elements of an energy conservation policy insofar as it affects land use, are reprinted in Appendix II, page 237. In addition, states and localities can adopt strategies discussed in the following chapters to implement the energy-conserving goals reviewed in Chapter 2.

RESOLVING TO PROMOTE ENERGY CONSERVATION

Though crucial, the effects of comprehensive state planning are seldom immediate. While waiting for plans to be formulated, governments should take the interim step of adopting a resolution that establishes an energy policy to be followed by the governing body. The Florida State Energy Office, working in conjunction with the state's ten Regional Energy Action! committees, has drafted an energy policy for that state that could be introduced in the 1977 legislative session. The proposed policy contains elements aimed at developing the effective use of energy and at discouraging all forms of energy waste, at encouraging local governments to consider energy in all planning, at giving the state government a leading role in developing and instituting energy management programs to promote energy conservation, and at furthering energy education. Like the energy element in a general state comprehensive planning act, the energy policy in a legislative resolution would guide actions of all government agencies, not only actions by designated land use agencies. (The full text of the proposed energy policy for Florida is reproduced in Appendix II, page 241.)

INCLUDING ENERGY CONSERVATION STANDARDS IN STATE LAND USE LEGISLATION

Conservation-conscious governments can also amend existing land use legislation to incorporate energy conservation considerations. Thirty states presently participate in the federally funded coastal zone management program; twenty-two states have the authority to plan or review local plans affecting wetlands or to control land use in wetlands; thirty-four states control the siting of power plants and related facilities; thirteen states have or are in the process of establishing rules, regulations, and guidelines for the identification and designation of areas of environmentally critical state concern; twenty-six states authorize flood plain regulation; five states authorize regulation of shorelands along significant bodies of water; and five states require permits for certain kinds of development with regional or statewide impacts [7]. Where appropriate, all of this state legislation should be amended so that development in areas subject to state control must be reviewed on the basis of the energy demands that the development will generate and actions taken by developers to mitigate those demands.

Indeed, states that have not already done so should consider asserting state control over developments whose statewide or regional impact will help determine where and how new growth occurs. By regulating such developments, states can direct major growth-shaping projects into energy-efficient locations; they can also set design, density, and use standards that will affect the energy efficiency of developments.

Vermont, for example, requires the promoters of all major developments (and of some minor developments in areas without zoning controls) to obtain state permits before beginning development. Permits are conditioned, in part, on the applicant's ability to demonstrate that the "planning and design of the subdivision or development reflect the principles of energy conservation and incorporate the best available technology for efficient use or recovery of energy" [8]. Vermont has also prepared a handbook setting forth guidelines for energy-efficient development [9].

States that do not require comprehensive state and local land use planning might follow Vermont's approach for promoting energy-conserving land use. Under Vermont's plan, those seeking development permits must file applications with a district environmental commission, which has the power to conduct investigations, examinations, tests, and site evaluations to verify information contained in the application. Notice of such applications must be given to munici-palities and regional planning commissions that wield authority over land that is subject to or adjacent to land affected by the development application. The state environmental board and any state agency directly affected by the proposed project must also be notified. Those groups, as well as adjoining property owners, may request a hearing on the application [10]. No application may be denied unless the district commission or state environmental board finds that the project is detrimental to the public health, safety, or general welfare, but conditions and requirements, including those pertaining to energy demand, may be incorporated in the permit [11]. In actual practice, most reviewers operating under the Vermont statute have looked at building insulation and orientation and landscaping to determine the energy efficiency of a proposed project. But there is no reason why other important energy conservation elements, such as project location (including proximity to transportation lines and activity centers), mixture of uses, and density, cannot also be reviewed.

Statutes in Florida and Oregon illustrate other ways to bring activities with large energy impacts under state control. The Florida statute [12] defines developments of regional impact (DRIs) as any development that because of its character, magnitude, or location, will have a "substantial effect upon the health, safety, or welfare of citizens of more than one county" [13]. When a DRI is proposed, the regional planning agency in its area must submit to the local government a report on the regional impact of the proposed project and recommendations regarding action on the DRI application. The go-ahead for DRIs is given by the local government in the area in which they would be located after that government evaluates the project's compliance with the state land development plan [14], local land development regulations, and the report and recommenda-tions of the regional planning council. DRIs may be approved subject to conditions or limitations [15]. Presumably, energy conservation can be included as a condition for approval, although the Florida statute does not require it.

To ensure that no large energy users escape the effects of the per-mit procedure and that the regional planning agency considers energy use when it prepares its report and recommendations for the local government, Florida amended its statute in 1976 to incorporate some energy considerations. Now the extent to which the development or subsidiary developments would create an additional demand for or use of energy is a factor that influences whether a development is presumed to be one of regional impact; in addition, the energy impact of the development must be assessed by the regional planning agency in its report to the local government [16]. Yet, the state legislation has still failed specifically to incorporate energy conservation requirements, as opposed to energy impact assessment requirements, for all DRIs [17]. A legislative proposal prepared by a public policy research organization in Florida [18] would compensate for this omission. It proposes that "the extent to which the development would discourage or encourage efficiency in energy use" be considered by those determining whether a development is presumed to be one of regional impact and by the regional planning agency in preparing its report and recommendations to the local government. It also proposes that "energy" be defined as a term that "includes, but is not limited to, heating, cooling, transportation, power generation, construction and operation of buildings, industrial and residential consumption" [19].

Perhaps the state land use legislation with the most far-reaching potential for energy conservation is Senate Bill 100, Oregon's 1973 land use legislation. Like the Florida statute, the Oregon law provides for regulation of development projects with broader than local impact. The state land use agency, the Land Conservation and Development Commission (LCDC), is authorized to designate activities of statewide significance, including planning and siting of public transportation facilities, public sewage and water supply systems, public solid waste disposal facilities, and public schools [20]. Once designated [21], these activities cannot be undertaken by a person or agency without a permit from LCDC, which may issue permits only after it determines that the activity complies with statewide goals and with the comprehensive plan of the county in which the activity is located [22]. What makes the statute so valuable is that energy conservation has been designated as one of the statewide goals with which major projects must comply [23]. Furthermore, the Oregon statute also requires all state agencies and special districts to carry out their planning duties, powers, and responsibilities, and to take actions with respect to programs affecting land use, in accordance with statewide planning goals, including the goal of energy conservation [24]. Thus Oregon's state land use legislation accomplishes comprehensive planning for energy-efficient land use to the same degree that would be achieved by the addition of an energy conservation element to a general comprehensive planning act [25].

ESTABLISHING REGIONAL
PLANNING COUNCILS TO PROMOTE
ENERGY-EFFICIENT LAND USE

In addition to asserting state control over developments with large energy impacts, another way to combat energy, as well as transportation, housing, and pollution, problems that extend beyond political boundaries is to establish regional councils of governments, or COGs, with authority over such larger-than-local issues. These councils are usually voluntary organizations that depend upon local and federal governments for financial support. Rarely do they possess implementing authority.

Regional councils can perform valuable energy conservation functions by educating local governments about the energy impacts of their land use decisions and by encouraging intergovernmental cooperation to combat energy waste. The often-cited energy and land use study of the Washington, D.C., metropolitan area, for example, grew out of COG–sponsored research [26]. Regional bodies can also prepare energy-conscious land use plans that will most likely have a greater impact on the location of state highways and other energy-related facilities than will a multitude of local plans.

Because COGs lack implementing authority and must depend on voluntary support and financial aid, however, the councils may be seriously set back if a participating governmental unit disagrees with its policies and withdraws support. Many excellent regional programs and plans never leave the drafting board because local governments refuse to adopt recommendations. Yet it is unlikely that many states will give regional councils authority to enforce their plans. In 1972, a study by the Advisory Commission on Intergovernmental Relations found that only 20 percent of surveyed local officials in regional council jurisdictions favored vesting councils with implementing authority [27]. Even purely advisory regional councils are perceived as a threat by some local governments.

A few states have managed to overcome these obstacles and have established strong regional agencies with the authority to develop regional comprehensive plans that provide a coordinated approach to issues (like the need for energy conservation) that require more than local attention. One notable example is the Columbia Region Association of Governments (CRAG) in the Portland, Oregon, metropolitan area, which has the power to adopt regional goals and objectives and to enforce them [28]. Another is the Minneapolis/St. Paul Metropolitan Council, which has authority to develop "metro system plans" dealing with transportation, airports, open space, and sewers in the

Twin Cities region and to disapprove local comprehensive plans that are inconsistent with any of the four metro system plans [29]. California also has regional planning districts created by statute and supported by assessments on each county within a district; the regional plans produced by the California regional bodies are, however, only advisory [30].

As a general rule, regional planning bodies are given implementing authority only when their region encompasses environmentally unique or critical land. The New York Adirondack Park Agency [31], the San Francisco Bay Conservation and Development Commission [32], the Tahoe Regional Planning Agency [33], and the Hackensack Meadows Redevelopment Agency [34] in New Jersey are examples. Already quite successful in protecting their special environments, these agencies could presumably incorporate energy conservation into their planning decisions.

Part of the opposition to vesting authority in regional councils may arise from an inherent dislike of bureaucracy and from a feeling that regional bodies move decisionmaking one step farther from the people affected. More tangible opposition may arise from the effect of regional planning on local revenues and community makeup. Most local governments rely on revenue from property taxes to support education and other local services. In trying to keep property taxes at a reasonable level, some local governments use their zoning and subdivision powers to exclude an undue number of families with school age children [35]. Other communities have used their land control tools to prevent people with low incomes or racial minorities from moving in and changing the character of the community. Unless these obstacles to strong regional planning are removed, planning bodies are not likely to be able to combat energy waste arising from improper location of new development. For unless there is coordination among adjacent communities, local controls imposed to save energy may simply drive new growth farther away from established activity centers, transportation lines, and public facilities to areas with less stringent land development regulations.

The trend in some state legislatures and courts to overturn fiscal zoning and exclusionary land use regulations can help remove obvious obstacles to regional cooperation. These actions must also be supplemented with reform in property tax laws so that localities are no longer forced to compete for "good" tax ratables [36]. Another strategy is to make all petitions for incorporation or for boundary changes subject to state agency review. The agency could use its power to ensure that jurisdictional boundaries within developing areas correspond to the physical area affected by the planning problem. Balkanization into many small governmental entities trying to insulate themselves from regional concerns would be avoided. California [37] and Oregon [38] already have provisions for state or regional agency review of boundary changes. With these reforms, energy-efficient land use planning on a regional scale will be possible [39].

MANDATING LOCAL COMPREHENSIVE LAND USE PLANNING IN ACCORDANCE WITH STATE ENERGY CONSERVATION GOALS

One promising way to achieve energy-efficient land use is to allow localities to develop their own land use plans, but to require these plans to conform to express state goals, including energy conservation. Oregon is already experimenting with such an approach.

With S.B. 100, adopted in 1973, Oregon established a Land Conservation and Development Commission charged with the responsibility of developing mandatory statewide land use goals and guidelines [40]. Fortunately, LCDC opted to include energy conservation as one of Oregon's statewide goals and selected several other goals that directly or indirectly promote energy-efficient land use [41]. In the same statute, Oregon requires all local governments to prepare and adopt comprehensive plans consistent with the statewide goals and guidelines, and calls for the enactment of zoning, subdivision, and other ordinances or regulations to implement the comprehensive plans [42].

S.B. 100 requires LCDC to review all local plans to determine whether they conform to statewide goals. Moreover, a governmental unit can petition LCDC to review a state or local action that it considers to be in conflict with statewide planning goals; and any person or governmental unit whose interests are significantly affected by a local comprehensive plan, zoning, or subdivision ordinance that allegedly violates statewide goals can get LCDC to review the provision [43]. LCDC can prescribe and administer a comprehensive plan for recalcitrant localities at the expense of the locality [44] and can enjoin any nonconforming land use or construction that violates the state-prescribed plan [45]. The rulings of LCDC may be appealed to the state court of appeals, where review is based on the administrative record, not on *de novo* proceedings, so the review process is relatively speedy [46].

By establishing statewide goals and guidelines with which all local comprehensive plans must comply and by subjecting those plans to state review, Oregon has helped to ensure coordination of local plans to promote specific land use goals. The state recognizes, however, that not all goals can be assigned equal weight in local plans. The goal of protecting individuals from natural disasters like flooding may, for example, conflict with the goal of energy-efficient land development. Yet to ensure that localities do not ignore statewide planning goals, the LCDC guidelines require that when a goal cannot be accommodated, the "compelling reasons and facts" behind the failure must be "completely" set forth in the plan [47]. These statements can form a basis for reviewing local comprehensive plans to determine whether they conform to state planning requirements.

Integration of land use plans is also enhanced by requiring each county to coordinate "planning activities" affecting county land use by cities, special districts, and state agencies, and by the county itself [48]. In addition, counties and cities can elect to form a regional planning agency to coordinate area plans. These two provisions form the foundation of an excellent framework for preparing plans that direct housing, employment centers, transportation, and utility lines into energy-efficient locations on a regional basis [49].

Excerpts from the Oregon land use legislation appear in Appendix II, page 243. Although the Oregon approach provides a first rate model for development and coordination of energy-efficient land use plans, states may opt to alter that approach in several ways.

Promoting Local Comprehensive Planning

First, states may simply encourage rather than require local governments to develop comprehensive land use plans designed in part to save energy. To do so, states can enact enabling legislation to authorize local comprehensive planning and can include in that legislation provisions for technical and financial support for such planning. Most local governments simply cannot act unless financial help is available, as their own coffers are empty. Indeed, the Council of State Governments reports that only 40 percent of the counties surveyed in 1971 used the basic development controls given to them [50]. Because so many jurisdictions have failed to use even fundamental land control tools, they are not apt to develop more complex comprehensive plans without first receiving encouragement and assistance from the state or federal government [51].

Alternatively, states can encourage localities to adopt comprehensive plans by conditioning grants of specific state benefits, or the allocation of specific planning powers, on the development of such a plan. The Model Land Development Code adopted last year by the American Law Institute takes this approach [52].

It is probably naive to assume, however, that the stick-and-carrot approach implicit in the ALI model code will provoke the flood of local comprehensive land use plans that energy-efficient land development and good land management in general require. California [53], Nebraska [54], Florida [55], Idaho [56], Wyoming [57], and Virginia [58] apparently share this view, for they have joined Oregon in passing laws that compel local governments to develop comprehensive land use plans following standards set by the state. Moreover, the Wyoming [59] and Florida [60] statutes, like Oregon's, direct state governments to take over the planning if local efforts prove inadequate [61]. The Wyoming State Land Use Planning Act also includes a section that explicitly authorizes planning grants of up to $10,000 per year to local governments and appropriates $460,000 for that purpose [62]. Oregon has appropriated $6 million to help localities with planning and has supplemented this financial assistance with a handbook on how to develop local comprehensive plans. In addition, field representatives from the Oregon Land Conservation and Development Department travel throughout the state to assist local planners and officials.

States that provide financial and technical assistance must still convince citizens of the merits of comprehensive planning—no easy task. In spite of the strongly entrenched legal precedents for the regulation of land uses [63], many persons continue to believe that land is a commodity, and not a resource subject to government control.

Citizens must be convinced that comprehensive planning gives them more, not less, control over their property and their lives. Consequently, the value of a comprehensive plan in terms of saving not only energy, but also money, natural resources, time, and the environment, should be emphasized. At the same time, states must also try to correct another common misconception about the effects of government involvement in land use—that planning is somehow inconsistent with economic development. They need to show property owners that the two goals need not be incompatible and that, in fact, planning coordinated on state, regional, and local levels can actually enhance economic growth. A land use official in Oregon has listed some economic benefits of coordinated comprehensive planning:

—A consistent local comprehensive plan which has been agreed to by affected local, state, and federal agencies speeds the review of project proposals, thereby decreasing the costs associated with unproductive capital and material. This applies to public as well as private investments.

- By eliminating the frustration and nuisance suits typically associated with mislocated urban growth, proper zoning based on comprehensive plans assures the property owner and operator that conflicting uses will not interrupt future operations.

- Developers or industries can make confident investments in land if they know that local, state, and federal facilities in the area (transportation, recreation, etc.) will be interrelated. Construction of the proposed development can also be staged with construction of public support services.

- The stability of the plan assures developers or industries that the resource and market conditions that justified their initial development decisions will exist in the future.

- The developers or industries are assured that their project is compatible with growth plans of the local area. Front-end investments can be made, with assurance that projects will be permitted [64].

In addition to the energy conservation made possible by local comprehensive planning, other considerations may motivate states to require comprehensive planning on a local, as well as regional and state, level. More and more local governments are engaging in planning to ensure that they do not find themselves overwhelmed by the burdens associated with growth while their neighbors attract only the benefits. The *Ramapo* [65] and *Petaluma* [66] cases, which tested the right of localities to control the timing and extent of their growth, provide evidence that localities are beginning to use their land management tools with more sophistication, although perhaps to the detriment of surrounding areas. If the effect of their actions is not only to guide growth but also to limit it, then neighboring localities, suddenly faced with unplanned and unmanageable development, will be prompted to develop growth control plans of their own that attract "good" tax ratables and exclude the poor. This competition among localities would appear to invite, if not to compel, the state to intervene in the land planning process to assure orderly growth. States can promote systematic energy-efficient growth by not only requiring all localities to plan comprehensively, but also requiring localities to coordinate their plans with each other and to make them conform to state goals and guidelines.

Comprehensive land use planning entails one additional benefit: the existence of comprehensive plans can make it more likely that courts will uphold the use of flexible land use techniques that can enhance energy conservation. These innovative techniques, such as planned unit development ordinances and growth management controls, give planning bodies useful and important discretion. But the exercise of such discretion without the backdrop of a comprehensive plan is vulnerable to legal challenge since piecemeal planning decisions may be struck down as being either arbitrary or capricious.

Since it is broad, unrestrained discretion that makes a planning agency's decisions vulnerable, those decisions can be strengthened if the comprehensive plan includes goals and standards to which the agency must adhere. At the same time, a flexible plan would still permit planning agencies to implement innovative land use controls. If a court can be persuaded that a comprehensive plan ensures that innovative land use controls are rational and are imposed fairly, it may find in the plan a basis for holding that flexible land use controls are constitutional [67]. For example, the sophisticated growth management system challenged in the landmark *Ramapo* case might not have been upheld if the comprehensive town plan (based on four volumes of land use studies) had not existed. The extensive research that culminated in the development of the plan and its implementing regulations helped convince the court that the growth management system adopted by Ramapo was a rational, fair response to the threat of unmanageable population pressures.

Securing citizen approval of the theory of comprehensive planning is only the first step in developing an energy-efficient plan. Citizen support during the planning process, which can be stimulated by encouraging citizen participation at all stages, is also crucial. Indeed, Oregon mandates citizen involvement in the planning process by requiring each county to appoint a broadly based citizen advisory committee to assist in preparing, adopting, and revising comprehensive plans within the county [68]. The support generated through citizen involvement in the early phases of comprehensive planning can be expected to provide a solid base for action during the implementation stage.

Incorporating Energy Conservation as a Goal

Once a locality decides to draft a comprehensive plan, it must next decide what elements to include in the plan. States that mandate local comprehensive planning will want to help select the elements addressed by the plan, and they should use their authority to make sure that energy conservation is one of the planning goals.

As noted, Oregon has established a state agency to develop mandatory statewide goals and guidelines for local comprehensive plans, relying in turn upon that agency to make energy conservation one of its goals. Because Oregon's approach leaves to the agency's discretion the matter of designating energy conservation as a statewide goal, a better approach may be to include in the local comprehensive planning statute the requirement that energy conservation be embraced as a goal by those developing the comprehensive plan. But this second approach is also less flexible. The state enabling statute for local comprehensive planning runs the risk of becoming a checklist, rather than a policy guide, if everything a comprehensive plan should consider, including energy conservation, is enumerated in the statute. Nevertheless, Florida [69] and California [70] have chosen this approach (albeit for goals other than energy conservation) to ensure that localities will consider elements deemed fundamental to good comprehensive planning. There is no reason why energy conservation cannot be added to the checklist [71]. Yet any state adopting this approach should also be prepared to create a state agency, as Oregon has done, to make certain that the local plans are consistent with the energy requirements of the state statute. Courts are ill-equipped to weigh the policy considerations inherent in development of an "energy-efficient" comprehensive land use plan.

Of course, states could, as a third approach, rely on local planners to voluntarily incorporate an energy conservation element into the plan. Although this approach requires no state regulation of local activity and may be preferable to some people for that reason, it is the least effective way of promoting energy-efficient land use plans precisely because it is the least stringent [72].

If energy conservation is made a required planning goal, the extent to which plans must promote energy-efficient land use must then be determined. On the one hand, localities can be required always to promote maximum energy conservation. At the other extreme, energy conservation can be designated a "consideration" to be weighed in developing a comprehensive plan. The more rigid requirement may backfire since many considerations other than energy consumption influence land use decisions. In some instances, a goal that conflicts with energy conservation may be more important. But simply designating energy conservation as a consideration may not be enough—localities may in practice ignore the potential energy impacts [73] of their proposed development. The Oregon method of requiring localities to state the reasons for failing to incorporate a goal—including the goal of conservation—in their comprehensive plans seems to represent a good compromise between concern for energy conservation and the need for flexibility in planning.

Coordinating Land Use Regulations with the Comprehensive Plan

Local comprehensive plans promoting energy conservation will be effective only if, as in Oregon, states require all zoning and subdivision ordinances, regulations, and other land use control tools to be consistent with the plan's policies. At present, comprehensive plans are often disregarded when requests for zoning amendments or variances come before local planning commissions, and previously adopted ordinances are seldom changed to conform to comprehensive plans [74]. Recently, however, the trend in several state courts has been to require zoning ordinances to conform to independently adopted comprehensive plans [75].

Supplementing such court opinions, several states have enacted legislation requiring consistency between land use regulations and separate comprehensive plans [76]. These statutes differ in their definitions of consistency, in the types of land use controls that they specify as subject to the consistency provisions, and in their handling of regulations that predate the consistency requirement.

California limits application of the consistency requirement to county and city zoning ordinances, but requires preexisting ordinances to conform to the comprehensive plan by a specified date [77]. "Consistency" in the California statute means that the "various land uses authorized by the ordinance are compatible with the objectives, policies, general land uses and programs specified in such a plan" [78]. In contrast to the California statutes, the Florida Local Government Comprehensive Planning Act of 1975 requires all land development regulations and amendments to the regulations—not just zoning ordinances—to be consistent with the adopted comprehensive plans [79]. The Florida act specifies that land development regulations include all zoning, subdivision, building, and construction regulations, as well as other regulations controlling the development of land [80]. Florida does not define "consistent."

If localities are to channel growth effectively into energy-efficient locations, they must adopt comprehensive plans designed to achieve that goal, and they must then make existing and future land use regulations conform to the plan. The best strategy is to combine the California and Florida approaches, requiring all land development regulations—including those predating the plan—to be made consistent with the adopted plan.

Requiring State Activities to Conform to Local Comprehensive Plans

Localities that adopt comprehensive plans often complain that their plans are ignored by state agencies that build roads, approve transmission lines, and construct state facilities that have tremendous influence over where public and private development will occur [81], and thus over energy consumption patterns. This disregard has generally been sustained by the courts [82].

One way to help guide development into energy-efficient locations is to encourage or even to require regional and state agencies to cooperate with local governments in the preparation of energy-efficient local comprehensive plans. A comprehensive plan based on such cooperation will not only serve local needs but will also reflect regional and statewide concerns. Cooperation reduces the possibility that a carefully prepared local comprehensive plan will be trampled upon by state or regional agencies.

The Virginia comprehensive planning law provides an example of a statutory mandate for cooperation between local governments and state agencies during the preparation of comprehensive plans. The statute requires state agencies responsible for construction, operation, or maintenance of public facilities within an area covered by a comprehensive plan to cooperate with local planning commissions. State agencies must furnish local comprehensive planning agencies with relevant information upon request [83].

A more effective strategy for bringing state activities in line with local comprehensive plans is, in addition to requiring agency cooperation, to require state agency actions to be compatible, or to comply with, approved local plans. Florida, Idaho, and Virginia comprehensive planning statutes require such conformity. Florida takes the strongest position regarding consistency by requiring all agency action that affects land covered by local comprehensive plans to honor the provisions of such plans [84].

In contrast to the Florida law, the Idaho and Virginia statutes recognize that broad state interests will occasionally differ from, and should override, local considerations. Idaho solves the problem by requiring governmental development to be consistent with local government plans and regulations except in those instances explicitly excused by statute [85]. Virginia, on the other hand, requires public streets, parks, other public areas, buildings, structures, utility facilities, and service corporation facilities (except railroad facilities) to conform "substantially" with adopted local plans [86].

A fourth approach for coordinating state agency action and local planning is Oregon's practice of making state agencies and special districts subject to the same statewide goals and guidelines (including the goal of energy conservation) that localities must follow in preparing comprehensive plans [87]. Oregon further enhances statewide coordination by requiring state and federal agencies and special districts to review local comprehensive plans in order to identify and to resolve conflicts between plans and projects of agencies and local comprehensive plans.

In sum, states and local governments can take a major step toward energy-efficient land use by establishing energy conservation as a policy goal to be reflected in all government actions and decisions. In addition, state and local governments should prepare comprehensive land use plans that identify where and how energy-efficient growth should occur. Though regional coordination of land use planning is essential, few states have created effective regional planning agencies. An alternative approach is to follow the Oregon model of requiring local governments to prepare comprehensive plans in accordance with the statewide goal of energy conservation. But, as Oregon has recognized, simple planning is not enough to ensure energy conservation. Consequently, that state has gone several steps further, and other states should follow its lead. Oregon subjects local plans to state agency approval, requires coordination of municipal plans with those of surrounding communities, and requires zoning, subdivision, and other land use controls to conform to and promote the comprehensive plans. Chapters 4, 5, and 6 contain specific suggestions for using those controls to give teeth to the adopted comprehensive plans.

NOTES TO CHAPTER 3

1. From 1950 to 1972, the number of metropolitan areas in the U.S. increased by 60 percent, while the number of metropolitan counties rose by 80 percent. The U.S. Commission on Population Growth and the American Future estimates that by the year 2000 there will be over three hundred standard metropolitan statistical areas and that about 25 percent of the nation's 3,146 counties will lie within the boundaries of a metropolitan complex. By the year 2000, there will be at least fifty SMSAs with populations over one million persons, whereas only fourteen SMSAs with that population existed in 1950. (Advisory Commission on Intergovernmental Relations, *Substate Regionalism and the Federal System/Regional Decisionmaking: New Strategies For Substate Districts*, I (Washington, D.C.: U.S. Government Printing Office, 1973), p. 317 (hereinafter cited as ACIR).

2. Although "community" usually refers only to local communities, here it refers to regional and statewide "communities" as well.

3. Donald G. Hagman, *Urban Planning and Land Development Control Law* § 22 (St. Paul: West Publishing Co., 1971), pp. 51–52.

4. "Community Goals and Policies/1974/Eugene" (Eugene, Oregon: Eugene Planning Department, 1974), p. 32.

5. "Albuquerque/Bernalillo County Comprehensive Plan/Policies Plan," (Albuquerque/Bernalillo County, New Mexico: Albuquerque/Bernalillo County

Planning Department, April 1975), p. 24. The policies plan also lists several specific techniques for achieving energy conservation goals.

6. "Transportation Goals and Policies" and "Energy Goals and Policies," adopted by the Lincoln City Council by Resolution A–62436 on January 26, 1976, and by the Lancaster County Board of Commissioners by motion on January 24, 1976.

7. The Council of State Governments, *State Growth Management*, prepared for the Office of Community Planning and Development, U.S. Department of Housing and Urban Development (Washington, D.C.: U.S. Government Printing Office, May 1976), pp. 24–25.

8. Vermont Land Use and Development Law, Vt. Stat. Ann. tit. 10, § 6086 (a) (9) (F) (Supp. 1975).

9. Vermont Public Service Board and the Agency of Environmental Conservation, "State of Vermont Energy Conservation Guidelines," (Montpelier: April 1974).

10. Vt. Stat. Ann. tit. 10, §§ 6083–6085 (Supp. 1975).

11. *Id.* at § 6087 (a), (b).

12. Florida Environmental Land and Water Management Act of 1972, Fla. Stat. Ann. § 380.012 et seq. (West Supp. 1977).

13. *Id.* at § 380.06 (1).

14. Florida has not yet adopted a state comprehensive land use plan, however.

15. Fla. Stat. Ann. § 380.06 (8) (11) (West Supp. 1977).

16. Fla. Stat. Ann. § 380.06 (2) (f), (8) (f) (West. Supp. 1977).

17. At least one regional planning agency has, however, voluntarily taken this step. *See* the discussion of Homestead, Florida, pp. 196–197, *infra.*

18. The Center for Governmental Responsibility, Gainesville, Florida.

19. A copy of the proposal is in the author's files.

20. 1973 Oregon Land Use Act, Or. Rev. Stat. § 197.400 (1) (1975–1976). Interestingly, power transmission lines are not listed among activities of statewide significance even though they strongly influence the location of new growth. The Oregon statute does, however, provide that the state planning commission can advise the state legislature to regulate other activities of statewide significance. *Id.* at § 197.405 (1).

21. LCDC has not yet exercised its designation power under the act.

22. Or. Rev. Stat. §§ 197.410, 197.415 (5) (1975–1976).

23. Oregon Land Conservation and Development Commission, "State-Wide Planning Goals and Guidelines," January 1, 1975, Goal No. 13.

13–ENERGY CONSERVATION

Goal:

> To conserve energy.
> Land and uses developed on the land shall be managed and controlled so as to maximize the conservation of all forms of energy, based upon sound economic principles.

Guidelines:

A. PLANNING:

1. Priority consideration in land use planning should be given to methods of analysis and implementation measures that will assure achievement of maximum efficiency in energy utilization.
2. The allocation of land and uses permitted on the land should seek to minimize the depletion of non-renewable sources of energy.
3. Land use planning should, to the maximum extent possible, seek to recycle and re-use vacant land and those uses which are not energy efficient.
4. Land use planning should, to the maximum extent possible, combine increasing density gradients along with capacity transportation corridors to achieve greater energy efficiency.
5. Plans directed toward energy conservation within the planning area should consider as a major determinant the existing and potential capacity of the renewable energy sources to yield useful energy output. Renewable energy sources include water, sunshine, wind, geothermal heat and municipal, forest and farm waste. Whenever possible, land conservation and development actions provided for under such plans should utilize renewable energy sources.

B. IMPLEMENTATION:

1. Land use plans should be based on utilization of the following techniques and implementation devices which can have a material impact on energy efficiency:
   a. Lot size, dimension and siting controls;
   b. Building height, bulk and surface area;
   c. Density of uses, particularly those which relate to housing densities;
   d. Availability of light, wind and air;
   e. Compatibility of and competition between competing land use activities; and
   f. Systems and incentives for the collection, reuse and recycling of metallic and nonmetallic waste.

24. Or. Rev. Stat. §§ 197.180, 197.185 (1975−1976).

25. Other elements of the Oregon Land Use Act that enhance energy-efficient land development are discussed later in this chapter.

26. James S. Roberts, *Energy, Land Use, and Growth Policy: Implications for Metropolitan Washington* (Washington, D.C.: Metropolitan Washington Council of Governments, 1975).

27. ACIR, *supra* note 1 at 345.

28. Or. Rev. Stat. §§ 197.705−197.795 (1975−1976).

29. *See* Fred P. Bosselman et al., *The Permit Explosion: Coordination of the Proliferation* (Washington, D.C.: The Urban Land Institute, 1976), pp. 12−15.

30. Cal. Regional Planning Law, Cal. Gov't Code §§ 65060.8, 65069, 65069.1, 65069.2 (West Supp. 1975) California also provides that two or more counties

may create a planning district upon resolution of the board of supervisors in each county, but recommendations made by such a district body are also merely advisory. Cal. Gov't Code §§ 66140, 66241 (West 1966).

31. N.Y. Exec. Law §§ 800−810 (McKinney Supp. 1975).

32. Cal. Gov.'t Code §§ 66600 et seq. (West Supp. 1975).

33. Cal. Gov.'t Code §§ 66800 et seq. (West Supp. 1975).

34. N. J. Stat. Ann. § 13: 17−1 et seq. (West Supp. 1974).

35. *See* City of Hartford v. Hills, ＿＿ F. Supp. ＿＿ (D.C. Conn. January 28, 1976); and Southern Burlington County NAACP v. Township of Mt. Laurel, 67 N.J. 151, 336 A.2d 713, *appeal dismissed*, 423 U.S. 808 (1975). *See also* Appendix I, pp. 221−225.

36. The Twin Cities region in Minnesota uses a fiscal disparities tax to distribute tax revenues on a regional basis. Fiscal Disparities Bill, Minn. Stat. Ann. §§ 473 F.01 et seq. (West Supp. 1975). See p. 147, *infra*.

37. Cal. Gov.'t Code § 35002 (West 1968).

38. Or. Rev. Stat. § 199.410 et seq. (1975−1976).

39. Aside from political difficulties, the establishment of powerful regional councils raises several legal issues. First, the state must ensure that the creation of a council with implementing authority does not conflict with constitutionally or statutorily granted local home rule power. If a conflict arises, home rule provisions would have to be amended.

In addition, the creation of regional councils raises issues related to voting and equal representation. Densely populated cities will advocate population-weighted one person, one vote systems. Suburban municipalities usually prefer a system in which each governmental unit has a vote, since this enhances their strength. Even though courts may uphold unit voting schemes in which council members are appointed rather than elected or in which the council performs proprietary functions (like supplying ranchers with water) rather than governmental functions, population-weighted voting may be required for regional councils with elected representatives who perform planning, administrative, and enforcement duties. *See* ACIR, *supra* note 1 at 335. Interestingly, however, the voting strength of CRAG, a regional planning body in Oregon, reflects governmental entities rather than population.

40. Or. Rev. Stat. §§ 197.030, 197.040 (2) (a), (d) (1975−1976).

41. Oregon LCDC, *supra* note 23. Guidelines for implementing several other statewide goals require, directly or indirectly, consideration of energy as a factor in the planning process: Goal Number 2 (To establish a land use planning process and policy framework); Goal Number 3 (To preserve and maintain agricultural lands); Goal Number 5 (To conserve open space and protect natural resources); Goal Number 8 (To satisfy the recreational needs of the citizens of the state and visitors); Goal Number 9 (To diversify and improve the economy of the state); Goal Number 10 (To provide for the housing needs of citizens of the state); Goal Number 11 (To plan and develop a timely, orderly, and efficient arrangement of public facilities and services to serve as a framework for urban and rural development); Goal Number 12 (To provide and encourage a safe, convenient, and economic transportation system); and Goal Number 14 (To provide for an orderly

and efficient transition from rural to urban land use). All of the above goals recommend that the energy impacts of actions to attain the goals be considered. In addition, Goal Number 7 (To protect life and property from natural disasters and hazards) indirectly promotes energy conservation by recommending creation of low density and open space uses in flood plains, and thus provides a growth management tool that may be used to promote more compact, less sprawling developments elsewhere.

42. Or. Rev. Stat. § 197.175 (1975–1976).

43. *Id.* at § 197.300.

44. *Id.* at §§ 197.325(1), 197.330. Proposed legislation would amend these provisions so that a noncomplying locality would be held in contempt of court.

45. *Id.* at §§ 215.510 (3), 215.535.

46. *Id.* at §§ 197.310 (5), 183.480.

47. Oregon LCDC, *supra* note 23 at 8.

48. Or. Rev. Stat. § 197.190 (1) (1975–1976). Portland is exempted from this requirement. *Id.*

49. Boundary commissions that must approve extension of sewer and water services and changes in municipal and service district boundaries also play an important role in coordinating regional growth. These commissions and their value as forceful instruments to promote energy conservation are discussed on pp. 143–145, *infra.*

50. The Council of State Governments, *1976 Suggested State Legislation,* XXXV (Lexington, Kentucky: The Council of State Governments, 1975), p. 75.

51. The Housing and Urban Development § 701 Comprehensive Planning Assistance Program has provided financial assistance to many local governments developing comprehensive plans, but Congress has drastically reduced funding for that program.

52. The ALI code requires local governments to adopt a "Local Land Development Plan" before they are granted the powers to (1) adopt special procedures for regulating planned unit developments; (2) designate "specially planned areas"; (3) incorporate by reference in their development ordinance criteria for development permits set forth in the land development plan; (4) establish special preservation districts without first preparing a written report that analyzes certain specified conditions; (5) reserve land for future acquisition by public agencies; and (6) enjoy broad powers for discontinuation of existing land uses. American Law Institute, *A Model Land Development Code,* §§ 3–101, 2–210, 2–211, 2–212, 2–209 (1) (b), 3–201, 4–102 (1) (Philadelphia, 1975).

53. Cal. Gov.'t Code § 65300 et seq. (West Supp. 1975).

54. Neb. L.B. 317, *as amended by* L.B. 410 (1975).

55. Fla. Stat. Ann. § 163.3161 et seq. (West Supp. 1977).

56. Idaho Local Planning Act of 1975, Idaho Code § 67–6508 (Supp. 1975).

57. Wyo. Stat. § 9–856 (Supp. 1975).

58. Va. Code § 15.1–446.1 (Supp. 1975).

59. Wyo. Stat. § 9.856 (e) (Supp. 1975).

60. Fla. Stat. Ann. § 163.3167 (8) (West Supp. 1977).

61. In Nebraska, a county within a standard metropolitan statistical area

must prepare plans and enforce zoning and subdivision regulations for municipalities that fail to prepare and to enforce adequately on their own plans and regulations. Neb. L.B. 317 §1, *as amended by* L.B. 410 §31 (1975).

62. Wyo. State Land Use Planning Act, Wyo. Stat. §9—862 (Supp. 1975).

63. *See* Village of Euclid v. Ambler Realty Co., 272 U.S. 365 (1926), which upheld zoning as a valid exercise of the police power of the state. Regulation of land use goes back as far as early nuisance cases prohibiting certain land uses deemed detrimental to the community. *See* Mugler v. Kansas, 123 U.S. 623 (1887).

64. Memorandum from Dick Mathews, land use economist at Oregon's LCDC to Edward Sullivan, legal counsel to Governor Robert W. Straub, dated October 13, 1976, on file with the author.

65. Golden v. Planning Board of the Town of Ramapo, 30 N.Y. 2d 359, 285 N.E.2d 291, 334 N.Y.S.2d 138, *appeal dismissed*, 409 U.S. 1003 (1972).

66. Construction Industry Association of Sonoma County v. City of Petaluma, 522 F.2d 897 (9th Cir. 1975), *cert. denied*, 424 U.S. 934, (1976).

67. Daniel R. Mandelker, The Role of the Local Comprehensive Plan in Land Use Regulation, 74 *Mich. L. Rev.* 900, 910—15 (1976).

68. Or. Rev. Stat. §197.160 (1975—1976).

69. Fla. Stat. Ann. §163.3177 (West Supp. 1977).

70. Cal. Gov.'t Code §65302 (West Supp. 1975).

71. As noted elsewhere, the Vermont Land Use and Development Law includes energy conservation as a criterion, but not in the context of comprehensive planning. Under Vermont law, all large and some small developments must show that ". . . planning and design of the subdivision or development reflect the principles of energy conservation and incorporate the best available technology for efficient use or recovery of energy." Vt. Stat. Ann. tit. 10 §6068(a) (9) (F) (Supp. 1975).

72. In any event, it is crucial that energy conservation be included as a planning element in the initial phase of local comprehensive planning. Once a comprehensive plan has been adopted, it will be extremely burdensome later to revise the plan to reflect energy conservation goals.

73. *See* Green v. Hayward, 23 Or. App. 310, 542 P.2d 144 (1975), *rev'd.* 275 Or. 693, ____ P.2d ____ (1976), which indicates the dangers inherent in making energy conservation a mere "consideration" in local planning. *Green* requires local boards to make detailed findings when approving or denying rezoning petitions. This process helps avoid the possibility that important policies like energy conservation might be overlooked in the decisionmaking process.

74. Comprehensive land use plans are given slight weight in large part because comprehensive planning enabling legislation has developed so haphazardly. The Standard Zoning and Enabling Act of 1926, which forms the basis for zoning enabling laws in forty-one states, empowers local goverments to zone "in accordance with a comprehensive plan." United States Department of Commerce, A Standard Zoning Enabling Act §3 (rev. ed. 1926), (hereafter referred to as SZEA). Ever since SZEA was adopted, confusion has arisen over whether zoning must comply with an independently adopted comprehensive plan or whether "comprehensive plan" simply refers to a rational, integrated zoning process. Part

of the confusion reflects the fact that it was not until two years after adoption of SZEA that the Department of Commerce promulgated the Standard Planning Enabling Act (SPEA), which authorizes local master planning and subdivision control. United States Department of Commerce, A Standard City Planning Enabling Act (1928), (hereafter referred to as SPEA).

Because nothing indicates that the comprehensive plan referred to in SZEA can be considered identical to the independently adopted master plan authorized by SPEA, most courts hold that SZEA does not require reference to an independent plan. (A leading example of this interpretation is Kozesnik v. Township of Montgomery, 24 N.J. 154, 131 A.2d 1 (1957). *See also* Citizen's Ass'n of Georgetown, Inc. v. Zoning Comm'n, 477 F.2d 402 (D.C. Cir. 1973); Bow & Arrow Manor, Inc. v. Town of West Orange, 63 N.J. 335, 307 A.2d 563 (1973). *See generally* E.J. Sullivan and L. Kressel, Twenty Years After—Renewed Significance of the Comprehensive Plan Requirement, 9 *Urban L. Ann.* 33 (1957).) Nevertheless, some courts consult independent comprehensive plans when examining land use regulations, even though the courts do not require that a separate plan exist for regulations to be upheld. *See* Udell v. Haas, 21 N.Y.2d 463, 235 N.E.2d 897, 288 N.Y.S.2d 888, (1968); Biske v. City of Troy, 381 Mich. 611, 166 N.W.2d 453 (1969). *See generally* Sullivan and Kressel, *supra*.

For a discussion of the history of local comprehensive planning, see Mandelker, *supra* note 67.

75. The landmark case on the subject is Fasano v. Board of County Commissioners, 264 Or. 574, 507 P.2d 23 (1973). *Fasano*, decided in 1973 by the Oregon Supreme Court, held that a county rezoning in Oregon must be consistent with an independently adopted county comprehensive plan. In a subsequent case, the Oregon Supreme Court further clarified the role of comprehensive plans when it ruled in Baker v. City of Milwaukie, ____ Or. ____ , 533 P.2d 772 (1975), that city zoning ordinances adopted prior to the adoption of a comprehensive plan must be changed to comply with the plan. Oregon courts are not the only ones to recognize the importance of comprehensive planning. Maryland, New York, Colorado, and Kentucky are some of the states whose courts have also given presumptive weight to independent comprehensive plans. *See* Norbeck Village Joint Venture v. Montgomery County Council, 254 Md. 59, 254 A.2d 700 (1969). Golden v. Planning Board of the Town of Ramapo, 30 N.Y.2d 359, 285 N.E. 2d 291, 334 N.Y.S.2d 138, *appeal dismissed*, 409 U.S. 1003 (1972); Fontaine v. Board of County Comm'rs, 493 P.2d 670 (Col. App. 1971); City of Louisville v. Kavanaugh, 495 S.W.2d 502 (Ky. App. 1973).

76. The California and Florida statutes are discussed in the text. *See also* Or. Rev. Stat. § 197.175 (2) (b) (1975–1976); Alaska Stat. §§ 20.33.090, 29.33.080, 29.33.085, (Supp. 1974); Ky. Rev. Stat. § 100.213 (1971) (note that Kentucky requires only map amendments, not zoning ordinances, to be in agreement with the comprehensive plan); and Neb. Rev. Stat. § 23.114.03 (1974). *See* Mendelker, *supra* note 67.

77. Cal. Gov't Code § 65860 (a) (West Supp. 1975).

78. *Id.* at § 65860 (a) (ii).

79. Fla. Stat. Ann. § 163.3194 (1) (West Supp. 1977).

80. *Id.* at § 163.3194 (2) (b).

81. Urban Systems Research & Engineering, Inc., *The Growth Shapers/The Land Use Impacts of Infrastructure Investments*, prepared for the U.S. Council on Environmental Quality (Washington, D.C.: U.S. Government Printing Office, 1976).

82. *See* Board of Regents of the Universities and State College v. City of Tempe, 88 Ariz. 299, 356 P.2d 399 (1960); The City of Des Plaines v. The Metropolitan Sanitary District of Greater Chicago, 59 Ill.2d 29, 319 N.E.2d 9 (1974).

83. Va. Code § 15.1–457 (Supp. 1975).

84. Fla. Stat. Ann. § 163.3194 (1) (West Supp. 1977). The Florida act defines governmental agencies to include federal governmental agencies. But case law has determined that the federal government is not subject to local or state regulation in the exercise of its constitutional powers. *See* United States v. Chester, 144 F.2d 415 (3d Cir. 1944).

85. Idaho Local Planning Act of 1975, Idaho Code § 67–6528 (Supp. 1975). This approach is also taken by the ALI Model Land Development Code, which requires government development to comply with local land use regulations except to the extent exempted by specific laws. ALI, *supra* note 52 at § 12–201 and accompanying Comment.

86. Va. Code §§ 15.1–456, 15.1–457 (Supp. 1975). The Virginia statute adds that even though state agencies must cooperate with local planning bodies, the act does not abridge the authority of state agencies over facilities coming under their jurisdiction. *Id.* at § 15.1–457. Whether this provision and a similar one in the Florida statute provide a loophole through which state agencies can circumvent local plans is a matter for judicial interpretation.

87. Or. Rev. Stat. §§ 197.180, 197.185 (1975–1976).

✳ *Part II*

Strategies for Energy-Efficient Land Use

Introduction

The following chapters review a variety of ways that states and local governments can use their regulatory, taxing, and spending powers to promote the energy-efficient land use goals outlined in Chapter 2.

The strategies included here are not touted as finished products. They are offered as suggestions and must in all instances be altered to satisfy state and local needs and laws. Table II−1, which lists some of the major participants and influences in the land development process, provides an idea of the numerous "entry points" for adapting strategies to achieve energy savings.

This book is designed to help states and localities decide not only what to do to save energy but also how to do it. Consequently, the following chapters contain considerable discussion of the legal issues that may arise when selected strategies are adopted. Additional discussion of legal issues may be found in Appendix I, pp. 213 to 236. Of course, these general discussions cannot replace expert legal analysis that is an essential part of any program for conserving energy through changes in land use. Readers are urged to consult attorneys before adopting techniques reviewed in the following pages.

Strategies rarely work in isolation; they should be combined and coordinated for maximum effectiveness. Yet, depending on what strategies are adopted and whether and how they are used in combination with other strategies, a program for conserving energy through land use can have secondary impacts that undermine the energy efficiency it is designed to promote. For example, a planned unit development (PUD) ordinance intended to save energy by clustering and

Table II–1. Major Participants and Influences in the Housing Market

Market Phase	Participants	Influences
Preparation: land acquisition, planning, and zoning amendments	Developer Landowner Lawyers Real estate brokers Title companies Architects and engineers Surveyor Planners and consultants Zoning and planning officials	Real estate law Recording regulations and fees Banking laws Zoning Subdivision regulations Private deed restrictions Public master plans
Production: site preparation, construction, and financing	Developer Lending institutions (interim and permanent) FHA, VA, or private mortgage insurance company Contractors Subcontractors Craftsmen and their unions Material manufacturers and distributors Building code officials Insurance companies Architects and engineers	Banking laws Building and mechanical codes Subdivision regulations Utility regulations Union rules Rules of trade and professional associations Insurance laws Laws controlling transportation of materials
Distribution: sale (and subsequent resale or refinancing)	Developer Real estate brokers Lawyers Lending institutions Title companies FHA, VA, or private mortgage insurance company	Recording regulations and fees Real estate law Transfer taxes Banking laws Rules of professional associations

| Service: maintenance and management, repairs, and improvements and additions | Owner
Maintenance firms and employees
Property management firms
Insurance companies
Utility companies
Tax assessors
Repairmen, craftsmen, and their unions
Lending institutions
Architects and engineers
Contractors
Subcontractors
Material manufacturers and distributors
Local zoning officials
Local building officials | Property taxes
Income taxes
Housing and health codes
Insurance laws
Utility regulations
Banking laws
Union rules
Rules of trade and professional associations
Zoning
Building and mechanical codes
Laws controlling transportation of materials |

Source: *A Decent Home*, Report of the President's Committee on Urban Housing (Washington, D.C.: U.S. Government Printing Office, 1969), p. 115.

properly orienting buildings may actually waste more energy than a conventional development if, as a condition for permitting the PUD, the community lowers the permissible density of development. Similarly, construction of a subway line may open up fringe areas that were previously considered too far away from the urban center to develop. Thus homes and jobs will be separated by an even greater distance unless jobs follow the residential development to suburban communities. Consequently, it is essential to consider the potential secondary energy impacts of proposed strategies.

Because other secondary effects—economic, social, environmental, and political—are likely to result from programs to encourage energy conservation through land use, state and local governments must also try to predict and consider the overall impacts that such a land use policy may have. The impact will vary according to the natural environment, degree of development, size, economic base, growth pressures, and climate of the community adopting the techniques. In some instances, energy conservation goals may have to be compromised.

The strategies suggested here are not all equally popular, simple, or easy to administer. Nevertheless, if state and local governments keep in mind their makeup, finances, technical skills, and the other goals with which energy conservation strategies must be meshed, they can design a land use program that will maximize energy savings while accommodating other important interests touched by land use policies.

Chapter 4

Energy-Efficient Density, Mixture of Uses, and Design

The density of development, the uses that will be permitted in a development, and how that development will be put together into an attractive, economical, and sound design are three issues that have consumed countless hours of negotiation between developers and planning boards. Although the issues are separable, it is often helpful to look at them as a unit since decisions regarding one factor will influence decisions regarding the other two. Particularly when energy efficiency is a major concern, the three questions should be treated together. This chapter reviews strategies that can remove barriers to energy-efficient development through optimum density, mixed uses, and design.

HIGHER DENSITY ZONING

Zoning and subdivision regulations are adopted to ensure that communities and neighborhoods will be designed to enhance the health, safety, and welfare of citizens. As the Standard Zoning Enabling Act states, the purpose of zoning regulations is to:

> lessen congestion in the streets; to secure safety from fire, flood, panic, and other dangers; to promote health and the general welfare; to provide adequate light and air; to prevent the overcrowding of land; to avoid undue concentration of population; [and] to facilitate the adequate provision of transportation, water, sewerage, schools, parks and other public requirements [1].

The traditional response to these goals has been adoption of unnecessarily rigid lot size, height, and use restrictions that prevent development at an optimal density to minimize energy use. This section examines modifications to zoning and subdivision ordinances that can remove impediments to higher densities while still preserving public health, safety, and welfare [2].

As noted in Part I, moderately high density development is the backbone of a multitude of energy-conserving land use goals. Multi-unit buildings can cut space heating and cooling costs by about 60 percent per unit since units are smaller and have fewer exposed surfaces that permit temperature exchanges. Dense development allows the use of total energy systems that reuse waste heat generated during the production of electricity. It also can permit and encourage the use of energy-efficient public transportation systems and, when it has the effect of bringing trip origins and destinations closer together, it will reduce the length of trips and can even make walking and bicycling reasonable substitutes for the automobile. Similarly, when higher density development is combined with energy-efficient locational choices, it will reduce the length of roads and utility systems whose unnecessarily extensive construction wastes fuel.

In spite of these energy efficiencies and the fiscal economies that accompany them, higher density development is not desirable everywhere, nor will it contribute to energy savings unless properly located. As the New York Regional Plan Association observed in a recent study [3], an isolated high-rise building will not permit use of public transit, but instead will increase dependence on automobiles for personal transportation. Doubling residential density from five to ten dwellings per acre within one mile of a downtown of ten million square feet will increase per capita public transit trips seventeen times as much as if the residential density is increased the same amount at a distance of ten miles from the downtown [4]. These figures emphasize the importance of locating dense development close to urban activity centers. In addition, they add evidence that Manhattan style development is not necessary for transportation energy savings. Indeed, as noted in Part I, super high-rises of fifty stories or more appear energy inefficient, while low-rise and small apartment buildings offer substantial energy savings.

Unfortunately, the multifamily housing market is suffering. Part of the problem may be attributed to greater financial risks associated with large-scale construction, higher mortgage interest rates applied to multifamily projects, and rent control that makes investment return uncertain [5]. These problems can be solved only through aggressive federal and state fiscal programs designed to make multi-family housing economically attractive to the investor. But other trends indicate that there are equally strong pressures operating to overcome the prejudice against multifamily housing. The economic recession and skyrocketing land and construction costs have removed the prospect of single family homeownership from three-fourths of the American public. Investment in cooperatives and condominiums has become an attractive way for builders to avoid the uncertainties raised by rent control. And, of course, the rising cost of energy will make the demand for multifamily housing even greater. These economic facts have been accompanied by changes in household preferences—people are getting married later in life and having fewer children, thus making multifamily housing a more attractive option. Many young couples no longer want to be saddled with the time-consuming home and yard maintenance chores imposed by single family housing.

Whatever the solution may be for removing economic obstacles to multifamily housing, state and local officials can with little effort ensure that outmoded regulatory barriers do not prevent energy-efficient, higher density development for those whose lifestyles or financial circumstances make it desirable.

In the energy-ideal world, all development would consist of multi-family structures at a density high enough to support use of public transit. Since the ideal is unrealistic for most communities, more practical, energy-efficient designs that communities should promote are (1) a community pattern where population is most dense near the urban center, (2) polynucleated development with high density clusters close to transportation lines, or (3) a "transit-oriented" pattern with high density residential and commercial growth located along transportation corridors that radiate from the urban center. Many cities already follow the first pattern—but few realize its energy-saving potential. Cities also may overlook the need to integrate higher density developments with transportation planning. And they may not recognize that, in many commercial and "buffer" residential areas, higher density than is presently permitted may be justified to save fuel.

By examining their comprehensive land use plans, localities can identify areas where more dense development can supplement space heating and cooling energy savings with transportation energy savings. They may spot areas where, even though single family housing is desirable, unnecessarily large lot sizes contribute to "urban spread" and hence longer automobile trips. Once they have identified target areas for multifamily development and smaller lots, the process of modifying existing ordinances to achieve higher densities is a relatively simple matter.

Zoning for Multifamily Structures

A first step communities can take to promote more dense development is to zone for multifamily structures. This step needs little elaboration: a simple change in the text of the zoning ordinance or a change in the zoning map to permit multifamily housing in areas where it previously was prohibited will accomplish the desired purpose. Some people have suggested that in addition to zoning for multifamily structures, communities should require developers of large projects to include a certain percentage of multifamily housing in the development. But, as discussed later [6], the legality of such a requirement is uncertain. On the other hand, communities may be on safer ground if they offer developers a *quid pro quo*, such as permitting cluster development or a planned unit development in exchange for the developer's including a certain percentage of multifamily housing in the project [7]. Although developers will have an economic incentive to put multifamily housing on land zoned for dense development, communities can spur the process along by making sure that the property assessments conform to the density permitted by the zoning. Oregon has accomplished this through an amendment to its tax laws [8]. It has also published a guide, reprinted in Appendix II on p. 260, that shows how assessors must value land in accordance with the comprehensive plan and zoning restrictions.

Modifying Height Restrictions

A second step in increasing density is to amend height restrictions to permit construction of energy-efficient, taller buildings such as garden apartments and low-rises. Two reasons communities impose height restrictions are to control congestion and to ensure that buildings will receive adequate light and air. Again, the health and safety goals are commendable, and should not be sacrificed for purposes of energy conservation. Nevertheless, multistory buildings may be desirable along major roads and transportation lines and near commercial centers. In those places, congestion that might otherwise accompany increased density may be reduced by integrating the more intense land use with transportation planning so that individuals can be pried out of automobiles and into conveniently located public transit. Montgomery County, Maryland, has acknowledged this interrelationship between high density development and public transit by creating transit station development zones for high density, multistory buildings within walking distance of transit stations [9]. The ordinance authorizing that development is reprinted in Appendix II, p. 266.

Reducing Lot Size Requirements

Another step to encourage more dense development is to reduce rigid lot size requirements in areas where single family housing will continue to be permitted. Conceivably, these requirements throughout an entire zoning district may need reduction. For example, with proper land use planning, most people can enjoy privacy or a sense of open space without living on a two acre lot. Yet those large lots that are increasingly evident on the developing urban fringe have the effect of a statutory mandate to encourage "urban spread" and discourage transportation energy husbandry. They also prevent later development at an energy-efficient density. Accordingly, rigid lot restrictions in developing areas should be modified to allow more compact development.

Even where relatively small lots are now permitted, the density could be increased without compromising public health, safety, or privacy. As Professor Norman Williams observes, in many instances, overly stringent zoning and subdivision requirements do not achieve the goals they pretend to advance. Some regulations specifying front, back, and side yard requirements are so modest that they serve no useful purpose. For example, a side yard requirement of eight feet does not greatly reduce congestion, guarantee a nice view, or even enhance privacy in many instances. Front yards border on public roads and essentially provide public, not private, space. And it is inconsistent to argue that yard requirements are imposed to protect individuals from noise and fumes, since the smallest front yard requirements are traditionally imposed on lots fronting on busy streets, while in quieter residential neighborhoods, the front yards must be considerably larger [10]. Rather than perpetuate application of these questionable requirements, it may be preferable to eliminate outmoded yard requirements and instead permit multifamily housing. Especially in existing single family neighborhoods close to urban centers, "infilling" with townhouses or garden apartments by special permit may be desirable. Since most jurisdictions allow restrictions to be attached to the permit to alleviate parking and other potential problems that multifamily housing may create, special permits can offer protection to existing residents while encouraging development of energy-efficient housing in an energy-efficient location.

Modifying Floor-to-Area Ratios

In lieu of imposing height, setback, and yard requirements to regulate density, some communities use floor-to-area ratio (FAR) requirements. As the floor-to-area ratio increases or decreases, the permitted size of the structure increases or decreases proportionately. To illustrate: a floor-to-area ratio of 1.0 or 100 percent, means that a one story structure can cover the entire lot or a two story structure can cover one-half the entire lot. A floor-to-area ratio of only 0.5, or 50 percent, allows the total square footage (of all floors) of the structure to equal only one-half the total square footage of its lot, so that a one story structure may cover only one-half the lot.

Because FARs eliminate traditional setback, yard, and height requirements, they allow flexibility of building shape and orientation that permits new buildings to optimize the energy-conserving features of their natural environments [11]. Nevertheless, many communities could amend their FAR ratio to permit greater density and still meet the health, safety, and general welfare requirements of the Standard Zoning Enabling Act [12].

Increasing Flexibility of "Use" Limitations

One additional easy to implement strategy for increasing density should be mentioned: permitting conversion of large single family units into multifamily structures. Often the use of single family homes is strictly regulated so that single family neighborhoods will not be "contaminated" by multifamily residences. This means that in older neighborhoods close to the urban center where high density is most valuable, zoning restrictions may prevent owners of large single family homes from renting unused rooms, converting an English basement into a rental unit, or dividing the house into separate apartments. As a result, urban space is wasted, while unnecessary, long commutes are forced on many persons who must accept housing in the suburbs.

Again, a special permit system governing conversion of single family homes would save energy and protect the established neighborhood. If, however, a special permit system is used, standards for granting and denying the permits must be included in the ordinance. A thirty year old Massachusetts case held invalid a special permit to convert single family homes into multifamily units because of the absence of such standards [13].

Other Considerations

Secondary Impacts. In spite of the substantial energy savings achieved through higher density development, there are also many disadvantages. Dense development can result in congestion, concentration of air pollution, fire hazards, loss of privacy, increased noise, overburdening of capital facilities, and degradation of scenic beauty. On the other hand, substantial but not drastic changes in density of development can safeguard aesthetic, health, and safety needs while saving energy. Without question, more dense, compact development must be accompanied by design changes and construction improvements such as better insulation to enhance privacy in multifamily structures; use of setbacks, tiered buildings, and narrow towers to ensure availability of light and air in tall buildings; and improved transit and traffic circulation to prevent congestion. In addition, localities must be certain that other capital facilities like water and sewer lines are adequate for the proposed density. A firm in Davis, California [14], has determined that more flexible fence setback requirements can compensate in part for loss of privacy due to higher density. This suggested ordinance for alleviating strict fence setback requirements is reprinted in Appendix II, p. 278.

The solution to the high density versus low density dispute clearly lies in a balancing of the various important considerations. Multiunit development realistically cannot be promoted throughout a community, but at a minimum it should be concentrated near employment centers, activity centers and along transportation lines. It should not be imposed on those for whom it is poorly suited. Getting families with children to help reduce transportation energy use by moving into single family houses on small lots instead of into houses on one to two acres may be enough of a victory for that group of citizens; but individuals without children should be encouraged to seek multifamily housing. In short, in establishing energy-efficient densities, each locality will have to weigh what density is best suited to its needs and where clusters of moderately high density development should be located.

Legal Issues. *Public Health, Safety, and Welfare.* A significant legal issue confronted by attempts to increase density through changes in height, lot, and use requirements is whether the zoning changes impinge on public health, safety, and welfare. The change may be challenged as an improper exercise of police power, or the right of state and local governments to regulate individual actions. In that situation, courts may look at the probable effect of the change on traffic congestion, safety, and noise; the adequacy of public facilities; the availability of light and air; and so forth. Because of the presumption that legislation is valid, it is unlikely that a comprehensive rezoning to higher densities will be struck, especially when the need for the rezoning is well documented. Nevertheless, the validity of the rezoning will be enhanced if it can be shown that rezoning to a higher density has no significant adverse impact [15]. The same reasoning applies when special permits are used to achieve higher densities in selected neighborhoods.

The principle that courts will sustain rezonings and special permits that uphold traditional zoning goals is illustrated in a Maryland case where a variance [16] rather than a rezoning was challenged, but the underlying concept is the same. The variance allowed a commercial building to be taller than was normally allowed in the zone it was in. Because of land characteristics, the building was constructed only on the front portion of the lot. The court upheld the variance on the ground that it would be illogical to forbid a structure that would allow adjacent buildings greater access to light and air than required under the original zoning regulation [17].

This case suggests that if one can show that the higher density that would result from zoning changes would be integrated with a transportation system designed to reduce congestion, or that adequate public facilities exist to serve an expanded population, or that other potential adverse impacts have been mitigated, the changes will withstand challenge.

Spot Zoning.   Spot zoning occurs when a zoning change permits uses different from those prevailing in an area to take place only in a small "spot" for a private benefit [18]. One expert points out that even though courts may refer separately to spot zoning and comprehensive plan doctrines, the concepts are often two sides of the same coin. If a rezoning conforms to a comprehensive plan, it is not spot zoning [19].

There is little chance that zoning changes to permit compact, higher density development would constitute spot zoning if the rezonings were not confined to small areas, but rather applied to entire communities, as would be necessary to achieve significant energy savings. These rezonings would be premised upon a review and revision of comprehensive plans to identify areas where higher density is desirable. Special permit procedures that allow multifamily development in designated residential areas should also be safe from spot zoning challenges since spot zoning does not occur where there are specific ordinance provisions permitting the use at issue [20]. On the other hand, if there has been no revision of the comprehensive plan on which to base a rezoning, spot zoning may be a credible argument even though developers may show that energy conservation will result [21].

Exclusionary Zoning.   During the first part of the twentieth century, apartment buildings were looked upon as parasites that would block light and air, promote "fire, contagion, and disorder," reduce property values, and stimulate juvenile delinquency [22]. But changes in lifestyles and in apartment design have made townhouses, apartments, and condominiums popular. There is growing awareness that the land use controls excluding multifamily housing from communities are not designed to protect the public welfare, but to exclude less wealthy individuals from the community.

In response to exclusionary attitudes pervasive in many developing communities, some courts have done an about face, and are now striking zoning ordinances that prohibit multifamily housing. In *Appeal of Girsh* [23], for example, the Pennsylvania Supreme Court held that a suburban township could not refuse to accommodate new growth by excluding apartments. Concern that housing be made available to low and moderate income persons recently resulted in a landmark decision by the New Jersey Supreme Court. In *Southern Burlington County NAACP* vs. *Township of Mount Laurel* [24], a case that is already influencing other states, the New Jersey court held that a developing community must provide an opportunity for construction within the community of its fair share of low and moderate income housing to meet present and prospective regional needs. The opinion requires rezoning to remove physical and economic barriers to low and moderate income individuals, including the failure to zone for multifamily units. The *Mount Laurel* theme was picked up in *Berenson* v. *Town of New Castle* [25], where New York State's highest court held that a community could not exclude multifamily housing if the result would be an imbalance of low and moderate income housing, either in the community or in the region.

Of course, not all multifamily units need be designed for low and moderate income dwellers. But, by calling for rezoning to permit construction of multiple family dwellings to meet low and moderate income needs and to accommodate increasing growth pressures, the courts in Pennsylvania, New Jersey, and New York may inadvertently have given a boost to energy conservation by prohibiting exclusion of multifamily housing from communities [26].

Unfortunately, a recent United States Supreme Court decision, *City of Eastlake* v. *Forest City Enterprises, Inc.* [27], has undermined some of the opportunities for multifamily construction required by the state courts. *Eastlake* upheld a mandatory referendum that barred the rezoning of land to allow high density residential development. The U.S. Supreme Court agreed with the state that rezoning was a "legislative" function that the people of Ohio had reserved to themselves. Consequently, residents could deny the rezoning by popular vote. The implications of this case for orderly planning and development are major. But its significance for this strategy is the additional obstacle to energy-efficient land use if communities can vote on a case-by-case basis to exclude dense development projects even though they may result in important energy savings. Perhaps the most compelling message of *Eastlake* is the crucial need to educate citizens regarding the advantages of good planning and well-designed, moderately high density projects, so that the prejudice against multifamily housing that prevailed early in the century will not cloud the future.

Implementation. *State.* Modifying zoning and subdivision ordinances to promote high density, compact development should require no new state enabling legislation or state action.

Local. This strategy would be implemented by localities. It may be accomplished through textual or map amendments to the zoning ordinances to reduce minimum lot requirements, permit additional multifamily housing, and modify maximum height limits and the FAR ratio.

If a special permit procedure is used to allow reductions in yard, lot, and setback requirements, or an increase in maximum height, the zoning board may attach conditions to ensure that the increased density does not create a nuisance, health, or safety hazard. No new administrative bodies are needed to implement this strategy, though use of special permits may increase administrative costs to a locality.

MIXED USE ZONING

Until fairly recently, it was not considered particularly chic to live above a candy store. It was, in fact, forbidden to live in a building tainted by commercial use, because that violated the notion that lawful and orderly urban life ought to be properly zoned and segregated. The notion originated earlier in the industrial revolution, when glue factories and such invaded residential districts and offended the nostrils of the inhabitants. Once they started restricting factories to industrial zones, there was no stopping the zoners. We now have zones for work and play, for people with high incomes, middle incomes, moderate incomes and low incomes, and for all manner of special uses. The result is that urban and suburban life is often dull, fragmented and wasteful. Business districts are dead at night. The fragmentation of people and activities leads to polarization and overspecialization. Most of us spend far too much time on the road flitting from one zone to another.
© *The Washington Post* 1976, reprinted with permission.

Wasted time and dull environments are not the only price we pay for segregating land uses. Zoning that prevents integration of activities is another major contributor to energy waste. As a result of separating commercial, residential, industrial, recreational, and cultural sectors, we increase transportation fuel demand by forcing people to leave their residential zone to shop, to leave their work zone to play, or to leave their school zone to go to the dentist.

Many localities recognize the inefficiencies, inconveniences, and monotony of use-restricted neighborhoods, and permit or encourage the integration of activities where mixed uses are desirable. Nearly all communities allow some "cumulative integration" of uses. This means that more restricted uses of land (for example, residential uses) are permitted in areas zoned less restrictively (as for commercial uses). The reverse, however, generally is not true—one cannot put an office building in an area zoned for single family residences.

There are, nevertheless, a few devices localities have used to break the concept of segregating uses. One is to adopt special permit systems that allow specified uses, such as daycare centers, neighborhood groceries, or small retail shops, in residential areas. Another is to construe liberally the term "accessory use" to allow small businesses and recreational uses in residential neighborhoods. Variances and nonconforming uses in older neighborhoods have also contributed to mixing of land uses. And in some larger new developments, communities have begun to accept the idea of combining uses. Mixing uses of land is, therefore, not a novel concept; but the haphazard fashion in which it has been accomplished is inadequate to meet the need for integrating land uses on a scale necessary to achieve significant energy savings. What is essential is a new commitment by localities to combine a variety of compatible land uses—not just homes and daycare centers—as well as a determination to invoke governmental powers to achieve that goal so that trip origins and destinations are brought closer together.

Zoning for "mixed uses," as used in this strategy, covers a broad range of options. First, the term includes combining buildings with different uses in the same zone—for example, commercial with residential, or institutional with recreational. Second, the term contemplates a mixture of uses within the same building, such as ground floor shops, business offices above, and apartments on top. Third, it means combining residential buildings of varying sizes and prices in the same area, (e.g., garden apartments, low-rise, and townhouses with single family homes) so that persons with different housing needs can find housing close to their jobs [28].

Mixing Buildings with Different Uses

As noted, some small mixture of uses is achieved by zoning ordinances that permit accessory uses to accompany major uses of land. Accessory uses are characterized as uses related, but subordinate and incidental, to the principal uses permitted in a zoning district. A garage that serves as a woodworking shop or a backyard swimming pool are examples of accessory uses that may slightly reduce traffic by bringing recreational activities close to home. Most courts balk at the idea of classifying a business as an accessory use [29].

Because accessory uses must be incidental, and in most jurisdictions customarily [30] incidental, to the principal use of a building, they have limited application, and, therefore, slight value for conserving energy by reducing transportation demands. In contrast, commercial, light industrial, institutional, and residential uses can often be compatibly combined and thereby offer a relatively self-sufficient neighborhood where the need for frequent automobile trips is reduced. Such a mixture, however, involves mixing principal, not accessory, uses. Those combinations are permitted only if they are allowed as a matter of right by the zoning ordinance or conditionally under a special permit system. Moreover, the mixture will not be allowed if it has a detrimental impact on the neighborhood, is noisy, generates excessive traffic, and so forth.

Nevertheless, some courts have recognized the desirability of mixing uses, noting that commercial centers are "often a convenience and sometimes a necessity in or near large residential areas" [31]. But where there is no special need to mix the uses, the result may be almost a presumption against the mixture [32].

In Montgomery County, Maryland, transit station zones provide one example of how specifically permitting the mixture of some uses, and allowing still others through special permits, may contribute to both energy conservation and an attractive environment. Montgomery County has created mixed use, high density zones near transit systems in order to maximize use of public transportation and minimize reliance on automobiles.

One mixed use zone, the transit station—residential zone (TS—R) [33] is designed to stimulate multifamily housing for all economic levels within walking distance of transit stations and consumer services. The TS—R zone provides for a combination of residential uses (including rental of guest rooms in single family homes), institutional uses (churches, libraries, museums, and homes for the elderly and handicapped), and some retail and personal service stores (florists, laundry, and medical offices). Hotels, restaurants, drug stores, and grocery stores are allowed by special permit. Flexibility in design, layout, and grouping are additional attractions of the TS−R zone.

Another zone, the transit station−mixed zone (TS M) [34], also provides for mixed uses, but is intended for locations near transit stations where substantial commercial or office uses already exist. The TS−M zone is designed to minimize automobile use by providing for "retail commercial uses and professional services that contribute to the self-sufficiency of the community" [35]. The zone also eliminates rigid height, bulk, and layout requirements. All uses allowed by right in the TS−R zone, as well as many retail sales and services allowed by special permit in the TS−R zone, are specifically allowed in the TS−M zone.

Montgomery County maintains tight control over developments in these zones by conditioning reclassification of land to a TS−M or TS−R zone on the approval of a development plan. The plan must not only show how it conforms to the purposes and requirements of the new zones, but must also state how the proposed development will be more efficient and desirable than standard methods of development. Even if the proposed plan complies with these requirements, the county can refuse to grant the rezoning. Site plans that conform to approved development plans are also required and provide additional opportunities to incorporate fuel-saving design features. Excerpts from the TS−R and TS−M zoning ordinance appear in Appendix II, p. 266.

High density mixed use zones such as those adopted by Montgomery County could result in significant energy savings if they were dispersed in clusters near public transportation stops [36]. But where neighborhoods have already been established and largely developed, high density mixed use zoning like that used in Montgomery County may not be an option. In those instances, energy efficiencies can be achieved through more liberal use of special permits to allow neighborhood retail sales shops, consumer service stores, medical and child care facilities, and other uses that would not impair the neighborhood welfare.

In some instances, special permit systems, which control the location of a use within a zoning district, offer advantages over allowing a mixture of uses as a matter of right. Because some uses, such as businesses, churches, or recreational centers, can create traffic congestion, noise, and safety hazards, or mar the appearance of a residential area, it may be preferable to allow such uses by permit only. With special permits, conditions may be attached to regulate the size, location, hours of operation, and the appearance of the regulated use. Moreover, the special permit system, by controlling location of the use, can further enhance energy conservation by making sure that uses cluster in an energy-efficient fashion. Thus, strip commercial development, which wastes land and transportation energy, can be avoided.

Of course, where the text of the zoning ordinance already provides for mixing land uses, only a map amendment will be necessary to expand the area where mixing uses is permitted.

Mixing Uses Within Buildings

Multiple use buildings, or buildings that combine under one roof residential, commercial, office, educational, or civic uses, have become increasingly popular. There are several explanations for the multiple use building trend. First, the attractiveness of a large apartment building is greatly enhanced if grocery and dry cleaning facilities, beauty shops, and recreational rooms are incorporated. As commuting distances and costs increase, people become more concerned with finding homes close to work and services. Some are attracted by the notion of a home literally on top of their office. Investors like the idea of multiple use buildings in downtown areas because they are a way to avoid temporary oversupplies of office space. City officials see multiple use buildings as devices to rejuvenate central cities by keeping activity downtown after business hours. Because they can be used twenty-four hours a day, rather than half that amount, multiple use buildings have greater operating efficiencies [37].

Regardless of their social and economic advantages, multiple use buildings can contribute to significant reductions in the demand for fuel for transportation. Multiple use buildings should be encouraged through removal of stringent use restrictions that prevent their construction and operation.

Penn Center in Philadelphia, Prudential Center in Boston, Century City in Los Angeles, Peachtree Center in Atlanta, Watergate in Washington, D.C., Marina Twin Towers in Chicago, and Olympic Tower in New York City are some of the most celebrated multiple use buildings that combine stores, office space, and residential units. In the same vein, the New York Museum of Modern Art is now considering building residential apartments on top of a new wing.

Even the federal government has gotten into the act with legislation encouraging the General Services Administration to build new buildings and recycle older ones for multiple use by combining government and commercial offices, restaurants, and shops [38]. In addition to helping preserve historic or culturally significant buildings and saving money, the legislation will, as the Senate Committee Report notes, save energy in more ways than cutting down on transportation fuel costs: "The design of older buildings is generally less extravagant in the use of energy than modern glass designs. A renovation approach would eliminate the consumption of energy needed to tear down and replace the older building" [39]. Although renovation of existing buildings may encounter more problems than the federal legislation acknowledges—it may, for example, require more flexible application of building and safety codes to older buildings—the strategy for multiple use of federally owned buildings is commendable. The federal bill, which may be adapted for state and local use, is reprinted in Appendix II, on p. 279.

Special zoning provisions are required for large multiple use projects like the ones listed above. But, in some instances, a mixture of uses can be achieved on a smaller scale through the "accessory use" theory. Vending machines, small grocery stores, and drug stores have sometimes been held to be accessory uses in multistory residential buildings [40]. On the other hand, small shops providing consumer conveniences have not always been approved as accessory uses [41]. And, as noted, the accessory use theory does not contemplate situations where apartments are built on top of shops, offices, or museums. Consequently, one way to assure approval of multiple use buildings that integrate commercial and residential uses is to modify the local zoning ordinance to permit specified multiple uses. This has been done in New York [42], Chicago [43], Baltimore [44], Washington, D.C. [45], San Francisco [46], Little Rock [47], White Plains, New York [48], and a host of other localities [49]. As with special permits, conditions may be attached to the uses so that they will not endanger the public or create a nuisance.

Home Occupations

As the preceding list of cities indicates, the concept of multiple use buildings is not confined to a megalopolis like New York; nor is it confined to high-rise office or apartment buildings. On a smaller scale, mixing uses within buildings can simply involve permitting lawyers, seamstresses, typists, or doctors to work in their homes. Although 36 percent of our automobile trips are for commuting to and from work [50], realistically, transportation energy savings resulting from home occupations will be relatively small when contrasted with energy savings that dispersed employment patterns or higher density contiguous growth can bring. Nevertheless, elimination of land use restrictions that prohibit home occupations is a step in the direction of transportation energy conservation. And if the reason for eliminating prohibitions on home occupations—to conserve energy—is sufficiently publicized, it may even spark a renewed interest in conservation that will carry over into other areas.

Depending on how strictly a locality interprets "accessory uses," offices in homes may or may not be allowed without explicit authorization. Because of the uncertainty, it is desirable to remove any question of legality by adopting appropriate home occupation legislation.

The American Society of Planning Officials (ASPO) has recently published a study analyzing ordinances that permit home occupations [51] and notes the advantages and disadvantages of the two major approaches. Ordinances that allow home occupations without requiring special permits usually consist of a definition of home occupation, crude performance standards, and a list of permitted and prohibited occupations. Staff time required to evaluate cases is minimal because the ordinance is usually clear on whether or not a particular occupation is allowed, but flexibility is lost. Ordinances requiring permits for home occupations do not usually list permitted and prohibited uses, but rather list performance standards and rely on case-by-case evaluation to determine whether a permit will be granted. Staff time is increased, but the permit approach gives the community greater leeway in deciding what kinds of occupations to allow. At the same time, the permit approach gives the community greater control over home occupations and allows nuisances to be detected and avoided on an individual basis before they arise [52]. Performance standards for both the permit and no permit approach must be reasonable and promote the public interest [53].

The ASPO publication examines in detail several localities' permit and no permit ordinances, and points out the merits and weaknesses of each. Readers are referred to that publication for a critical analysis of ordinances that may be adapted for use by their own localities. In addition, states might consider adopting the following suggested legislation to ensure that all localities will permit home occupations:

No regulation may infringe on the right of any resident to use a minor portion of a dwelling for gainful employment that does not change the character of the surrounding residential area.

Mixing Building Types to Accommodate
Income Ranges

One particularly harsh side effect of large lot, leapfrog development in urban areas is the extent to which it has separated individuals' homes from their jobs. While some may choose to spend an hour or two commuting each day, others, by virtue of their low or moderate incomes, are forced into housing miles away from their work. The separation has been aggravated by the flight of businesses to suburbs where low and moderate income housing is hard to find. The problem has become so severe that some communities are even having trouble providing middle income housing for teachers, police officers, and mail carriers [54].

As noted elsewhere [55], the elimination of zoning restrictions that completely ban multifamily housing in communities, and the state court cases calling for regional "fair share" accommodation of low and moderate income housing, can help blue collar and service workers locate near their jobs. An alternative is to mandate the inclusion of a fixed percentage of low and moderate income housing in large, multifamily developments. Such a provision may or may not withstand challenges, depending on the state court's view of the role of zoning. A Fairfax County, Virginia, ordinance was struck as being outside the scope of the enabling legislation and as being a taking of property without just compensation [56], but a similar Montgomery County, Maryland, ordinance remains intact [57]. These issues are discussed in more detail in a later section on incentive zoning [58], which examines use of density bonuses to compensate developers for including multifamily income housing in their developments.

Other Considerations

Secondary Impacts. Pollution, noise, congestion, the reduction of property values, and other problems that have led to segregation of uses can be minimized through zoning controls that condition mixed uses on adherence to strict requirements regarding size, landscaping, lighting, hours of operations, and other important factors. Mixed uses may enhance consumer convenience, actually raise the value of buildings and complexes, save money by cutting transportation expenses, and stimulate rejuvenation of cities. Perhaps the main obstacle to mixing land uses is public opposition to the concept. No one wants a heavy industrial plant next door. But better design and construction practices, imposition of strict performance standards, and the rising cost of commuting—both in terms of time and money— auger well for a change in public attitude and acceptance of mixed uses.

Legal Issues. Most of the legal issues raised by mixed use zoning have been discussed in the context of particular strategies available to promote mixed uses. For example, enabling legislation may have to be broadened to mandate the inclusion of multifamily housing in developments. Uses must be carefully controlled to ensure that they do not become a nuisance or create health and safety hazards. Relying upon interpretation of "accessory use" clauses may not ensure that a mixture of uses will be upheld. Rezonings for mixed uses should be in accordance with a comprehensive plan or they will be attacked in some jurisdictions as spot zoning.

Legal issues surrounding the use of special permits deserve a somewhat closer review. Special permit uses are a well-recognized way to control uses that may be inherently compatible with uses specifically permitted, but that may have some characteristics that may make them undesirable unless carefully regulated. They are an accepted form of land use regulation in most states. In many jurisdictions, special permit uses must be granted if the ordinance's requirements are met. In others, this requirement does not exist [59]. In drafting ordinances to permit mixed land uses, localities may, therefore, want to specify that if conditions of the ordinances are met, the special permit must be granted. One of the conditions should be energy-efficient location of the proposed use.

Zoning ordinances with special permit provisions may be held invalid if the standards for granting the permit are impermissibly broad or vague. Hence, the more explicit the standards (e.g., the project must be located within 500 feet of a transit station; a neighborhood grocery must be located on a collector street, be in a "residence type" building, and must not draw heavy traffic through a local street), the greater the chance that the special permit system will be upheld. Surprisingly, a majority of courts has upheld issuances and denials of special permits that were judged according to vague standards like the promotion of the "public interest," the "public health, safety and welfare," or the "public convenience and welfare" [60]. Most courts always uphold special permits based on only slightly more precise standards, such as requiring conformity with the intent, purpose, or spirit of the zoning ordinance, or not being a nuisance, or not being a use that is incompatible or injurious to the surrounding area [61].

In addition to requirements specified in the zoning ordinance, most courts have upheld the power of zoning boards to attach reasonable conditions to the granting of special permits [62]. Conditions may range from landscaping requirements to make the project more visually pleasing to restrictions on hours of operation [63]. Because they can mitigate potential detrimental side effects that may arise from construction of energy-efficient mixed use developments and multiple use buildings, conditions are particularly valuable for the protection of a community when standards for granting permits are vague.

Implementation. *State.* No special enabling legislation to permit mixed uses is required, but states may wish to pass legislation encouraging mixing of uses.

Local. The strategy can be implemented at the local level through existing legislative and zoning bodies. Creation of mixed use zones may require amendment of zoning texts and maps, and amendment of master plans, to indicate where mixed use zones may be appropriate. When mixed uses are allowed by special permits, it will be necessary to amend zoning texts to specify these new uses.

EFFICIENT BUILDING LAYOUT, ORIENTATION, AND LANDSCAPING

Rigid lot size, setback, yard, and street requirements are primary obstacles to energy-efficient development design. Those requirements encourage developers to think in terms of lot-by-lot construction and discourage overall planning for total communities. The result is often a pattern like a huge waffle. Complete leveling and grading of property that requires ripping out natural landscaping may be the only alternative for developers who must build on rectangular lots laid out in a grid pattern that is determined by a rigid street plan. Long and duplicative road and utility systems must be provided to serve each unit. Natural land contours are ignored or destroyed so that natural drainage swales must be replaced by energy-intensive concrete curbs and gutters. New vegetation should be planted, but often is ignored in an effort to cut corners. Hence, heating and cooling bills rise. In addition, the rigid yard and lot requirements prevent proper building orientation and arrangement to capture cool breezes, deflect strong winds, and take advantage of warm solar rays. Since many developers use mass-produced building plans rather than plans drawn for a specific lot, the orientation options are further narrowed. Although some architects and builders will always produce energy-inefficient, inferior developments, there are some steps localities can take to ensure that energy-conscious developers have the flexibility to produce fuel-saving projects that also meet health, safety, environmental, and aesthetic standards.

Cluster Zoning and Subdivision Ordinances
One solution is to permit clustering of buildings. Cluster zoning or subdivision ordinances relax yard, setback, and lot size requirements,

thereby permitting developers to group buildings that would have to be put on separate lots under traditional land use controls. Land saved by the reduction in yard size for individual houses is preserved as undeveloped, open space that may be enjoyed by all development residents. In some cases, the common open space may be owned by the residents. In other cases, it may be donated to the public. Figure 4–1 contrasts a cluster design with more common residential patterns.

Cluster development should naturally lead to energy conservation because it permits developments to preserve and make use of energy-saving features of the natural environment. Flexible orientation is possible since houses are not forced into a grid pattern that ignores the free energy offered by the sun. Moreover, buildings can be arranged so that they shelter each other from the wind in the winter while allowing air flow between structures in the summer. Because clustering reduces the need for grading land and preserves open space, natural vegetation that protects us from temperature extremes can be saved.

Other energy savings should also be noted, for the advantages of clustering extend far beyond space heating and cooling energy benefits. Energy consumed to construct streets and utilities and to provide public services is reduced, since clustered developments typically have shorter road and utility lines. Private transportation energy demands can also be minimized by bringing trip origins and destinations closer together. Public transportation is enhanced since clustering creates a common origin point convenient to many passengers. Open space preserved by clustering may be used for recreational activities close to home, thus cutting back on the need to drive to enjoy such activities. And clustering on a large scale may make it possible for developments to take advantage of centralized heating and cooling systems that are now being developed through federal research grants [64].

Clustering does not, by itself, guarantee maximum fuel conservation. Developers may group buildings in a spot that is not sheltered from the wind or they may destroy a stand of trees that could provide needed shade. Where clustering is allowed by special permit or where cluster ordinances call for site plan review, however, the cluster development can be subjected to energy-efficiency standards pertaining to building orientation, street and building arrangement, and landscaping [65]. In addition, communities should amend the purpose clauses of their cluster ordinances to include energy conservation as a goal.

Figure 4—1. Cluster Development

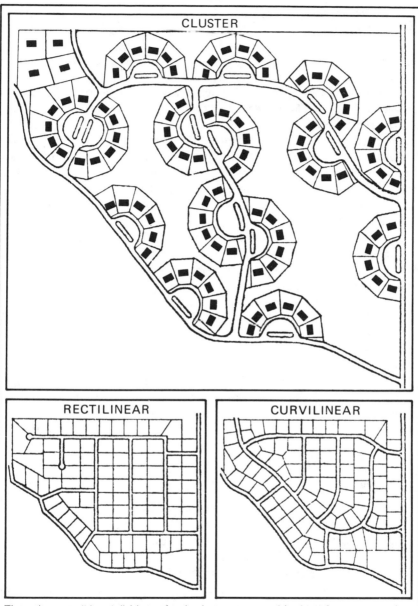

CLUSTER

RECTILINEAR

CURVILINEAR

These three possible subdivisions of a development tract with ninety-four one acre plots show cluster layout, top, rectilinear pattern, bottom left, and curvilinear plan, bottom right. Only 6,000 feet of streets are needed for cluster. Grid calls for 12,000 feet, curvilinear layout needs 11,600 feet.

Reprinted from:
New Approaches to Land Development/A Study of Concepts and Innovations, Technical Bulletin 40 (Washington, D.C.: The Urban Land Institute, 1961), p. 29.

Street Design Requirements

While cluster ordinances may provide the best way to promote energy-efficient building arrangement and orientation and to preserve natural vegetation, they are not the only effective device. Another important step localities can immediately take to enhance energy-efficient design is to eliminate any language in their subdivision ordinances that perpetuates construction of streets in a grid pattern [66]. Street layout essentially determines the orientation and shape of the lot, and therefore, the orientation and shape of the building placed on the lot. Consequently, an ordinance that requires all proposed streets to be "continuous and in alignment with existing streets" [67] almost guarantees adherence to grid patterns that prevent flexible, energy-efficient design.

In earlier times, when service alleys were built into developments (something that is prohibitively expensive in new subdivisions), it made sense to design streets in a grid pattern. The grid permitted houses to face the streets and the back door to be located next to the service alley where the garage and garbage cans were located. But these "efficiency" considerations are now almost obsolete, since many modern houses have built-in garages and garbage disposals [68]. Now developers must focus on different building concerns sparked by the energy shortage—the need to take advantage of the sun, to arrange buildings so they shelter each other from harsh winds, to preserve natural vegetation so that buildings are protected from temperature extremes, and to take advantage of natural drainage swales so that concrete curb and gutter systems and storm drainage systems are unnecessary. All this can be furthered through more flexible subdivision laws pertaining to street design. Perhaps the best kind of residential streets are those ending in cul-de-sacs that encourage clustering of houses. Those streets can not only preserve natural, open spaces, but also prevent "through" traffic, thus making streets safer for pedestrians and bicyclists. When, however, cul-de-sacs are used, localities must also be careful to permit flexible building orientation so that houses may optimize solar energy.

Flexible Orientation Through Special Permits

When only one or two small buildings are involved, clustering and flexible street layout may not be applicable, since the arrangement of the buildings in relation to one another probably has been determined by preexisting land development patterns. But the orientation of buildings may still warrant attention. Use of special permits to allow optimal orientation is one way to avoid the rigidity imposed by traditional lot and yard requirements.

What is slightly unusual about using special permits to enhance efficient building orientation is that it is not the *kind* of use, but the orientation of a structure that is the subject of the permit. A Buchanan, New York, zoning ordinance that allows for variation in the orientation of structures that are themselves allowed only by special permit provides language that could be adapted to allow the energy-efficient orientation of *all* buildings:

> Recognizing that there are trends in the planning of dwellings and groups thereof and in lot arrangements that seek to secure the benefit of solar orientation [and] climate control . . . which may necessitate variation in the front, rear and side yard requirements of this ordinance . . . and in the regulations applying to accessory buildings, fences, and walls, the planning board, on application, may permit variations in such regulations for the accomplishment of the foregoing purposes, provided that such variations shall be so devised and applied that:
>
> (a) the distance between buildings in the same block shall not be less than would result from the application of the regulations prescribed by this ordinance for the district;
>
> (b) air, daylight, and sunlight shall not be obstructed from adjacent buildings to a greater degree than would result from the application of the regulations prescribed for the district;
>
> (c) the proposed location and arrangement of buildings will not be otherwise detrimental to adjacent buildings or to the neighborhood generally; and
>
> (d) the variations will conserve and promote health and safety [69].

Landscaping Requirements

In addition to permitting optimal building arrangement and orientation, clustered development may go a long way toward optimizing energy-saving features of the natural landscape. Yet there are other possibilities for improved landscaping through regulation, even when clustering is not possible. A planning and design firm in California has drafted model resolutions and ordinances, reproduced in Appendix II, pp. 279, 280, that are designed to increase tree shading in existing developments, and require functional landscaping in commercial developments. These ordinances provide an excellent start for energy-conscious communities who can use them as a base for further legislation. One additional need is to include an ordinance requiring as a condition of development approval that all residential developments preserve a maximum practicable amount of natural vegetation and incorporate energy-conserving landscaping in their design. The ordinance could provide, for example:

The landscape shall be preserved in its natural state, insofar as practicable, by minimizing tree and soil disturbance or removal. If development of the site necessitates removal of trees of [insert size] or more, special attention should be given to the planting of replacement trees or other landscape treatment that offers maximum protection from temperature extremes and high winds [70].

Another useful ordinance is one adopted in Fairfax County, Virginia, that requires any developer who proposes to clear five or more acres of land to secure a permit from the county for tree removal [71]. Although probably motivated by aesthetic rather than energy concerns, the ordinance nevertheless can have an impact on energy demand if there is a presumption against removal of large shade and buffer trees.

Other Considerations

Secondary Impacts.   In addition to saving energy, strategies reviewed in this section can enhance the attractiveness of new developments by eliminating monotonous grid patterns and preserving the natural environment. They can also save both money and time by reducing the length of roads and utility lines and by discouraging unnecessary grading and landscaping. Clustering can promote pedestrian safety (by often eliminating "through" traffic), encourage community cohesiveness, and stimulate integrated planning [72]. In view of its benefits, it is hard to imagine that developers and homebuyers continue to find traditional residential patterns attractive. There are a few explanations, however.

Cluster development requires residents to give up large private open space in return for large community open spaces. This arrangement may not be palatable to persons who fear a loss of privacy or who want a big rear yard for children. But good landscaping and design can overcome privacy problems. And others may welcome cluster development as a way to enjoy open space without being personally responsible for its upkeep [73].

Another consideration is that if common open space is dedicated to the public, there may be a loss of property tax revenues since public lands generally are not subject to property taxes. In addition, dedication of land to the public essentially means that residents of the clustered development have paid the cost of acquiring public open space.

Legal Issues.   There are no unusual legal problems raised by the use of special permits to allow optimal building orientation, provided that clear standards for awarding them are in the ordinance. SZEA specifically authorizes the use of special permits.

Cluster ordinances may, however, raise some legal issues, although such ordinances have been the subject of little litigation. The foremost issue concerning clustering is whether the Standard State Zoning Enabling Act authorizes it. Clustered zoning is clearly a way to regulate the density of development and to provide open space, two purposes explicitly contained in the act; but SZEA also contains a list of authorized zoning devices that does not include clustered zoning. Nevertheless, one expert in land use notes that since clustered zoning promotes the general purposes stated in SZEA, authority for clustered zoning probably exists even where there is no specific statutory authorization for the technique [74]. Indeed, clustered zoning has been upheld in the absence of special enabling legislation [75].

Cluster zoning has also been found to meet the uniformity of zoning requirements of state zoning enabling legislation, which calls for zoning to be equally applicable to the same kind of building in the same zoning district. Because the use of cluster provisions is available to all developers, one case has held that the uniformity requirement is met, even though clusters will differ within the same district [76].

Another potential legal issue involves ownership and maintenance of open space created by clustering. Some ordinances require the land to be held in corporate ownership by owners of lots within the development or maintained by neighborhood associations. Others mandate that the open space be dedicated to the locality for public use. When open space is dedicated to, and administered by, a neighborhood association, localities must ensure that they have the right to enforce maintenance responsibilities of the association. An American Society of Planning Officials survey of planned unit developments that incorporate clustering concludes that one of the most effective ways localities can avoid the maintenance problem is to retain the right to enforce the articles of a homeowners' association, including the collection of maintenance fees, whose assessment may constitute a lien against the property [77].

Requiring dedication of the land to the community for public use may be a little stickier than having it held in corporate ownership by development residents or maintained by neighborhood associations. There has been substantial litigation about the constitutionality of mandatory dedication requirements, even when there is enabling legislation authorizing mandatory dedication. The outcomes differ, depending on the purpose for which the dedication is made (e.g., streets, utilities, schools, recreation). But the clear trend is to uphold mandatory dedications for recreational purposes, provided the dedication requirement is tied to the demand for services created by the new growth [78].

Most cases challenging dedication requirements have not involved the mandatory dedication of open space created solely in clustered subdivisions, but rather have examined mandatory dedication of open space by all kinds of subdivision development. Conceivably, cluster dedication requirements could raise legal problems, since the entire amount of open space left by clustering may be more than that required to serve residents' recreational and other open space needs. Though the problem would be unusual, should it arise, a logical solution may be to limit land dedicated to the public to an amount needed to meet subdivision requirements. The rest could be left to a homeowners' association, or otherwise restricted. This is the approach taken in Fayston, Vermont, where the local planned unit development provision contemplates clustering [79].

Implementation. *State.* As noted, cluster zoning appears to require no special state enabling legislation or other action for adoption and implementation. Some states may need to adopt enabling legislation permitting the creation of neighborhood associations to oversee open space resulting from clustering; such legislation already exists in most states.

Local. No new administrative body is required to implement cluster provisions, although site plan review of the proposed cluster will be necessary. Even when clustering is available, a community may have to stimulate its use by educating developers and homebuyers to the energy efficiency and fiscal advantages of the technique. The planning board itself will, of course, have to learn to recognize an energy-efficient cluster plan when an application is made for cluster development [80].

OTHER DESIGN FEATURES

Several miscellaneous, but noteworthy, design features that can contribute to energy-efficient land development are the incorporation within neighborhoods of recreational land, the construction of bicycle and pedestrian paths that lead to activity centers, and the elimination of unnecessarily wide streets. This section serves as a "catchall" to discuss those three miscellaneous design strategies; energy-conscious localities will surely think of other strategies that can be added to this list.

Conveniently Located Recreational Land

No one would argue that taking the family on a picnic is a chief cause of energy waste. But that activity is representative of many others (such as driving children to school) that, when added together, consume considerable amounts of energy. Alteration of land development patterns to bring recreational and other facilities closer to their users is one way to cut back on needless energy demand.

Both the energy shortage and the increasing urbanization of America [81] make it plain that conveniently located parks in urban areas can contribute to energy savings. Yet only one thirty-second of the 320 million acres of public recreational land exists in our cities. As a result, people often have to drive to state and national parks located three or four hours outside urban areas for leisure and recreational opportunities. Although large regional parks will remain important, one expert advocates that localities also provide many small neighborhood parks that are accessible by walking or bicyling [82]. Several small parks, dispersed throughout communities and designed to serve an identifiable neighborhood, instead of one large park that serves a more diverse community can contribute to energy efficiency. The proximity and human scale of small parks will make them more accessible and more inviting to users [83]. Consequently, people may be more inclined to use those facilities than to hop into the car for more distant destinations when they have leisure time. To complement neighborhood parks, large regional parks should be located close to metropolitan areas and designed to discourage or prohibit automobile use in them.

Another solution to providing conveniently located parks may be to require developers to set aside land for public recreational use within their subdivisions or to make payments in lieu of land dedication when dedication is impractical. Subdivision exactions have become a popular way to require the developer to "pay" for the increased burden the new development will put on the community. Developers have long been required to provide paved streets, sewer lines, drainage facilities, and other "infrastructure." More recently, they have been required to set aside land for public recreational, park, and school facilities. When the development is too small to permit dedication of land or where the land is not suitable for dedication, developers have been required to pay a fee into a community fund for the purchase of public recreational or school land elsewhere.

Required dedication of recreational land can conserve energy while it preserves local coffers. Because land set aside for neighborhood recreation is within, or convenient to, the residential development it serves, trip generation can be reduced [84]. Moreover, because subdivision exactions cause developers to internalize costs of expensive infrastructure and amenities that the locality would otherwise pay for, the increased costs may discourage premature, marginal developments.

On the other hand, the exactions will encourage sprawling growth if marginal developers are encouraged to leapfrog to distant areas where subdivision exactions are not imposed, or where lower land prices can make up for the cost of the required dedication. Another consideration is that if the amount of impact fees paid in lieu of land are based on the density of development rather than on acreage, low density development rather than more energy-efficient higher density may be encouraged [85]. Hence, developer exactions will be ineffective in reducing energy consumption if their purpose is to curb non-contiguous, low density urban development. Instead, their energy conservation value lies in providing conveniently located facilities that can be reached by means other than the automobile.

Secondary Impacts. A locality may be able to stabilize its taxes if the developer must assume the cost of providing recreation land (as well as school land and infrastructure including streets and sewers). But cutting community expenses simply means that the costs to the developer will be passed on to the consumers in the form of higher housing prices. For this reason, some argue that subdivision exactions are exclusionary and a double tax. Present residents counter with the argument that they should not be saddled with higher taxes that will benefit only new residents. Still others argue that subdivisions must be designed with certain basic amenities, even if they are intended for low and moderate income individuals, and that amortization of the cost of amenities over the life of the mortgage has a less noticeable economic impact than increased taxes [86].

The dilemma is not easily solved. But all agree that it is important to set aside land for basic recreational needs, and that the land set aside should be both adequate for, and convenient to, the people who will be using it. Consequently, regardless of whether the developer dedicates land or the local government furnishes it, land must be located and designed to discourage automobile use.

Legal Issues. *Legitimate Exercise of Police Power.* Developer exactions for streets and utilities are generally accepted as a legitimate exercise of the police power, but the dedication of land for parks and recreation has been the subject of greater controversy. This questioning has begun to wane in the last ten years, as several states and localities have passed statutes and ordinances incorporating dedication and fees-in-lieu provisions that have withstood court challenge [87].

Taking. Courts have applied various tests to determine whether the dedication of land for parks constitutes a taking of property without just compensation. Illinois, Rhode Island, and Ohio require the need for dedicated subdivision land to be "uniquely attributable" to the subdivision and have invalidated dedications that failed to meet this strict requirement [88]. New York and California, however, have upheld land dedications that meet a less stringent standard: the need must be "reasonably related" to the burdens generated by the subdivision [89].

California, New York, Connecticut, and Wisconsin have upheld statutes requiring dedication of money in lieu of land where subdivision land is unsuited for public purposes because the subdivision is too small to permit a dedication of a useable size [90]. Significantly, the California statute authorizing subdivision exactions gives credit for facilities, such as recreational facilities, already built into the development. This is consistent with the requirement that the dedication be reasonably related to needs generated by the subdivision.

In sum, where land dedicated for recreational use will be used to benefit subdivision residents, rather than the entire locality, most courts will find that mandatory dedication is not a taking. Where exaction of fees for recreational use is involved, the judicial trend is to uphold the requirement if the money is earmarked for use to the benefit of the subdivision residents [91].

Even though the dedication of land for park and recreational uses will be upheld in most states, it is less likely that courts will approve a requirement that developers provide recreational facilities like tennis courts, swimming pools, or baseball fields that may encourage people to relax close to home. Such a requirement would probably raise the issue of "arbitrary and capricious" regulation, although there are precedents for requiring developers to include similar "nonessential" items such as proper landscaping, covered pedestrian walkways and other amenities [92]. Of course, many developers voluntarily offer both recreational land and facilities because they add to the attractiveness of the development.

Equal Protection. Along with the claims of "taking," opponents of mandatory dedications may claim that the requirement discriminates against subdivision residents by forcing them to pay for benefits formerly born by the entire community. They may find additional grounds for challenging the requirements if the exactions are not imposed on other kinds of construction, such as apartment buildings, that also create growth pressures but do not come under the definition of "subdivision." Courts have held the classification to be reasonable, however, and have refused to set aside subdivision exactions for park and recreational land on either ground [93]. Similarly, courts have rejected arguments that subdivision residents will suffer a double tax because they must both dedicate the land and pay for its maintenance through property taxes imposed on the general public [94].

Enabling Legislation. The Standard Planning Enabling Act authorizes communities to exact dedications for streets, sewers, utilities, and other improvements. Many jurisdictions have interpreted the last category to include park and recreational land. But there is no specific mention of park and recreational land in the statute, and at least one case has held that imposing a park and recreation facility fee is a tax and therefore beyond the scope of planning enabling legislation [95].

Implementation. *State.* In view of the uncertainty discussed above, enabling legislation that specifically authorizes dedication of park and recreational land or fees in lieu of land is advisable. Good examples of such legislation may be found in the California statutes [96], and the model subdivision regulations developed for the American Society of Planning Officials [97].

Local. Although mandatory dedications and fees in lieu of land may be administered by officials responsible for subdivision approval, several implementation issues are presented. First, a method of computing the amount of required dedication must be agreed upon. Although many localities compute the dedication as a percentage of the size of the development, others contend that it is more rational to vary the percentage according to the density of development. The number of residents is, after all, a clearer indicator of the amount of open space that may be required [98]. But, as noted, if the amount of dedication is directly proportional to the density of development, low density sprawl may be encouraged. Consequently, the dedication should relate to the needs of the residents, but not be so stringent that it encourages low density development. It may also be desirable to provide that subdividers must put the open space at the fringe of the subdivision, where it can be combined with land from other developments to create a sizable park [99]. In any event, dedication provisions should require land to be suitable for recreation and to be conveniently located.

Fees paid in lieu of land should be required as an alternative to dedication to prevent developers from avoiding the mandatory dedication provision by only subdividing parcels of land too small to permit dedication, or by choosing land where portions not built upon are unsuitable for dedication. If money rather than land is received, several additional implementation issues must be addressed. A formula for computing fees will have to be established. A simple approach, used in California, is to require the subdivider to pay an amount equal to the value of the land that would have to be dedicated. Complicated formulas have also been suggested. They factor in the density and other requirements of the development and eliminate the need for land appraisals [100].

Another matter to be considered in connection with mandatory dedication is whether the locality will apply for federal financial assistance in creating neighborhood parks. Under the 1961 Housing Act, the federal government will match municipal funds set aside for acquiring park land [101]. Hence, a community can double the value it receives from fees.

Bicycle and Pedestrian Paths

Riding bikes, jogging, and old-fashioned walking have suddenly been transformed into favorite pastimes of the American public. Whether stimulated by health concerns or simply by a desire to be chic, these nonmotorized forms of transportation can have beneficial energy-saving side effects. One study, for example, reports that in new communities with two or more pedestrian paths leading to schools, 49 percent of the children walk to school; in contrast, only 22 percent walk to school in new communities that provide no pedestrian paths [102].

States and localities should take vigorous steps to make bicycling, jogging, and walking attractive means for people of all ages to do errands, get to work, or simply enjoy themselves. Paths must be safe, easy to use, well lighted, and must connect residential areas with activity centers. Bike and pedestrian routes should be planned at the same time that future roads are charted on a coordinated land use and transportation plan. Although a companion book in this series [103] treats bicycling strategies in greater detail, a few land-use-related techniques are briefly reviewed here.

Oregon enacted, in 1971, a bicycle and footpath law [104] that can serve as a model for other states. The law requires that 1 percent of state highway funds awarded to a city or county be used to establish footpaths and bicycle trails along highways, roads, and streets that are being constructed or relocated. Though the amount allocated to paths and trails is small, and hopefully will be increased in Oregon and in other states adopting similar legislation, the funding at least provides a start. Moreover, by permitting localities to purchase enough right of way for bike and pedestrian paths at the same time that land for highways is acquired (instead of having to buy up additional land later), the statute can save localities considerable amounts of money. Oregon's law also permits additional expenditures for establishing and maintaining footpaths and trails along other highways, roads, and streets, and in parks and recreation areas.

Another recent development in Oregon may be of assistance to localities concerned with the cost of providing pedestrian and bicycle paths. The Oregon Court of Appeals recently held that a locality could establish a local sidewalk and bikeway improvement district and charge the cost of the improvements to abutting property that was deemed to "specially benefit" from them [105].

California's Bikeways Act [106], somewhat longer and more complex than the Oregon version, provides for bikeway planning and utilization of highway rights of way as bikeways. It also establishes priorities for construction of bikeways and related facilities, with bikeways serving mass transit terminals receiving top priority. Safety factors are stressed. The bikeways are funded by removing a cigarette tax exemption on federal installations in the state. Both the Oregon and California statutes are reprinted in Appendix II, pp. 281–282.

Another alternative available to localities is to require developers of large-scale projects to include bike and pedestrian paths connecting residential areas to activity centers within the project. Subdivision regulations already include tree-planting requirements, sidewalk requirements, and road installation requirements. It seems a small step to add pedestrian and bike paths to the list of necessary improvements.

Yet another way to stimulate nonmotorized travel is to make pedestrian paths convenient and pleasant to use. A firm in California has drafted a resolution for the city council of Davis, California, that would promote those goals by calling for preparation of a plan that recommends routing, shading, easement acquisition, and construction of facilities needed along pedestrian paths [107]. The resolution is reprinted in Appendix II, p. 290.

Street Widths

Oftentimes our streets, particularly those in residential areas, are excessively wide for the traffic they bear [108]. Most of the unnecessary width is taken up by cars parked along both sides while garages provided for cars (a zoning requirement in most cities) lie empty or fill up with bicycles and garden equipment. Streets that are too wide cost money and energy to build and maintain and can force us to waste energy on air conditioners by increasing the ambient air temperature [109]. By narrowing streets, particularly local ones that serve residences rather than function as major arteries or collectors, energy can be saved without compromising safe access and design. The change would simply require altering the street width requirements in subdivision ordinances. As noted in Chapter 2, one study recommends that collector and subcollector streets, which are typically built at widths of about thirty-six feet, be reduced to twenty-six feet [110]. Cul-de-sac streets could be safely constructed at eighteen feet [111]. A resolution drafted by a California firm that encourages energy-efficient street standards is reproduced in Appendix II, p. 290.

ENERGY EFFICIENCY STANDARDS

Another direct way for localities to promote energy savings through land use is to amend zoning and subdivision ordinances to require developers to meet energy efficiency standards when they select sites, when they determine the density and kinds of land uses to be included in a development, and when they choose among alternative building layouts and orientations and landscaping possibilities.

One option is for localities to adopt language requiring developers to design projects for "maximum practicable energy efficiency." Such a broadly written ordinance would, however, give headaches to administrative agencies in charge of implementation, since there are no standards in the statute for measuring energy efficiency or practicability. The vague language may also be so pierced with loopholes that almost any development plan could slip through untouched. On the other hand, a wordy, rigid statute spelling out requirements may be too inflexible to accommodate a variety of plans and natural environments. Good landscaping and proper orientation may be the best land use alternatives that a builder of one or two single family homes can use to enhance energy efficiency, but a developer of a large project has many other options. The ideal ordinance would require each to maximize energy-saving potential.

One solution to the dilemma of drafting a flexible, yet effective, ordinance is to require developments to be as energy-efficient as practicable in terms of density, mixture of land uses, site selection, building layout and orientation, and landscaping; at the same time, the ordinance should provide a checklist of standards that, if met, would result in a presumption of energy efficiency. Subdivision approval or development permits could be conditioned on a finding of energy efficiency. Developers would bear the burden of showing that a particular standard, as applied to their development, is not practicable, is energy-inefficient, or that an alternative approach would save more energy.

In Vermont, for example, where state development permits are required for all major developments [112], the reviewing agency uses the checklist of site planning objectives found in Figure 4-2 to determine whether the development permit should be awarded. Because of Vermont's cold climate, the checklist emphasizes preventing heat losses. A different checklist would be appropriate in warmer climates. Building design considerations, such as the amount of insulation used, size and placement of windows, use of vestibules on door openings exposed to prevailing winds, lighting choices, and so forth, could also be added to the list of land use considerations. Such factors are discussed in a companion book on energy conservation through building technology [113]. In addition, localities may want to add the following density, mixed use, locational, and design considerations:

1. Large developments (specify size) must contain a mixture of multifamily and single family housing at a variety of prices. (Minimum percentages for each kind of housing may be useful.)
2. The site must be ____ feet (specify distance) or less from public transportation lines that provide convenient access to shopping, recreational, school, cultural, and medical facilities and major employment centers.
3. Large developments (specify size) must include conveniently located commercial, public, and recreational facilities adequate for use by development residents.
4. The development must be contiguous with existing development.
5. Pedestrian paths and bikeways must connect residential developments to activity centers and provide convenient access to public transportation.

Planning agencies can be assisted in determining whether a project meets energy efficiency standards if the developer is required to submit a statement of energy efficiency when seeking necessary permits and approvals. Colorado had this approach in mind when it considered House Bill 1166 in 1975 [114]. Although the bill failed to muster sufficient votes, it would have required subdividers to provide evidence of future availability of energy to support a proposed sub-

Figure 4−2.   Check List of Site Planning Objectives

	Employed by developer	Partially employed by developer	Considered, but not employed	Not considered
A. Efficiency of Site Design				
1. Most efficient road, water and sewer, and electric utility layout	___	___	___	___
2. Cluster development	___	___	___	___
3. Use of party walls	___	___	___	___
4. Centralized heating for development	___	___	___	___
5. Alternative energy source for development	___	___	___	___
B. Orientation of Development				
1. Land is gently sloping and faces southeast to southwest	___	___	___	___
2. Building(s) face southeast to southwest	___	___	___	___
3. Building(s) positioned in most favorable topographic situation allowed by existing land form (midway up slopes is best)	___	___	___	___
4. Building(s) in wooded or otherwise sheltered sites rather than open sites	___	___	___	___
C. Wind Protection for Developments				
1. Shelterbelts* used or existing	___	___	___	___
2. Most effective possible shelterbelt	___	___	___	___
3. Most of development within 10−20 times the average height of shelterbelt	___	___	___	___
4. Shelterbelts serve more than one purpose	___	___	___	___
D. Wind Protection for Individual Buildings				
1. Wind screen** used for each building	___	___	___	___
2. Wind screen optimal distance from building (not further than 5× height or closer than 1/2× spread)				
3. Building oriented between 45° and 90° prevailing wind	___	___	___	___
4. Nonheated building spaces on windward	___	___	___	___

(Figure 4−2. continued overleaf . . .)

Figure 4–2. continued

	Employed by developer	Partially employed by developer	Considered, but not employed	Not considered
5. Maximum pitched roof areas and minimum wall areas on windward side of building	___	___	___	___
6. Optimal wind protection to three sides of building	___	___	___	___
7. Use of wind barriers that direct cold winter winds away from buildings and direct cooling summer breezes into it	___	___	___	___
8. Use of snow or other devices for wind protection	___	___	___	___

E. Natural Ventilation

1. Plants or detached structural elements used for directing air flow for natural ventilation	___	___	___	___
2. Mechanical air conditioning eliminated by using physical devices to manipulate air	___	___	___	___

F. Shading

1. Outside shading devices used to shade major window areas from 10 A.M. to 5 P.M. during summer months	___	___	___	___
2. Deciduous shade trees used for shading placed in optimal location for summer shade	___	___	___	___
3. Vines used on sunny brick, stone, or concrete walls	___	___	___	___
4. Grass or other plant materials used against buildings rather than paving	___	___	___	___

Source: "State of Vermont Energy Conservation Guidelines," prepared by the Vermont Public Service Board and the Agency of Environmental Conservation (Montpelier, April 1974).

   *A shelterbelt is a mass of tree plantings used to reduce wind velocity.

   **A wind screen also gives protection from the wind. A wind screen can be provided by a structural part of the building, a structure separate from the building, orientation of the building, plants, or any combination thereof.

division, of energy-conserving measures incorporated in the proposed subdivision, and of site platting and layout changes to permit use of sun, wind, and other natural energy sources. The text of the proposed amendments to the Colorado subdivision regulations is printed in Appendix II, p. 291. (Energy impact statements are discussed in more detail in Chapter 6.)

Compliance with energy efficiency standards like the ones above must, of course, be judged according to the natural and manmade environment of the region involved. For example, the orientation of buildings in a southeasterly direction may be important in temperate zones, but less desirable in hot-humid zones. In a highly developed neighborhood, street layout may be permanently established; by contrast, developers of open space can lay out road systems for maximum energy efficiency. An energy efficiency ordinance must account for such differences.

An ordinance with specific standards that result in a presumption of energy efficiency should allow developers the option of showing that the standards are inapplicable in their case, or that other strategies may provide comparable or more energy savings. For example, if a development is far from transportation lines, the developer might propose to compensate by providing convenient bus service connecting the development to established public transit. The ordinance would also allow exceptions when natural features, economic realities, or social conditions outweigh the need for energy savings. For example, if some special natural feature exists in the center of a development, the developer should be excused from locating public facilities there, even if that spot would be most convenient to residents. Similarly, if a public housing project is proposed, the municipality might have to shoulder part of the expense of an energy-efficient design in order to keep costs down. The community could provide a neighborhood park rather than requiring dedication of land for that purpose by the developer.

A different approach to overall energy-efficient design is to award energy conservation points for various land use features and to withhold subdivision and development permits unless a project accumulates a fixed number of points. This concept is similar to one used in Ramapo, New York, where the timing of development is controlled by conditioning the approval of a development on the adequacy of public facilities that would serve it [115]. But the law proposed here would condition development approval on a design's overall energy efficiency, in addition to the availability of public facilities. For example, points could be granted for proximity to transportation lines, proximity to other developments, cluster zoning, percentage of multifamily homes, self-sufficiency of the development, availability of bikeways, etc. Developers would have to accrue a certain number of points before a subdivision or site plan would be approved. Variances could be given to projects unable to meet the energy efficiency requirements due to unique circumstances. The value of this approach is that it removes discretion from administrative agencies that must determine whether or not a development is energy-efficient. It also gives the developer maximum flexibility for designing a development that meets the overall efficiency goal.

Other Considerations

Legal Issues. *Vagueness and Improper Delegation of Authority.* Legislation that conditions development permits and subdivision approvals on proof that the development is as energy-efficient as practicable can be attacked for vagueness and for improperly delegating legislative authority to administrative bodies which must flesh out the ordinance with specific standards. Yet many equally vague land use control laws, including special permits and variances, have been judicially upheld. For example, a majority of courts have upheld special permits conditioned on provisions for promoting the "public interest," "public convenience," "spirit of the zoning ordinance," or on not creating "an excessive nuisance" [116]. Even allowing for the difficulty in quantifying energy impacts of alternative land use development patterns, the term "energy-efficient" arguably is more objective than vague standards like "excessive nuisance," "public interest," or "public convenience." Courts that have upheld such vague terminology would probably also enforce language requiring energy-efficient land development. Other courts, however, require more precise standards, and have declared some ordinances to be invalid even when they were relatively specific [117]. Such courts may have difficulty with an ordinance that merely requires developments to be as energy-efficient as practicable.

Statutes with detailed standards for presumption of energy efficiency, especially those relying on a point system for development approval, are less subject to typical vagueness and improper delegation of authority challenges. They may, nevertheless, still be subject to attack on the ground that energy-efficient land use is incapable of sufficiently precise measurement to justify regulation. Such a challenge goes not so much to a law's vagueness as to the rationality of the standards applied. Courts are inclined to defer to legislative determinations, but even if they do look at the reasons behind a governing body's action requiring energy conservation through land use, there is a great deal of authority in the area to back up the rationality of such ordinances.

Taking. Energy-conserving requirements will undoubtedly impose additional costs on developers during the planning and permit review stages. But the payoff will be in enhanced convenience, energy savings, and perhaps improved visual aesthetics. Some requirements may even save money for the developers and ultimate homeowners. For instance, shortened, energy-efficient streets and utility systems will cost less to construct. Clustering can save the developer several hundred dollars per acre in clearing costs and the cost of replacing vegetation [118]. Moreover, by making the development a more convenient and aesthetically pleasing place to live, the value of the development will be enhanced. Thus, the developer will recoup some of the extra expense. There should not, therefore, be any taking in the way of a substantial diminution in value of the property.

Other factors further remove the likelihood of a "takings" challenge by mitigating the regulatory impact of the ordinance. Developers may show that standards are not applicable to their situation, or that they would not be practicable. Or, developers may suggest ways to compensate for an inability to meet a particular energy standard. In essence, the regulations would merely provide a minimum standard for energy efficiency, and that minimum standard would itself be subject to a variance procedure in case of undue hardship.

Some conservation standards may raise more credible "taking" challenges than others. Standards that pertain to the degree of urbanization of an area (e.g., availability of roads, sewers, and water lines) are one example. Although conditioning development permits on the availability of public facilities has been upheld in New York [119], that law gave developers explicit time schedules specifying when public facilities would be available to their lots and, therefore, when development would be permitted. In contrast to the New York law, the developer would be awarded a development permit under the standards proposed here only when random, external growth pressures, not set time limits, indicate that an area is ripe for urbanization. The legal implications of such an indefinite time schedule are discussed more fully on p. 149.

Enabling Legislation. As noted in Appendix I, existing zoning and subdivision enabling legislation does not explicitly permit land use regulation for the purpose of energy conservation. Yet many of the energy efficiency standards proposed here incorporate land use restrictions already legitimately imposed by localities to achieve other goals. With respect to those restrictions, it is unlikely that a challenge to the authority of the locality would succeed. For example, landscaping requirements are common, and approval of street and layout width is regularly required. Many localities have ordinances requiring developers to provide pedestrian paths and open spaces for recreation. High densities can be mapped along transportation corridors with no legal problem. Nevertheless, states should consider adopting zoning and subdivision legislation like that outlined in Appendix I, p. 226 to bolster the validity of local requirements imposed to conserve energy.

Implementation. *State.*   State, regional, and local governments may adopt legislation applying energy conservation standards to developments subject to government permitting requirements. States will have to assist regional and local governments during the initial implementation of standards by providing technical expertise and money to train staff members evaluating energy efficiencies.

Local.   Energy efficiency standards implemented at the local level should be incorporated in existing zoning and subdivision regulations, and their review should be conducted simultaneously with subdivision and site plan reviews when possible. Integration into existing procedures will avoid creation of an additional layer of time-consuming and expensive development approvals.

Planning staffs may review energy efficiencies based on information provided by the developer. This strategy may require expansion of planning staffs and will probably result in some administrative delays until the procedure becomes familiar to both developers and officials. But the initial delays should ultimately result in valuable land use plans that will provide an energy-efficient model for future developments.

Some efficiency standards may be impossible to comply with and thus not "practicable" until conflicting zoning and subdivision ordinances are identified and amended. For example, a zoning ordinance may prohibit multifamily zoning in an area, or may impose rigid yard and lot size requirements that prevent optimal building orientation. Other strategies discussed in this chapter have suggested ways to modify existing ordinances so that barriers to energy-efficient land use can be removed and energy efficiency standards can effectively be applied.

PLANNED UNIT DEVELOPMENT ORDINANCES

Planned unit developments (PUDs) offer an exciting opportunity to design energy-efficient, environmentally sound, and aesthetically pleasing developments that promote the traditional health and safety goals of land use planning. PUDs vary in size, but they are characterized by a single, integrated plan for an entire project. Rigid lot size, use, and density regulations are relaxed to permit a mixture of building types and uses, flexible building design and siting, and clustering of structures to preserve the natural environment. The unitary plan ensures that buildings will be related both to each other and to the transportation and utility infrastructure, thus opening the way for maximum energy efficiency.

Because of their flexibility and emphasis on planning, PUDs combine many of the energy-saving techniques discussed earlier, although few PUDs have energy conservation as a stated goal. This section reviews ways that PUD ordinances can be used to help accomplish energy-efficient land use [120].

Adopting PUD Legislation — The First Step

In 1973, six states had PUD enabling legislation, six others had approved PUDlike techniques, such as cluster subdivisions, and one hundred communities had adopted PUD legislation without benefit of state enabling legislation [121]. Although the interest in PUDs has increased since then [122], the possibility for energy conservation through PUDs has barely been tapped.

PUDs' energy-saving potential is unique, for they can incorporate and integrate every energy conservation strategy discussed in this chapter. By eliminating rigid setback, yard, lot, and height requirements, PUDs can permit the clustering of buildings; the utilization of natural shading and ventilation systems; shortened road and utility systems; shared walls, ceilings, and floors; and optimal building arrangement and orientation. Depending on their size and the availability of flexible use restrictions, PUDs can combine residential, commercial, institutional, light industrial, and recreational uses. They can create relatively self-sufficient communities where jobs, homes, shopping centers, schools, churches, and doctors' offices are within easy reach. Bonuses that permit higher density development in exchange for including amenities are often part of PUD ordinances [123]. And because PUDs are subject to site plan review, opportunities are provided for analyzing the energy efficiency of the road network, landscaping, and other individual features as well as the overall project.

Removing institutional barriers to flexible, innovative land use does not guarantee that all PUDs will take advantage of the opportunity for energy savings. Not all PUDs cluster buildings, many do not integrate uses, and it is safe to say that few consciously incorporate energy-conserving design features [124]. Nevertheless, replacing rigid ordinances with laws that enable and encourage localities to promote PUD development can be a strong step in the direction of energy conservation.

Incorporating Energy Efficiency Requirements in PUDs

Although several model PUD enabling statutes exist [125], none reflects an overt concern for energy conservation. This neglect is understandable, as most PUD enabling legislation was written when few Americans realized we faced an energy shortage. Now, however, PUD enabling legislation and ordinances adopted thereunder should be brought up to date.

Energy Conservation as a Goal. As a first step, the "purposes" section of PUD legislation and ordinances should be amended to incorporate energy conservation. The following language, excerpted from the purposes section of the Montgomery County, Maryland, PUD ordinance [126], shows how, with only minor changes, a typical PUD ordinance can be converted into one that explicitly encompasses energy conservation; adaptive language is italicized. Note that the ordinance already contains many energy conservation considerations, but fails to acknowledge their energy impacts:

> ... It is intended that this [Planned Unit Development] Zone provide a means of regulating development which can achieve flexibility of design, the integration of mutually compatible uses, *maximum practicable energy-efficiency*, and optimum land planning with greater efficiency, convenience, and amenity than the procedures and regulations under which it is permitted as of right under conventional zoning categories . . .
>
> It is intended that development in this Zone produce a balanced and coordinated mixture of residential and convenient commercial uses, as well as other commercial and industrial uses shown on the area master plan, and related public and private facilities, *all conveniently located for easy access by residents of the planned unit development with minimum reliance upon motorized transportation.*
>
> It is furthermore the purpose of this Zone to provide and encourage a broad range of housing types, comprising owner and rental occupancy units, and single-family, multi-family, and other structural types.
>
> Additionally, it is the purpose of this Zone to preserve and take the greatest possible . . . advantage of exiting topography and other natural

features *to promote* aesthetic *and energy-conserving goals*, and, in order to do so, minimize the amount of grading in the construction of development *and optimize siting, orientation, layout, and design of structures to take advantage of shading, cooling, windbreak, drainage, and other natural features that can reduce the impact of temperature extremes and otherwise enhance energy conservation.*

It is further the purpose of this Zone to encourage and provide for open space . . . conveniently located with respect to points of residential and commercial concentration so as to function, for the general benefit of the community and public at large, as places for relaxation, recreation, and social activity; and, furthermore, open space should be so situated as part of the plan and design of each development as to achieve the physical and aesthetic integration of the uses and activities within each development.

It is also the purpose of this Zone to encourage and provide for the development of comprehensive pedestrian *and bicycle* circulation networks, separated from vehicular roadways, which constitute a system of linkages among residential areas, open space, recreational areas, commercial and employment areas, and public facilities and thereby minimize reliance upon the automobile as a means of transportation.

Since many of the purposes of the Zone can best be realized with developments of a large scale in terms of area of land and numbers of dwelling units which offer opportunities for a wider range of related residential and nonresidential uses it is therefore the purpose of this Zone to encourage development on such a scale [127].

Once an energy-conserving purpose has been identified, it is necessary to set out ways to achieve that purpose. Five considerations of prime importance are (1) the overall size of the PUD; (2) whether the PUD will incorporate a mixture of uses, including regionally based commercial and industrial uses, or whether uses will be limited to those necessary for the convenience of PUD residents; (3) the location of the PUD; (4) PUD density; and (5) PUD design.

Size. Planned unit developments vary in size from large-scale "new towns" such as Twin Rivers, New Jersey, which covers 714 acres and will house 10,000 persons, to developments of five acres or less. The American Society for Planning Officials (ASPO) views the PUD as a process, not a product. Consequently, ASPO recommends that localities permit the construction of PUDs on small parcels of under five acres [128]. Obviously, the potential for energy savings is greater in large projects, since the developer has more siting, orientation, and building and street layout options; nevertheless, the application of flexible techniques to any size development can save fuel. It is particularly desirable to apply PUDs to small parcels in urban areas, since large-scale land assembly is difficult there.

Permitted Uses. Although many PUDs are now limited to residential developments, large-scale PUDs can cut transportation energy demands by mixing commercial, and even industrial, establishments with residential development. But before this decision is made, its consequences must be carefully evaluated. Large commercial or industrial centers may actually stimulate commuting unless individuals employed in those centers can afford housing in the PUD. A large-scale PUD may not be economically viable without at least one commercial or industrial element designed to serve regional needs. But some have suggested that such a development may be a "singular local occurrence" that prevents development of other large scale PUDs [129]. And PUDs with mixed uses catering to regional needs may stimulate premature development on the urban fringe unless surrounding areas are zoned for less intensive development [130]. Another problem is that large-scale PUDs that hope to attract big businesses and industry may fail to do so. Consequently, residents of PUDs located outside developed urban areas may end up commuting long distances to jobs in urban centers [131]. In view of these potential problems, the location of PUDs become crucial (see below). The best course may be for localities to require that, where practicable, PUDs provide commercial establishments and community facilities to serve PUD residents. Localities can, if they desire, allow incorporation of larger scale businesses, but only after the local governing body has made a careful analysis of energy and other impacts.

Location. Location of large-scale PUD projects is a particularly important consideration since, as noted, PUDs may generate a lot of traffic. It is important to encourage construction of PUDs close to urban centers and public transportation so that whatever commuting occurs can be done in an energy-efficient manner. Some localities use a "floating zone" approach to control locations of PUDs. Areas are designated where PUD zones may be appropriate, but the locality refuses to map a PUD zone prior to careful consideration and approval of the development plan [132]. The energy impacts of the proposed PUD location should be a factor in the decision.

Another approach is to make PUD development a special use in designated zoning districts close to the urban center. Again proximity of the PUD to transportation lines should be a factor in determining whether the PUD will be approved. A special permit system does not require an amendment to the zoning map, and some argue that it gives the locality greater control over the planning and location of PUDs than do floating zones [133]. But as long as areas where PUDs may be appropriate are spelled out in the ordinance, it seems unimportant whether the PUD is approved by the floating zone or special permit technique [134].

Density and Design. A primary concern with all PUDs, and particularly with the development of energy-efficient PUDs, is the density that will be allowed. Sometimes the density of development permitted under traditional zoning is decreased to permit PUD zoning. This action should be strongly discouraged, for a well-designed PUD offers an opportunity to accommodate high densities much more attractively and pleasantly than can most conventional subdivisions. Development at a density sufficient to support public transportation should be permitted and encouraged. One way to encourage higher densities and other energy-saving design features is to allow higher densities as a matter of right when specified energy-efficient design and location "amenities" are provided. This approach provides an element of certainty that developers will appreciate.

The following language gives a very rough suggestion of how density increases and amenities may be balanced:

Density increases. Density increases shall be governed by the precepts listed below, which are to be treated as additive, and not compounded:

Transportation, siting, layout, landscaping, and design features incorporated in a development shall be considered cause for density increases in the number of dwelling units not to exceed thirty (30) percent, provided these factors make a substantial contribution to the energy conservation objectives of a Planned Unit Development. The degree of energy efficiency and the social and environmental desirability of energy-efficient features shall govern the amount of density increase which the Planning Commission may approve. Such features may include, but are not limited to, the following:

1. Transportation (a maximum increase of fifteen (15) percent):
   a. location close to existing roads, public transportation lines, and stations and activity centers
   b. location contiguous to previously developed land
   c. location close to employment centers
   d. pedestrian and bicycle lanes separate from road systems and connecting residential areas and major activity centers
   e. minimal central road network (width and length), that nevertheless preserves the natural landscape insofar as practicable
   f. facilities for convenient use of public transportation (e.g. transit shelters, restrooms)

2. Siting, layout, and landscaping (a maximum increase of five (5) percent):

    a. maximum preservation and use of energy-efficient landscaping, drainage swales, and other natural environmental features

    b. lot and building arrangement and orientation to permit solar, wind, or total energy systems and to shelter buildings from temperature extremes

    c. energy-conserving vegetation planted where most effective

    d. minimized grading of land

3. Design (a maximum increase of ten (10) percent):

    a. buildings arranged in a cluster pattern to follow contour of land

    b. availability within the development of conveniently located public facilities and shopping facilities

    c. mixture of housing types with _____ percent multifamily housing

    d. adequate open space and recreational land for residents

    e. provision of recreational facilities [135]

Of course, other energy-conserving features discussed in this book and in companion books on building technology and transportation could be added to these provisions.

In some instances, the amenity may be too important to rely on an incentive system; mandatory provisions may be in order. For example, because PUDs should generally be designed for higher densities than most developments, it is extremely important that streets and traffic lights be planned so that traffic will flow smoothly, as much fuel is wasted when cars idle. Pedestrian and bike paths should exist and should lead to major activity centers within the PUD. One PUD ordinance requires, for example, that:

> At least 30 per cent of the dwelling units in the Planned [Unit] Development area shall have access to commercial areas by pedestrian paths suitable for use in all weather. Such access shall not involve the crossing of any street serving more than ten (10) dwelling units, nor any collector or primary street.
>
> All nonresidential land uses within a PUD should have direct access to a collector or primary street, especially where large parking areas are included [136].

Modifications could be made to that ordinance to require even higher numbers of dwelling units to have access to commercial areas by pedestrian paths.

In addition, the energy efficiency standards reviewed earlier should be applied during the site plan review to ensure that the energy conservation goal cited in the "purpose" section of the PUD ordinance is met.

To summarize, PUDs can combine energy-efficient location, layout, design, orientation, landscaping, mixed uses, nonmotorized transportation systems, and energy-efficient technology to attain large-scale energy savings. This goal can be achieved through energy-conscious PUD ordinances backed up by planning staff efforts to assist developers in preparing integrated plans that meet strict energy-conserving standards of the PUD ordinance.

Other Considerations

Secondary Impacts. In addition to saving energy, planned unit developments may enhance environmental protection since they can cluster buildings and thereby direct development away from critical or hazardous areas. PUDs also can reduce both air pollution (by reducing the amount of fuel burned for transportation) and the cost of infrastructure (by eliminating duplicative road and utility systems through integrated planning). The cost of grading also can be considerably reduced, since flexible design standards allow PUDs to preserve much of the natural environment.

One big advantage of PUDs is that even though they do away with the traditional notion of a single family home on a large plot, they offer proof that many people welcome compact, higher density development when it is properly designed. Hence localities that may be generally unwilling to permit multifamily housing may agree to the development of a PUD that incorporates a mixture of dwelling types [137]. Other advantages include better design, more amenities for residents, conveniences stemming from mixed uses, attractiveness to corporate investors, and some marketing plusses [138].

On the minus side, PUDs may result in higher costs, in part attributable to the need for greater planning, development, and managerial expertise, longer review processes, and increased amenities. They may also be more susceptible to economic recession [139]. One commentator suggests that PUDs may encourage exclusionary practices because the large degree of bargaining and discretion institutionalized in the PUD process offers easy opportunities to veto projects with mixed cost housing [140].

The most disappointing aspect of PUDs has been the failure of developers and communities to take advantage of their design flexibility. An ASPO survey of PUDs found that "few of them were innovative . . . many of them were unimaginative and possibly inadequate" [141]. Many were built at the same density as the surrounding conventionally zoned districts; few offered incentives for more amenities; most were limited to residential use [142]. If PUDs are to fulfill their promise of energy-efficient land use, localities must find ways to reward developers who do propose well-planned developments and to assist those whose plans fall below standards.

Legal Issues. *Enabling Legislation.* Although PUDs depart from traditional zoning concepts by eliminating strict yard, setback, height, and use requirements, they do not represent any radically new thinking. Many localities have long histories of substituting bulk requirements for strict yard measurements, and almost all allow some mixture of uses, either through cumulative zoning or accommodation of nonconforming uses [143]. Nevertheless, some states have passed PUD enabling legislation and others have adopted enabling legislation for PUD like techniques to ensure the legality of mixing residential and nonresidential uses (including commercial uses serving a region, not just the PUD, in some instances); to permit use of innovative design techniques including clustering; and to allow shifting of some planning decisions to administrative bodies. They have also created legal mechanisms for dealing with private open space [144]. Many municipalities without PUD enabling legislation have permitted PUDs as a special use [145].

Uniformity Requirements. A potential legal issue may be that PUD zoning violates uniformity requirements since each PUD incorporates different types of buildings and uses of land that cannot possibly be duplicated in another PUD [146]. Another legal issue is that the uniformity clause prevents the mixture of uses contemplated by PUDs. The latter argument was dismissed in *Orinda Homeowners Committee* v. *Board of Supervisors* [147]. Both arguments may be avoided by including a provision in PUD enabling legislation that exempts PUDs from zoning uniformity requirements.

Floating Zones. In several states, PUD zones are included in the text of the zoning ordinance, but are not mapped until an applicant requests that the PUD zone be attached to a specific plot of land. If the application is approved, the PUD zone is then "anchored" and development proceeds [148]. This "floating" zone technique has been popular in Maryland, New York, Connecticut, and Pennsylvania (after an initial adverse decision). But other states see floating zones as the antithesis of comprehensive planning required by the Standard Zoning Enabling Act, and also find them an invalid delegation of legislative authority to local administrative bodies. Consequently, any state contemplating PUD floating zones must carefully check its case law.

One alternative to floating zones is to attach PUD provisions to existing zoning ordinances as special uses. This approach avoids the need for zoning map amendments, and has been used by many localities [149]. It is necessary, however, to include in the ordinance standards for approval of special permits. Otherwise, agency approval of a special permit may constitute an improper delegation of legislative authority [150].

Implementation. *State.* States without PUD ordinances should pass legislation to enable localities to adopt this form of development. States should be careful to include energy conservation as a purpose of the legislation. In addition, states should authorize a mixture of residential, commercial, and industrial uses where feasible.

One main obstacle to developing energy-efficient PUDs is that they have very heavy front end planning costs. High interest rates encourage developers to build a development as quickly as possible, thereby preventing a thorough analysis of energy-efficient design [151]. States can assist developers in this respect by providing low interest loans to finance preconstruction development.

A study of the Twin Rivers, New Jersey, planned unit development suggests that even if an ordinance requires PUDs to evaluate the possibility of total energy systems, solar systems, and other energy-conserving systems, local planning boards may lack the expertise and sophistication to evaluate their desirability [152]. State technical assistance to the local planning boards in evaluating the energy efficiency of PUDs may be essential.

Local. Local governments will be primarily responsible for adopting and implementing PUD ordinances. As noted, the ordinance should incorporate energy efficiency standards and use the rezoning and site plan review process to ensure that the standards are met. In addition, because PUD ordinances leave so much discretion to administrative bodies, those bodies should use their authority during negotiating sessions to ensure energy-efficient design, layout, and landscaping. According to one study, 50 percent of the way a PUD will be developed is settled during the negotiating process [153].

Because developers involved in PUD applications may be discouraged by the various plans and written documents they must prepare, as well as by the length of the review process, localities must take steps to minimize these administrative burdens. A first step may be to encourage or require preapplication conferences with developers, so that both the developer and the local planning staff can educate each other regarding the proposed PUD, the standards it must meet, and ways to meet those standards. Perhaps PUD applications can be given priority on review dockets; or perhaps permit requirements can be consolidated [154]. Use of bonus provisions, discussed in the following section, is another way to help make red tape feel less sticky [155].

INCENTIVES FOR ENERGY-EFFICIENT DEVELOPMENT

This chapter almost exclusively has discussed regulatory techniques for promoting energy-efficient density, mixed uses, and designs. Another approach to achieve the same goals is to give the developer financial incentives to plan and build developments that conserve energy. Localities can also use their control over extension of services and facilities as leverage for bargaining with developers to secure energy-efficient projects. This section looks at two techniques—density bonuses and annexation agreements—that incorporate those two nonregulatory approaches for achieving energy conservation.

Density Bonuses

Density bonuses are a form of incentive zoning that allows developers to build at a density higher than normally permitted if they include specified amenities or other specified features in their development. Density bonuses should logically enhance energy conservation in two ways. Properly located dense development can help cut back transportation and space heating and cooling energy demands. In addition, many of the "amenities" that developers exchange for density bonuses can be energy-conserving design features. For example, communities may grant density bonuses for locating developments close to public transportation lines; for including a certain percentage of multifamily housing; and for offering pedestrian paths and bikeways, covered public transportation stations, multiple use buildings, recreational facilities, energy-saving landscaping, or clustered housing. The list is limited only by the imagination of energy-conscious planners and local legislatures.

Density bonuses take the form of increasing the floor-to-area ratio of buildings above what is normally permitted, changing height limits to permit taller buildings, reducing lot requirements, or otherwise increasing the number of permitted units per parcel of land. Because density bonuses are designed to give the public a benefit in exchange for allowing the developer to build at a density higher than normal, they can help forestall neighborhood objections to increased density.

Although most bonus systems are voluntary, some communities *mandate* that developers include specific amenities, and grant valuable density bonuses as compensation. In New York City, new buildings near Lincoln Center were required to build connecting arcades that provide an overhead pedestrian path. Certain buildings in the Fifth Avenue district had to put in subway stops. Other mandatory facilities were spelled out for the Greenwich Street district and the Brooklyn Center district. In some instances, construction was required to follow a development plan prepared by the city [156].

Similarly, Fairfax County, Virginia [157]; Montgomery County, Maryland [158]; and Lakewood, Colorado [159]; have experimented with requiring large developments, or those in multifamily districts, to include a fixed percentage of low and moderate income housing in exchange for density bonuses. This approach to promoting the inclusion of low and moderate income housing in suburban developments is one promising way to attack the problem of providing homes for nonprofessionals close to their jobs [160].

Where amenities are mandatory, density bonuses serve chiefly as a device to compensate developers for the potentially adverse economic impacts of including the required amenity. They thereby make land development requirements more politically acceptable. Mandating inclusion of energy-saving amenities will be more effective than using voluntary bonus systems to promote energy-efficient land development. On the other hand, mandatory bonus systems may be more susceptible to legal attacks. Fairfax County's effort to encourage low income housing through the use of mandatory density bonuses has been found unconstitutional by that state's supreme court. Some commentators believe the case is an aberration [161].

Even voluntary bonus systems can lead to fuel-saving project designs and locations. The previous section on planned unit developments contains an example of a voluntary density bonus ordinance designed to save fuel. Eugene, Oregon, offers density bonuses to developers who dedicate land for bike paths [162]. San Francisco awards density bonuses for buildings that are close to transit stations or that provide access to rapid transit [163]. Prince George's County, Maryland, gives density bonuses to developers who provide pedestrian paths that link housing to major transportation terminals, who offer common open space for recreation, and who preserve stands of trees [164]. New Castle County, Delaware [165], and Freemont, California [166], provide density bonuses to developers who include low income housing in planned unit developments, while Arlington County, Virginia, grants density bonuses for the provision of low income housing in multifamily units as well as in planned unit developments [167]. Olympic Tower, a multiple use building in New York City, demonstrates how voluntary incentive zoning can be advantageous to the developer and the public. Although not designed primarily for energy conservation, Olympic Tower qualified for bonuses that entitled it to a 44 percent floor-to-area ratio increase by providing amenities that serve stated public goals [168]. Comparable incentives can stimulate developers to promote fuel-saving land use [169].

Secondary Impacts.   Density bonuses will, as their name suggests, increase the density of an area. The resulting secondary impacts, like congestion, loss of privacy, and noise, should be minimized if the bonuses are accompanied by proper planning, design, and landscaping. Other secondary impacts of density bonuses will vary according to the amenity that is provided in return for the bonus. Pedestrian paths, bikeways, jitney services, public transportation stops, recreational land, and other energy-conserving amenities can enhance the convenience, attractiveness, and environmental soundness of projects. Density bonuses for low and moderate income housing may provide an acceptable means for the economic integration of neighborhoods.

For a bonus system to be a true incentive, it must give developers an economic benefit. Under mandatory bonus systems, increased density may or may not fully compensate developers for the cost of the required amenity, but the amenity itself may enhance the project's value and economically benefit the developer. Developers who had always planned to include a particular amenity would get a windfall if they later discovered they were eligible for a density bonus. A bonus is worthwhile even in this situation, however, as it allows localities to ensure that an amenity is designed in the most energy-efficient manner possible.

Legal Issues.   Optional bonus provisions have been widely used in planned unit developments, multiunit structures, and downtown business areas in major cities. In spite of their broad use, there have been few legal challenges to optional density bonuses, perhaps because developers who receive the bonuses are not inclined to attack their legality, and neighbors who might be opposed to them have been assuaged by the provision of amenities [170].

Mandatory bonus provisions, on the other hand, are more susceptible to legal challenge [171]. Although there are only a few cases involving mandatory provisions, localities should carefully draft such ordinances to avoid legal challenge. The following suggestions apply to both optional and mandatory bonuses unless otherwise specified.

Rational Relationship. Some argue that a density bonus must be rationally related to the amenities it induces if it is to be a legitimate exercise of the police power [172]. If this requirement exists, it nevertheless presents no problem with respect to many energy-saving amenities. Potential adverse side effects resulting from an increase in density can be balanced by amenities such as providing pedestrian paths and bikeways, locating buildings close to public transportation stations, clustering buildings so that the length and number of streets are reduced, and providing sufficient and appropriate landscaping to enhance privacy. It may be somewhat harder to show that the potential problems of increased density can be lessened by providing a mixture of housing types, costs, or uses within a development, or by preserving natural drainage swales and vegetation.

On the other hand, since the enhancement of energy conservation is arguably a legitimate basis for land use regulation, density bonuses that induce a developer to incorporate fuel-saving design features should not be held arbitrary. At any rate, it is not likely that courts will closely examine the relationship of a density bonus to an amenity, especially when the bonus provisions are optional, since legislative actions enjoy a presumption of validity [173].

Even if courts fail to fault the general relationship between a bonus and an amenity, they may be less hesitant to strike the provision if the size of a bonus is unrelated to the value of the amenity provided. In other words, it may be arbitrary to allow developers to build twenty additional homes on a block when the only amenity they provide is a single bus stop.

Taking. Another legal issue that goes to the constitutionality of density bonuses is whether the bonus system constitutes a taking of property without just compensation. If a locality makes the regulations underlying an optional bonus system so stringent that the developer is "forced" to try to get a bonus, courts may find the ordinance to be unreasonable. Consequently, in adopting a bonus provision, a locality should be wary of modifying preexisting regulations applicable to the land to "encourage" use of density bonuses [174]. In any event, reducing the intensity of development permitted in the zoning ordinance and substituting density bonuses to try to encourage both high density development and provision of an energy-efficient design may backfire: unless developers take advantage of the density bonuses, there may be an overall decrease in density and a decrease in energy savings.

Mandatory bonus ordinances also run the risk of violating the taking clause if they do not sufficiently compensate the landowner for the cost of providing the amenity. The Virginia Supreme Court held that Fairfax County's mandatory bonus provision, which required the inclusion of 15 percent low and moderate income housing in multifamily projects, constituted a taking even though the developer was awarded a density bonus of one unsubsidized unit for every two subsidized units built [175]. The Virginia court appeared opposed to density bonuses on principle, and it is unlikely that lesser requirements would have received a favorable response. Other localities have been more successful. A Montgomery County, Maryland, ordinance [176] requiring 15 to 20 percent moderate income units in developments of fifty units or larger in exchange for density bonuses is still in effect (although it is now being challenged), and a Los Angeles ordinance [177] that conditions building permit approval on the inclusion of low and moderate income housing still stands, even though developers receive no bonus in return.

Enabling Legislation. In addition to constitutional challenges, bonus provisions may be subject to charges that they are not authorized by state enabling legislation. Although special state legislation that allows localities to adopt incentive zoning is desirable, strong arguments can be made that voluntary and mandatory incentive zoning is proper even without it, since SZEA clearly authorizes localities to regulate density of development. Density bonuses are one way to exercise that authority.

Alternatively, courts may find that bonuses granted in exchange for transit stops, pedestrian and bicycle paths, etc. fall within the scope of most state enabling legislation since SZEA authorizes zoning to "lessen congestion in the streets; . . . [and] to facilitate the adequate provision of transportation" [178]. Localities with home rule charters may be able to adopt density bonuses without relying on separate enabling legislation since bonuses are matters of local concern. It should be noted that the Virginia Supreme Court has held that *mandatory* bonus provisions for low and moderate income housing are outside the authority delegated to counties by state enabling legislation [179].

Because of the uncertainty regarding the need for enabling legislation, states should adopt legislation to permit the use of optional and mandatory density bonuses to save energy. In addition to removing doubts generally about the use of density bonuses, such enabling legislation should also enhance the validity of offering density bonuses in exchange for amenities that do not seem to alleviate problems caused by density and for requiring the inclusion of other amenities in exchange for bonuses.

Statutory Claims. Municipalities must take pains to establish clear standards of what amenities qualify for a bonus. Without such standards, municipalities may find themselves stuck with setbacks they never wanted, or a plethora of duplicative transit stops, or they may be subject to suit for failure to provide bonuses in exchange for undesirable "amenities" offered by a developer.

Implementation. *State.* As noted above, states should adopt enabling legislation authorizing localities to set up mandatory and optional density bonus programs for the purpose of promoting energy-efficient land use.

Local. Density bonus ordinances are adopted and implemented at the local level. The crux of designing an effective density bonus system is ensuring that the bonus provides a true incentive for the developer. San Francisco, California, accomplishes this by first deciding what amenities it wants to encourage. Next, the city does an economic analysis to determine how much of a bonus has to be offered to induce developers to provide the amenities. This analysis compares the cost of each amenity to the value of each benefit the developer will receive from the bonus. By computing the building development costs and revenues per square foot for an average building, the value of the added density and the cost of the amenity can be established. San Francisco assumes that the bonus should exceed the estimated cost of the amenity to be a genuine incentive [180]. As experience in Prince George's County, Maryland, demonstrates, it may at times be difficult to estimate whether the increased densities compensate for the cost of public benefit features. The first developer to opt for density bonuses in that county is still involved in cost accounting to figure out which densities are feasible [181].

Optional density bonuses raise other administrative issues. Localities must decide, for instance, whether the granting of bonuses will be discretionary or a matter of right if a developer meets the amenity requirements. One advantage of discretionary bonuses is that localities can control their distribution, so that they are granted only for desirable amenities in desirable areas.

On the other hand, although discretion may enhance a locality's bargaining power with small developers, it may put the locality at a disadvantage when bargaining with large developers. Moreover, discretion may give rise to equal protection challenges and may open the door to corruption since approval of higher density enhances the value of the land [182]. New York City initially left bonuses to the discretion of the city planning commission, but later, to prevent favoritism and corruption, followed the policy of precisely delineating when bonuses would be awarded [183].

In adopting optional density bonuses, communities will want to set maximum limits so that a developer cannot exceed desirable density levels no matter how many amenities are provided. Of course, it is essential in drafting a bonus provision that amenities be specified in great detail so reviewers may determine whether developers' plans conform to the bonus requirements and so the developers can be sure that the amenity they provide will qualify for a bonus.

Annexation Conditions

In an effort to cut costs, many developers prefer to buy less expensive property outside of municipal boundaries and then apply to the municipality for annexation. Upon annexation, the municipality will be requested to install public facilities and provide other necessary municipal services. Municipalities can use their leverage arising from provision of public facilities and services to condition annexation on the construction of energy-efficient developments. For example, a city could require developers to lay out their homes and streets in a clustered fashion rather than in typical grid fashion, to include a certain percentage of multifamily housing, or to include a mixture of land uses.

The idea of conditioning annexation on obtaining certain development concessions is not new, although there appear to be no instances of cities' using annexation agreements to further energy conservation. Courts in several states have upheld the power of municipalities to impose conditions on landowners seeking annexation [184]. In 1963, the Illinois legislature passed legislation that authorizes municipalities and property owners to enter into annexation agreements that give municipalities detailed control over development design, density, and land uses [185]. In addition, the threat of deannexing the parcel and the ability of cities to enforce the agreement in court give cities assurance that the terms of the contract will be met. Presumably, developers also benefit from annexation agreements, since the agreement can spell out obligations of the municipality and thereby remove uncertainties inherent in the development process. One disadvantage of annexation agreements is that if two municipalities are competing for the same parcel of land, they may bargain away important elements, including, perhaps certain energy-saving features [186].

Although energy conservation is not one of its purposes, a recent annexation agreement between Aurora, Illinois, and a developer of a new community near the expanding city shows how annexation agreements can work. Under the contract, the proposed community, which will accommodate about 30,000 people on more than 1,500 acres, must contain no less than 15 percent low and moderate income housing. The developer is required to submit yearly progress reports and plans for future low income housing before building permits will be issued [187]. In another example, a developer of a 783 acre planned unit development agreed with the city of Naperville, Illinois, to develop his property "only in accordance with the Plan as shown on said preliminary plat, as approved or subsequently amended . . ." [188]. Any community entering into similar agreements could help conserve energy by making sure that the approved agreement required compliance with an energy-efficient land use plan designed along the lines described in earlier sections of this chapter.

Implementation. *State.* Municipalities in several states, including those in Illinois prior to 1963, have entered into annexation agreements without benefit of state enabling legislation [189]. Nevertheless, states should enact legislation authorizing annexation agreements between cities and landowners in order to remove doubts about the validity of those agreements.

Local. Local governments will be responsible for entering into energy-saving agreements and for ensuring that developers comply with the agreement. Additional staff time to negotiate the agreements will be required. Localities must also find ways to minimize delays associated with negotiation of the agreement, or expenses to developers caused by delay may prevent the project from going forward.

NOTES TO CHAPTER 4

1. United States Department of Commerce, A Standard Zoning Enabling Act, §3 (rev. ed. 1926).
2. Another method for promoting higher density development, use of density bonuses, is discussed on pp. 116–122, *infra.*
3. "Where Transit Works: Urban Densities for Public Transportation," *Regional Plan News*, no. 99 (New York: Regional Plan Association, August 1976), p. 10.
4. *Id.* at 7.
5. Rep. Henry Reuss, "Stimulus Seen Available for Multi-Family Housing," *The Washington Post*, January 3, 1976, p. B–1.
6. *See* pp. 118–121, *infra.*
7. *Id.*
8. Or. Rev. Stat. §308.235 (1975).

9. Montgomery County, Md., Ordinance No. 7–75 (Jan. 29, 1974), Montgomery County, Md., Code §§59–51.6, 59–51.7 (Michie Supp. 1975).

10. Norman Williams, Jr., *American Land Planning Law*, vol. 3, §68.05 (Chicago: Callaghan & Co., 1975).

11. *See* pp. 18–23, *supra*.

12. One potential problem with FARs is that they may encourage developers to divide buildings into as many living units as possible so that profit may be increased. Accordingly, localities using floor-to-area ratios may wish to modify the FAR to allow larger structures, but also protect health and aesthetic needs by maintaining control over the number or size of units within each structure.

13. Smith v. Board of Appeals of Fall River, 319 Mass. 314, 65 N.E.2d 547 (1946). *See* Williams, *supra* note 10 at vol. 5 §149.09, p. 174, for a discussion of the case. Cases involving special permits for multifamily housing are summarized in Williams, *supra* note 10 at vol. 2 §54.06–54.12, pp. 418–21.

14. Living Systems, "Planning for Energy Conservation, Draft Report," prepared for the City of Davis, California, pursuant to HUD project grant No. B–75–51–06–001 (Winters, California, June 1, 1976) p. 8.

15. *See* Williams, *supra* note 10 at vol. 2 §§50–56 for a more complete discussion of the case law concerning multiple dwelling zoning.

16. Variance proceedings are administrative proceedings and, therefore, may be subject to greater judicial scrutiny than rezonings, which in most states are considered legislative. *But see* Fasano v. Board of County Commissioners of Washington County, 264 Or. 574, 507 P.2d 23 (Or. 1973).

17. Loyola Federal Savings and Loan Ass'n v. Buschman, 227 Md. 243, 176 A.2d 355 (1961).

18. *See* Williams, *supra* note 10 at vol. 1 §27.02, p. 563.

19. *Id.* at vol. 1 §27.01, p. 561, *citing* Jones v. Zoning Board of Adjustment, 32 N.J. Super. 397, 108 A.2d 498 (App. Div. 1954).

20. *See, e.g.*, Duggins v. Board of County Commissioners, 179 Kan. 101, 293 P.2d 258 (1956); White v. Zoning Board of Adjustment of Arlington, 363 S.W.2d 955 (Tex. App. 1962); and Wicker Apartments, Inc. v. City of Richmond, 199 Va. 263, 99 S.E.2d 656 (1957).

21. Challenges to less restrictive zoning amendments may have greater success in Maryland, where zoning changes depend on showing either that there was a mistake in the original zoning or that a change in the neighborhood justifies rezoning.

22. *See generally* Williams, *supra* note 10 at vol. 2, §50.01–50.09, pp. 252–82.

23. 437 Pa. 237, 263 A.2d 395 (1970).

24. 67 N.J. 151, 336 A.2d 713, *appeal dismissed*, 96 S.Ct. 18 (1975).

25. 38 N.Y.2d 102, 341 N.E.2d 236, 378 N.Y.S.2d 672 (1975).

26. In addition to enhancing space heating and cooling energy savings through construction of multiunit buildings, these decisions may also promote transportation energy savings since construction of low and moderate income multifamily buildings in the suburbs may enable blue collar and service workers to live closer to their jobs. *See* Regina B. Armstrong, "Linking Skills, Jobs, and

Housing in the New York Urban Region" (New York: Regional Plan Ass'n., March 1972).

27. ____ U.S. ____ , 96 S.Ct. 2358 (1976).

28. A recently published book, *Mixed-Use Developments: New Ways of Land Use*, Technical Bulletin 71, by Robert E. Witherspoon et al. (Washington, D.C.: The Urban Land Institute, 1976), analyzes institutional changes necessary for successful mixed use developments, but the concept as used in that book applies to large scale projects in urban centers.

29. *See, e.g.*, Boreth v. Philadelphia Zoning Board of Adjustments, 396 Pa. 82, 151 A.2d 474 (1959); Perron v. City of Concord, 102 N.H. 32, 150 A.2d 403 (1959). *But see* City of Rockford v. Eisenstein, 63 Ill. App.2d 128, 211 N.E.2d 130 (1965); and Dellwood Dairy Co. v. City of New Rochelle, 7 N.Y.2d 374, 165 N.E.2d 566 (1960).

30. "Customarily" has been defined as a use so necessary as to be commonly expected, such as a garage for a house or a parking lot for a church. *See* Williams, *supra* note 10 at vol. 3, §74.16, pp. 421–23, for a summary of decisions interpreting "customary" uses.

31. Town of Marblehead v. Rosenthal, 316 Mass. 124, 126, 55 N.E.2d 13, 14 (1944).

32. *See* Williams, *supra* note 10 at vol. 4, §88.4, p. 77.

33. Montgomery County, Md., Ordinance 7–75 (Jan. 29, 1974), Montgomery County Code §59–51.6 (Michie Supp. 1975).

34. *Id.*, Montgomery County Code §59–51.7.

35. *Id.* at §59–51.7(a)(4).

36. Another strategy applicable to developing areas is to zone for planned unit developments with a mixture of land uses. This strategy is discussed on p. 110, *infra*.

37. Kenneth M. Friedman, "Are Multi-Use Buildings Here to Stay?" *Real Estate Review* 5, no. 2 (Summer 1975): 70.

38. Public Buildings Cooperative Use Act of 1976, Pub. L. No. 94–541 (1976).

39. Senate Comm. on Public Works, "Public Buildings Cooperative Use Act of 1975," 1st sess., S. Rep. No. 94–349 (July 31, 1975), p. 2.

40. Dellwood Dairy Co., Inc. v. City of New Rochelle, 7 N.Y.2d 374, 165 N.E.2d 566 (1960); Kushner v. Lawton, 351 Ill.App.422, 115 N.E.2d 581 (1953); *See generally*, Williams, *supra* note 10 at vol. 3, §74.37–74.38, pp. 469–75.

41. *See In Re* 140 Riverside Drive, Inc. v. Murdock, 276 App. Div. 550, 95 N.Y.S.2d 860 (First Department 1950).

42. *See* City of New York, N.Y., Zoning Resolution (effective Dec. 15, 1961), which contains numerous provisions allowing mixed uses.

43. Chicago, Ill., Municipal Code Ch. 194 A, Arts. 8, 9 (1957) (mixed uses permitted in business and commercial zones).

44. City of Baltimore, Md., Zoning Ordinance, No. 1051 §5.1 and §§6.1–6.5 (1971).

45. District of Columbia Zoning Ordinance, §5102.1 (1972) (mixed use buildings permitted in commercial zones) and §2101.13 (1974) (mixed use buildings permitted in commercial-residential zones).

46. City of San Francisco, Cal., Municipal Code, City Planning Code, Part 2, Ch. 2 (1974).

47. City of Little Rock, Ark., Zoning Ordinance, No. 12857, §4030–6 (1937).

48. *See generally* Zoning Ordinance of City of White Plains, N.Y. (1949) (*as amended*).

49. *See* Williams, *supra* note 10 at vol. 3, §74.38, p. 474, n. 352, for a more complete listing of zoning ordinances permitting multiple use buildings in high density districts.

50. Nationwide Personal Transportation Study, "Household Travel in the United States," Report no. 7 (Washington, D.C.: U.S. Department of Transportation, Federal Highway Administration, December 1972), p. 4.

51. William Toner, "Planning for Home Occupations," Planning Advisory Service Report No. 316 (Chicago: American Society of Planning Officials, April 1976).

52. *Id.* at chapters 2, 3 at 5–12.

53. *Id.* at 13.

54. *See* Armstrong, *supra* note 26; and Ernest Erber and John Prior, "The Trend in Housing Density Bonuses," in *Planning* (Chicago: American Society of Planning Officials, November 1974), p. 14.

55. *See* Appendix I, pp. 221–225.

56. Board of Supervisors of Fairfax County v. DeGroff Enterprises, Inc., 214 Va. 235, 198 S.E.2d 600 (1973).

57. Montgomery County, Maryland, Code, Ch. 25A, (Michie Supp. 1975).

58. *See* pp. 116–122, *infra*.

59. *Cf.*, Bonhage v. Cruse, 233 Md. 10, 194 A.2d 803 (1963); Illinois Bell Telephone Co. v. Fox, 402 Ill. 617, 85 N.E.2d 43 (1949).

60. *See* Williams, *supra* note 10 at vol. 5, §150.03.

61. *Id.*, *see generally* vol. 5, §150, for a discussion of standards for special permits.

62. *See* Borough of North Plainfield v. Perone, 54 N.J. Super. 1, 148 A.2d 50 (App. Div. 1959); and Pearson v. Shoemaker, 25 Misc. 2d 591, 202 N.Y.S.2d 779 (Sup. Ct., Rockland County, 1960).

63. *See* Williams *supra* note 10 at vol. 5, §151, for a discussion of conditions that may be attached to special permits.

64. *See* p. 23, *supra*, for a discussion of total energy systems.

65. *See* pp. 99–106, *infra*, for a discussion of energy efficiency standards.

66. David Mosena et al., "Institutional Factors Influencing the Acceptance of Community Energy Systems and Energy-Efficient Community Design: Public Planning, Administration, and Regulation," prepared for Energy and Environmental Systems Division of Argonne National Laboratory, Contract No. 31–109–38–3078 (Chicago: American Society of Planning Officials, September 1976), p. 104.

67. *Id.* This language is found in the ordinances of the Maryland–National Capital Park and Planning Commission.

68. National Association of Homebuilders, *Land Development Manual* (Washington, D.C., 1974), p. 74.

69. Buchanan, N.Y., Zoning Ordinance, §8, excerpted in Williams, *supra* note 10 at vol. 5, §150.11, p. 208.

70. Adapted from proposed Princeton, N.J., Ordinance §6(a-d), excerpted in Williams, *supra* note 10 at vol. 5, §152.02, pp. 224–25.

71. Fairfax County, Va., Zoning Ordinance, Site Plan Ordinance, ch. 30–11; Fairfax Co., Va., Subdivision Ordinance, ch. 101; and Fairfax Co., Va., Erosion Sediment Control and Conservation Ordinance, ch. 104. Tree removal standards are found in vol. 3 of the Fairfax County *Public Facilities Manual.*

72. *New Approaches to Land Development/A Study of Concepts and Innovations*, Technical Bulletin 40 (Washington, D.C.: The Urban Land Institute, 1961), p. 23.

73. The homeowner may, however, be required to contribute to a homeowner's association that maintains property.

74. Williams, *supra* note 10 at vol. 2, §47.02.

75. *See* Chrinko v. South Brunswick Township Planning Board 77 N.J. Super. 549, 600–601, 187 A.2d 221, 225 (Law Div. 1963), where the court found that the clustering ordinance "reasonably advances the legislative purposes of securing open spaces, preventing overcrowding and undue concentration of population, and promoting the general welfare." A later New Jersey case holding a clustering and zoning ordinance to be invalid does not address the issue of whether separate legislation is necessary. Mountcrest Estates, Inc. v. Mayor & Tp. Committee of Rockaway Tp., 96 N.J. Super. 149, 232 A.2d 674 (App. Div. 1967).

76. Chrinko v. South Brunswick Township Planning Board, 77 N.J. Super. 549, 187 A.2d 221.

77. Frank S. So et al., "Planned Unit Development Ordinances," Planning Advisory Service Report No. 291 (Chicago: American Society of Planning Officials, 1973), pp. 32–34.

78. *See* Associated Homebuilders of the Greater East Bay, Inc. v. City of Walnut Creek, 4 Cal. 3d 633, 94 Cal. Rptr. 630, 484 P.2d 606, (1971). Unlike most states, California does not require the dedication to be precisely related to the needs of the subdivision residents. Dedication requirements are discussed more fully on pp. 93–97, *infra.*

79. Town of Fayston, Vt., Zoning Ordinance §6.0.5 (Jan. 1975).

80. *New Approaches to Residential Land Development*, *supra* note 72 at ch. 2, pp. 23–25.

81. By 1980, over 70 percent of all Americans will live in 125 metropolitan areas with populations of 250,000. (Dr. Seymour M. Gold, "Energy Conservation and Urban Recreation Planning," Paper submitted for presentation at Confer–In 75/American Institute of Planners Conference, San Antonio, Texas [October 27, 1975], p. 10.)

82. *Id.* at 12—13.

83. *Id.*

84. The effectiveness of the mandatory dedication in keeping people close to home will be doubly enhanced if, in addition to setting aside open recreational space, the developer provides recreational and other facilities that will induce residents to stay close to home. A requirement to that effect may run into legal problems, but bonuses used to persuade developers to include such amenities may be less controversial.

85. Mary E. Brooks, "Mandatory Dedication of Land or Fees-in-Lieu of Land for Parks and School," Planning Advisory Service Report No. 266 (Chicago: American Society of Planning Officials, 1971), p. 16.

86. Robert H. Freilich and Peter S. Levi, *Model Subdivision Regulations/ Text and Commentary* (Chicago: American Society of Planning Officials, 1975), p. 105.

87. Associated Home Builders of Greater East Bay, Inc. v. City of Walnut Creek, 4 Cal.3d 633, 94 Cal. Rptr. 630, 484 P.2d 606 (1971); Jenad, Inc. v. Village of Scarsdale, 18 N.Y.2d 78, 218 N.E.2d 673, 271 N.Y.S.2d 955 (1966); Jordan v. Village of Menomonee Falls, 28 Wis.2d 608, 137 N.W.2d 442 (1965) *cert. denied*, 385 U.S. 4 (1966).

88. Pioneer Trust and Savings Bank v. Village of Mount Prospect, 22 Ill.2d 375, 176 N.E.2d 799 (1961); Frank Arsuine, Inc. v. City of Cranston, 107 R.I. 63, 264 A.2d 910 (1970); McKain v. Toledo City Planning Commission, 26 Ohio App.2d 171, 270 N.E.2d 370 (1971).

89. Jenad, Inc. v. Village of Scarsdale, 18 N.Y.2d 78, 218 N.E.2d 673, 271 N.Y.S.2d 955 (1966); Associated Home Builders of Greater East Bay, Inc. v. City of Walnut Creek, 4 Cal. 3d 633, 94 Cal. Rptr. 630, 484 P.2d 606 (1971); Jordan v. Village of Menomonee Falls, 28 Wis.2d 608, 137 N.W.2d 422 (1965) *cert. denied*, 385 U.S. 4 (1966).

90. Associated Home Builders of Greater East Bay, Inc. v. City of Walnut Creek, 4 Cal.3d 633, 94 Cal. Rptr. 630, 484 P.2d 606 (1971); Jenad, Inc. v. Village of Scarsdale, 18 N.Y.2d 78, 218 N.E.2d 673, 271 N.Y.S.2d 955 (1966); Aunt Hack Ridge Estates, Inc. v. Planning Commission, 160 Conn. 109, 273 A.2d 880 (1970); Jordan v. Village of Menomonee Falls, 28 Wis.2d 608, 137 N.W.2d 422 (1965), *cert. denied*, 385 U.S. 4 (1966).

91. The most unsettled area is the validity of mandatory dedication or payments in lieu of dedication for school sites. New Jersey and Illinois have rejected such mandatory dedications, (West Park Ave., Inc. v. Ocean Tp., 48 N.J. 122, 224 A.2d 1 (1966); Pioneer Trust and Savings Bank v. Village of Mount Prospect, 2 Ill.2d 375, 176 N.E.2d 799 (1961)), while Wisconsin has specifically upheld them (Jordan v. Village of Menomonee Falls, 28 Wis.2d 608, 137 N.W.2d 442 (1965) *cert. denied*, 385 U.S. 4 (1966)). Experts have expressed different opinions on the issue. *See, e.g.*., Freilich and Levi, *supra* note 86 at 127—28. Accordingly, the issue awaits further resolution by the courts. One thing is clear—the amount of the dedication must be reasonable and somehow related to the needs of the subdivision, or the dedication will be struck as a taking. *Id.* at 128.

92. Williams, *supra* note 10 at vol. 4, §100.08, p. 273.

93. Associated Home Builders of Greater East Bay, Inc. v. City of Walnut Creek, 4 Cal. 3d 633, 94 Cal. Rptr. 630, 484 P.2d 606 (1971).

94. *Id.*

95. Home Builders Association of Central Arizona, Inc. v. Riddel, 109 Ariz. 404, 510 P.2d 376 (1973).

96. Cal. Gov.'t Code §66477 (West Supp. 1976).

97. Freilich and Levi, "Requirements for Improvements, Reservations and Design," *supra* note 86 at §4.9, pp. 98–101.

98. *Id.* at 122.

99. *Id.* at 129.

100. *Id.* at 128. For a fuller discussion of the issues raised by implementation and administration of mandatory dedications, and for descriptions of approaches used by several localities, *see* Brooks, *supra* note 85.

101. Housing Act of 1961, Pub. L. 87–70, 75 Stat. 183, tit. VII, *as amended*, 42 U.S.C. §1500 et seq. (Supp. 1976).

102. Raymond J. Burby, III, and Shirley F. Weiss, *New Communities U.S.A.* (Lexington, Massachusetts: D.C. Heath and Co., 1976), p. 339.

103. Durwood J. Zaelke, *Saving Energy in Urban Transportation* (Cambridge, Massachusetts: Ballinger Publishing Co., 1977).

104. Oregon Bicycle Trails and Footpaths Law, Or. Rev. Stat. §366.514 (Supp. 1975).

105. Chrysler Corp. v. City of Beaverton, 25 Or. App. 361, 549 P.2d 678 (1976).

106. California Bikeway Act, S.B. 244 (approved September 30, 1975), Cal. Streets and Highways Code, §§2370 et seq. (West Supp. 1975).

107. Living Systems, *supra* note 14 at 44.

108. *Id.* at 20–40; Urban Land Institute et al., "Residential Streets/Objectives, Principles & Design Considerations" (Washington, D.C., 1974), pp. 32–33.

109. Living Systems, *supra* note 14 at 23. Living Systems asserts that sometimes temperatures are increased by as much as ten degrees because of excessive paving.

110. Urban Land Institute et al., *supra* note 108 at 32.

111. *Id.* at 33.

112. Vermont Land Use and Development Law, Vt. Stat. Ann. tit. 10, §6086(a)(9)(F) (Supp. 1975).

113. Grant P. Thompson, *Building to Save Energy: Legal and Regulatory Approaches* (Cambridge, Massachusetts: Ballinger Publishing Co., 1977).

114. Second regular session, 50th general assembly, state of Colorado (1975).

115. Town of Ramapo Zoning Ordinance, *as amended* in 1969. These amendments and the ensuing litigation, in which New York's highest state court upheld them, are discussed on pages 139, 148–152, *infra*.

116. *See* Williams, *supra* note 10 at vol. 5, §150.03, p. 195.

117. *See* Pacesetter Homes v. Village of Olympia Fields, 104 Ill. App.2d 218, 244 N.E.2d 369 (1968), where the excessive similarity and dissimilarity requirements applied only to structures within 1,000 feet, and where excessively similar and dissimilar features were defined. The case is discussed in Williams, *supra* note 10 at vol. 3, §71.18, p. 323.

118. Philip Goldberg, "Planning With Energy" (Philadelphia: Rahenkamp, Sachs, Wells & Associates, Inc., 1975).

119. Golden v. Planning Board of the Town of Ramapo, 30 N.Y. 2d 359, 285 N.E.2d 291, 334 N.Y.S.2d 138, *appeal dismissed*, 409 U.S. 1003 (1972).

120. For an overview of planned unit developments, suggested PUD legislation, and general legal issues raised by PUDs, see So et al., *supra* note 77. The report does not, however, incorporate energy conservation considerations in its discussion of PUDs. *See also* Jan Z. Krasnowiecki, *Legal Aspects of Planned Unit Residential Development*, Technical Bull. No. 52, Part I (Washington, D.C.: The Urban Land Institute, 1965); George Sternlieb et al., Planned Unit Development Legislation: A Summary of Necessary Considerations, 7 *Urban L. Ann* 71 (1974); and John A. Couture, "Land Use Law for the Builder & His Attorney" (Washington, D.C.: National Association of Home Builders, 1972).

121. So et al., *supra* note 77 at 47.

122. There now appear to be at least eighteen states with some form of PUD enabling legislation.

123. *See* pp. 116–122, *infra*, for a discussion of density bonuses.

124. For an analysis of the development process for a large-scale planned unit development in East Windsor, New Jersey, and a discussion of barriers to incorporating energy-efficient design in the PUD, see Harrison Fraker and Elizabeth Schorske, "Energy Husbandry in Housing: An Analysis of the Development Process in a Residential Community," Center for Environmental Studies Report No. 5 (Princeton, New Jersey: Princeton University, December 1973).

125. *See, e.g.*, Richard S. Babcock, Jan Z. Krasnowiecki, and David N. McBride, The Model State Statute, 114 *U. Pa. L. Rev.* 140 (1965); Advisory Commission on Intergovernmental Relations, "State Legislative Program No. 5/Environment, Land Use and Growth Policy" (Washington, D.C., November 1975), pp. 120–36.

126. Montgomery County, Md., Code §59–64A (Michie Supp. 1975).

127. *Id.* at §59–64A(a).

128. So et al., *supra* note 77 at 29–30.

129. Robert W. Burchell, with James W. Hughs, *Planned Unit Development/New Communities American Style*, (New Brunswick, New Jersey: Center for Urban Policy Research, Rutgers University, 1972), p. 195.

130. *Id.* at 198.

131. One disappointing aspect of PUDs has been that most residents do not work in the PUD. *See* Burchell, *supra* note 129 at 187 and Fraker and Schorske, *supra* note 124.

132, Montgomery County, Maryland, uses a floating zone approach. Montgomery County, Md., Code §59–64A (Michie Supp. 1975).

133. See Williams, *supra* note 10 at vol. 1, §28.01–28.03, pp. 575–83.

134. *See* Michael J. Meshenberg, "The Administration of Flexible Zoning Techniques," Planning Advisory Service Report No. 318 (Chicago: American Society of Planning Officials, 1976), for a discussion of special permits and floating zones, as well as a discussion of planned unit developments.

135. The language is heavily based on a PUD ordinance in So et al., *supra* note 77 at 27.

136. *Id.* at 37.

137. Williams, *supra* note 10 at vol. 2 §48; and Burchell, *supra* note 129 at 130.

138. Dr. Mary Alice Hines, "Analysis of PUD Profitability Possible Through Computer Analysis," *Mortgage Banker*, March 1976, p. 41.

139. *Id.* at 42; *see* So et al., *supra* note 77 at 8.

140. Williams, *supra* note 10 at vol. 2, §43.02, pp. 228–29.

141. American Society of Planning Officials, "Survey of Innovative Land Use Provisions," p. 93, cited in Williams, *supra* note 10 at vol. 2, §48.11, p. 242.

142. *Id.*

143. *See* Williams, *supra* note 10 at vol. 2, §48.01, pp. 226–27, and §48.04, pp. 230–31; Frank A. Aloi, Legal Problems in Planned Unit Development, 1 *Real Estate Law Journal* 5, 9–10 (Summer 1972); So et al., *supra* note 77 at 45.

144. So et al., *supra* note 77 at 30–34. Mixing of residential and nonresidential uses within a PUD has been specifically upheld in Cheney v. Village #2 at New Hope, Inc., 429 Pa. 626, 241 A.2d 81 (1968); and Rudderow v. Tp. Comm., Township of Mount Laurel, 121 N.J. Super. 409, 297 A.2d 583 (1972).

145. So et al., *supra* note 77 at 47.

146. *See* Williams, *supra* note 10 at vol. 2, §48.04, pp. 230–31.

147. 11 Cal. App.3d 768, 90 Cal. Rptr. 88 (1970).

148. *See* Meshenberg, *supra* note 134, for a discussion of the floating zone.

149. So et al., *supra* note 77 at 49.

150. *See* Lund v. City of Tumwater, 472 P.2d 550 (Wash. App. 1970), where failure of the ordinance to list PUDs as a special use resulted in invalidation of a PUD permit.

151. *See* Fraker and Schorske, *supra* note 124 at 21–26.

152. *Id.* at 18–19.

153. So et al., *supra* note 77 at 6.

154. *See* Fred P. Bosselman et al., *The Permit Explosion: Coordination of the Proliferation* (Washington, D.C.: The Urban Land Institute, 1976), for a discussion of techniques for reducing delays during the development approvals process.

155. For a more complete discussion of administrative issues raised by planned unit developments, *see* Meschenberg, *supra* note 134 at 19–24.

156. *See* Williams, *supra* note 10 at vol. 4, §100.08–100.09, pp. 273–74. *See also id.* at §100.03–100.07, pp. 266–73.

157. Fairfax County, Va., Zoning Ordinance, Amendment No. 249 (1975).

158. Montgomery County, Md., Code, ch. 25A (Michie Supp. 1975). In lieu of providing the required housing, developers in Montgomery County may transfer land to the county so that it may provide the housing. *Id.* at §25A–4(b).

159. "Low- and Moderate-Income Housing Related to New Developments," Policy no. 15, City of Lakewood, Colo., Planning Commission (May 16, 1973).

160. Some commentators report that opposition to privately built low cost housing is much less than to publicly funded projects, even when the housing in question is scattered throughout middle and upper income developments. *See* Erber and Prior, *supra* note 54 at 14.

161. Board of Supervisors of Fairfax County v. DeGroff Enterprises, Inc., 214 Va. 235, 198 S.E.2d 600 (1973).

162. Eugene Planning Department, *Eugene Community Growth and Policies* (Eugene, Oregon, 1974), *cited in* Mosena et al., *supra* note 66 at 65.

163. San Francisco, Cal., Municipal Code, City Planning Code, part 2, ch. 2 §122.3 (1974).

164. Prince Georges County, Md., Zoning Ordinance, §18(a)–(e) and §30 (Oct. 30, 1976).

165. New Castle County, Del., Zoning Code, §23–80(1)(c)3 (Feb. 1970).

166. Resolution No. 1059 §1(d), Development Policy for Planned Districts, adopted by Freemont, Calif., City Council (June 1963).

167. Arlington County, Va., Zoning Ordinance §36–H(5)(c)(1973) (as found in Appendix of the Arlington County Code).

168. Judith C. Lack, "Olympic Tower: Dwelling Above the Shop," *Real Estate Review* 5, no. 2 (Summer 1975): 73.

169. For a review of incentive zoning and how it has worked in New York and San Francisco, *see* Norman Marcus and Marilyn W. Groves, eds., *The New Zoning: Legal, Administrative, and Economic Concepts and Techniques*, pt. III (New York: Praeger Publishers, 1970). *See also* the discussion of density bonuses in PUDs, pp. 111–112, *supra*.

170. Mary Brooks, "Bonus Provisions in Central City Areas," Planning Advisory Service Report No. 257 (Chicago: American Society of Planning Officials, May 1970), p. 3.

171. David J. Benson, Bonus or Incentive Zoning—Legal Implications, 21 *Syracuse L. Rev.* 895–906 (Spring 1970); Dan Yurman, "Can Density Bonuses Pay Off?" *Practicing Planner*, April 1976, pp. 14–20.

172. Benson, *supra* note 171.

173. Mandatory bonus ordinances may, however, be subject to closer scrutiny. *See* Board of Supervisors of Fairfax County v. DeGroff Enterprises, Inc., 214 Va. 235, 198 S.E.2d 600 (1973).

174. *See* Benson, *supra* note 171 at 897.

175. Board of Supervisors of Fairfax County v. DeGroff Enterprises, Inc., 214 Va. 235, 198 S.E.2d 600 (1973).

176. Montgomery County, Md., Code, ch. 25A (Michie Supp. 1975).

177. See Erber and Prior, *supra* note 54 at 15–16.

178. United States Department of Commerce, A Standard Zoning Enabling Act §3 (rev. ed. 1926).

179. Board of Supervisors of Fairfax County v. DeGroff Enterprises, Inc., 214 Va. 235, 198 S.E.2d 600 (1973).

180. Brooks, *supra* note 170 at 14.

181. Yurman, *supra* note 171 at 19.

182. Brooks, *supra* note 170 at 16.

183. Williams, *supra* note 10 at vol. 4, §100.07, p. 272.

184. *See* Mayor and Council of Rockville v. Brookeville Turnpike Construction Co., Inc., 246 Md. 117, 228 A.2d 263 (1967); Child v. City of Spanish Fork, 538 P.2d 184 (Sup. Ct. Utah 1975); City of Colorado Springs v. Kitty Hawk Development Co., 154 Colo. 535, 392 P.2d 467 (1964).

185. Ill. Stat. Ann., ch. 24 §11–15.1–1 et seq. (Smith-Hurd Supp. 1975).

186. *See* Donald Priest et al., "State and Local Policy on Large Scale Land Development" (Washington, D.C.: The Urban Land Institute, 1977), for a discussion of the advantages and disadvantages of annexation contracts.

187. The Potomac Institute, "Metropolitan Housing Program Memorandum 76–3" (Washington, D.C., March 31, 1976), pp. 12–13.

188. Agreement dated September 17, 1973, cited in Priest, *supra* note 186 at 204.

189. *See* note 184, *supra*.

Chapter 5

Energy-Efficient Location
of New Development

In Chapter 2 we noted that for maximum energy efficiency, a community should be relatively small and densely
populated and should be served by efficient public transportation. It should also contain the job, shopping, civic, and recreational opportunities necessary to satisfy the needs of its residents. In
practice, though, communities are spreading out at low densities,
leapfrogging over pockets of developable land, segregating residential
land uses from commercial land uses, and rendering public transportation an impossibility. The term "urban sprawl" is used here to
refer to such haphazard development that wastes energy by increasing transportation and space heating and cooling demands and by
requiring the extension of services and facilities to distant locations.

Undoubtedly, an ideal energy-conserving community is not always
practicable. Land development patterns predetermined by existing
land uses may prevent contiguous growth that flows out from the
center of an urban area. Or, health problems arising from sewer over-
loading or a desire to protect ecologically sensitive lands may require
planners to leave some areas sparsely populated and to zone other
areas farther away from urban centers for higher densities. Yet even
in the face of these planning constraints, applying the design standards reviewed in Chapter 4 is not the only way to help save energy
through land use. Controlling the location of new growth, to the
extent permitted by existing land development patterns, can also
help conserve significant amounts of fuel.

The emphasis in this chapter is on methods to promote orderly,
energy-efficient growth—growth that is characterized primarily by

urban containment and concentration of development along adequate transportation lines. Communities that for health or other reasons must develop in a nonideal energy fashion, such as in a polynucleated pattern (that is, with small pockets of dense development separated from the urban center by considerable amounts of undeveloped land) can nevertheless benefit from the locational strategies discussed here. Those communities can, for example, use energy-saving location techniques to ensure that, where practicable, the new growth in the development nodes occurs in a compact, contiguous fashion and is not scattered at low densities between the node and the urban center. Similarly, communities that develop in corridor patterns (with development stretched out along transportation lines) can use these strategies to keep growth centered near transportation facilities.

Some of the strategies reviewed in the following pages have been used for years for purposes other than energy conservation; others are just emerging as new solutions to old land use problems. All, however, can be used to make energy conservation figure strongly in the land development process.

CAPITAL FACILITIES PROGRAMMING

The location of roads, sewer lines, airports, civic centers, municipal office buildings, hospitals, and other public facilities has a major impact on transportation energy consumption. The placement of these capital facilities, dubbed "growth shapers" by a recent report prepared for the Council on Environmental Quality [1], is in fact a prime determinant of the location of new development [2]. Extending a road or sewer line into a previously undeveloped area nearly guarantees that development will spring up alongside the facility, unless the development leapfrogs to more distant territory slated soon to receive capital facilities of its own. As a result, residents of the new development must spend more energy, time, and money on transportation as the distance increases between home and trip destinations (jobs, shopping, etc.). Although roads and sewers probably influence the location of development more than does any other kind of public facility, the locations of civic centers, hospitals, or community colleges can also induce development in surrounding areas. Such facilities can have a particularly severe energy impact when placed in isolated, fringe areas since they generate considerable traffic.

Faced with rapidly increasing population pressures and with the fiscal burdens that governments must shoulder when they provide services to inefficiently located residents, many localities have begun to use their power to furnish, withhold, or govern the location of capital facilities to shape the pattern of growth. In those localities where governments are trying to influence development through their capital facilities programs, public facilities are no longer being built in a haphazard fashion dictated by the vagaries of sprawling developments. Instead, they are being extended only into areas where the comprehensive plan indicates that growth is advisable. Still others have taken a tougher approach. Along with a carefully planned program of capital improvements, they have adopted zoning techniques that condition development permits on the adequacy of the public facilities that serve the development. This technique can be a forceful tool to stimulate energy-efficient land development.

This section reviews some of the energy policy considerations that state and local governments should weigh before deciding whether and where to provide capital facilities and services. It then looks at two strategies that states and localities can use to achieve orderly, energy-efficient growth.

Policy Considerations

If energy efficiency were the only development goal, the first rule for localities trying to decide where to locate capital facilities would be to build those facilities within developing or developed areas, not on the urban fringe where they might induce premature growth and encourage traffic. Capital facilities that provide services, such as water and sewer lines, would be extended to serve legitimate growth demands, but would not be constructed in areas outside designated growth centers until all vacant land within those centers had been filled. Consequently, if a plan called for a growth center in a node outside the main urban center, the public service and traffic-generating facilities would be concentrated in the node and the urban center, and not spread between the two focal points. Although sewer, road, and utility lines may have to be extended from the urban center to the new growth center, other techniques, including open space zoning, which is discussed later in this chapter, would be used to discourage development along those facilities between the two growth centers.

A second principle guiding construction of service facilities would be to ensure that the new facilities are large enough to accommodate the desired density of development. Merely zoning for a PUD that contains low-rise and small high-rise apartments will not guarantee construction of those energy-efficient buildings if the supporting infrastructure of roads, sewer, water, and utility lines is not adequate.

Third, all major traffic-inducing facilities would be located along adequate transportation routes so they could be reached by public transportation and, at a minimum, would not encourage traffic congestion, unnecessary stops and starts, and unnecessary "idling."

Fourth, when possible, traffic-generating facilities would be clustered together in many small groups so that they would form a single destination point that could easily be served by public transit. Clustering a library, school, and museum, for example, could also reduce the number of necessary automobile trips, since a single trip could often serve more than one purpose.

Fifth, communities would disperse their public buildings (although in small clusters located near transportation routes) throughout developing areas so that the mixture of uses discussed in Chapter 4 could be accomplished. Adopting this policy should help reduce trip lengths.

Sixth, communities would view their capital facilities as tools for assisting private developers who undertake projects that could stimulate energy-efficient land use. For example, a large-scale mixed use project proposed for a central city might rejuvenate the central city and attract people from the suburbs back into urban neighborhoods. A locality interested in constructing a civic auditorium might give the proposed mixed use project a boost by including the auditorium in it.

In sum, capital facilities are enormously valuable land management tools, and they should be used to shape growth, not merely to respond to it. Policies adopted in Oregon and the township of Ramapo, New York, provide examples of two approaches that state and local governments can use to get maximum leverage for energy-efficient land development through control over capital facilities.

Adequate Public Facilities Ordinances

One way to encourage orderly, energy-efficient growth is to adopt an ordinance that conditions development permits on a showing that the applicable project will be served by adequate public facilities. Simultaneously, the locality should prepare and adopt a capital facilities plan that shows where and when facilities will be extended to energy-efficient locations.

The value of adequate public facilities ordinances is that they can inhibit leapfrog growth by guiding development in a predetermined, preplanned fashion. Thus, growth can be shaped to conform to the energy-ideal model (concentric, compact, contiguous development) or, when that kind of development is impossible, the growth can be channeled into energy-efficient locations that are close to transportation lines and activity centers. Consequently, transportation energy demands associated with urban sprawl—long trips, frequent use of automobiles because destinations are spread out and public transportation is not practical—can be significantly reduced. In addition, by promoting contiguous development, adequate public facilities ordinances can help reduce the length of roads, sewer lines, and curb and gutter systems, and hence the energy that goes into construction of those systems.

In spite of the possible energy savings, adequate public facilities ordinances could actually stimulate energy consumption rather than conservation if curbing growth on the fringe of a community means that growth will merely leapfrog to exurban areas. This happened when the imposition of sewer moratoria halted almost all construction in counties surrounding the District of Columbia. Growth skipped over those counties and took root farther out—miles from the capital. Clearly, any program that seeks to conserve energy by limiting sprawl in fast-growing metropolitan areas will require cooperative efforts on a regional basis to contain growth within designated boundaries. As discussed later, Oregon has helped solve the need for interjurisdictional cooperation through establishment of regional boundary commissions that control sewer and water extensions [3].

Ramapo, New York. The celebrated land use plan of Ramapo, New York, illustrates how to stage development in accordance with capital facilities extensions. Ramapo is a rapidly expanding suburban township within commuting distance of New York City. Faced with an exponential population growth—from 35,000 in 1960 to 76,702 in 1970, and an estimated 120,000 in 1985 [4]—Ramapo found itself unable to provide sufficient public facilities to meet the demands of its burgeoning population. In an effort to channel growth into an orderly pattern whose service needs would be manageable, Ramapo amended its zoning ordinance to prohibit residential developments unless a prospective developer obtains a special permit. That permit can be issued only upon a showing that the site is served by adequate sewers, drainage facilities, public parks, public schools, roads, and firehouses [5]. A point system based on the sophistication of the facilities and their proximity to the proposed development determines whether the "availability of services" test is met. For example, an "improved public park" within a quarter mile of a development is worth five points while one within one mile is worth only one point. To be successful, applicants must collect a minimum of fifteen points. Excerpts from Ramapo's adequate public facilities ordinance are reprinted in Appendix II, p. 292.

Complementing Ramapo's adequate public facilities ordinance, the town's capital facilities and services program designates where public facilities and services will be extended over the next eighteen years. Hence developers who hope to build in a particular area know how long they will have to wait before the city services will be available to qualify the site for a special permit. If they do not want to wait for public facilities to be built, developers can build facilities themselves and thereby meet the ordinance requirements. To meet constitutional objections, the township provides for reduced tax assessment for land incapable of immediate development. To further lighten the burden, some uses of property are permitted during the delay. For example, landowners may construct one single family home, but they may not build a "development." The land may also be used for recreation and farming.

Energy conservation was not an issue in 1969 when Ramapo passed its adequate public facilities ordinance. Consequently, Ramapo did not consider the energy impacts of the ordinance, nor has any attempt been made to quantify the extent of energy savings attributable to its implementation. The orderly development will probably contribute to energy conservation by discouraging fringe development, but additional savings could have been possible if individually built single family homes and commercial and industrial developments were also subject to the permit process, thereby ensuring contiguous growth. Instead, Ramapo allows scattering of those structures throughout the township. (Probably Ramapo's lawyers feared that a provision tying all development to availability of public facilities might unreasonably restrict use of land and raise the issue of taking without just compensation. This issue is discussed later.) Even further energy savings would have been possible if lot size requirements had been reduced to encourage more compact development. This technique was used as early as 1951 in Clarkstown, New York— not to save energy, but to create "urban development clusters" where individuals with varying incomes could live.

Clarkstown, New York. The Ramapo plan is actually a more refined version of two Clarkstown, New York, growth management ordinances. The ordinances created three rings around the town center, with the innermost ring zoned for residential development (with a minimum lot size of 15,000 square feet) and the outer two rings zoned for larger lots. The town allowed residential development in the second ring and, upon application, reduced the minimum lot size to 15,000 square feet if the land met certain conditions. First, it had to be feasible to service the land with adequate public facilities; second, the land had to be located adjacent to existing development [6].

Hence, there was an incentive to develop land close to the urban center since the land could be developed at a higher density than was permitted for land in the third ring. In this respect, the Clarkstown plan was superior to that of Ramapo, for it combatted both leapfrog growth and "urban spread," the complementary elements of urban sprawl. Of course 15,000 square feet is still a sizeable lot, but it nevertheless represents an improvement over Ramapo's zoning plan where no attention was paid to the problem of large, sprawling lots. Clarkstown's plan could have been more energy-efficient if multi-family housing had also been allowed, perhaps through a special permit process.

The success of Clarkstown's attempt to manage the location and timing of growth is debatable. The validity of its plan was upheld in *Matter of Josephs* v. *Town Board of Clarkstown* [7], but shortly thereafter, an amendment to the ordinance significantly altered its growth management provisions. Nevertheless, one commentator reports that development has in fact concentrated near the county seat and along a transportation corridor, as intended under the plan [8].

Other Localities. Other localities also have attempted to use less complex forms of adequate public facilities ordinances and capital improvements programming to control the location and sequence of growth. Montgomery County, Maryland, has had in effect since 1973 an ordinance [9] that conditions subdivision approval on adequacy of roads and public transportation facilities, sewerage and water service, and street access within a tract. In addition, the proposed development must be located so that it does not endanger the health, safety, or welfare of residents by being too far from police, fire stations, schools, and other facilities. Unlike Ramapo, Montgomery County does not use a point system; nevertheless, its ordinance sets out detailed standards for determining the adequacy of facilities.

Interestingly, the enabling legislation on which the Montgomery County ordinance is based states that counties may prepare subdivision regulations that provide for:

> ... the avoidance of scattered or premature subdivision of land as would involve danger or injury to health, safety or welfare by reason of the lack of water supply, drainage, transportation or other public services or necessitate an excessive expenditure of public funds for the supply of such services [10].

Because the enabling legislation lists specific conditions that justify a subdivision regulation to prohibit scattered development, yet fails to mention energy, the legislation may preclude the use of "orderly growth" regulations solely to save energy. As a practical matter, one would expect to find that most developing areas face sewer, water, and transportation problems along with energy shortages. In some instances, efforts to relieve the transportation problems may coincide with efforts to reduce energy demand. Nevertheless, to ensure that energy conservation is a recognized goal of subdivision controls, language to that effect should be added to state enabling legislation authorizing sequential growth controls.

For Montgomery County's neighbor across the Potomac River, Fairfax County, Virginia, a combination of circumstances has resulted in apparent abandonment of plans to adopt an adequate public facilities ordinance similar to Ramapo's. The plans fell victim to politics, the unfavorable judicial reaction to Fairfax County's sewer allocation program as a means for managing growth, and the difference in size between Fairfax County and Ramapo—a difference that raises tough legal problems regarding the general transferability of Ramapo's plan [11]. (This legal problem and others are discussed below.)

Other localities that have used their capital facilities programs to check sprawl include Boulder, Colorado; Brooklyn Park, Minnesota; Sacramento County, California; and Salem, Oregon [12]. Not all programs are tied into an adequate public facilities ordinance like Ramapo's, but they all are characterized by an intent to make public facilities available only where growth is desired. For example, as early as 1958, Boulder created a water service boundary line beyond which municipal water services would not be offered [13]. Brooklyn Park has discouraged development in some areas by rezoning them for agricultural and large lot development and by imposing an off-site storm drainage system requirement that has virtually precluded development in these areas. A staged extension of facilities program will eventually permit development to take place in the restricted section [14]. Sacramento County is avoiding destruction of valuable agricultural land by refusing to extend urban services into land zoned permanently for agricultural use and by temporarily withholding facilities from agricultural urban "reserve" areas that are to absorb future population expansions when needed. County subdivisions must by law have public sewers and water [15]. In a refreshing display of intergovernmental cooperation, Marion and Polk counties, Oregon, which bisect the city of Salem, have recognized Salem as the exclusive supplier of sewerage services in the Salem urban area. Salem has created an urban boundary within which it will encourage growth over the next twenty years through orderly annexation and capital improvements programs. Developments will not be provided city water or sewer facilities unless annexed [16].

Boundary Commissions

Although combining capital facilities programming with adequate public facilities ordinances is a useful technique for exercising control over development patterns, one unintended result may be that development will leapfrog to more distant areas outside the jurisdiction of the locality imposing the stringent development controls. Regional coordination of land management tools is essential to avoid the effect of actually encouraging growth in energy-wasteful locations distant from urban centers rather than close to them.

One way to promote energy-efficient growth on a regional basis is to establish a state agency to review proposals for capital facilities expansion outside municipal boundaries. The agency could be given the right to deny applications for extensions that would lead to energy waste by encouraging development in fringe areas or areas distant from transportation lines. Oregon has taken this approach through the use of regional boundary commissions, established by statute in 1969 [17]. The commissions are charged with the responsibility

> to provide a method for guiding the creation and growth of cities and special service districts in Oregon in order to prevent the illogical extensions of local government boundaries and to assure adequate quality and quantity of public services and the fiscal integrity of each unit of local government [18].

While only three boundary commissions—each with jurisdiction over counties surrounding one of the three major metropolitan areas in Oregon—were established [19], the statute contains a provision for creating more boundary commissions as the need arises [20]. Each boundary commission has control over major or minor boundary changes [21] and over the extension of water and sewer services in its territory. Each territory consists of all areas beyond either the corporate limits of a city or the boundaries of a service district, but within the counties included in the boundary commission's jurisdiction.

No extraterritorial extension of a special district or city sewer or water line may be undertaken without the approval of the boundary commission with jurisdiction over the affected area [22]. The same requirement applies to privately owned community water supply systems and to privately owned sewerage and waste disposal systems

[23]. In addition, since the boundary commissions have jurisdiction over the extension of services outside city limits and outside boundaries of service districts, the commissions can, by their authority to approve or deny boundary changes, regulate whether extension of services will be subject to commission review. Once the boundary commission has approved annexation of land by a city, for example, the commission loses its authority to regulate extension of services within the annexed territory.

The boundary commission decides on a petition for major and minor boundary changes or for an extension of capital facilities outside a city or service district by studying the petition and holding one or more public hearings on the proposal [24]. Its decisions are subject to judicial review by the circuit court in the county where the commission is located [25]. The review is based on the administrative record.

By inhibiting leapfrog development and unnecessary duplication of services and facilities [26], orderly growth promoted by the boundary commission can by itself be a major contributor to energy conservation. But the boundary commissions have a more direct mandate to help conserve energy through land use. Through the statewide planning goals promulgated under the 1973 Oregon Land Use Act, the boundary commissions are required to take into account the planning goal of energy conservation in making their determinations regarding capital facilities extensions and boundary changes [27]. The strength of this mandate is bolstered by an additional requirement: both local comprehensive plans, which are required under the act, and actions taken by the boundary commissions and service districts must promote the statewide planning goal of development of timely, orderly, and efficient arrangements of public facilities and services [28]. A third goal, one providing for the orderly and efficient transformation of rural land to urban land, requires localities to establish urban growth boundaries to identify and separate urbanizing lands from land that should remain rural [29]. These growth boundaries, established by cities with county concurrence, serve as a guide to boundary commissions when they review petitions for the extension of water and sewer lines. Among other things, the establishment of the urban growth boundaries must reflect energy considerations and the need for "orderly and economic provision for public facilities and services" [30]. Land outside the urban growth boundary typically is zoned for agricultural use so that development will be discouraged.

Presently only two cities in Oregon have had their comprehensive plans formally acknowledged by the Land Conservation and Development Commission (the state land use agency) as being consistent with the state goals [31]. The other cities and counties are operating under interim plans that have not yet been approved by LCDC [32]. Once the comprehensive plans of localities within their jurisdiction have been approved, the boundary commissions must assume that the plans conform to the state energy conservation goal, and that any proposal to extend services in accordance with the plans is appropriate. Until that approval is granted, however, the boundary commissions are not required to follow local interim comprehensive plans. Instead they must assess proposed capital facility extensions to determine independently whether such extensions comply with statewide goals. If they decide that the petition, though in accordance with the local interim plan, does not promote the goal of energy conservation, and if no reasonable explanation for the petition's failure to observe the conservation goal is given, the boundary commission may deny the petition. The fact that facilities have previously been extended to other individuals in an area is insufficient grounds upon which to require boundary commission approval of facility extension to other similarly situated individuals when the extension conflicts with statewide planning goals [33].

In addition to controlling sewer and water locations that may determine whether growth occurs in an energy-efficient fashion, boundary commissions can also help save energy by controlling the timing of capital facilities extensions within urban growth boundary lines. Most comprehensive plans cover a ten to twenty year period. The boundary commission can, without violating the plan's provisions, postpone projects outlined in the plan—including the extension of water and sewer lines—until growth pressures make development appropriate in the urban fringe. Thus, the boundary commission can retain control over where and when growth may occur, and can thereby ensure that the timing of development serves energy efficiency, something that long range comprehensive plans cannot accomplish. (The text of Oregon's statute establishing boundary commissions is reprinted in Appendix II, p. 299.)

Other Considerations

Secondary Impacts. *Social.* If a community's capital facilities are not expanded at a rate demanded by growth pressures, the cost of existing housing and developable land will soar. The result may be an unconstitutional exclusionary impact on low and moderate income individuals [34]. Some communities may use their capital facilities programs to shift growth elsewhere, but growth management systems that spring from a parochial determination to isolate the community from the burdens of growth are unrealistically simplistic. Ignoring growth or keeping it in somebody else's back yard will not eliminate the problem.

Capital facilities programming, even when used in combination with adequate public facilities ordinances, can promote energy-efficient land use as well as economic, environmental, and social well-being without being unconstitutionally exclusionary. Limiting the *amount* of growth is not crucial to the promotion of energy-efficient land use. What is essential, however, is that new growth be accommodated in a carefully planned and, where possible, compact and contiguous fashion.

Several ways to avoid potential exclusionary impacts of land development controls are discussed in Appendix I, p. 225.

Economic. The use of capital facilities extension programs to induce development in energy-efficient locations has an advantage over the land acquisition growth management techniques discussed in the following sections. In contrast to acquisition techniques, capital facilities programming requires no additional expenditure of funds by localities. It simply forces localities to look at the energy impacts of their capital facilities decisions and to design their programs to achieve maximum energy efficiency.

Economic impacts of growth management through capital facilities planning are, however, unclear. A study analyzing the economic impacts of the Ramapo system has been sharply criticized as inadequate [35]. *The Costs of Sprawl* [36] estimates that planned communities can save 15 percent of the road and utility costs incurred by sprawling communities. In contrast, a study of Sacramento, California, estimates that the costs of providing public services to sprawling developments are only marginally higher than the costs of providing identical services to "contained" developments [37]. That study did not, however, look at the cost of providing roads, nor did it review the personal transportation costs associated with sprawl. In spite of the extreme differences in the results of these two studies, it seems likely, in any event, that curtailing sprawl will at least delay expenditures for providing, operating, and maintaining public facilities and services even if it does not greatly reduce their ultimate amount. This savings over the short run may make up for the reductions in property taxes that may accompany the reduction in value of land not serviced by facilities.

Another possible economic advantage of adequate public facilities ordinances used in combination with staging of capital facilities expansions is that they may control speculation and thus the inflation of land prices by removing doubt about the development status of land. Developers who know when and where land will be serviced with facilities will no longer have an incentive to buy or sell land based on a hunch or tip that the land will soon be served by a public facility that will greatly enhance the land's value. This assumes, of course, that enough land is available for development to prevent the price of land that has adequate facilities from skyrocketing.

One serious economic issue that may be raised by an urban containment policy, whether it is achieved through capital facilities programming or other techniques reviewed in this chapter, is that competition for tax revenues may prevent the intergovernmental cooperation necessary to prevent growth from leapfrogging to outlying rural areas. Underdeveloped jurisdictions on the fringe of developing areas may resent being deprived of revenues generated by growth that is prevented from spreading prematurely to those undeveloped territories [38].

The Minneapolis/St. Paul (Twin Cities) region of Minnesota has developed an innovative approach to promote regional solutions to the tax competition problem. Special state enabling legislation [39] created a tax-sharing system that allows governments in the Twin Cities area to pool a percentage of their incremental commercial-industrial property tax base. The collected funds are then redistributed to communities in a manner that favors communities with large populations (and, therefore, high public service costs) but with low property market values (and, therefore, a low capacity to meet fiscal requirements). Consequently, communities have little economic incentive to compete for high tax ratables or to engage in fiscal zoning that excludes individuals (such as large families whose children attend public schools) whose high public service costs exceed the revenue they generate for the locality. The fiscal disparities tax presumably can have an additional energy conservation benefit by permitting industries and employment centers to settle in efficient locations; now localities often offer concessions to desirable businesses to lure them into their area, even though the location may be energy-inefficient. The tax-sharing program should reduce this problem. The program has, however, been criticized for giving "money grants . . . to wealthy bedroom communities" that lack financial need and that have habitually discouraged industrial expansion in their area [40].

Environmental. The potential environmental benefits of inhibiting sprawl, discussed on pages 28—29, are an additional benefit of using adequate public facilities ordinances and capital improvements programming as an energy conservation technique.

Legal Issues. A development phasing ordinance similar to Ramapo's, but which does not control the rate or amount of growth, will involve several legal issues that, at least for Ramapo, were resolved in the township's favor. Other legal issues not covered in the *Ramapo* case are unique to the use of capital facilities programming to promote energy conservation.

Taking. In a landmark decision in 1972, New York's highest court upheld Ramapo's use of an adequate public facilities ordinance as a growth management device [41]. A central issue in the *Ramapo* case was whether timing and sequential land development restrictions constituted a taking without just compensation. Ramapo's ordinance passed the taking test, but there is no guarantee that the same ordinance, if adopted elsewhere, would be upheld. Judicial determinations will turn on the facts unique to each locality. For example, the extensive growth pressures and the fact that all the undeveloped land in Ramapo could be serviced with public facilities by a specified date were crucial factors in the court's decision; not all localities can show similar circumstances. In fact, Fairfax County, Virginia, determined that because of its size—410 square miles as opposed to eighty-six square miles in Ramapo—it could not reasonably prevent subdivision development in outlying areas until public facilities were available. It would take decades to service the areas, and no one knew whether facilities would ever be needed in some places. Consequently, on the advice of its legal consultant, Fairfax County decided that development rights [42] would have to be acquired in outlying areas in order to prevent premature development there [43].

There are several important steps that Ramapo took, and that other localities can take, however, to minimize the risk that adequate public facilities will create a taking. First, Ramapo convinced the court that it was making reasonable efforts to provide the facilities demanded by new growth. Its assertions were supported by an extensive four volume study of the town's existing and projected land needs. The study had formed the basis for the town's comprehensive plan. Based on this study, Ramapo could show that, temporarily, growth demands exceeded the locality's ability to provide public services and that the ordinance was a reasonable response to growth pressures. Ramapo also skirted the taking issue by requiring a development permit only for subdivisions of two or more houses. Consequently, all reasonable use of land was not restricted. Recreational, single family, and other uses previously permitted in residential districts were still allowed. In addition, property taxes were reduced on land that was not available for immediate development, thus compensating owners in part for the restrictions [44].

An additional way the Ramapo ordinance sufficiently softened the restrictive blow to avoid a taking was by permitting developers to go forward with their plans if they installed the necessary infrastructure themselves. If developers were consistently to take advantage of this concession, however, the resulting scattered development would greatly reduce the effectiveness of sequential controls in conserving energy. Nevertheless, the concession was deemed essential to prevent courts from finding a taking.

Ramapo's chief arguments for upholding its ordinance were that the restrictions were "temporary" in nature—even though they lasted up to eighteen years in some places, a length that may be an outer limit in terms of constitutionality—and that the dates for extension of capital facilities and for qualifying for a development permit were in effect guaranteed. For if the town fails to adhere to its capital improvements schedule, the Ramapo ordinance provides for issuance of development permits on the date the plan indicates adequate public facilities will be available, regardless of whether the facilities have been built. Hence the restrictions, while severe, do not permanently prevent development of land.

An interesting question is raised whether, for purposes of promoting maximum energy efficiency of land development, a locality such as Ramapo could design a capital facilities extension program that would guarantee that by a specified year, facilities would be extended to a specified point, *provided* the development pressures continued at the rate at which they were anticipated when the facilities schedule was set. In other words, the comprehensive plan, zoning, and the capital facilities expansion program itself would be predicated on continued growth pressures. If those pressures developed as anticipated, the town would be required to expand its capital facilities as scheduled. If, however, the growth pressures did not develop as anticipated, the town would be under no obligation to extend capital facilities, since there would be vacant developable land still available within the area already being served by facilities. By imposing such a condition, communities could avoid an obligation to extend facilities under circumstances that would encourage premature, energy-inefficient development. Arguably, if growth pressures do not develop in the anticipated fashion, then landowners will not have suffered because of the failure of capital facilities to be extended to their property: it is not the unwillingness of the community to extend facilities, but rather the changing circumstances due to reduced growth pressures, that has prevented development of the property [45].

The technique of staging capital facilities expansion and thus development according to actual rather than anticipated growth pressures has already been tried in several localities. Oregon and Montgomery County, Maryland, have adopted this approach without apparent legal repercussions. And a federal court in California has upheld growth management restrictions that not only limit the number of building permits a community can issue each year, but also effectively create indefinite "greenbelts" that restrict development in certain sections surrounding a city [46]. The legality of such a technique would be enhanced if there were precise standards for determining when additional capital facilities expansion would be needed to accommodate growth pressures. Standards might involve determinations of whether a community had accepted its fair share of regional growth and whether there was remaining vacant land served by public facilities. Communities would be required to reevaluate their comprehensive plans on a regular basis to determine whether growth pressures warranted comprehensive plan amendments.

Arbitrary Means. In addition to questioning the reasonableness of the regulations in terms of their impact on land uses and values, some critics of Ramapo's plan have questioned the court's apparent attitude that "because the town's own planning supports its ordinance, the ordinance is therefore legal and constitutionally valid" [47]. There is no question that the court relied heavily on the extensive studies and comprehensive plan on which Ramapo's ordinance was based as evidence of the rationality and reasonableness of Ramapo's growth management techniques. The importance of facts, figures, and a comprehensive plan in establishing the validity of any growth management strategy cannot be underestimated. Yet, as one commentator has pointed out, even though extensive studying and planning went into creation of Ramapo's phased zoning ordinances, standards contained in the ordinance were in many ways arbitrary or unduly burdensome [48]. For example, availability of firehouses was one criterion, yet Ramapo not only planned to build no new firehouses, but also lacked authority to do so. Hence, the township could not guarantee that the facility would be available within the eighteen year time limit promised in the ordinance. In addition, distance to public facilities was measured in a straight line, rather than according to the length of access routes, which would have been the logical measurement [49]. Criticism of the irrationality of portions of Ramapo's ordinance points out the need for localities that plan to use adequate public facilities ordinances or other growth management techniques to evaluate carefully their proposed criteria to guarantee that the standards are rationally related to the needs of the area for which the controls are designed.

Exclusion. Conditioning development permits on availability of adequate public facilities may, as noted earlier, have an unconstitutionally exclusionary impact. This legal issue and ways to avoid exclusionary impacts are discussed in Appendix I, p. 225. Nevertheless, it is interesting to note the reasons that the *Ramapo* court found that the township's ordinance was not exclusionary. The decision rested in part on the finding that the ordinance (1) did not set a limit on population (yet even use of population caps was later upheld in a controversial California decision) [50]; and (2) was supported by extensive studies of the need to achieve orderly growth consistent with the community's ability to provide municipal services. Moreover, the court noted that Ramapo had attempted to overcome the exclusionary impact of its zoning ordinance by creating a public housing authority and proposing to construct biracial, low cost family housing [51]. As noted in Appendix II, subsequent cases in New York and New Jersey suggest that in the future those states and others following their lead will take a stricter look at adequate public facilities ordinances that have a potential for exclusionary impact. Consequently, those ordinances must be complemented by programs or circumstances that mitigate or avoid exclusionary effects.

Enabling Legislation. A strongly disputed issue in *Ramapo* was whether the state's zoning enabling act, modeled on the Standard State Zoning Enabling Act, authorizes localities to control the timing of growth. The New York statute, like SZEA, explicitly lists devices that localities may use to promote the general welfare, but nowhere mentions the device of regulating timing of development. Yet, over a strong dissent, the *Ramapo* majority held that timing controls do fall within the ambit of the New York enabling legislation. Whether the court would reach the same conclusion today is open to question, especially in view of the fact that the composition of the court has changed dramatically since the Ramapo opinion was written. Consequently, states that wish to guarantee authority to use timing or sequential controls should pass enabling legislation to that effect. The Maryland statute on page 141, provides a model, although it pertains to subdivision, not zoning controls. It also should be modified to include energy shortages as a condition justifying regulation to stop scattered development [52].

Proprietary Obligations.   A remaining legal issue, and one of great significance, relates to the authority of governments to regulate where capital facilities will be extended. Can a locality withhold public utility service from some areas to discourage energy-inefficient growth there, or does the locality have a "proprietary" obligation to extend its facilities wherever they are demanded? A "proprietary" obligation exists whenever the government acts like a private contractor or utility company rather than in its capacity as a government body. In carrying out proprietary obligations, a government generally must serve all customers similarly situated. Yet even when acting in a proprietary capacity, the government usually can refuse to extend services within its service districts if it can show that economics, health hazards, environmental hazards, or the sheer inability to meet the demands placed on public facilities by unrestricted growth prevents the offering of public services [53].

The authority to refuse to extend public services in crises or unusual circumstances does not, however, address the broader issue of whether a locality that has the capability to extend services may refuse to do so in order to promote energy-efficient land development. A recent Colorado case, *Robinson* v. *The City of Boulder* [54], indicates that where a locality has created, served, and monopolized a sewer service area outside of its boundaries, the locality has a proprietary obligation to make sewer facilities available to all alike within that area [55]. The effect of that decision is that a locality cannot use its control over sewer and water extensions to influence the sequence or intensity of growth in areas where it has already extended facilities and created a monopoly.

Nevertheless, the *Robinson* case does not completely undermine the concept of combining a capital facilities expansion program with an adequate public facilities ordinance to promote sequential growth for the purpose of energy conservation. First, the *Robinson* court emphasized that the city of Boulder had no authority to regulate land use in the area in which it proposed to withhold facilities. This suggests that, where the locality has authority over both zoning and sewer facilities, courts may uphold staging public facility expansion to avoid scattered development, provided the staging is in accordance with a carefully designed and articulated comprehensive plan. In addition, where capital facilities and land planning powers do not coincide, *Robinson* nevertheless leaves open the possibility that a locality can refuse to extend services to an area it has never served.

This points out the need for localities to recognize the possible long term effect of a decision to extend services to new areas.

One argument against extension of services that has never been tested is that the energy shortage constitutes an environmental crisis that warrants withholding additional public facilities in outlying areas until land closer to developed areas had been filled. Similar environmental arguments have been successfully used to prevent sewer hookups [56], but the relationship between land development and sewer overloads may be easier to prove to the court than the relationship between sprawling growth and energy waste. This problem would be minimized if states adopted enabling legislation that authorized localities to use a combination of capital facilities expansion programs and zoning powers to promote sequential development goals of their comprehensive land use plan. To avoid the jurisdictional problems posed by *Robinson*, states should follow the example of Oregon and create regional bodies to regulate capital facilities expansions outside city limits [57].

Implementation. *State.* States do not implement adequate public facilities ordinances, but, as noted, state enabling legislation is desirable to ensure that localities, assisted by regional bodies, have adequate authority to enhance energy conservation by controlling the sequence of development through police power regulations and public facilities programs. In addition, since states often control utility extensions, school and road construction, and the development of other public facilities that are a major determinant of where development occurs, they must make sure that the state public facilities programs do not interfere with local efforts to use adequate public facilities ordinances to control the sequence of new development. This can be accomplished if states require that any new state facilities conform to the adopted local comprehensive plan unless a compelling need prevents that compliance [58].

Local. Although individual localities can adopt adequate public facilities ordinances, growth management should be coordinated on a regional basis so that growth cannot leapfrog the area imposing the controls. Boundary commissions and tax-sharing schemes can enhance orderly development on a regional basis.

A prerequisite to use by a locality of an adequate public facilities ordinance designed to save energy is the development of a comprehensive plan and an extensive record demonstrating how the proposed location and sequence of development can result in energy conservation. The ordinance itself may be adopted as a zoning ordinance, with special permits issued to those who can show the availability of adequate facilities, or it may be adopted as a subdivision ordinance that conditions subdivision approval on the existence of adequate public facilities. Montgomery County, Maryland, has taken the latter approach [59]. Of course, the zoning or subdivision ordinance must be accompanied by a capital facilities program designed to expand facilities to meet the demands of a growing population. This requires that capital facilities planning departments and land use planning departments be merged or their work closely coordinated.

OPEN SPACE ZONING

Open space zoning is another technique for reducing energy waste by discouraging premature development in areas isolated from employment, shopping, and other traffic-generating destinations. Through open space zoning on the urban fringe, both the kind and intensity of development may be restricted; growth can be guided back toward urban centers where land is zoned for small lot or multifamily development and is already serviced by public facilities. Open space zoning, like other growth management regulations, should be accomplished in accordance with a comprehensive plan that demonstrates the rationality of the zoning provisions and ensures that adequate land, housing, public facilities, and other services are available in areas where development is welcomed. It should also complement capital facilities expansion programs.

Although there are many kinds of open space zoning designed to prevent or minimize land development, this section looks primarily at three: large lot zoning, agricultural zoning, and sensitive area zoning.

Large Lot Zoning

The simplest form of open space zoning is large lot zoning, where minimum lot sizes of several acres or more prevent high density development. Although court cases suggest that large lot zoning has sometimes been used illegally to exclude low and moderate cost housing from communities [60], large lot zoning can be used in a way that avoids exclusionary impacts and, at the same time, serves as a useful land planning tool for promoting energy conservation. This is the case when the large lot requirements are imposed on the urban fringe, leaving smaller lots for development close to the urban center. Withholding capital facilities from the large lots reinforces the effect of the zoning. When available small lots have been built upon and legitimate growth pressures reach out to the large lot zone, the area may be rezoned for higher intensity use, provided the rezoning is accomplished in accordance with the comprehensive plan and is coordinated with capital improvements programming.

There are, however, several problems with relying on large lot zoning to promote urban containment. One is that some development will occur in the restricted area. Hence, houses may be built on two to ten acre lots, making lifelong commuters and long distance shoppers out of the residents. On the other hand, if a choice must be made, it is probably better to have a few people living on large lots than to have dense development out in the fringe areas where employment and shopping opportunities do not exist. Another potential problem with large lot development is that it may establish land development patterns sufficiently strongly so that later development at desired densities is hindered. A partial solution may be to indicate in the comprehensive plan that the area will be rezoned for higher density development when growth pressures warrant a rezoning. This at least puts large lot owners on notice that the area will not permanently retain its semirural character. A third, more serious, problem is that, as with all other open space zoning techniques, large lot zoning will not achieve its goal of conserving energy by curbing sprawl unless it is imposed on an area large enough to discourage leapfrog growth [61]. The solution to this problem lies in regional coordination of land use planning. Boundary commissions [62] and local comprehensive planning subject to state review [63] can help ensure the necessary coordination.

Considering the problems with large lot zoning, one may ask why it is included as a technique for saving energy. In short, its value lies in its simplicity and in local governments' familiarity with its application. Unlike sensitive area or agricultural zoning, large lot zoning can be imposed on any type of land regardless of its physical characteristics. Thus it can be strategically mapped for maximum effectiveness in suppressing sprawl. Because there are no physical conditions that govern where large lot zoning can be imposed, it can be removed when development of the land is desirable without causing the detrimental side effects that may occur when other kinds of open space zoning restrictions are lifted. For example, removal of agricultural zoning or sensitive area zoning may result in development that can destroy valuable crop land or ecologically important land.

The simplicity and flexibility of large lot zoning that make the technique valuable for inhibiting sprawl are also its legal nemesis. Because there is often no unique natural characteristic that can justify imposition of large lot zoning on land where the locality wants to discourage development, large lot zoning may be more vulnerable to legal challenges than other forms of open space zoning, especially when it is not coordinated with comprehensive planning and capital facilities programming. On the other hand, because it does permit some use of land, large lot zoning may at times be legally acceptable when other, more restrictive, land use controls would fail. These legal issues are discussed later.

Agricultural Zoning

The need to protect agricultural land from development that spills out of urban areas has long commanded the attention of state and local governments. Farmers who are being crowded out by urban developers suffer double burdens: the market value of their property rises with the increasing demand for developable land, thus causing their property taxes to go up; and as development moves into rural areas, tax rates are increased again in order to pay for public services demanded by new residents [64]. It is easy to understand why many farmers, faced with soaring taxes and premature developments that interfere with farming efficiencies, are eager to sell to developers who offer urban prices for rural land.

On the theory that rising rural land taxes are a major cause of land conversion, the response to encroachment upon agricultural land in forty-two states has been adoption of legislation that taxes rural farmland at a preferential rate. Sometimes forest, open space, and recreational land are also given preferential treatment. Rather than being taxed at its market value, which increases as development presures increase, eligible land is taxed at its "use" value, or value when used as agricultural, forest, or recreational land or as open space. Sometimes taxes are partially deferred and the previously excused taxes are recaptured when the land is converted to ineligible uses. Five states condition preferential treatment on landowners' agreements not to convert their agricultural and/or open space and recreational land to ineligible uses for a specified length of time. Penalties are imposed on those who cancel the contract before its expiration.

A recent study for the Council on Environmental Quality (CEQ) [65] concludes that preferential taxation schemes and their variations, when used independent of other land use controls, have failed at keeping development out of agricultural land and open spaces on the urban fringes. One reason is that taxes are only one of many factors influencing farmers' decisions. In addition, tax savings from preferential assessment usually do not adequately compensate the farmers for keeping their property in agricultural use rather than selling it to developers. The study speculates that farmers owning less than 1 percent of existing farms may be influenced yearly by preferential assessment to maintain their land in agricultural uses [66]. Techniques such as restrictive contracts that force farmers to continue farming their land for an agreed upon length of time are not popular, since farmers do not want to forgo the opportunity to sell their land at high prices [67].

In addition to being ineffective, preferential taxing schemes are costly, and they may have inequitable impacts because they shift tax burdens from owners of land eligible for preferential taxation to owners of ineligible land. To make up for the tax shifts and loss in revenues, California makes payments to counties whose tax revenues are reduced by preferential taxation. Although officials estimate that localities lost $45–$50 million from preferential taxation in 1973 to 1974, the state reimbursed counties for only one-third that amount [68].

The CEQ study concludes that preferential taxation is a valuable tool for preserving open space only when used in combination with regulatory devices to prevent premature development. The report recommends creation of agricultural zones to protect farmland from urban encroachment.

Various forms of agricultural zoning are already used in many states to preserve crop land and open space. Exclusive agricultural zoning prohibits the construction of all buildings unrelated to farm purposes in the zone. Less restrictive forms of agricultural zoning appear to be little more than large lot zoning that permits residential uses along with the raising of crops and livestock in rural areas. For example, Loudoun County, Virginia, has established two agricultural use districts that allow residential structures on lots of a minimum size of three and ten acres, respectively [69]. Pinellas County, Florida, permits single family homes only on lots of two acres or more in its agricultural district [70]. Two acre lots are also required in the agricultural-residential areas of Sacramento County, California [71].

Agricultural zoning may be imposed only in those rural areas where agriculture is the major activity. But even though the use of agricultural zoning is so restricted, that condition poses no problems to the goal of urban containment since many urban areas are surrounded by prime agricultural land. The major obstacle to urban containment through exclusive agricultural zoning lies in the fact that courts may find that exclusive agricultural zoning (i.e., nothing but farm-related buildings) in an area subject to development pressures raises the taking issue [72]. Although courts have approved such zones where agriculture is the predominant activity, they are likely to take a more critical view of exclusive agricultural zoning in areas subject to development pressures on the urban fringe. This

explains why many agricultural zones near urban areas permit residential uses. Zoning for agricultural uses in accordance with a comprehensive plan, documenting the value of the agricultural land for
food production as well as its contribution to energy conservation
and a pleasing environment by promoting orderly growth, showing
that there is sufficient land elsewhere that is available for development, and providing preferential tax treatment will help significantly
to avoid "taking" challenges.

Sensitive Area and Other
Environmental Zoning

Other techniques designed to create areas of low density development surrounding areas where higher density is desired are sensitive area zoning and permit controls that restrict development on
hazardous or ecologically valuable (critical) land. Hazardous and
critical land include floodplains, steep slopes, eroded areas, earthquake zones, shorelands, wetlands, and important wildlife habitats.
As with agricultural zoning controls, environmentally related zoning
and permit controls may be imposed only on those areas that exhibit
the characteristics with which the ordinance or regulation is concerned. Environmental regulations may prevent all construction in
regulated areas, may permit some carefully regulated construction,
or may restrict the land to agricultural or recreational uses when
intense development would be dangerous or ecologically unwise.

Environmental zoning and permit controls have merited increasing
attention and approval both from state and local legislatures and
courts. States have asserted control over environmentally sensitive
land that spans local jurisdictions, and localities have used environmental zoning to protect sensitive or hazardous lands within their
borders.

For purposes of urban containment, however, environmental controls are perhaps a less valuable tool than large lot or agricultural zoning because environmentally unique or hazardous land may not exist
in a location where its regulation would encourage development to
flow back toward the urban center. A floodplain, for example, may
exist in a developing area and, if protected from construction, may
push growth farther from the urban center rather than channel it in-
ward. Consequently, it will be necessary to coordinate the sensitive
area zoning with other land management techniques that can direct
growth into desired locations. Another drawback to depending on
environmental controls to influence the location and timing of
growth is that presumably the physical characteristics that qualify
the land for environmental zoning and permit requirements make it

permanently unsuitable for development. Therefore, when legitimate development pressures push out to the sensitive or unique land, the result may be that development is forced to leapfrog the land because construction on the land would be unwise. The solution, again, is to try to channel the growth into more energy-efficient locations by combining sensitive area zoning with other forms of open space zoning and other growth management techniques. This approach may provide communities with a host of secondary benefits in addition to energy conservation and protection of sensitive land. A recent study predicts that coastal zone management in California will channel new development into or adjacent to built-up areas, thus reducing the cost of capital facilities investment, protecting the environment, and presumably conserving energy resources as well [73].

Other Kinds of Open Space Zoning

Large lot, agricultural, and environmental zones are only a few of the many kinds of open space zones that may be established to preserve rural land. Some communities preserve open space through a method simply termed "open space zoning" that restricts location, use, and intensity of development in the open space zone. Open space ordinances often combine several goals of ordinances that are more narrow in scope. A typical example states as its purpose the protection of "agricultural, recreational, and scenic land, the prevention of development in hazardous areas, and the *containment of urban sprawl*" [74]. Scenic area zones are another kind of open space zone for the protection of undeveloped, ecologically sensitive, or unique land.

Other Considerations

Secondary Impacts. *Social.* The major social obstacle to open space zoning in general, and large lot zoning in particular, is the potential exclusionary impact on low and moderate income individuals. Large lot zoning clearly increases the cost of housing both by increasing the size of minimum lots and by forcing developers to build expensive houses commensurate with the price of the lot. Whereas low cost housing will not be practical on large lots, large lot zoning and other forms of open space zoning by themselves will not have an unconstitutional exclusionary impact, provided the community zones other areas for multifamily housing or low cost housing on smaller lots.

Economic. Open space zoning should not cause prices of less restricted land to rise dramatically if enough small lot zoning is available elsewhere in a community to meet growth pressures. Any increase in the price of developable land close to municipal and urban centers should be accompanied in part by tax savings that result from a reduced need to extend costly public facilities and services into the suburban and exurban fringe. These savings, however, will accrue to the community as a whole and will not fully compensate individuals who must pay increased land prices.

Other cost savings can be achieved through regulation of development in hazardous and ecologically important areas. By preventing or limiting development in floodplains or earthquake zones, it is possible to avoid the economic devastation that falls not only on residents of an area but also on taxpayers across the country when natural disasters occur. The economic importance of other kinds of environmental zoning is equally apparent. Environmental zoning, for example, can preserve wetlands that in turn both protect us from flooding and provide food and spawning grounds for the countless fish on which our commercial and sport fishing industry depend [75]. In addition, the protection of prime agricultural land through agricultural zoning near urban areas may preserve the productivity of those farms [76].

Environmental. Whereas large lot, agricultural, and general open space zoning may inadvertently provide useful protection for ecologically sensitive areas, zoning tailored to meet specific environmental needs is likely to be more effective in achieving environmental goals. Nevertheless, large lot, agricultural, and open space zoning all restrain development in fringe lands and, therefore, can help protect both the ecological and visual environment.

Legal Issues. *Exclusion.* As noted repeatedly in this book, land use policies that produce exclusionary effects will be struck down in many state courts. Pennsylvania has been particularly strict in rejecting large lot zoning of two and four acres on the ground that the zoning has an improper exclusionary impact. Beginning with *National Land and Investment Co.* v. *Easttown Township Board of Adjustment* [77], the Pennsylvania Supreme Court has on several occasions held that zoning may not be used to restrict population growth: "Zoning is a means by which a governmental body can plan for the future—it may not be used as a means to deny the future" [78]. The Virginia Supreme Court reached a similar result in *Board of County Supervisors of Fairfax County* v. *Carper* [79] when it held a two acre zoning requirement imposed on outlying areas of the county to be invalid because the zoning resulted in economic exclusion. And decisions in New Jersey and New York have also put localities on notice that zoning practices will be scrutinized for exclusionary impacts [80].

While the above cases demonstrate the importance of avoiding exclusionary impacts, they do not suggest that large lot zoning is always improper. In contrast to the New Jersey cases, a leading federal decision in New Hampshire, *Steel Hill Development Inc.* v. *Town of Sanbornton* [81], upheld the conversion of a residential zone to a minimum six acre lot size "forest preserve" zone. The rezoning took place in response to second home development pressures that threatened the community's ecological balance, scenic value, open space, and rural character. Several facts distinguish the *Sanbornton* case from cases where exclusionary impacts have been found. In *Sanbornton*, vacation homes, not principal residences, were involved; the rezoning was temporary, not permanent; and there were strong environmental policy reasons for upholding the large lot zoning. The case was not one involving development pressures to meet natural growth demands. Hence the *Sanbornton* ruling is consistent with the established principle that zoning may not be used to exclude unwanted "natural" growth. Nevertheless, it is important to note that the *Sanbornton* court criticized the community for hastily approving the rezoning without benefit of a comprehensive plan or studies to justify the ordinance; in addition, the court suggested that future rezonings without a basis in carefully researched land use studies may not be approved.

Like adequate public facilities ordinances, large lot zoning may be justified if, in addition to serving energy efficiency goals, it is used to avoid a health problem such as inadequate sewerage, provided the community has made reasonable efforts to provide the facilities. But again, allegations must be backed up by concrete data [82].

Agricultural and sensitive area zoning should be less vulnerable to exclusionary attacks than large lot zoning for several reasons. Because agricultural and sensitive area zones are created to serve a specific and self-limiting purpose—the protection of agricultural and environmentally unique or hazardous land—it will be difficult to show that the real purpose is exclusion of low cost housing. This is especially true with respect to sensitive area zoning, which, at least in the case of floodplain and other hazardous area zoning, is directly tied to the health and safety of individuals.

A second reason why agricultural and environmental zoning will probably withstand exclusionary challenges is that these zones can be imposed only on land whose natural characteristics qualify it for special zoning. Since it is unlikely that such zoning will apply to all developable land, the charge that it eliminates significant potential for low and moderate cost housing would probably not be raised.

Rational Means.   Even if an open space zoning ordinance proposes to advance a legitimate objective, such as urban containment for the purpose of saving energy, and does not get bogged down in exclusionary challenges, the locality must show that the zoning classifications are reasonable means for achieving the intended goal. In creating agricultural and environmental zones, states and localities must ensure that the land mapped for a particular kind of zone actually displays the physical characteristics implied by the zone classification. Hence, in establishing an exclusive agricultural zone, a locality must be prepared to defend the boundaries it has drawn with evidence that the climate, soil, typical crops, and water supply support the result. Similarly, in critical area and hazardous area zoning, the boundaries must reflect the natural characteristics of the land or the zones may be struck down as arbitrary and capricious [83].

Taking.   Intertwined with the issue of whether the physical characteristics of the land reasonably qualify it for open space zoning is the question of whether the zoning so unreasonably restricts the use of property as to constitute a taking without just compensation. Although the determination will turn on the facts of each case, there are several basic propositions and trends in court cases that should be noted.

Exclusive agricultural zoning may be vulnerable to taking challenges when it is imposed on land subject to development pressures. Some have argued, however, that such zoning should be upheld if (1) the restrictions are imposed on a regional basis, (2) there is adequate land available elsewhere in the area for growth, (3) it can be shown that farmland is a natural resource essential to health and welfare of community residents, and (4) farming on the restricted land can produce a reasonable financial return [84]. Another expert contends that exclusive agricultural zoning may be upheld if it is temporary and is accompanied by tax adjustments and an adequate variance procedure [85]. Still others argue that preferential taxation by itself may sufficiently mitigate the harsh impacts of regulation to avoid a taking [86].

The taking question is less likely when the agricultural zone permits additional uses, such as residential structures on large lots, or when the zone is purely a large lot zone that permits a mixture of residential and other uses. Combining agricultural or large lot zoning with other land management techniques (such as capital facilities programming) that reduce development pressures on the urban fringe can also enhance its legality. Evidence of health and safety problems (e.g., the possibility of a sewer overload) is another important justification for open space zoning. As noted, temporary large lot restrictions to prevent second home development have been upheld [87].

Environmental zoning raises taking problems similar to those of agricultural and large lot zoning, although the direct importance of floodplain or hazardous area zoning to the health and safety of a community enhances its validity. For example, in *Turnpike Realty Co.* v. *Town of Dedham* [88], the Massachusetts Supreme Court upheld floodplain zoning that resulted in an 88 percent loss in land value to the landowner. State courts have also become more sympathetic to regulation of development in coastal land, marshes, and other environmentally sensitive areas. The Wisconsin Supreme Court has held that "landowners do not always have a right to fill wetlands for development" and that limiting the land use to other activities, such as farming, golf courses and so forth does not constitute a taking [89].

Although many cases protecting environmentally sensitive land do so in the context of development permit applications rather than sensitive area zoning, they nevertheless demonstrate a trend toward judicial acceptance of regulations that restrict development on sensitive lands. But the advances have been accompanied by setbacks [90], causing some states to supplement their environmental protection statutes with schemes to compensate landowners to ensure that development restrictions will be upheld [91].

Implementation. *State.*   General open space zoning may be implemented at the local level, but, as stated in Chapter 3, many states have reasserted their power to regulate development in hazardous and critical areas.

States have also gotten involved in open space preservation through preferential tax treatment of agricultural and other land. Although agricultural zoning is handled at the local level, specific statutory authorization may be necessary to empower localities to create agricultural districts where preferential assessment is available [92].

Finally, and perhaps most importantly from the standpoint of saving energy, states must support or require regional cooperation to prevent growth from leapfrogging from one locality to areas with less stringent development controls. This problem was discussed earlier in the context of comprehensive planning and capital facilities programming.

Local. Whether sensitive area and open space zoning is implemented at the local level or by the state, it is essential to maximize local input, since the localities are most familiar with those physical characteristics of their land that may qualify it for special zoning restrictions. Localities that adopt open space, large lot, agricultural, and sensitive area zoning will need to change their zoning texts and maps to implement the new zoning requirements. In addition, where these zones are used as temporary holding zones to check premature development, the locality will be required to provide regular reviews of the comprehensive plan to determine when and what zoning changes are necessary to accommodate growth. Localities must anticipate and be able to withstand piecemeal rezoning requests. Prior to imposing open space zones, local governments must be able to substantiate with studies and facts the need for such zones. Finally, local governments should complement their open space zoning plans with programs to make land available for development close to the urban center.

LAND ACQUISITION PROGRAMS

Regulation of land use to prevent energy-inefficient development costs little to implement and is a major land use tool for that reason if for no other. Yet regulation by itself sometimes can prove legally and politically unpalatable. Overharsh regulation may be unconstitutional. Even if a regulation meets legal tests, public opinion may block the imposition of stringent regulations on the way individuals use their land. In addition, land use regulations have been criticized as inflexible, negative, difficult to administer, and vulnerable to amendments that undermine overall goals.

As a response to the increasing realization that traditional regulatory methods cannot singlehandedly meet the challenges of orderly growth, more and more state and local governments are supplementing land regulatory programs with land acquisition programs. Land, or a partial interest in land, is acquired on the urban fringe where regulation is impracticable but where land development is permanently or temporarily undesirable.

Controlling land development through acquisition rather than regulation offers two primary advantages. Acquisition avoids the taking issue because just compensation is given to landowners in exchange for property rights. In addition, land acquisition programs may be more politically acceptable since they compensate landowners for giving up rights that often could be taken away through regulation without compensation.

Because of the expense of land acquisition, the technique is un-likely to become a primary instrument for land management. Never-theless, several alternative land acquisition techniques now being used, both in this country and elsewhere, can supplement regulation and capital facilities programming techniques to help save energy by encouraging orderly land development. This section reviews two kinds of acquisition programs that can be used to guide growth into energy-efficient locations [93].

Examples of Acquisition Programs to Promote Orderly Growth

In designing land acquisition programs that promote urban con-tainment, state and local governments have two basic choices: they can select a program that permanently restricts land development on the urban fringe, or they can adopt one that withholds land from development only so long as is necessary to prevent premature devel-opment. The latter is typically known as land banking. Permanent restriction programs are a familiar land management device. By con-trast, except in Puerto Rico, land banking has never been tried in this country [94], although it has been used successfully in Canada and Europe.

Programs with Permanent Restrictions. Traditional open space conservation programs that permanently restrict development are not designed primarily to influence development patterns. Instead, they are intended to promote complementary interests—to preserve scenic land surrounding urban areas, to protect prime agricultural land, or to guard environmentally critical areas. For example, in an effort to stem the increasing encroachment of development on agricultural land, New Jersey recently enacted legislation that will enable the state to spend $5 million to buy development rights, (the right to build upon or otherwise develop land) from farmers in Burlington County. The state will "retire" the development rights after they have been purchased, thus permanently reserving the land for agri-cultural use [95]. Over thirty-eight states have adopted enabling legislation for use in acquiring scenic easements [96], while New Jersey, Massachusetts, California, and Pennsylvania permit acquisi-tion of open space through eminent domain [97]. Numerous locali-ties have bought open space. Boulder, Colorado, for example, has purchased development rights on 172 acres at 30 to 60 percent of the full fee purchase price [98].

These programs can, as a secondary effect, retard the haphazard spread of development from urban centers; but the kind of land whose purchase is authorized is often not strategically located for growth management purposes. Traditional land acquisition programs to shape growth involve another problem too: if the land is purchased on the theory that it will be permanently reserved for open space, later development of that land is prevented even though energy-efficient land use would require its development when legitimate growth pressures arise.

Two simple but far-reaching changes in these traditional acquisition programs could greatly enhance their usefulness in shaping urban growth. The first, already adopted by Pennsylvania, would authorize acquisition of any land needed to direct growth toward urban centers [99]. The second, a logical extension of the first, would permit governments to dispose of acquired land when that land is ripe for development and to impose conditions that regulate the way that the released land is developed. Several countries are now using such a program, called land banking, to end land speculation and to ensure orderly growth.

Land Banking. Land banking entails governmental acquisition and disposal of undeveloped land in sufficient quantities to control growth patterns [100]. In theory, the government could acquire undeveloped land on the urban fringe and withhold it from development until growth pressures require release of the "banked" land for development in an orderly fashion. In addition, the land bank could prepare land for development, and, when the land was released, it could attach restrictions on the way that the land could be used. By controlling the timing, location, and method of land development, the land banking entity could enhance energy-efficient land use.

The chances are slim that any community would ever have the financial means or political support to accomplish land banking on a scale that, by itself, would discourage urban sprawl. Nevertheless, the technique could be useful on a smaller scale when combined with comprehensive planning, land regulation, taxing, and capital facilities expansion programs designed to enhance orderly growth. Moreover, the possibility that the locality could attach energy-efficient development and use restrictions to the banked land upon its release could be extremely valuable if the land controlled by the land-banking entity were strategically located, such as along transportation and utility lines.

Precedents for Land Banking. Numerous localities in this country have confused their advance land acquisition programs with land banking. For example, Fairfax County, Virginia, has established a multimillion dollar revolving fund to purchase sites for low income housing development. Milwaukee and Philadelphia use advance acquisition techniques to set aside industrial land. In fact, small-scale advance acquisition programs exist in about one-third of all cities with more than 50,000 people [101]. But these programs and similar ones in other localities are not land-banking programs as the term is used here. They are not aimed at managing growth, but rather at obtaining land for specified uses or at saving money through early acquisition of land for public uses. In contrast, model land-banking legislation proposed by the American Law Institute (ALI) would give the state, whether it is acting on its own or on behalf of a local government, broad authority to acquire, hold, and dispose of land in a manner that promotes orderly development [102]. Under the ALI provisions, land or land interests could be acquired for an indefinite period for an "unspecified" use.

The concept of general land banking has been applied to shape growth patterns in Saskatoon, Canada, in Stockholm, and in Puerto Rico. In Saskatoon, the initial "bank" was virtually cost-free, since the city obtained land through tax defaults during the Depression. Stockholm's land bank, which began in 1904 and now encompasses 200 miles or 70 percent of all land outside the central city, is credited with making possible the construction of eighteen attractive new communities near subway systems that provide convenient access to Stockholm [103]. A more recent land bank project merits note because it is the only extensive land-banking program adopted by a U.S. governmental body and because it has withstood direct legal challenge: Puerto Rico created a land bank in 1964 to promote the dual goals of stabilizing land supply (and hence land prices) and of controlling the direction of growth. The need to reduce land prices to discourage speculation in Puerto Rico has, however, precipitated the premature release of land and the simultaneous subordination of the urban containment goal [104].

Land Bank Structure. Choosing a body to develop and control the land bank represents a major policy decision. Some commentators urge reliance on a public corporation akin to the Urban Development Corporation in New York or to the Puerto Rican Land Administration. Such public corporations would be free from political pressures and yet would enjoy tax advantages that can reduce landholding costs [105]. But others contend that state governments should administer the land bank in order to make it politically accountable [106]. The ALI Model Land Development Code represents a middle course, calling for creation of a land reserve agency within the state government with powers "analogous to those of a large public corporation" [107]. The land bank would operate on a state level and have authority to work with local governments [108].

Other Considerations

Although land acquisition programs may vary, depending on whether their goal is the permanent or the temporary restriction of land development, land acquisition programs raise many common economic, political, and legal issues.

Interest to be Acquired. Planners must decide whether to acquire full ownership of land or merely development rights, provided either would be sufficient to achieve the land use goal of urban containment. In theory, the major advantage of acquiring less than full title to land is thrift. However, a partial interest may actually cost as much as the full title where intense development pressure exists. Since the value of land lies in its development potential, acquiring an interest to prevent development can be as expensive as acquiring full title once development pressure mounts. Therefore, a program of acquisition of less than full title should precede the onset of significant development pressure.

Timing of Acquisition. At least two difficulties stand in the way of an early start. First, the need for acquisition may not be recognized until development pressure begins to assert itself. Second, development pressure may gather force prematurely, owing to government activity. Once the government removes land from the market, the development potential of remaining land will be that much more valuable [109]. The ALI Code attempts to avoid this problem by allowing the use of private agents to purchase land for land banks [110]. Presumably, the anonymity of the agents will help prevent land prices from being driven up.

Method of Acquisition. Governments interested in shaping growth through land acquisition will have to make other decisions, too. Should they exercise their power of eminent domain to acquire land, or should they secure title or an interest through negotiated purchase or other means? Eminent domain may not be a legal alternative, depending on state laws and upon their interpretation. Moreover, even if legal obstacles do not prevent use of eminent domain, political considerations may, since eminent domain represents the harshest form of government intrusion on private property rights. Opposition to eminent domain may be particularly strong since the importance of orderly growth, while immediate, is not as apparent as the need, for example, to take land for a school site or for road construction or for some other purpose for which eminent domain has been traditionally been exercised. Because of political opposition, eminent domain should generally be used only as a backup tool when land purchase by bid, negotiation, or some other means is impossible. A kind of legal heavy artillery, eminent domain may be rarely used, but it remains a crucial part in a government's battery of urban containment tools. Without the power of eminent domain, a government may have to pay inflated prices to acquire urban fringe property. Significantly, the ALI Model Code grants state governments the authority to require sale of strategically located lands to land banks [111].

Whether land is acquired by the exercise of eminent domain, by purchase, by gift, or by other means, governments must anticipate a clash between urban and suburban interests if premature development in the urban fringe is prevented through acquisition programs while growth within urban boundaries flourishes. Because publicly owned land is generally not taxable, local governments adjacent to municipalities trying to contain sprawl will surely resent the loss of property tax revenues, even though there may be long term savings in infrastructure costs.

As a practical matter, few local governments can legally condemn land beyond their borders. And, as the ALI Code notes, it is equally unlikely for political reasons that central cities will be able to buy surrounding suburban land. The code attempts to circumvent these problems in the land-banking area by giving the state land reserve agency the authority to acquire land on behalf of a local government [112]. It also suggests that state governments engaged in land banking pay reduced property taxes on acquired land to reduce the local financial impact of the land acquisition program [113]. But, as the code points out, such taxes will increase the cost of holding land and may result in the forced sale of property before development is desirable [114]. Moreover, paying reduced property taxes does not help solve local financial problems if the acquisition program is conducted by a local, rather than state, government. In that instance, the local government would be paying taxes to itself. A partial solution may be to permit interim use of the land for agricultural or some other nondevelopment, revenue-generating activity. But interim use may raise legal problems if the land in question has been acquired through condemnation.

Financing the Acquisition. Along with the tax consquences of a land acquisition policy, finding funds for purchasing or condemning land presents another major financial question. The most common method for raising money is the general obligation bond [115]. In Wisconsin, a special cigarette tax finances the acquisition of scenic and conservation easements [116]. In New Jersey a 0.4 percent state tax on all real estate transfers provides funds for land acquisition [117]. North Marin County, California, has created a special assessment district to finance the purchase of 180 acres of open space [118]. Boulder, Colorado, enacted a 1 percent additional sales tax in 1967 and designated 40 percent of the proceeds for greenbelt acquisition. Similarly, Jefferson County, Colorado, pays for its open space acquisition program through a 0.5 percent sales tax [119]. As still other alternatives, acquisition could be funded by federal revenue-sharing funds available under the Housing and Community Development Act of 1974 [120], which allows use of such funds for acquiring property for "community development"; or land purchase may be funded through revenues collected from land speculation taxes like the one adopted in Vermont [121].

Impact on Land Prices. Before embarking on a land acquisition program, governments must also explore the effects of large-scale land acquisition on surrounding land prices. Interestingly, land banking is often considered a tool for diminishing land speculation and stabilizing land prices. Land banking, advocates claim, will make speculation less attractive because of the threat that the government can sell land at less than the prevailing market value, thereby undercutting speculative prices. In addition, by freeing more land for development, land banking deals land speculation an additional blow. But its critics argue that land banking will have the opposite effect if it is used to achieve simultaneously the goals of urban containment and stabilization of land prices. They argue that withholding land from the market—even temporarily—will drive up prices of privately held land. Holding costs will, they say, also increase the sale price of banked land [122]. Furthermore, the value of land released by the bank will be enhanced and the goal of stabilizing land prices will be subverted if the land bank is successful in promoting orderly growth [123]. Of course, where the acquired land is permanently restricted from development, the possibility that the land acquisition program will drive up land prices looms even greater.

Legal Issues. Although several legal obstacles hinder the development of extensive public land acquisition programs, legal questions probably will not pose as severe a threat to acquisition as will economic and political problems—provided proper enabling legislation is adopted. Nevertheless, some fundamental legal questions must be addressed so that potential barriers can be anticipated and avoided.

The method of acquisition that is adopted will influence whether legal barriers will exist. Acquisition by condemnation raises by far the most extensive questions, while acquisition by purchase will generally be more legally acceptable. As noted elsewhere, land may be condemned only for a public use. "Public use," while strictly construed in the past, has been more liberally interpreted in recent years and has now become almost synonymous with "public purpose" [124]. Indeed, the ALI Model Code provisions authorizing large-scale land acquisition has declared such acquisition through eminent domain "for the purpose of facilitating future planning" to be for the "public purpose" [125].

As one commentator observes, whether or not courts will allow the exercise of eminent domain to promote orderly growth will largely turn on whether they regard orderly growth as beneficial to the public [126]. Strategies to promote energy conservation unquestionably benefit the public [127], and many courts have declared unequivocally that localities can use delegated police powers for the public purpose of promoting orderly growth [128]. Consequently, condemnation of land for the purpose of conserving energy through urban containment should also fall within the meaning of public purpose. This view has been legislatively supported by the adoption in some states of open space statutes that authorize land acquisition through the exercise of eminent domain [129]. Nevertheless, state and local governments should study their state eminent domain statutes carefully to determine the exact purposes for which condemnation is allowed. Governments may find that revising statutes along the lines suggested by the ALI Model Land Development Code is in order.

A constitutional issue raised by land banking, one applicable to acquisition by either condemnation or purchase, is whether the land may be acquired for an unspecified future use. A strong argument can be made that evidence of the present use of the land to promote orderly growth in order to save energy should be legally sufficient to permit the acquisition without addressing the issue of an unspecified future use. But even if that argument is rejected, the issue may nevertheless be of little consequence. In the only direct challenge in the United States to land acquisition where no future land use had been specified, the Puerto Rican Supreme Court upheld the acquisition [130]. One key factor in the court's approval of the acquisition scheme, which was accomplished through land banking, was that land banks were seen as a potential solution to the problems of overcrowding and soaring land prices in Puerto Rico. The facts may differ in other localities where land banking is proposed, however. Because circumstances vary from state to state, those states adopting land-banking programs should anticipate and attempt to avoid charges that unspecified future uses do not serve the public purpose; to do so, they can adopt legislation similar to that found in the ALI Model Code, which declares that land acquisition to facilitate future land planning is for a public purpose [131].

Implementation. *State.* In most states, as the commentary to Part 4 of the ALI Code has pointed out, the state's authority to acquire, hold, or dispose of land is either spelled out in a scattered fashion throughout statutes or it does not exist at all. Moreover, statutes rarely identify orderly growth as a legitimate part of land acquisition programs. Consequently, enabling legislation that clearly authorizes state and local governments to acquire land or an interest in land for the purpose of orderly growth is needed.

Legislation enabling governments to become involved in land banking should authorize the establishment of a land bank entity with broad powers of acquisition, holding, and disposition for implementing the state land use policy. A state agency may serve as the land-banking entity, or, as discussed earlier, the land bank may be operated at the local level or by a public corporation.

In addition to providing adequate enabling legislation, the state must provide a means for financing land acquisition programs. They may be compelled to issue new bonds, new sales taxes, new real estate transfer taxes, or land gains taxes as sources of revenue.

Local. Local governments with proper enabling authority may set up land acquisition programs themselves, or they may assist the state governments in land acquisition. If the second approach is taken, state governments should seek local assistance in identifying both land that should be purchased and land that should be disposed of. The ALI Model Land Development Code provides a statutory model for creating a land bank that incorporates local land use goals [132] and for giving local governments the power to acquire and to dispose of land [133].

TRANSFER OF DEVELOPMENT RIGHTS

A description of the transfer of development rights (TDR) is a necessary part of any discussion of strategies to conserve energy by promoting higher density development near urban centers and along transportation corridors while inhibiting premature fringe growth. Yet, as the title of a recent publication on the technique states, TDRs are presently only a "Promising But Unproven New Approach to Land Use Regulation" [134].

Under a TDR plan, "development rights," or the right to modify the natural environment, such as by building structures on land, are severed from one parcel of land and transferred, usually by sale, to another. The parcel to which the development rights have been shifted may then be built upon at a higher density than would have been allowed under the zoning ordinance prior to transfer of the development rights. Many TDR systems appear to be almost identical to clustering: they allow development rights to be transferred only between contiguous pieces of land owned by the same individual. But the TDR system proposed here is a much more refined device. Based on a comprehensive plan for orderly growth, this TDR plan establishes development districts in which higher densities are desired and preservation districts in which development should be discouraged. It involves the creation and allocation of development rights according to anticipated growth pressures, and the right to transfer (for compensation) development rights from land located in the preservation district to noncontiguous land in the development district. Land that loses and land that receives development rights may be owned by different individuals.

A concrete example best illustrates how TDRs should work in practice. Farmer Jones, whose land is threatened by urban expansion, may find that preferential taxation is an insufficient incentive for him to continue farming in the face of encroaching urbanization. Raising crops has become difficult and Farmer Jones can reap big profits from the sale of his farmland to developers. On the other hand, Developer Smith owns a plot of land close to the urban center that would be ideal for townhouses and garden apartments, but the existing zoning ordinance permits only single family homes on 15,000 square foot lots. The town in which Smith's plot is located has decided that it can no longer afford to extend capital facilities, schools, and roads far out into the countryside where developments have been springing up willy-nilly over the past five years. It also wants to preserve the open space offered by Farmer Jones' land, to protect the wetlands alongside the river that runs through Jones' property, and to reduce the air pollution and energy waste caused by long distance commuting.

The town fathers are reluctant to zone Farmer Jones' land for open space because they fear that Jones will contest that zoning as a taking of his property without just compensation. They know that although Jones would like to continue farming, he also would be more than slightly annoyed if the zoning forced him to give up the profit he could derive from the sale of his land to eager developers. And even if the open space zoning were legal, the goals of such zoning ordinances would probably be undermined by variances, rezonings, and the like. Yet, the town lacks the money to buy Jones' land and to thereby ensure that development would be prevented. Moreover, buying the land would remove valuable property from the tax rolls. So the town decides to experiment with the transfer of development rights, a new approach that falls somewhere between regulation and condemnation, yet promises to shape growth rather than to let the town be shaped by overweening development pressures.

The first step the town takes is to designate a development district in which it wants new growth to concentrate. The town particularly wants to confine the new growth it encourages to an energy-efficient spot where public transportation already exists or is easily accessible, where shopping and employment opportunities are close at hand, where utility systems are already in place, and where the natural environment is well-suited for the energy-efficient layout and design of new development. After a careful analysis of several alternative sites, it selects a sparsely settled area that is close to the urban center and that includes Developer Smith's property. The area the town chooses can easily support more development than the present single family zoning will permit.

At the same time that the town selects an area for higher density development, it also designates outlying land, including Farmer Jones' farm, as a preservation district. The town tells Jones and others owning land in the preservation district (which is presently zoned for five acre minimum lots) that for every five acres of land that they own, they may sell one TDR to developers who wish to build in the development district. Under the TDR scheme, the TDRs cannot be sold until the farmer agrees to reduce the density of development on his land to one dwelling unit per twenty-five acres. Meanwhile, the TDR system permits the developer who buys the development rights to build in the development zone one additional dwelling unit for each TDR purchased, up to a maximum of eight units per acre. Consequently, even though the basic zoning has not been changed, the developer can build at a considerably higher density than the zoning regulations would normally permit [135]. Before the additional development is approved, however, the developer must demonstrate that his plan accords with the town's comprehensive plan; with the public facilities ordinance; and with the energy efficiency standards, environmental standards, and other requirements that may be imposed on new development.

If all works as expected, Farmer Jones will be happy because he can continue farming and still receive compensation for the development potential of his land, and Developer Smith will be content because he can build economical and more lucrative high density housing (the cost of the TDRs is presumably outweighed by profits accruing from the higher density development). The town is also pleased: the land remains on the tax rolls, premature expansion of capital facilities is halted, energy conservation is promoted through orderly, compact growth, and no municipal capital has been laid out other than the money needed to develop the TDR system itself.

Plusses and Minuses of TDRs

The system described above roughly approximates the features of the TDR system now existing in Buckingham Township, Pennsylvania [136]. Other localities, including Chesterfield Township in New Jersey, Collier County in Florida, Montgomery County in Maryland, and Southampton Township in New York [137], have also adopted some form of TDR ordinance to enhance open space preservation. The New Jersey, New York, and Oregon legislatures have considered adoption of TDR enabling legislation designed to preserve open spaces [138].

The reasons for the sudden flurry of excitement over TDRs as a new land management device are numerous. Proponents assert that TDRs provide a way to preserve open space and to curtail sprawl while avoiding the stifling threat of the takings challenge to which other land management methods are subject. In addition, TDRs avoid the dual expense of condemnation, which not only requires tax dollars for the purchase of the land, but also reduces tax revenues because it removes the property from the tax rolls by taking it out of private ownership. Although restrictions on land development are permanent once the development rights have been transferred (at least until the local government amends its comprehensive plan and zoning ordinances [139], the land nevertheless may be used for farming, recreational purposes, or other nondevelopment uses. Since the landowners who keep their land in low density development are compensated for giving up their development rights, the economic windfalls and wipeouts that can result from government action affecting land—such as the construction of a road near one's property or the downzoning of land from a one acre to a fifteen acre minimum lot size—presumably are eliminated [140].

A technique with such promise should have taken the country by storm. But several thorny problems have dampened the urge of governments to hop on the TDR bandwagon. Not the least of the problems associated with TDRs is the fact that, as a new technique, it is the subject of suspicion; no one is sure what secondary impacts it may have on land prices and housing costs or whether a TDR system can be successfully administered. Another big problem is that land speculators, who already own much of the land in developing areas, thrive in the current windfall-wipeout system; they stand to make great fortunes if they own land in the right spot at the right time. Thus, many oppose a system that would stifle gambling with land values even though speculation wreaks havoc with land prices, promotes graft, and makes implementing efficient land use plans next to impossible [141]. Several TDR systems have run into trouble because citizens opposed the construction of multifamily structures that would be permitted in the transfer zone [142]. Other major obstacles to adoption of TDRs are the uncertainty over whether such a system would be economically viable and the legal problems that a hybrid system, falling somewhere between regulation and condemnation, creates. Significantly, the legality of TDRs will depend in large part upon their economic merits.

Setting Up a TDR System

Setting up a TDR system that relies on the free market to effect the transfer of development rights is no small feat. On the one hand, developers must be given an economic incentive to buy available TDRs. On the other, landowners in the preservation district must be offered enough compensation to stimulate them to sell their development rights. Trying to accommodate both parties and, at the same time, to control the direction and intensity of growth through TDR programs requires considerable planning and analytical skill.

Economic Issues. The prime rule is to ensure that there are neither so few available TDRs that owners of development rights are able to charge exhorbitant prices nor so many TDRs that prices crash, leaving landowners with little incentive to sell their development rights. Thus, the amount of anticipated development activity must be fairly accurately calculated, so that the number of TDRs issued corresponds to development demand.

A recent study of TDR systems lists several requirements for balancing the number of TDRs with market demand [143]. Designating transfer districts in areas where development demand is strong, making the number of TDRs that may be used in the transfer districts larger than the number of TDRs available from the preservation district, restricting the granting of zoning variances and density bonuses that allow greater densities than zoning permits (thereby eliminating the need for TDRs), and allowing developers to build at a sufficiently high density to make TDRs economically attractive are suggested as basic ground rules [144].

Development rights can be allocated in various ways—by tying the number of TDRs to the amount of development that is possible under existing zoning, or to the land's assessed or market value (which presumably reflects its development potential), or to the amount the landowner loses in land value when a land use plan that identifies development and preservation areas is designed and published [145]. Under the last system, only land that depreciates in value would be awarded any TDRs. Similarly, TDRs may also be priced in various ways, ways that vary from locality to locality. One TDR may be sufficient to build one residential unit in one place, while another locality may require developers to purchase two or more TDRs per residential unit.

If the development demand has been properly anticipated, so that the number of TDRs issued corresponds to the market demand, developers should purchase TDRs for use in the transfer district, thus compensating landowners in the preservation district for their loss of development rights. Upon the sale of TDRs, a restrictive covenant, enforceable by the locality, that extinguishes development rights in the preservation district, should be recorded to ensure that the preservation land is not developed. Thus the landowner in the preservation district is encouraged, but not required, to sell development rights and to maintain the preservation land in its existing undeveloped state. Some have proposed prohibiting development altogether in the preservation district so that landowners would be forced to sell their TDRs to compensate for the loss of development potential, but, as noted below, a mandatory system is likely to run into legal problems.

Because TDRs are taxable property rights that are not attached to specific parcels of land, cheap TDRs may flood the market as farmers with development rights but without the intention of developing their land try to unload unused rights that otherwise merely constitute an economic drain. Preferential taxation of the unused rights may stem the flood, but they may also reduce the incentive to sell the development rights. Another alternative is to have the locality purchase the development rights and thereby to regulate their flow. But this alternative may be too expensive for most localities to consider. The TDR market may also become glutted if transfer zones are developed at densities lower than those anticipated. In such cases, the government may be forced to create other transfer zones to keep the demand for TDRs steady.

Other economic questions are also raised by the use of TDRs. Although some proponents assert that TDRs will discourage land speculation by removing windfalls and wipeouts, in fact it seems logical that speculation will continue. Development districts will increase in value because of their development potential and because the amount of land available for high density development is limited. Hence the possibility for high risk development will still exist, but its impacts may be tempered somewhat by the need to purchase or the ability to sell development rights.

These economic issues leave open the question whether TDRs can effectively promote energy conservation through orderly growth. Although TDR systems may help protect isolated, environmentally sensitive lands or particularly good agricultural soil, placing all fringe land in a preservation district would probably glut the market with TDRs; alternatively, if only a limited number of TDRs is issued for a large preservation district, the TDR sellers may not be adequately compensated, since the sale of a few expensive TDRs could not make up for the accompanying loss of development rights. Thus, the initial preservation district should consist of imminently threatened land on the fringe. Land beyond the fringe could be regulated to prevent development—through the use, for example, of exclusive agricultural zoning. Additional threatened land may be added to the preservation district as required and as the supply of existing TDRs is exhausted. In this manner, a TDR system may channel growth into compact, urban locations [146].

Other Considerations

Legal Issues. *Taking Versus Just Compensation.* It is difficult to judge the legality of a TDR system without first defining a TDR and establishing the standards by which a TDR system should be tested. Yet that task is deceptively difficult, especially when mandatory TDRs are involved.

A mandatory TDR system is different from the one described in the example at the beginning of this section. A mandatory TDR system would prohibit development in the preservation district and thereby force the sale of development rights for use in the transfer zone. It constitutes neither police power regulation nor the exercise of the power of eminent domain. If mandatory TDRs are viewed strictly as a regulatory mechanism, the permanent restrictions imposed on development in the preservation district might constitute a taking of property without just compensation, especially if the demand for TDRs is not high enough to give landowners a reasonable return on the sale of their development rights. This potential problem may become a reality in Puerto Rico where the proposed TDR system would not only impose mandatory use restrictions in the preservation district, thus forcing the sale of TDRs, but would also lower the intensity of land uses in the transfer zone, thereby forcing landowners in that zone to buy TDRs [147].

TDR systems might also pose problems if viewed strictly as a form of eminent domain, since the TDR certificates are not money and since their value depends solely on the creation of a TDR market [148]. Indeed, a mandatory TDR system in New York City that zoned two parcels in Manhattan as public parks and proposed to award the landowners development rights certificates as compensation was found to be a taking by the trial court. The court reasoned that because of the uncertain value of the development rights, TDRs did not qualify as "just compensation" [149].

Taking problems would be more severe in a mandatory than in a voluntary TDR system in which landowners in a preservation district can either develop their land or sell TDRs at will. In fact, the voluntary TDR system gives landowners the additional right to sell development rights; it does not remove any property rights [150].

Equal Protection and Uniformity Requirements. If landowners who buy TDRs are permitted to build at higher densities than landowners in the same district who do not buy TDRs, constitutional and zoning uniformity problems may arise. The legal issue is whether such a system violates either constitutional equal protection rights or state laws that require zoning regulations to be "uniform for each class or kind of building(s) throughout each district" [151]. This issue has been examined in the context of landmarks preservation by a noted TDR expert, John J. Costonis, but Costonis' analysis can be applied to the use of TDRs to preserve open space and to contain urban sprawl as well [152]. Costonis compares TDRs to PUD [153] and clustering ordinances that relax building use and/or bulk requirements. Developers taking advantage of these flexible ordinances may build at densities that exceed the level normally permitted within the zoning district. Yet PUDs and cluster zoning, when challenged on uniformity grounds, have been upheld on the theory that uniformity does not require all buildings in the district to be alike, but merely requires all landowners within the district to have the same development options [154]. TDR schemes are based on the idea that all landowners in a transfer district have an equal opportunity to purchase development rights from landowners in preservation districts. The fact that only wealthier landowners will be able to purchase the rights does not appear to raise significant equal protection problems [155].

Enabling Legislation.   Some localities have adopted TDR systems without benefit of state enabling legislation, but such systems are always voluntary supplements to existing zoning controls [156]. TDR systems may fall within the zoning powers delegated to localities for regulation of the density and intensity of land use [157]. But the novelty of TDRs may make state enabling legislation desirable, even though it is, arguably, inessential. In contrast, mandatory TDR systems most certainly require state enabling legislation, although such legislation does not guarantee that mandatory TDR systems will withstand constitutional challenges.

Proposed TDR enabling legislation, largely based on a New York bill, is included in Appendix II, p. 309. In addition, the TDR ordinance adopted in Buckingham Township, Pennsylvania, is included for review. Note that the Buckingham ordinance does not establish transfer zones, but rather permits use of TDRs anywhere outside the preservation district. Because such a system does not ensure that the new growth will be located in the most energy-efficient spots, any locality using the Buckingham ordinance as a model should also consider establishing transfer zones.

Implementation. *State.*   State enabling legislation is desirable for the development of an effective voluntary TDR system and is essential to the adoption of a mandatory system.

Local.   The locality devising a TDR system must enact a TDR ordinance based on a careful examination of the areas to be conserved, the areas to be developed, and the number of TDRs needed to accomplish the goal. Local governments are also responsible for creating and allocating the TDRs. Some governments may wish to be directly involved in the trading of TDRs, either by making approval of a TDR exchange contingent upon the buyer's compliance with development standards or by manipulating the market through government purchases of TDRs to maintain reasonable TDR prices. Local governments must also exercise enforcement powers to ensure that, once development rights are sold, landowners in the preservation district do not build beyond the reduced development limit.

NOTES TO CHAPTER 5

1. Urban Systems Research & Engineering, Inc., *The Growth Shapers/The Land Use Impacts of Infrastructure Investments*, prepared for the U.S. Council on Environmental Quality (Washington, D.C.: U.S. Government Printing Office, May 1976). *See also* Richard D. Tabors et al., *Land Use and the Pipe* (Lexington, Massachusetts: D.C. Heath and Co., 1976), for an analysis of sewerage policies that can shape development.

2. *Urban Systems, supra* note 1.

3. See pp. 143–145, *infra*.

4. Israel Stollman, "An Editorial and the Ordinance as Amended," in Randall W. Scott, ed., *Management and Control of Growth*, vol. II (Washington, D.C.: The Urban Land Institute, 1975), p. 5.

5. Ramapo, New York, Proposed Amendments to Building Zone Amended Ordinance of 1969, §8 (Sept. 22, 1969), reprinted in Scott, *supra* note 4 at 4–13.

6. For a description of the Clarkstown plan, *see New Approaches to Residential Land Development/A Study of Concepts and Innovations*, Technical Bulletin 40 (Washington, D.C.: The Urban Land Institute, 1961), p. 74; R. May, "Comment," in Scott, *supra* note 4 at 50; and Norman Williams, Jr., *American Land Planning Law*, vol. 3, §73.09 (Chicago: Callaghan & Co., 1975), pp. 354–57.

7. 24 Misc.2d 366, 198 N.Y.S.2d 695 (Sup.Ct., Rockland County, 1960).

8. Williams, *supra* note 6.

9. Montgomery County, Md., Adequate Public Facilities Ordinance No. 7–41 (June 26, 1973), Montgomery County, Md., Code §50–35(j) (Michie Supp. 1975).

10. Maryland Code Ann., Art. 66D §87–116(a) (Michie Supp. 1976).

11. Grace Dawson, "No Little Plan: Fairfax County's PLUS Program for Managing Growth" (Washington, D.C.: The Urban Institute, December 1976).

12. Michael E. Gleeson et al., "Urban Growth Management Systems: An Evaluation of Policy-Related Research," Planning Advisory Service Reports Nos. 309, 310 (Chicago: American Society of Planning Officials, August 1975), pp. 10–27.

13. *Id.* at 11.

14. *Id.* at 12.

15. *Id.* at 23–25.

16. *Id.* at 25–27. The Salem experience will be replicated throughout Oregon as a result of state-imposed local comprehensive planning requirements and the use of boundary commissions that must approve extensions of sewer and water lines.

17. Or. Rev. Stat. §§199.410 et seq. (1975–1976).

18. Or. Rev. Stat. §§199.410(2).

19. Or. Rev. Stat. §199.425. The boundary commissions were established in (1) the Portland metropolitan area (Columbia, Washington, Multnomah, and Clackamas counties); (2) the Salem area (Marion and Polk counties); and (3) the

Eugene area (Lane County). These three boundary commissions cover seven of the thirty-six counties in Oregon.

20. Or. Rev. Stat. §199.430.

21. A major boundary change includes the formation, merger, or dissolution of a city (or cities) or service district. Or. Rev. Stat. §199.415(12). A minor boundary change includes the annexation or withdrawal of a territory to or from a city or district. Or. Rev. Stat. §199.415(3).

22. Or. Rev. Stat. §199.464(3).

23. Or. Rev. Stat. §199.464(4).

24. Or. Rev. Stat. §199.461(1)(a).

25. Or. Rev. Stat. §§199.461(3), 199.464(1).

26. *See, e.g.*, the "Interim Regional Development Policy" adopted by the Columbia Region Association of Governments in January 1974, which states that the boundary commission should "encourage development on vacant land lying within already developed areas where services are available, thus eliminating the proliferation of public services into undeveloped areas and thereby lessening the degree of urban sprawl."

27. Or. Rev. Stat. §197.180 (1975-1976). *See* pp. 42, 45-53, *supra*, for a fuller discussion of the 1973 Oregon Land Use Act and, Chapter 3, note 23, p. 54, for the text of Oregon's State-Wide Goal No. 13, "Energy Conservation."

28. Oregon Land Conservation and Development Commission, "State-Wide Planning Goals and Guidelines," January 1, 1975, Goal No. 11, "Public Facilities and Services."

29. *Id.*, Goal No. 14, "Urbanization."

30. *Id.*

31. Telephone interview, Mr. Dale McGee, member of the Land Conservation and Development Commission, November 5, 1976. The cities are Medford and Central Point.

32. *Id.*

33. Conversation with Edward J. Sullivan, legal counsel to Governor Robert W. Straub of Oregon. By using boundary commissions, the Oregon legislature has avoided the problem raised in California and Virginia—namely, that capital facility expansion constitutes a proprietary obligation and cannot be exercised by municipalities to control land development patterns outside city limits. *See* discussion on pp. 152-153, *infra*.

The boundary commissions' authority to exercise independent judgment until final plans are approved is presently being tested in the Portland area. There a boundary commission denied permission to extend a water system into an agricultural area, saying that such an extension was not in accord with the statewide goal of preserving rural lands, even though the interim plan for the area included urbanization of the affected area.

34. If the supply of housing in developing areas is extremely restricted, prices of urban housing and urban property taxes will also skyrocket, forcing the poor out of their inner city homes into even more inferior housing. The sewer moratoria in counties surrounding Washington, D.C., have had precisely this effect, resulting in runaway housing prices and public outcries for tax reform to dampen speculation in inner city housing.

35. Gleeson et al., *supra* note 12 at 98−99.

36. Real Estate Research Corporation, *The Costs of Sprawl, Detailed Cost Analysis* (Washington, D.C.: U.S. Government Printing Office, 1974), pp. 7−8. Even higher savings in road and utility costs are possible with high density planned communities.

37. Gleeson, *supra* note 12 at 99.

38. Ramapo's experience demonstrates, however, that growth does not always bring an increase in revenues; it may result in an increase in expenditures to provide costly public services.

39. Fiscal Disparities Bill, Minn. Laws (1971), Minn. Stat. Ann. §§473 F.01 *et seq.* (West Supp. 1975).

40. Village of Burnsville v. Onischuk, 222 N.W.2d 523, 541 (Minn. 1974), *appeal denied*, 420 U.S. 916 (1975). *See* Katherine C. Lyall, "Tax Base-Sharing: A Fiscal Aid Towards More Rational Land Use Planning," *Journal of The American Institute of Planners* 41, no. 2 (March 1975): 90−100; and Mary E. Brooks, "Minnesota's Fiscal Disparities Bill," Planning Advisory Service Memo No. M−9 (Chicago: American Society of Planning Officials, 1972), for a more complete discussion of the Minnesota fiscal disparities tax plan.

41. Golden v. Planning Board of the Town of Ramapo, 30 N.Y.2d 359, 285 N.E.2d 291, 334 N.Y.S.2d 138, *appeal dismissed*, 409 U.S. 1003 (1972).

42. *See* note 93, *infra*, for a discussion of acquisition of development rights.

43. Dawson, *supra* note 11.

44. The tax reduction raised the question whether Ramapo had authority to grant differential property tax rates, since the state constitution required uniformity of taxation. The majority of the court ignored the question, but it was noted in the dissenting opinion.

45. *See* Daniel R. Mandelker, The Role of the Local Comprehensive Plan in Land Use Regulation, 74 *Mich. L. Rev.* 900 (1976), for the argument that if development proposed by a comprehensive plan does not materialize, that plan should not be accorded a presumption of validity, and communities should not be obligated to comply with the capital facilities expansion program outlined in the comprehensive plan.

46. Construction Industry Ass'n of Sonoma County v. Petaluma, 522 F.2d 897 (9th Cir. 1975), *cert. denied*, 424 U.S. 934 (1976).

47. Randall Scott, "Comment," in Scott, *supra* note 4 at 46.

48. *Id.*

49. *Id.*

50. Construction Industry Ass'n of Sonoma County v. Petaluma, 522 F.2d 897 (9th Cir. 1975), *cert. denied*, 424 U.S. 934 (1976).

51. Critics of the Ramapo plan have pointed out that of the 200 biracial, low cost units that have been built, only about forty house low income families, of which only 10 to 20 percent are occupied by blacks. Fred P. Bosselman, "Town of Ramapo: Binding the World?" in Scott, *supra* note 4 at 107.

52. As noted elsewhere, even in the absence of explicit legislative authority to promote energy conservation, zoning and subdivision controls designed to save energy by regulating location of growth may also promote other goals that

SZEA or the Maryland enabling legislation presently authorize—such as facilitating the economical provision of municipal services and preserving open space. These regulations should withstand enabling authority challenges for that reason. *See* Appendix I, p. 225, for additional discussion of this issue.

53. Reid Development Corp. v. Parsippany—Troy Hills Township, 31 N.J. Super. 459, 107 A.2d 20 (App. Div. 1954); *See* Smoke Rise, Inc. v. Washington Suburban Sanitary Commission, 400 F. Supp. 1369 (D.Md. 1975) (involving a sewer hookup, not an extension), and Golden v. Planning Board of the Town of Ramapo, 30 N.Y.2d 359, 285 N.E.2d 291, 334 N.Y.S.2d 138, *appeal dismissed*, 409 U.S. 1003 (1972), (the inability of the township to meet demands of growth was not disputed).

54. 547 P.2d 228 (Colo. 1976) (*en banc*).

55. *Id.* at 232.

56. Smoke Rise, Inc. v. Washington Suburban Sanitary Commission, 400 F. Supp. 1369 (D.Md. 1975).

57. *See* Environmental Law Institute, *Approaches to Water Quality Management Planning and Implementation*, prepared for the U.S. Environmental Protection Agency (Washington, D.C.: March, 1977), for an excellent discussion of the phasing of capital improvements and conditioning land development on availability of adequate public facilities.

58. *See* pp. 51—52 on comprehensive planning.

59. Montgomery County, Md., Adequate Public Facilities Ordinance No. 7—41 (June 26, 1973), Montgomery County, Md., Code §50—35(j) (Michie Supp. 1975).

60. *See* National Land and Investment Co. v. Easttown Township Board of Adjustment, 419 Pa. 504, 215 A.2d 597 (1965); Appeal of Kit-Mar Builders, Inc., 439 Pa. 466, 268 A.2d 765 (1970); and Board of County Supervisors of Fairfax County v. Carper, 200 Va. 653, 107 S.E.2d 390 (1959).

61. A further problem unrelated to energy waste is that so many houses may be built in the area subject to large lot zoning that a health hazard will be created unless sewer and water lines are extended there. For this reason, as well as for energy conservation reasons, minimum lot sizes in areas designated for open space should be as large as legally permissible in order to discourage development.

62. *See* pp. 143—145 for a discussion of boundary commissions.

63. *See* pp. 45—51 for a discussion of local comprehensive planning.

64. Regional Science Research Institute, *Untaxing Open Space/An Evaluation of the Effectiveness of Differential Assessment of Farms and Open Space*, prepared for the U.S. Council on Environmental Quality (Washington, D.C.: U.S. Government Printing Office, April 1976), p. 4.

65. *Id.*

66. *Id.* at 65.

67. *Id.*; Gregory C. Gustafson and L.T. Wallace, "Differential Assessment as Land Use Policy: The California Case," *Journal of the American Institute of Planners* 41, no. 6 (November 1975): 379.

68. Regional Science Research Institute, *supra* note 64 at 96.

69. Gleeson et al., *supra* note 12 at 16.

70. *Id.* at 20.
71. *Id.* at 24.
72. *See* Thomas Norman and Donn A. Derr, "The Legal Aspects of an Agricultural Open Space Preserve through Exclusive Agricultural Zoning in New Jersey," and "Addendum," *Environmental Comment*, 21 (May 1975): 11—14.
73. Real Estate Research Corporation, "Business Prospects Under Coastal Zone Management," prepared for the U.S. Department of Commerce, National Oceanic & Atmospheric Administration, Office of Coastal Zone Management (March 1976).
74. Palo Alto, Cal., Municipal Code, Ch. 18.71.010—.140 (1972) (emphasis added).
75. The commercial fishing industry earned $75 million in 1965; commercial fishermen earned $30 million and sports fishermen spent about $400 million in gear, hotel rooms, meals, and other direct and indirect expenses while catching fish whose existence depends on wetlands. John and Mildred Teal, *Life and Death of the Salt Marsh* (New York: An Audubon/Ballentine publication, 1969), p. 204.
76. One study, however, disputes the national economic significance of preserving such farmland. George E. Peterson and Harvey Yampolsky, "Urban Development and the Protection of Metropolitan Farmland" (Washington, D.C.: The Urban Institute, 1975).
77. 419 Pa. 504, 215 A.2d 597 (1965).
78. *Id.* at 610. *See also* Appeal of Kit-Mar Builders, Inc., 439 Pa. 466, 268 A.2d 765 (1970); and Appeal of Girsh, 437 Pa. 398, 263 A.2d 395 (1970). But note that recently a commonwealth court of Pennsylvania held that three acre zoning was not unreasonable per se. DeCaro v. Washington Township, 344 A.2d 725 (Pa. Cmwlth. 1975).
79. 200 Va. 653, 107 S.E.2d 390 (1959).
80. Southern Burlington County NAACP v. Township of Mount Laurel, 67 N.J. 151, 336 A.2d 713, *appeal dismissed*, 423 U.S. 808 (1975); Berenson v. Town of Newcastle, 38 N.Y.2d 102, 341 N.E.2d 236, 378 N.Y.S.2d 672 (1975).
81. 469 F.2d 956 (1st Cir., 1972). *See* Senior v. Zoning Commission of Town of New Canaan, 146 Conn. 531, 153 A.2d 415 (1959), *appeal dismissed*, 363 U.S. 143 (1960).
82. *See, e.g.*, Kennedy Park Homes Ass'n v. City of Lackawana, 436 F.2d 108 (2d Cir. 1970), *cert. denied*, 401 U.S. 1010 (1971); Appeal of Kit-Mar Builders, Inc., 439 Pa. 466, 268 A.2d 765 (1970).
83. *See* Mary Cranston et al., *A Handbook for Controlling Local Growth* (Stanford, California: Stanford Environmental Law Society, September 1973), pp. 45—46.
84. Norman and Derr, *supra* note 72 at 13.
85. Robert H. Freilich and John W. Ragsdale, Jr., Timing and Sequential Controls—The Essential Basis for Effective Regional Planning: An Analysis of the New Directions for Land Use Control in the Minneapolis—St. Paul Metropolitan Region, 58 *Minn. L. Rev.* 1009, 1067 (1974).
86. Gustafson and Wallace, *supra* note 67 at 386. Indeed, the *Ramapo* court noted that one of the reasons it did not find the town's phased zoning ordinance

to constitute a taking was that owners of land ineligible for development received preferential tax treatment. Exclusive agricultural zoning is, however, more restrictive than the phased zoning scheme upheld in *Ramapo.*

87. Steel Hill Development Inc. v. Town of Sanbornton, 469 F.2d 956 (1st Cir. 1972).

88. 362 Mass. 221, 284 A.2d 891 (1972).

89. Just v. Marinette Co., 56 Wis.2d 7, 201 N.W.2d 761 (1972).

90. *See* MacGibbon v. Board of Appeals, 340 N.E.2d 487 (Mass. 1976).

91. *See, e.g.*, R.I. Gen. Laws §§2-1-18-24. The statute is discussed in J.M. Mills, Inc. v. Murphy, 6 Envir. L. Rep. 20455 (1976).

92. California specifically authorizes the creation of agricultural districts. California Land Conservation Act of 1969, Cal. Gov't Code §51230 (West Supp. 1976).

93. States and localities can choose among several methods of land acquisition and can acquire several kinds of interests in land.

Methods of Acquisition

Eminent Domain. The exercise of eminent domain, or the inherent power of sovereign governments to condemn, or to take, property for public use, is the most severe method of acquiring public land. Landowners of property condemned in accordance with the requirements set forth in condemnation laws and regulations must turn their property over to the government, but they are entitled to compensation for the fair market value of their condemned land. Thus one advantage of eminent domain as a land management tool is that once a government has carefully planned where acquisition of land or of partial interests in land is desirable, it can acquire the land it needs to fulfill the purposes of its plan without worrying about many of the legal uncertainties that would accompany regulation. In contrast, where there is no power to require sale of land, landowners may hold on to their land and exercise their right to develop it within the bounds permitted by applicable land use regulations, even though development may be carried out in an energy-inefficient location or manner or may otherwise be inappropriate.

Eminent domain is not, however, a land control tool to be used lightly. Aside from political opposition to landowners' involuntary forfeiture of their property rights, another factor limits the use of eminent domain: it is not clear whether condemnation of land on the urban fringe to prevent sprawl meets the "public use" test. (This legal issue and others pertaining to land acquisition through eminent domain are discussed more fully in the text in the legal issues section.)

Purchase. Purchase of land by bid, negotiation, or fixed price is another common means of acquiring land. The basic restriction on this method is that public funds must be expended for public purposes only. However, spending decisions are not likely to be overturned for failure to fulfill a "public purpose" since courts generally defer to legislative interpretations of that phrase. Land purchase is usually made easier when it is backed by the power of eminent domain, even though that power may not be used.

Land can be purchased outright or by installment. If installment buying is done from a revolving fund, the government can acquire interest in more parcels of property than if it ties up the entire sum at its disposal in full payment for one parcel. Because the transfer of title may be delayed under installment purchase until full payment is made, the extent to which government can control the use of the land in the interim is open to question.

Leasing.   Long term property leasing by the government may be useful if condemnation and purchase prove unsuccessful or infeasible. This method of acquisition can forestall undesired development for as long as the government holds the lease, but it also burdens the government with all maintenance expenses and ultimately requires the government to relinquish the property to the landowner. A better solution would be to negotiate a lease with a purchase option that could be exercised if property development remains undesirable when the lease expires.

Gifts and Bequests.   Though of limited value for promoting orderly growth, another backup land acquisition technique consists of the dedication of private land to the public. Several major problems prevent widespread reliance on gifts and bequests as a land management tool. First, the location of the dedicated land may be haphazard and may bear no relation to the land use plan for managing growth. Donated land may or may not fall within the area in which development is to be discouraged, and properties from several donors will most likely be widely scattered so that an effective greenbelt, or development-restricted area for containing urban development, cannot be formed. Second, donors may attach conditions to the dedication that could hinder the goals of the acquisition program. And finally, it is naive to think that sufficient land will be donated to achieve all the land use goals of a particular area. Nevertheless, dedication of land can effectively supplement an acquisition program.

Kinds of Interests Acquired

Fee Simple.   Numerous rights, including the right to develop, sell, donate, lease, and grant easements, are connected with ownership of land. Collectively, these rights, called fee simple ownership, give landowners fullest control over the use and disposition of their land. Because acquiring a fee simple interest means acquiring all the interests in a piece of property, such an interest is the most valuable and the most expensive form of land ownership.

Less than Fee Simple.   In many instances, obtaining full fee ownership of land is not necessary to carrying out an urban containment or other land use policy. For example, premature growth may be prevented and open space preserved if a government acquires and withholds from development only the right to develop the land. In addition, acquisition of less than a fee simple interest may also be less expensive than a full fee purchase, both because the base cost of a partial interest is less than the cost of the full interest in the land and because the original owner must still maintain the property and pay taxes on the land. (Lowering of property assessments to reflect the loss of development rights may be a necessary part of this technique.)

Several kinds of interests in land entail less control than do fee simple interests, but it is the partial interest known as development rights that is particularly important in urban containment programs. If a state or local government owns the right to develop urban fringe property, it can withhold that land from development and thereby help ensure that growth will not spread prematurely to distant areas, where it will probably consume prime agricultural, scenic, and environmentally unique land and add to transportation and possibly space heating and cooling energy costs as well.

94. As noted on p. 166, *infra*, many communities have advanced acquisition programs that they call land banking, but these programs are much narrower in scope and purpose than the general land banking discussed in this section.

95. 1976 N.J. Laws, ch. 50. *See* "New Jersey Sets up Project for Farmlands Preservation," in *Planning* (August 1976): 7.

96. James F. Wagenlander, The Urban Open Space Game, 6 *Urban Lawyer* 950, 959 (1974).

97. New Jersey Green Acres Land Acquisition Act of 1971, N.J. Stat. Ann. §13:8A–19 et seq. (West Supp. 1976); Mass. Gen. Laws Ann. ch. 184, §31 (West Supp. 1974); Cal. Open Space Easement Act of 1974, Cal. Gov't. Code §51070 et seq. (West Supp. 1976); and Pa. Stat. Ann. tit. 32 §5001 et seq. (Purdon Supp. 1976).

98. R. Lehr, "Boulder Acquires Land for Open Space Program," in *Planning* (February 1975): 5.

99. 32 Pa. Stat. tit. 32 §5005(7). (Purdon Supp. 1976).

100. *See* American Law Institute, *A Model Land Development Code*, Art. 6, "Land Banking" (Philadelphia, 1975) (hereinafter cited as *ALI Code*); and Harvey L. Fletcher, *Land Banking in the Control of Urban Development* (New York: Praeger Publishers, 1974), pp. 3–9.

101. Public Land Banking: A New Praxis for Urban Growth, 23 *Case Western Reserve L. Rev.* 897, 914 (1972).

102. *ALI Code, supra* note 100.

103. "Land Banking Can Ease Some Growing Pains," *Conservation Foundation Letter* (Washington, D.C.: The Conservation Foundation, December 1975), p. 3, *quoting* Sherry S. Kraus, Land Banking: New Solutions for Old Problems, 4 *Albany L. Rev.* 784 (1975).

104. Richard P. Fishman, "Public Land Banking: Examination of a Management Technique," in Scott, *supra* note 4 at vol. III, pp. 64–65. Critics of land banking have in fact suggested that its two principal objectives—controlling development patterns to discourage sprawl and reducing land prices through elimination of speculation—are incompatible. See, American Law Institute Endorses Land Banking, 5 *Envir. L. Rep.* 10152, 10154 (September 1975).

105. Fishman, *supra* note 104 at 67.

106. Sylvan Kamm, "The Realities of Large-Scale Public Land Banking," in Scott, *supra* note 4 at vol. III, p. 90.

107. *ALI Code, supra* note 100 at §6–201 and following Note, pp. 269–71.

108. *Id.* at §6–501; "American Law Institute Endorses Land Banking," *supra* note 104 at 101.

109. Kamm, *supra* note 106 at 89.

110. *ALI Code, supra* note 100 at §6–302(1).

111. *Id.*

112. *Id.* at §6–501(1) and following Note.

113. *Id.* at §6–203 and following Note.

114. *Id.*

115. E. Smith and D. Riggs, eds., *Land Use, Open Space, and Government Process—The San Francisco Bay Area Experience* (New York: Praeger Publishers, 1976), p. 110.

116. Gleeson et al., *supra* note 12 at 37.

117. *Id.*

118. Smith and Riggs, *supra* note 115.

119. Wagenlander, *supra* note 96 at 953.

120. 42 U.S.C. §5305(a)(1) (Supp. 1976).

121. Vt. Stat. Ann. tit. 32, §§10001 et seq. (Supp. 1976).

122. Kamm, *supra* note 106 at 88.

123. "American Law Institute Endorses Land Banking," *supra* note 104, *citing* S. Kamm, "Land Banking: Public Policy Alternatives and Dilemmas 16," Urban Institute Paper No. 112–28 (December 31, 1970).

124. See, *e.g.*, Berman v. Parker, 348 U.S. 26 (1954); *see generally* Fishman, *supra* note 104 at 68–73.

125. *ALI Code, supra* note 100 §6–101.

126. Fishman, *supra* note 104 at 69.

127. *See* discussion in Appendix I, pp. 214–216.

128. *See* Golden v. Planning Board of the Town of Ramapo, 30 N.Y.S.2d 359, 285 N.E.2d 291, 334 N.Y.S.2d 138, *appeal dismissed*, 409 U.S. 1003 (1972); Construction Industry Ass'n of Sonoma Co. v. City of Petaluma, 522 F.2d 897 (9th Cir. 1975) *cert. denied*, 424 U.S. 934 (1976).

129. *See* text accompanying note 97, *supra*. The open space statutes do not envision large-scale condemnation of land to prevent urban sprawl, but rather authorize smaller scale condemnation for related goals of preserving environmentally unique or scenic lands.

130. Commonwealth of Puerto Rico v. Rosso, 95 P.R.R. 488 (1967), *appeal dismissed*, 393 U.S. 14 (1968) (land acquisition by eminent domain was attacked in this case).

131. *ALI Code, supra* note 100 at §6–101.

132. *ALI Code, supra* note 100 at Art. 6.

133. *Id.* at Art. 5.

134. Margaret M. Bennett, "Transfer of Development Rights: Promising But Unproven New Approach to Land Use Regulation," (Philadelphia: Pennsylvania Environmental Council, Inc., February 1976).

135. The number of TDRs that farmers can sell and the number developers must buy to build at a higher density are carefully worked out in advance by the town to ensure that the number of available TDRs corresponds as much as possible to the development pressures the town should experience in the next few

years. This close correlation is important to ensure that farmers are neither over-paid nor underpaid for their development rights and that developers have an incentive to buy the TDRs. The crucial nature of this calculation is discussed more fully on pages 176—178, *infra*.

136. Buckingham Township, Pennsylvania, Zoning Ordinance, Article II, Section 216; Article III, Section 304; Article V, Section 502; Article VI (1975).

137. Chesterfield Township, New Jersey, Zoning Ordinance, Sections 329 and subsection 701E (December 11, 1975); Collier County, Florida, Zoning Ordinance, Section 9, "Special Regulations for (ST) Areas of Environmental Sensitivity," (1974); Montgomery County, Maryland, Ordinance No. 7—30 (1972); Southhampton Township, New York, Building Zone Ordinance No. 26, sections 2—10—20, 2—40—30 (1972).

138. New Jersey Assembly Bill No. 3192 (Senate Reprint, November 24, 1975); New York Assembly Bill No. 8928 (July 11, 1975); and Oregon Senate Bill No. 27 (1975).

139. *See* Buckingham Township Pennsylvania, Zoning Ordinance, Article II, Section 216; Article III, Section 304; Article V, Section 502; Article VI (1975).

140. The advantages of TDRs do not stop with the preservation of open space and prime agricultural land and the saving of energy by directing higher density development close to urban centers; TDRs have also become a popular and sometimes successful device for preserving historic buildings by transferring development potential to adjacent property. New York has had some success in using TDRs to preserve landmarks. *See* Bennett, *supra* note 134 at 64. Illinois has adopted enabling legislation authorizing use of TDRs to preserve historic landmarks. Ill. Historical Preservation Enabling Act, Ill. Rev. Stat. Ch. 24, §§ 11—48.2—1 et seq. (1971).

141. *See* Audrey Moore, "TDRs as the Solution to Failure of Existing Land Use Controls: Fairfax County, Virginia," in Frank S. Bangs and Conrad Bagney, eds., "Transferable Development Rights," Planning Advisory Service Report No. 304 (Chicago: American Society of Planning Officials, March 1975), p. 29; *see also* Bennett, *supra* note 134 at 74.

142. *See* discussion of plans of Southampton Township, New York, and Upper Makefield Township, Pennsylvania, in Bennett, *supra* note 134 at 72—73.

143. Bennett, *supra* note 134 at 41—44.

144. *Id.*

145. *See generally* Bangs and Bagney, *supra* note 141.

146. This discussion has examined some of the economic considerations involved in the development and implementation of TDR systems. Readers interested in a more detailed outline of the issues raised by TDRs should consult the Urban Land Institute's list of 146 questions raised by TDRs. Frank Schnidman, "Transfer of Development Rights: Questions and Bibliography," in *Urban Land* (January 1975): 10—15.

147. *See* Robert S. DeVoy, "The Puerto Rico Proposal: Preserving the Environment While Protecting Private Property Rights," in Bangs and Bagney, *supra* note 141 at 13; and John J. Costonis and Robert S. DeVoy, "The Puerto Rican Plan: Environmental Protection Through Development Rights Transfer,"

in Jerome G. Rose, ed., *Transfer of Development Rights* (New Brunswick, New Jersey: Center for Urban Policy Research, Rutgers University, 1975), p. 200.

148. Jerome G. Rose, "Psychological, Legal, and Administrative Problems of the Proposal to Use the Transfer of Development Rights as a Technique to Preserve Open Space," in Rose, *supra* note 147 at 296—97.

149. Fred F. French Investing Co. v. City of New York, 77 Misc. 2d 199, 352 N.Y.S.2d 762 (1973). The court was disturbed by the fact that there was no specific parcel of land to which the rights were being transferred. Hence landowners adjacent to the land where the transferred development rights ultimately would attach arguably had no voice in a rezoning that affected their property. A further argument could be made that TDRs do not satisfy requirements of eminent domain because the development rights are not condemned for public use. But, as is the case with urban renewal, a counter argument would be that if a public purpose is served by the condemnation (or, in this case, the prohibition of development), it makes no difference that private interests profit as well. *See* Berman v. Parker, 348 U.S. 26 (1954).

150. *See* Bennett, *supra* note 134 at 54—55.

151. United States Department of Commerce, A Standard Zoning Enabling Act §2 (rev. cd. 1926).

152. John J. Costonis, "The Chicago Plan: Incentive Zoning and the Preservation of Urban Landmarks," published in Rose, *Transfer of Development Rights*, *supra* note 147 at 311—16.

153. *See* pp. 107—116 for a discussion of planned unit developments.

154. Costonis, *supra* note 152 at 314, *citing* Chrinko v. South Brunswick Township Planning Board, 77 N.J. Super. 594, 187 A.2d 221 (L.Div. 1963), and Orinda Homeowners Committee v. Board of Supervisors, 11 Cal. App.3d 768, 90 Cal. Rptr. 88 (1970).

155. *Id.* at 316, *citing* James v. Valtierra, 402 U.S. 137 (1971), and Dandridge v. Williams, 397 U.S. 471 (1970), for the proposition that a law whose impact discriminates against the poor is not unconstitutional unless there is no rational basis for the classification.

156. *See*, *e.g.*, the Montgomery County, Maryland, Ordinance No. 7—30 (1972); Buckingham Township, Pennsylvania, Zoning Ordinance, Article II, Section 216; Article III, Section 304; Article V, Section 502; Article VI (1975); and discussion of Upper Makefield Township Ordinance in Bennett, *supra* note 134.

157. Bennett, *supra* note 134 at 52.

Chapter 6

Energy Impact Statements

The design and location strategies reviewed in Chapters 4 and 5 outline techniques for attacking specific barriers to energy efficiency. In contrast, energy impact statements provide a means for state and local governments to assess the overall energy impacts of a proposed project and to determine whether efforts have been made to reduce the energy demands that the project may generate.

Energy impact statements modeled on federal environmental impact legislation and its progeny in the states can provide state and local governments with information on which to base land management decisions. Their function would be similar to that of an environmental impact statement, which acts as an "alarm bell . . . to alert the public and its responsible officials to environmental changes before they have reached ecological points of no return" [1]. By focusing attention of developers and the public on the importance of energy conservation during the formative stage of projects—before developers are irrevocably committed to inefficient plans—energy impact statements can save money and conserve fuel. In addition, energy impact statements can provide an important educational service. They can increase awareness of the need to save energy and encourage training of energy conservation experts who can recommend more efficient approaches. Experience with environmental impact statements suggests that educational fallout is one of the most important aspects of this genre of legislation.

ENERGY IMPACT ASSESSMENT
IN THE STATES

The National Environmental Policy Act of 1969 (NEPA) has spawned an impressive number of state, county, and local progeny modeled after the federal statute [2]. Most state statutes require a consideration of "the environmental impact of the proposed project" and "any adverse environmental effects." The consumption of energy itself can be read into the statutes as constituting a reviewable environmental impact [3].

Of the twenty-five states that have adopted environmental impact legislation or regulations modeled on NEPA, nine explicitly require analysis of the energy demand generated by the project and of the sources of energy that will meet the demand [4]. New York and California have gone further, however, by requiring an analysis of measures to *conserve* energy resources [5]. Unfortunately, the New York measure has not been tested, since that state has temporarily suspended implementation of its environmental policy act.

California

California's approach to energy impact analysis is more advanced, yet could still be improved. It requires state and local governments to prepare, or to have prepared, an environmental impact report (EIR) on all projects they carry out or approve that may have a significant effect on the environment, including enactment and amendment of zoning ordinances, issuance of zoning variances, issuance of conditional use permits and approval of tentative subdivision maps by a public agency [6]. No EIR is required, however, if the project involves a "ministerial" rather than a "discretionary" act by the government [7]. Even with this exemption, it appears that all major energy-consuming projects would be required to examine their energy efficiency.

In California, an environmental impact report must contain "[m]itigation measures proposed to minimize the impact, including but not limited to, measures to reduce wasteful, inefficient, and unnecessary consumption of energy" [8]. Prior to their amendment, which was effective in January 1977, the guidelines gave several examples of land use/energy conservation measures that could mitigate adverse environmental impacts. One item concerned the orientation of structures to maximize natural heating and cooling sources, and others involved ways to reduce the energy consumed by transportation. Access to energy-efficient modes of transportation was covered: bus lines, mass transit, bicycle lanes, pedestrian facilities, and carpooling were mentioned specifically [9].

The new guidelines [10] are far less specific than the old ones with respect to land use measures that can reduce energy consumption. Indeed, they ignore many useful suggestions that were contained in proposed amendments to the old guidelines. One proposal, for example, specifically mentioned consideration of site conditions including the existence of cold-ponding areas, downslope winds, and extreme solar exposure in summer. Applicants would also have been required to discuss the following in relation to their proposed development:

1. the degree to which current energy conservation technology was used;
2. ways to encourage energy conservation by shifting to less energy-intensive transportation modes and fuels;
3. proximity to existing resources, including labor and material supplies;
4. measures to eliminate unnecessary grading during construction; and
5. the use of total energy systems and other technological innovations to reduce the energy needed for heating and cooling.

Now, however, these specific factors affecting energy-efficient land development must be read into more general phrases like:

Potential measures to reduce wasteful, inefficient and unnecessary consumption of energy during construction, operation, maintenance and/or removal.

*

The potential of siting, orientation, and design to minimize energy consumption.

*

Alternate fuels (particularly renewable ones) or energy systems [11].

The adopted language may provide state and local governments more flexibility in assessing the energy impacts of proposed projects. It is essential, however, that agencies responsible for applying these guidelines develop detailed standards so that developers are given an idea of what the agency deems important and so that the agency itself is prompted to give energy considerations the thorough attention they merit.

Florida

Energy impact statements required by the South Florida Regional Planning Council (SFRPC) demonstrate how energy conservation can be encouraged on a regional level. As noted in Chapter 3, under Florida's land use legislation, the Environmental Land and Water Management Act [12], developments of regional impact (DRIs) are subject to review by regional bodies, which may propose conditions for the granting of a development permit. One of the factors in determining what is a DRI is the extent to which the development would create an additional demand for energy [13].

The SFRPC has used its review authority to incorporate energy conservation policies as a major factor in the review and permitting process. A developer applying for a development permit must answer a broad range of questions, some designated as energy-related and many others not so designated, but equally important in assessing the energy efficiency of the development's land use.

Aside from questions specifically pertaining to energy sources and requirements, most questions asked by the SFRPC staff focus directly and indirectly on the development's transportation energy demands:

1. effect of the development on public transportation facilities;
2. ability of residents to find adequate housing reasonably accessible to their places of employment;
3. accessibility to neighborhood or community parks;
4. availability of community facilities and services such as telephones, schools, ambulances, and fire protection (an indication of the urbanization of an area);
5. trip generation rates anticipated by the development for both internal and external traffic; and
6. availability to residents of energy-efficient transportation systems (including transit, bicycle, and pedestrian systems).

Developers also must note whether the development incorporates a mixture of uses (i.e., residential, commercial, industrial or wholesale), and whether housing will be available for low and moderate income persons. Heating and cooling energy demands are covered by questions pertaining to the extent of landscaping and grading, and by the question, "What provisions have been made for solar energy and on-site generating facilities?" [14].

The energy impact assessment under DRIs has had some favorable results. In a case involving a large-scale development in Homestead, Florida, questions asked by the SFRPC prompted the developer to discuss possibilities for energy conservation through site design, lay-out and landscaping, building design and construction, use of solar energy and other alternative energy sources, as well as the provision of park-and-ride facilities, and bicycle and pedestrian paths. On the basis of the information provided by the developer, the council staff prepared an impact assessment report recommending that the development be approved, provided that, among other conditions, there was an overall 30 percent reduction in the electrical energy consumed per residential unit. It also recommended that prior to the approval of each major phase of development, the applicant submit to the city of Homestead a written statement of proposed energy conservation measures and of progress made toward the overall goal. These recommendations were formally adopted by the SFRPC and incorporated in the development order that was issued. Interestingly, although some provisions were included in the order to reduce transportation energy demand, such as requiring the applicant to provide land for a park-and-ride bus facility, transportation energy demand was largely ignored [15].

DRAFTING ENERGY
IMPACT LEGISLATION

A threshold problem in drafting energy impact legislation is determining when the required statement must be filed. In the analogous area of environmental impact legislation, California and the federal government require impact statements for actions that would have a significant impact on the environment. California, as noted, exempts ministerial actions from the EIR requirement. In remaining cases, an applicant submits information on which a preliminary review of the project is made to determine the necessity of an EIR. The environmental review staff looks at the existing environmental impacts of the project and at alternatives that would eliminate or minimize the impacts. On the basis of these studies, a determination is made of whether a project is a major action significantly affecting the environment. If the answer is negative, an environmental clearance, or declaration of negative impact, is issued and an environmental impact report is not required. A positive finding means that an environmental impact report and public hearings for review of the report are necessary [16].

The same approach can be used for determining whether an energy statement is required. Although it is clear that all projects will demand at least some energy, it would not be desirable to require the preparation of a detailed energy impact statement for every project.

In the case of small projects, simple requirements in the zoning ordinance—a requirement, for example, that all projects be oriented and landscaped for maximum energy efficiency—may be sufficient. But energy impact statements should be considered where there are large potential energy savings in the density, design, location, layout, orientation, or landscaping of a project.

One solution is to use a preliminary energy impact statement approach to determine whether a formal statement is necessary. Alternatively, one could simply set an arbitrary acreage limit and require any development covering more than that amount of ground to produce an energy impact statement. North Carolina, for instance, requires environmental impact statements for "major development projects" that are not less than two contiguous acres in size [17]. Of course, the two strategies can be combined, so that a preliminary statement would be required only when a project is above a certain size. A third approach is to require all public projects, all subdivisions and developments subject to subdivision or site plan review, and all requests for rezoning to undergo a formal energy impact review. This approach would guarantee that major projects would come under energy impact scrutiny.

In drafting energy impact statement guidelines, state, regional, and local governing bodies may model their reviews on the California and SFRPC guidelines pertaining to transportation, space heating and cooling, and construction energy impacts. The energy conservation goals reviewed in Chapter 2 suggest other areas that should be addressed if impact statements are to be truly comprehensive.

Jurisdictions that currently require environmental impact statements should incorporate energy impact review as part of the process. Those jurisdictions that do not have environmental impact requirements should either adopt "little NEPA" legislation containing an energy impact requirement or adopt separate energy impact legislation. The broader environmental impact approach is preferable, however, since it allows energy and closely linked ecological concerns to be addressed in the same procedure. A model local resolution requiring energy impact statements, primarily adapted from a Penfield, New York, resolution requiring environmental impact statements for new developments, appears in Appendix II, p. 319. The local resolution is followed by a model energy impact ordinance based on an ordinance approved for environmental impact statements in Holden Beach, North Carolina.

OTHER CONSIDERATIONS

Secondary Impacts

The development and analysis of an energy impact statement for a project would probably delay a project and would impose additional expense on the developer. Often preparation of analogous environmental impact statements has required developers and planning offices to hire consultants whose fees may exceed several thousand dollars. In addition, holding charges mount while environmental impact statements are being prepared. Both of these charges generally fall directly on the developer and ultimately on the consumer. Including the energy impact statement as part of environmental or site plan requirements should help reduce administrative delays and expenses. In addition, costs should wane as the impact process becomes more familiar. A recent study of California local governments shows that the cost of environmental impact statements has declined with their increased use. Delays have become shorter because developers are now familiar with the process, and therefore less likely to propose projects that ignore the environmental review requirements. Developers are also proposing more environmentally acceptable projects. In addition, as the environmental planning process and evaluation have become more standardized, and as skill and data bases for evaluating impact reports have grown, the time for preparation and analysis of EIRs has been reduced. In particular, the EIR administrators have become more sure of what factors they feel to be significant in individual projects, and have begun to collect and synthesize information from past projects that will be useful in evaluating new projects [18]. These trends should be repeated as energy impact statements become widely used. In fact, the information requested in the energy impact statement may often parallel, and be no more onerous than, that ordinarily requested by a planning board educated to the need for energy conservation.

Nevertheless, the costs incurred remain substantial during preparation and analysis of impact reports and those costs are passed on from developers to purchasers. Yet one study asserts that the additional costs to purchasers arising from EIR requirements may be a bargain. The same reasoning is applicable to energy impact statements. First, the cost is applied to the entire project, and therefore may result in only a small expense to the ultimate purchaser. Indeed, the owner of a house may amortize the cost with the mortgage. An increase in cost of $100 for the energy impact statement for a home with a $40,000 mortgage may only result in an actual increase of about $1 per month. This assumes a monthly mortgage payment of \$390 at 10 percent for 20 years [19]. Consequently, an energy impact statement would be a good buy even if it saves the home-owner only \$12 per year.

Nevertheless, efforts are needed to cut the red tape that plagues developers. Streamlined permit procedures now being advocated [20] may offer some relief, provided energy and other environmental considerations are not compromised during the review procedures.

Legal Issues

Legal Effect of Impact Statements. Energy impact statements, like environmental impact statements, would be informative only. Their usefulness is in forcing developers and planning boards to consider the impacts of a proposed project or subdivision or zoning change so that enlightened decisions can be made. Hence, the approval or denial of a permit or zoning change, or the construction of a state or municipal facility, would not usually be mandated by the findings in a statement. But the statement may influence decision-makers, just as the Homestead, Florida, development order requiring a 30 percent reduction in residential electrical energy consumption grew out of the impact report.

Some state courts have, however, taken a stronger position, at least with regard to environmental impact statements, and have implied that in some situations agencies must withhold approval when adverse impacts are forecast. In the landmark case of *Friends of Mammoth* v. *Mono County* [21], the California Supreme Court observed that "[o]bviously if the adverse consequences to the environment can be mitigated, or feasible alternatives are available, proposed activity, such as the issuance of a permit, should not be approved." Similarly, the Washington Supreme Court remarked in *Eastlake Community Council* v. *Roanoke Associates, Inc.*:

> Though a substantive result is not dictated [by the state environmental policy act] where adverse environmental impact is indicated, the approval of such a project may reveal an abuse of discretion by the public agency where mitigation or avoidance of damage was possible [22].

Due Process. Careful attention to the due process requirements of notice and hearing must be accorded applicants for development permits, but no unusual problems are raised by the energy impact analysis process. Analogous environmental cases point out the importance of carefully defining the kind of projects subject to energy impact review.

Enabling Authority. The authority to require energy impact statements on a state and local level clearly falls within the ambit of the police power. But it is not clear whether enabling legislation is necessary for localities to impose their own energy impact report requirements. Bowie, Maryland, and Penfield, New York, have adopted environmental impact statement requirements without state enabling legislation [23]. Nevertheless, to be on the safe side, states should adopt enabling legislation permitting or requiring local governments to impose energy impact requirements on projects funded by, or subject to, local approval. The following language may be used:

> The governing bodies of all cities, counties, and towns, acting individually, or collectively, [are hereby authorized to require] [shall require] preparation of an energy impact report for all projects that they carry out or approve that may have a significant energy impact. The report shall include a detailed statement setting forth the energy impact of the proposed project and mitigation measures proposed to minimize the impact.

Implementation

State. Adopting energy impact legislation is only a first step. States also must build technical expertise in energy conservation and planning to enable them to review state level projects and to provide technical assistance to localities. Localities will, of course, want to develop expertise of their own, and may require financial assistance from the state to do so.

Most commentators agree that the best impact statements are prepared by governmental staff members who draw on information gathered from the developers. Because a developer who has worked on a project since its inception may not be sufficiently objective to recognize or consider appropriate alternatives, it would be unwise to leave preparation of the statement to the developer.

It is also important at both the state and local levels that staff members confer with developers before they apply for development permits, so that extensive commitment to energy-inefficient plans can be avoided. At such conferences, the governmental officials and staff members can advise developers of what energy impact statements require, so that proper information can be gathered with the least possible waste of time and money.

Local. The same considerations applicable to implementation of energy impact reports at the state level are also applicable at the local level. The overriding consideration is to integrate energy impact statements in the planning review process, or an energy analysis will otherwise simply add to the "paper pollution" problem.

NOTES TO CHAPTER 6

1. County of Inyo v. Yorty, 32 Cal. App.3d 795, 810, 108 Cal. Rptr. 377, 388 (1973).

2. See Nicholas C. Yost, "State Legislation Patterned On NEPA—Overview," *The Environmental Impact Statement Process Under NEPA*, a conference co-sponsored by the Center for Administrative Justice of the American Bar Association and the Environmental Law Institute (Washington, D.C.: June 3–5, 1976), pp. 116–117.

3. State courts often apply federal NEPA case law in interpreting state acts. *See* Friends of Mammoth v. Board of Supervisors of Mono County, 8 Cal.3d 247, 260–61, 502 P.2d 1049, 1057–58, 104 Cal. Rptr. 761, 769–70 (1972); and Secretary of Environmental Affairs v. Massachusetts Port Authority, 323 N.E.2d 329, 339 (Mass. 1975). Hence it is noteworthy that the United States Court of Appeals for the District of Columbia circuit has ruled that a federal environmental impact statement on an application for a nuclear power plant was fatally defective for failing to examine energy conservation as an alternative to plant construction. Aeschliman v. United States Nuclear Regulatory Commission, _____ F.2d _____ (D.C. Cir. 1976). There are other indications that NEPA requires assessment of energy impact. In interpreting NEPA, the Council on Environmental Quality has recognized energy as an area of environmental impact. 38 Fed. Reg. 20550, 20558 (1973); 40 C.F.R. § 1500 (a) (4) (1976).

4. *See* Michael Gerrard, "Disclosure of Hidden Energy Demands: A New Challenge for NEPA," *Environmental Affairs* 4, no. 4 (1975): 665–66.

5. New York Environmental Conservation Law, Art. 8 § 8–0109 (2) (f) (McKinney Supp. 1976); Cal. Pub. Res. Code § 21100 (c) (West Supp. 1976).

6. Cal. Pub. Res. Code § 21080 (a), *as amended* by A.B. 2679 (effective Jan. 1977) (West Supp. 1976).

7. *Id.* at § 21080 (b) (1). In the absence of a local ordinance that states what is and is not a "ministerial" duty, the environmental impact report (EIR) guidelines, effective in January 1977, assume that issuance of building permits and business licenses and approval of final subdivision maps and individual utility service connections and disconnections are exempt from EIR requirements. 14 Cal. Admin. Code, Ch. 3, § 15073 (b) (effective Jan. 1, 1977).

8. Cal. Pub. Res. Code § 21100 (c) (West Supp. 1976).

9. 14 Cal. Admin. Code, Ch. 3, Appendix F (West Supp. 1975).

10. *Id.*, *as amended* effective Jan. 1, 1977.

11. *Id.* at § II.D.

12. Florida Environmental Land and Water Management Act of 1972, Fla. Stat. Ann. § 380 (West 1974 & Supp. 1977).

13. *Id.* at § 380.06 (2) (f), (8) (f) (West Supp. 1977).

14. South Florida Regional Planning Council, "Information Requested for an Application for Development Approval" (copy in the author's file at the Environmental Law Institute).

15. Homestead, Florida, Ordinance No. 75–11–70 (Dec. 11, 1975).

16. Robert W. Burchell and David Listokin, *The Environmental Impact Handbook* (Rutgers: Center for Urban Policy Research 1975), pp. 60–61.

17. North Carolina Environmental Policy Act of 1971, N.C. Gen. Stat. §113A 8 (1975).

18. Arthur W. Jokela, "Self-Regulation of Environmental Quality/Impact Analysis in California Local Government," Environmental Series Studies No. 6 (Claremont, California: Center for California Public Affairs, 1975), p. 67.

19. *See id.* at 67–68.

20. Fred P. Bosselman et al., *The Permit Explosion: Coordination of the Proliferation* (Washington, D.C.: The Urban Land Institute, 1976).

21. 8 Cal.3d 247, 263 n. 8, 502 P.2d 1049, 1059 n. 8, 104 Cal. Rptr. 761, 771, n. 8 (1972).

22. 82 Wash.2d 475, 497 n. 6, 513 P.2d 36, 49 n. 6 (1973).

23. See Nicholas C. Yost, NEPA Progeny: State Environmental Policy Acts, 3 *Envir. L. Rep.* 50090 at 50093 (1973), for a list of localities that have adopted environmental impact statements without relying on special state enabling legislation.

❋   *Part III*

Conclusion

Conclusion

As the introduction made clear, the purposes of this book have been to identify, insofar as possible, energy-efficient land use patterns that state and local governments should emulate and to set forth strategies that governments can select to achieve those patterns. Studies conducted by several research groups and described here have helped identify land use changes that can lead to greatest energy savings. For several reasons, however, this book has not set out a single detailed, energy-efficient land use model. One reason is that research is still being conducted to refine the broad conclusions established in earlier studies. Another is that the natural and manmade environment unique to each community makes only generalizations, not specific suggestions, useful. Even the roughly described development patterns advocated in this book must be modified to accommodate other land use constraints and policies.

This book has invited readers to "pick and choose" among the implementation strategies presented here, and reminded readers that coordinating selected approaches increases the effectiveness of those strategies. At the same time, it has urged readers to integrate those energy policies and techniques with social, political, economic, and environmental goals. But while this book has briefly noted some of the land use considerations that must be weighed along with the policies designed to reduce energy waste, it has made no attempt to reconcile the many, and often competing, interests that will affect ultimate decisions. Instead, it holds that only state and local governments can balance the different goals and arrive at an integrated land use policy that satisfies their unique requirements.

Some readers may be discouraged by recommendations for additional regulatory controls at a time when bureaucratic red tape has slowed and, in some cases, permanently paralyzed construction projects. Yet recent literature cited elsewhere in this book has offered some solutions to the perplexing problem of how to reduce the delay and expense associated with the development approvals process while ensuring that energy conservation, the environment, and other interests affected by land use decisions are not compromised. Coordinated permitting procedures, informal conferences to clear up questions about land use requirements, and time limits on agency decisions are some of the most frequently suggested approaches. Most techniques discussed here, such as energy efficiency standards and capital facilities programming, can easily be incorporated into the existing planning and regulatory process, thereby avoiding delays that a separate proceeding might cause. Even when some delay and higher costs are exacted in the short run in exchange for energy efficiency, insulation from another energy crisis and from long term energy price increases may be well worth the expense.

By focusing on methods to save energy in developing areas, this book has looked at only part of the energy conservation/land use question. Additional research is needed on ways to husband existing resources—our developed, urban areas—to save energy. Cities already offer essential energy conservation features: many are densely populated and many offer a mixture of land uses within easy access of residents. In addition, the necessary infrastructure and buildings are in place, and efficient public transportation systems either exist or can be provided much more easily than new lines can be extended to low density suburbs. Yet cities are losing, not gaining, population.

Programs aimed at revitalizing urban areas and luring middle and upper income people back to the cities figure centrally in an urban energy conservation program. The blueprints for this revitalization must include policies that encourage preservation of existing buildings, government assistance to private urban redevelopment projects, and a renewed commitment to reliable, inexpensive, and convenient public transportation systems. Many of the land use goals that developing areas have embraced are relevant to remaking the city into a model of energy efficiency. But, since cities already have established identities and patterns of development, as well as social and economic problems that may be difficult to alter, cities may find it harder to act in accord with those goals. Fortunately, the goal of energy-efficient land use neatly fits into ongoing and proposed programs to cure urban ills.

Whether government officials focus their attention on developed or developing areas, they must immediately take the lead in the attack on our energy problems. Savings will not occur at the private level until citizens see a determined public commitment to energy-efficient land use. Three effective ways to demonstrate an immediate commitment are engaging in symbolic acts, setting up educational programs for public officials and private individuals, and offering technical and financial assistance to local governments carrying out conservation strategies.

Well-publicized, symbolic energy savings can create a feeling of community comraderie and focus attention on the importance of energy savings; they may trigger private actions to conserve energy. During the oil embargo of 1973, for example, Governor Tom McCall of Oregon turned off display advertising lights—a gesture that resulted in some direct energy savings, but that probably had the greatest energy impact in reminding citizens of the fuel shortage and of the need to conserve energy. Similarly, everyone is familiar with President Carter's "sweater campaign." Governments promoting enlightened land use should also engage in symbolic acts; local governments contemplating construction of a public building could, for example, make the building a mixed use facility (i.e., a public office/civic building) and could locate it next to a major transportation line. The energy conservation choices that go into site selection and design of the building could be emphasized in public statements so that developers will learn how to build energy-efficient structures and so that consumers will know what energy-saving features to look for when purchasing homes or renting office space.

Though important, symbolic energy-saving action is only a first step. Governments must also demonstrate their commitment to energy conservation by providing educational programs; both public officials and private citizens need to be able to recognize inefficient habits and choices so that they can modify them. Educational programs should emphasize the costs of energy waste and tout the tangible benefits—in terms of financial savings, increased leisure time, and cleaner environments—that may flow from a decision to save energy. They should delineate the costs and benefits borne by the individual and those assumed by the locality or nation. Energy information offices, radio and television programs, printed materials, and workshops can all be used to disseminate conservation ideas.

In addition, states must make technical and financial assistance available to local governments so that they will have the ability to implement the energy conservation programs they select. Energy-conserving land use strategies are not as simple to understand or implement as a strategy to save fuel by buying smaller cars. Outside assistance may be necessary to develop a local staff with land use/ energy conservation expertise. Yet few local governments have un- committed funds to hire energy consultants or to add planning staff members to review development applications for energy efficiency. State funding, supplemented by money allocated through the federal energy conservation acts, is essential to ensure effective local action.

In short, state and local governments now have an opportunity to mitigate through land use policies the impact of the inevitable hardships that energy shortages and price increases will produce. Before those problems again reach the crisis proportions experienced nationwide during the oil embargo of 1973 and in many parts of the country during the winter of 1976–77, governments should seize this opportunity to lead, and not merely respond to, the appeals of their constituents.

Appendices

Common Legal Issues

State governments enjoy four powers on which energy conservation strategies discussed in this book depend: the powers to regulate, condemn, tax, and spend. Although federal as well as state constitutional and statutory guidelines limit the exercise of each power, the United States Supreme Court has, from the 1920s until recently, shied away from substantive involvement in land use decisions [1]. This self-imposed silence has been relieved in part by decisions of lower federal courts, but much of the land use case law has been formulated at the state, not federal, level [2]. Hence any state or local government adopting innovative land management programs to conserve energy must be as familiar with state land use case law as with federal.

While it is easy to note the importance of state land use law, it is not a simple matter to outline that law in a short book, particularly since the law differs from state to state. It is possible, however, to provide in the following pages an overview of land management powers available to state and local governments and an analysis of major constitutional issues that may be raised by use of those powers to achieve energy-efficient land use. Other constitutional and nonconstitutional questions stemming from use of land management techniques to save energy are examined in Part II of the book in the context of particular strategies [3].

REGULATION

The majority of land management policies are carried out through regulatory programs, even though use of taxing, spending, and land condemnation powers can have a tremendous impact on development patterns. The power to regulate stems from what is known in legal jargon as the "police power," or the inherent power of a sovereign government to act in its discretion to promote the public health, safety, morals, and general welfare [4]. These four concerns—and the concept of "general welfare" in particular—carve out rather enormous domains subject to police power regulation.

The United States Supreme Court has often emphasized the elastic scope of the police power and its capability to expand to meet the complex needs of a changing society [5]. This section first looks at whether energy conservation fits within that elastic scope as a legitimate objective that can be advanced through police power regulations. It then examines an additional requirement for regulatory schemes: use of reasonable means for achieving energy conservation. If a regulation is arbitrary and unreasonable in that it has no likelihood of achieving the stated goal or has an unduly harsh impact on a class of individuals or piece of property, it will be struck down. There are two primary areas in which energy-land use controls may be attacked as unreasonable and both are examined in the following paragraphs. The most frequent challenge will probably be that the regulation constitutes a "taking" of property without just compensation. The second major potential challenge may be on grounds that legislation to save energy through land management has an exclusionary impact. Neither argument appears to pose a significant threat to saving energy through land use regulations.

Energy Conservation As A Legitimate Objective

Unless courts accept energy conservation as a legitimate objective for police power regulation, regulatory strategies designed to save energy through changes in land use will be invalid. There is little reason to fear, however, that energy conservation will fail to pass the legitimate objective test. Just as societal concern over the fate of our environment brought environmental objectives under the police power umbrella, so the pervasive and nearly unanimous desire to "save" energy should also be accepted.

Energy conservation falls naturally within the mushrooming categories of general welfare goals on which changing values, resource scarcities, and broadened public concern have focused. Because of the economic importance of energy conservation and the threat to our lifestyle posed by shortages of energy, energy-conserving regulations may be even more readily recognized as legitimate objectives than presently accepted land use regulations to protect "family values, youth values, and the blessings of quiet seclusion and clean air . . ." [6]. Nevertheless, states and local legislatures that adopt energy-conserving policies and litigators charged with defending them would be wise to use a "Brandeis brief" approach—that is, to fill their legislation, plans, and briefs with data to support the need for energy conservation through land use policies—so that there will be no question about the rationality of the legislation if it should be challenged [7].

Although state legislatures cannot bootstrap energy conservation into a position of unassailable legality, the states' response to our energy shortage is some measure of public concern that energy waste be minimized through governmental action under the police power. The Energy Conservation Project has in the last two years monitored thousands of state energy conservation measures implicitly adopted pursuant to police power authority. New Mexico has been more explicit about its ability to mandate or encourage energy savings through police power regulation. In 1975, it enacted legislation declaring an intent to enact "energy resource conservation and control legislation under the police power of the state . . . " [8]. The outpouring of legislation designed to protect Americans from energy shortages leaves little doubt that conserving energy is a legitimate public objective under even the most strict construction of the general welfare clause of the police power.

Many energy-conserving land use measures should also withstand court scrutiny because they promote other land use objectives that have been blessed with judicial sanction. Innovative zoning ordinances already contain requirements for energy-efficient landscaping, pedestrian paths, and clustering. Strategies to save energy by withholding premature development from fringe areas is being accomplished to some extent through open space zoning, agricultural zoning, floodplain zoning, and other techniques that have been upheld under the police power [9]. The growing trend toward controlling community development patterns, an essential aid to energy-efficient land development, has received judicial sanction by New York's highest state court and by a federal court in California [10]. In sum, many economic, health, and environmental goals that courts have approved coincide with efforts to promote energy-efficient development patterns.

Energy conservation legislation whose primary objective is not to save energy but to achieve some other purpose not sanctioned by the police power will, however, be struck down. Regulation to serve private, not public interests, to restrict private property for governmental use without compensation, or to exclude an economic class from a community are prime examples of the way regulatory powers may be abused for the ostensible purpose of energy conservation [11]. These problems are discussed below in the context of "taking" and "exclusionary" land use patterns. Although in some instances legislation honestly designed to save energy may have undesirable secondary impacts, well thought out legislation will be drafted to minimize such implications or impacts and will be founded upon studies documenting at length the need for such legislation to achieve energy efficiency.

Taking

Whenever a government restricts the use of land without providing compensation to the landowner for the diminished use of the land, legal challenges to the regulation as a "taking" of private property are possible. The federal constitutional basis for a taking challenge to an ordinance is derived from the Fifth Amendment ("nor shall any person . . . be deprived of . . . property, without due process of law") and is applied to the states through the Fourteenth Amendment ("No state shall . . . deprive any person of . . . property, without due process of law"). State constitutions contain similarly worded provisions prohibiting uncompensated confiscation of property. Consequently, landowners who contest energy-efficient land regulation as a taking can do so on federal and state constitutional grounds.

Individuals challenging an ordinance that restricts land use can argue that the ordinance is generally arbitrary or unreasonable as applied to all property and thus is an illegal "taking" on its face; or they can assert that the regulation has an unreasonably harsh impact on a specific piece of property and is invalid insofar as it pertains to that specific property. Because of the presumption of validity accorded acts of legislatures in most states, it may be more difficult to show that land use regulations are generally unreasonable than to show that they are arbitrary and unreasonable as applied to individual parcels of land. Hence, a court reviewing a police power regulation may find that the regulation promotes a legitimate objective through use of reasonable means but still declare the regulation to be a taking when its impact on a specific piece of property is evaluated.

Regulation Never Constitutes Taking.   Perhaps no other issue has stirred as much controversy among land use experts as the question of whether and when a regulation equals a "taking." Such experts argue that the test most courts have developed to determine when a taking occurs—the balancing test which weighs the loss in property value caused by the regulation against the benefit of the regulation to the public—has no historical validity nor special justification and should be abandoned [12]. They suggest that just as government can strictly regulate commerce without providing compensation, it should also regulate land use without fear of a takings challenge and invalidation of the regulation, even though the regulation may result in denying use of the property for a profitable purpose. Compensation should be required only where the government physically invades or confiscates property; otherwise, the legislature should determine whether or not and how much it wants to compensate property owners whose land is subject to regulation [13]. A recent case in Wisconsin is heralded for refusal by the state court to invalidate land use controls on the basis of their adverse economic impact on landowners [14].

This approach, if adopted nationwide, would offer a tremendous boost to energy conservation as well as to other goals that land use regulations have been developed to promote. Mere regulation to conserve energy would never constitute a taking, because there would be no physical invasion of property. At the same time, legislators could vote to compensate property owners so that they would not shoulder a disproportionate burden arising from the public need to save energy. The concept, though not yet widespread, could be enhanced if state legislatures provided enabling legislation permitting localities to regulate land uses for the purpose of conserving energy and simultaneously provided a mechanism for compensating landowners who suffer economic losses as a result of the regulation.

The Balancing Test. Other experts disagree that regulation can never result in a taking [15]. They subscribe to the balancing theory, although they point out that many factors other than the balancing of private versus public interests can and do explain state court takings decisions. They nevertheless wish that courts would be more explicit in setting standards to be used while balancing interests.

Insofar as one can articulate the state of the takings law as it exists in most states, several general rules seem to apply. Courts have long held that development restrictions on land do not necessarily deprive that land of a reasonable use [16]. The majority of state courts agree that property owners are not guaranteed the highest and best (i.e., the most profitable) use of their land, but only a reasonable use. In reaching a determination of what is a reasonable use, those courts typically impose a balancing test, and generally place the burden on the landowner to show that the regulation is unreasonable [17]. Some of the factors state courts look to in determining injury to the landowner include:

Diminution in Value.   At some point the financial return on a piece of regulated property will be found so low as to constitute an "unreasonable" restriction. No formula exists to compute the allowable diminution in value, and studies show that a certain percentage diminution in value can result just as often in an invalidation as an upholding of a regulation [18]. This indicates that though an important factor, diminution in value will not be determinitive in any case except where *all* value is taken.

Permanence of Regulation.   Along with the right to a reasonable return on their property, it is generally accepted that landowners have a right to enjoy that return within a reasonable period of time. Consequently, permanent restrictions on land use may be more subject to a takings challenge than are temporary restrictions, at least where health or safety does not necessitate the burden on land use. Although courts appear more willing to accept temporary measures that promote the general welfare, the acceptable length of a "temporary" restriction is open to question. The New York Supreme Court has approved use of temporary controls that last up to eighteen years [19]. Again, however, the acceptable time limit for land use restrictions will vary from state to state and from case to case.

Adaptability of Land.   The issue of adaptability or the suitability of land for the permitted uses looks at the reasonableness of the permitted land use in light of the size, shape, topography, subsoil, and neighborhood surrounding the property. Many design strategies proposed in this book call for greater, not less, flexibility in the way land may be used and therefore should not be susceptible to lack of adaptability arguments. Strategies governing development location may be more vulnerable, however. For example, open space zoning permitting only agricultural uses in areas where development would be premature may be a taking because it is both arbitrary and unreasonable if the land is unsuited for raising crops.

After looking to the effects on the individual property owner, the courts turn to the interests sought to be protected by the state. Three primary areas are looked at by the court:

Immediacy of Harm.   If the effect of a regulation is to protect the public from an immediate threat of harm, then the courts are inclined to allow more substantial restrictions on land use. Although the energy shortage presents an immediate threat to the security of this country, the complacency of the public except in crisis situations makes it questionable whether courts will permit substantial land restrictions solely to save energy unless states provide statutory authorization for such action. Hopefully courts reviewing energy conservation legislation will recognize the grave problem that the energy shortage poses.

Magnitude of Harm.   The magnitude of threatened harm will also be a factor. The possibility of serious flooding or earthquakes may justify strict land use controls. It is impossible to predict how much the public will be willing to sacrifice before it considers the energy shortage a similarly serious crisis.

Nature of Interest.   Every person and, more importantly, every state has a different pecking order of the most important public interests to be protected. Community health and safety are very high on all lists. Other interests may include protecting the local economy, providing adequate public services and facilities, protecting the environment, and preserving scenic and historic sites. Depending on how each court ranks the various interests, more or less rigorous restriction of land uses will be tolerated before a taking is found. For example, some state courts have increasingly granted deference to regulations restricting ecologically sensitive land to its natural state [20]. This is definitely not to say that all regulations restricting land to its natural state will be found to be reasonable, but it does show a trend on the part of the courts to flex the already flexible standards of the police power to include broader land use goals. Because each balancing test is subjective, predictions are difficult. It seems, however, that energy-oriented regulation may be well-received in the balancing test. The threat and magnitude of an energy crisis, the universal effect, and the basic values and lifestyle that are at stake seem to point to great latitude in development of energy-efficient land use controls.

Inverse Condemnation.   One additional element of the taking issue should be noted. Some challenges to land use regulations have been grounded on the theory that the land has been the subject of "inverse condemnation" by the government. The theory is that the regulation or governmental activity has been so harsh that it actually results in appropriation of the land for public use. This form of government land appropriation is "inverse" because the property owners, rather than the government, must initiate proceedings to show that some portion of their property has been taken for public use without just compensation [21].

Actions in inverse condemnation may stem from actual physical damage to property caused by government activity, such as blasting or dam building on nearby land. That is the easy situation; compensation clearly will be awarded. The harder question arises when a landowner alleges inverse condemnation because government regulations result in nonphysical harm (usually diminution in value) to property. If the regulation were challenged as a taking of property, then landowners and the government are in an "all or nothing" situation. Either the regulation is declared illegal or, if it is upheld, the landowners must submit to regulation without compensation for its impact on their property. Inverse condemnation, by constrast, would permit the regulation to stand, but would compensate landowners for the hardship the regulation imposes.

There are very few cases supporting the proposition of allowing inverse condemnation challenges to government regulations [22] and two strong arguments against inverse condemnation. First, awarding inverse condemnation as a remedy to successful challengers of zoning or other police power regulations will have a chilling effect on the initiation of innovative control techniques by localities. If a city knows that it may be saddled with huge inverse condemnation awards if its new land use regulations are declared invalid, it will be very hesitant to try anything but the established techniques. Second, a locality will lose control over allocation of its financial resources [23]. With inverse condemnation awards available for invalid zoning acts, the locality's treasury will be subject to an indeterminate demand generated by judicial grants of inverse condemnation.

The opponents of compensation for zoning challenges draw support from an inverse condemnation case in California that held that compensation was not an available remedy where only loss of market value due to regulation is alleged [24]. In that case, although the loss involved an 80 percent reduction in market value, the court held that the challenger's only recourse was to try to have the regulation declared invalid as a taking. If the California approach becomes generally accepted, so that invalidation remains the only remedy for an unreasonable regulation, the chilling effect that inverse condemnation might have on adoption of innovative, energy-efficient land use techniques would be removed.

In summary, the "regulation does not equal a taking" approach offers the greatest promise for energy-efficient land use. But until that concept gains greater acceptance, the balancing test, whether implicitly or explicitly applied by state courts, will continue to dominate judicial review of land use regulations in those cases where regulation results in a significant private burden as well as a significant public benefit. Regardless of the judicial approach, however, legisla-tors should draft regulations as narrowly as possible so that energy goals may be achieved with the least imposition on private property rights. In addition, as discussed earlier, it is imperative that the need for energy-conserving legislation and the value of the particular legis-lation in enhancing energy savings be documented at length.

Exclusionary Regulation

Another volatile area of land use challenges now emerges from charges of the intentional or unintentional use of land regulations to exclude a particular class of persons (usually racial minorities and the poor) from living in a community [25]. Because poorly thought out energy conservation statutes may well have an exclusionary impact, planners, legislators, and legislative drafters should be familiar with developing case law on exclusionary challenges to land use programs. Equipped with this knowledge, state and local officials should be able to prepare legislation that will promote energy efficiency and at the same time avoid exclusionary impacts and the threat that the legislation will be invalidated because of its detrimental secondary effects.

Banning multifamily dwellings; requiring developers to pay "im-pact" fees to cover school, utility, and other costs of new growth; adopting subdivision regulations that mandate inclusion of expensive recreational amenities in developments; and imposing open space zoning that diminishes the amount of land available for development and drives up the cost of remaining land are some of the many tech-niques that can work to exclude the poor (and, by implication, racial minorities) from wealthy areas. Communities that have employed these tactics have defended them with a variety of rationales, some legitimate, others less so. Justifications for exclusionary land policies include a desire to protect the character of a community (and its property values); to check unrestrained growth that will overburden sewer systems, water supplies, and schools; to prevent construction of ugly, low cost housing; and to prevent congestion in streets and an increase in crime. How realistic these fears are varies from community to community. Some problems, such as sewer capacity, are measur-able; some, while difficult to measure, clearly exist; others can be avoided through expansion of existing facilities [26]; still others may be imaginary. Whether the problems a community associates with growth are real or fictitious, the fact is that more and more localities are closing their doors to newcomers through land use laws that exclude not simply the very poor, but middle income individuals as well.

As unrelated as these exclusionary policies and energy conservation may appear, many techniques used to keep people out of a community may also be used to promote orderly, energy-conserving growth. For example, large lot and open space zoning, if properly used, can reduce energy consumption by discouraging urban sprawl. Requiring a developer to include recreational facilities or to dedicate land within the development for recreation may increase costs to the developer and homeowner, and thus price the poor out of a community; but it may also encourage residents to relax near home rather than hop in a car to drive to a local tennis court or public park. Similarly, pedestrian and bike paths may cost money, but they can save fuel by keeping people out of automobiles.

This is not to say that growth management and energy conservation strategies are necessarily exclusionary [27]. Many techniques, such as promoting clustered, multiunit development, can reduce the cost of housing and thereby open up a community to individuals with a variety of incomes, provided the developer does not use the savings to build luxury units. Other techniques with potential exclusionary impacts can be implemented in a manner that avoids economic exclusion. For example, large lot zoning on the urban fringe to stop sprawl can be complemented with sufficient small lot zoning to house moderate and lower income individuals closer to the urban center. Nevertheless, in some instances techniques may price housing out of reach for all but the wealthy. In those instances, the government may have to assist private developers in providing low income, energy-efficient housing. In effect, the government would be subsidizing those who cannot afford the rising cost of energy.

Equal Protection Argument. The "equal protection" clause found in the Fourteenth Amendment to the United States Constitution requires all people to be treated equally under the law unless classification with different treatment for each class is necessary to achieve (or, in legal terminology, is "rationally related to") a permissible state objective. That federal constitutional requirement is imposed on both the federal and state governments. In addition, state constitutions also contain equal protection clauses whose interpretation is often based on interpretations of the federal provision. It seems logical to expect that challenges to exclusionary land use policies would focus on denial of equal protection to the poor and racial minorities who, in contrast to the wealthy, are prevented from finding housing in desirable communities. But for several reasons, equal protection has not provided the key to unlock exclusionary patterns.

One reason is that local land use policies and regulations rarely contain an explicit racially discriminatory purpose. If they did, under federal equal protection standards, the government would have to show a *compelling* reason for the discrimination, a difficult test to meet. When there is no explicit racially discriminatory purpose, litigants have argued that the policies have a discriminatory impact on minorities. This argument has resulted in decisions by federal courts of appeals that localities have no affirmative duty to provide housing for low and moderate income individuals [28], but that localities may not obstruct attempts to correct racially segregated housing patterns [29]. In several cases localities have been ordered to undertake affirmative remedial action to plan for minority housing in white neighborhoods where there was a consistent pattern of racial exclusion by the municipality [30]. But recent U.S. Supreme Court cases indicate it may be more difficult to show unconstitutional discrimination. They hold that a racially disproportionate impact of a land use regulation would be insufficient under the federal constitution to invalidate legislation; a racially discriminatory purpose must also be found [31].

Because race discrimination through exclusionary land use policies has been difficult to establish, a more promising equal protection argument would seem to be that wealth-related land use policies unreasonably discriminate against the poor, regardless of race. The problem with this approach is that wealth or poverty classifications in the land use area are generally not viewed by the federal courts as "suspect" and therefore are not subject to the "strict scrutiny" or "compelling interest" test applied to racial classifications [32]. Many land use experts argue that race and poverty go hand in hand and that to afford only one of the two the strictest equal protection review is illogical. That is, nonetheless, the situation today in the U.S. Supreme Court.

General Welfare Argument. The greatest success in attacking exclusionary land use policies has come in state courts where the challengers have argued that zoning or some other regulatory control is an unreasonable use of the police power because it prevents poor people from settling in the community.

Pennsylvania was one of the first states to invalidate land use techniques used to "prevent the entrance of newcomers" [33]. Two, three, and four acre minimum lot requirements have been struck down in that state, and another Pennsylvania decision found invalid an ordinance that effectively excluded multifamily dwellings from a town, allegedly for the purpose of avoiding the increased responsibility and financial burden of population growth [34]. The courts in these decisions implied in their holdings that these exclusionary goals were impermissible police power objectives because they failed to promote the regional general welfare. Indeed, in a later Pennsylvania case, the state supreme court explicitly adopted the regional general welfare test [35]. Of course, any opinion making multifamily housing more accessible to prevent exclusionary impacts can simultaneously, although perhaps unwittingly, promote energy conservation through higher density development, provided the development is properly located.

New Jersey courts have handed down some of the strongest anti-exclusionary case law in the country. New Jersey has not only found "wealth" to be a suspect category for purposes of state equal protection cases but has also interpreted the state police power to include an affirmative duty, based on the general welfare concept, to shoulder a portion of the burden of regional housing needs. These cases, of course, are binding only on New Jersey courts, but that state's decisions are part of a trend toward recognition of housing obligations on the part of municipalities to individuals of all income ranges.

In one New Jersey case challenging the validity of an ordinance prohibiting multifamily dwellings, the lower court grounded its invalidation of the ordinance on the individual's "right to be free from discrimination based on economic status" [36]. The court found the ordinance violated the equal protection clause and was inconsistent with the "general welfare" of the community. Later, in a landmark decision, *Southern Burlington County NAACP* v. *Township of Mount Laurel* [37], the New Jersey Supreme Court held as violative of the general welfare (and hence violative of the police power) an ordinance that in effect excluded the poor by prohibiting multifamily housing. The court went further than simply invalidating the ordinance; it also placed an affirmative duty on the township to provide an opportunity for its fair share of low and moderate income housing needed in the region [38].

New York's highest court has followed the example set by New Jersey. In *Berenson* v. *Town of New Castle* [39], the court set out tests to be applied in determining whether an ordinance excluding multifamily housing is permissible. Building on an increasingly strong concern that localities should be required to take into account the regional general welfare in developing land use controls, the *Berenson* court held that ordinances excluding multifamily housing are permissible only if the locality can show that (1) it is a "balanced, cohesive community"; and (2) the regional needs for multifamily housing have been or are being met.

In one important respect these cases challenging exclusionary practices assist energy conservation efforts. By focusing attention on regional rather than local general welfare, they may spur interjurisdictional cooperation not only in housing but possibly in other areas as well. This would certainly be a boost to energy conservation since, as noted in Chapter 3, many land use programs designed to save energy require rational land use, transportation, and utility coordination.

Energy-efficient, orderly, and inclusionary land development goals are not necessarily mutually exclusive. Although the importance of comprehensive planning is discussed at length in Chapter 3, it is worthwhile to note again that a comprehensive plan can be an immensely valuable tool to assist communities in achieving energy-efficient land use while avoiding exclusionary impacts. The plan can help show whether provisions for additional low and moderate cost housing is needed, and can assist in documenting the reasonableness of the policies designed to promote energy efficiency. Where affirmative action is needed to avoid an unconstitutional exclusionary impact, several steps can be taken. Communities can zone for multifamily housing and specifically provide for inclusion of low and moderate cost housing through density bonuses or mandatory quotas for such housing in large developments [40]. They can also subsidize low cost housing or, where environmental or health problems require allocation of available water and sewer facilities, localities can give priority to projects with housing for low income individuals. This practice is being followed in Montgomery County, Maryland [41]. In short, any community that achieves energy efficiency at the expense of low and moderate income individuals simply has failed to take advantage of land management techniques that can be used to achieve simultaneously a variety of land use goals.

Enabling Authority

A nonconstitutional issue, but one that can just as swiftly cause the demise of energy-efficient land use legislation, is the adoption of energy regulations by localities that have not been given authority by the state to adopt such legislation. The Tenth Amendment of the U.S. Constitution reserves to the states all powers not delegated to the federal government. The police power, unmentioned in the constitution, is therefore reserved to the states, which may transfer or "delegate" to localities through "home rule" or enabling provisions the authority to regulate land uses to save energy.

"Home rule" is the legal device developed to give cities broad discretionary power to act in areas of municipal concern. Presumably energy conservation is as much a matter of municipal concern as it is a legitimate objective under the general welfare provision of the police power. Hence, it is arguable that additional authority for achieving energy conservation through land use practices will not be needed by municipalities with home rule authority.

Localities without home rule powers must rely for regulatory authority on constitutional provisions or statutory grants of power called enabling legislation. Rather than being broad conferrals of power, enabling provisions delineate specific areas in which localities may act. States differ on how specific a grant of power must be in order to authorize an action [42].

The Energy Conservation Project has found no state that includes energy conservation as a purpose in traditional zoning and subdivision enabling provisions [43], but energy conservation may with little effort be read into some of the existing enabling acts. For example, a strong argument can be made that energy conservation falls within the "promotion of general welfare" clause found in the Standard State Zoning Enabling Act [44]. In addition, as noted in Chapter 4, many localities currently use new kinds of regulatory devices, such as planned unit development and clustering ordinances, that can save energy in addition to accomplishing other land use goals. If these new devices are authorized under enabling legislation that already exists in a state, there will be no need to adopt additional enabling legislation simply because we now recognize that these devices may be used to save energy. But other energy-saving techniques—transfer of development rights, for example—may require additional legislative authority before they can be employed at the local level. Consequently, states should provide enabling legislation for energy-efficient land use regulation in order to minimize legal challenges to local action. As a first step, states might consider adapting the following language to their particular requirements:

Zoning and subdivision ordinances may include reasonable regulations to promote energy-efficient location, density, and design of development. The regulations may apply to, among other things:

1. proximity of site to urban centers, transportation, and utility lines; employment, shopping, and cultural facilities; medical facilities, schools, and recreational areas;
2. layout of transportation systems, buildings, and utility lines;
3. lot and yard size;
4. orientation of buildings;
5. landscaping;
6. design, height, and uses of buildings;
7. income ranges accommodated by the development; and
8. construction standards.

Delegation of Power

A related issue, but one that raises constitutional questions, arises when the local legislative body enacts vague ordinances that in effect require nonlegislative bodies to make legislative decisions in order to implement the ordinances. Courts may invalidate such vaguely written legislation. Consequently, as emphasized in the section on energy efficiency standards in Chapter 4, energy conservation ordinances should be written with explicit performance standards in order to avoid this legal pitfall.

EMINENT DOMAIN

Eminent domain, the inherent power of government to appropriate private property for public use, is another power that states and localities may be able to use to stimulate conservation. The U.S. Constitution, and every state constitution except North Carolina's, contain "eminent domain" clauses that explicitly prohibit appropriation of property without just compensation [45]. From this phrase spring the two primary issues raised in legal challenges to eminent domain: Has the property been taken for a proper "public use"; and, Was "just compensation" paid for the taking of the property?

The definition of "public use" has been drawn very broadly by federal and state courts in deference to the legislatures' determination that a particular purpose is a proper one for the exercise of eminent domain. Traditionally, eminent domain has been used to acquire land on which to build public facilities. It has also been used to aid public housing development and urban renewal. Eminent domain is now viewed as a potential tool for shaping land use through condemnation programs that prevent development in valuable scenic or environmentally sensitive areas. It remains to be seen whether the "public use" concept will be extended to large-scale land acquisition programs designed specifically to promote energy-efficient growth by stopping premature, noncontiguous development. Unless large-scale land acquisition programs backed up by the power of eminent domain are approved, eminent domain would appear to have little value as an energy conservation tool. One exception may be in situations where small parcels of land are condemned to provide public facilities. In those instances, governments must be careful that the condemned land is conveniently located so that the traffic-generating facilities are accessible to the public by walking, bicycling, or energy-efficient public transportation.

If land acquisition by eminent domain meets the "public use" test, the second major issue will be whether "just compensation" has been paid for the land. The fact that land is condemned to save energy will not influence determinations of what constitutes "just compensation." As a rule, the fair market value of the land at its highest and best use is the measure of compensation. These vague phrases leave a great deal of room for controversy and often result in court battles to determine the value of the condemned property.

TAXING POWER

The third power that states can use to promote energy-efficient land development is the power to tax. An inherent state power, the power to tax, like the police power and the power of eminent domain, can be exercised by local governments only when localities have been delegated that authority by the state.

The power to tax entails not only the right to raise money, but also the authority to influence policy, including land use policy, depending on how and where the tax is applied. Some taxes may unintentionally affect land use practices. Long debates have raged, for example, over whether property taxation contributes to urban sprawl [46]. Other taxes are specifically designed to influence land use. A prime example is preferential agricultural land taxation, now used in forty-two states for the purpose of preventing urban development from consuming prime farmland. Several recent studies have determined, however, that preferential agricultural taxing policy by itself has failed to achieve its goal [47]. Nevertheless, the principle behind preferential taxation is a good one: by imposing additional taxes on undesirable (energy-inefficient) land practices, or by giving "tax breaks" through credits, deductions, preferential assessments, and other tax incentives to desirable (energy-efficient) land practices, taxation can become a useful instrument for influencing land development patterns. The caveat illustrated by the property tax and preferential tax examples is that using taxes to influence policy requires great skill, for sometimes unexpected side effects occur, while at other times the intended result is never achieved. Frequently taxes must be combined with regulatory and spending programs in order to achieve the desired goal.

Another book in the ELI Energy Conservation Project series is devoted to use of the taxing power to influence energy policy choices [48], and readers are referred to that book for a fuller discussion of legal ramifications involved in using the taxing power to save energy. What follows is a much briefer look at a few federal and state constitutional issues that taxing strategies noted in the text of this book may raise.

Taxation as a Means of Regulation

The first issue, whether state taxes may be used for regulatory purposes, has been clearly answered by the United States Supreme Court. In *Magnano Co.* v. *Hamilton* [49], the U.S. Supreme Court upheld a Washington state tax of 15 cents a pound on butter substitutes even though the obvious purpose of the tax was to discourage the use of margarine. It observed that a tax within the lawful power of a state should not "be judicially stricken down ... simply because its enforcement may or will result in restricting or even destroying particular occupations or businesses" [50]. It is likely that the U.S. Supreme Court would give a similar stamp of approval to land regulatory taxes designed to save energy, provided they meet other constitutional criteria.

Recently, the Vermont Supreme Court addressed the issue of using state taxes for regulatory purposes in the context of a challenge to an innovative state land gains tax [51]. Ostensibly adopted to raise revenue for a property tax relief program, the tax without question was largely intended to deter land speculation and slow up second home development that was destroying Vermont's environment. The Vermont Supreme Court upheld the tax and noted that the legislature could properly intend the tax to serve dual purposes of raising revenue for the property tax relief program and deterring land speculation. The Vermont case, along with the U.S. Supreme Court's approval of regulation through taxation, suggests that tax policies may be used to provide an incentive for energy conservation by making individuals pay directly for energy they consume.

Uniformity

The uniformity requirement poses the greatest barrier to use of tax incentives to encourage energy-efficient land use and tax disincentives to discourage land practices that waste energy. All state taxation measures are subject to the federal equal protection provision prohibiting discrimination. The U.S. Supreme Court has, however, permitted classification of property for taxation purposes so long as property within the same class is uniformly taxed and the classification system bears a rational relationship to a legitimate state purpose [52]. Where the tax scheme affects a "fundamental interest," such as freedom of speech or worship, or is applied differently to a racial minority ("suspect class"), the tax classification system will be upheld only if the state can show a compelling interest in the classification. There is no reason for any energy-conserving land use tax measure to affect a fundamental interest or apply unequally to a "suspect" class. Because legislative acts are accorded a presumption of validity, rarely will the U.S. Supreme Court overturn a state tax policy on the ground that the tax classification is not rationally related to a legitimate goal.

Added to the federal equal protection requirement, however, are uniformity provisions found in state constitutions. Although the language and interpretation of the uniformity provisions vary from state to state, uniformity clauses are often interpreted as prohibiting or severely limiting property classification for tax purposes [53]. The precise wording of the clause is crucial in interpretation. Issues in dispute may include (1) taxes subject to the uniformity clause; (2) permissible classifications, if any; (3) permissible exemptions; (4) effect of uniformity requirements on property assessments; and (5) limitations on use of revenue raised by the taxes. Generally the state uniformity clause applies only to property taxes. In some states, constitutional amendments are needed to authorize property classification [54], but in others, judicial interpretation of the constitutional language may permit classification [55].

Classification is crucial to implementing energy-saving property tax strategies. For example, property tax incentives for people who rehabilitate inner city homes may encourage individuals to give up suburban life for housing located close to jobs, shopping, and entertainment attractions. Although preferential agricultural land assessment by itself has not been successful, preferential assessment combined with restrictive zoning and stiff rollback penalties on profit when land is sold may help retard energy-expensive sprawl. In sum, each state and local government should look for opportunities to complement its land regulatory programs with tax strategies that can heighten the effectiveness of those programs. But care must be taken to ensure compliance with uniformity requirements of the state constitution.

SPENDING POWER

The final major power that state and local governments can exercise to conserve energy is the spending power. Perhaps the most politically acceptable means for promoting energy-efficient land use, spending, unlike regulation, condemnation, or taxation, neither infringes on individual property rights, forces landowners to give up property against their will, nor necessarily subjects individuals to higher taxes than they would ordinarily pay. Using the spending power to save energy in the context of land use may simply require evaluation of ongoing public facilities programs so that expenditures promote energy efficiency, not waste. For example, states and localities can refuse to extend sewers or roads into undeveloped areas, thus discouraging premature spillover of urban growth [56]. At the other extreme, spending may require raising large sums of money to permit large-scale land acquisition that can shape growth in energy-efficient patterns [57]. In addition to influencing land development patterns simply by spending or withholding money from public programs, government can also affect land use by imposing conditions or restrictions on the way money awarded by states to localities or government contractors may be spent [58]. Oregon, for example, has given localities money to develop comprehensive land use plans, but as a condition to use of that money, the localities must take energy conservation into account in developing the plans [59].

Public Purpose Requirement

State governments must spend public money for public purposes. The same rule applies to local governments, whose spending programs may also be subject to state-imposed spending limitations. Although the main issue surrounding spending programs seems to be what comprises a public purpose, that is a matter over which legislators have broad discretion. Courts have, however, established that while an expenditure need not benefit everyone in a community in order to serve a public purpose, it must be reasonably related to the operation of the government and must serve a public, not private interest. It appears unquestionable that energy conservation can fit easily into the scope of acts undertaken for a public purpose.

Other Limitations

There are several other constitutional and nonconstitutional limitations on the spending power with which legislators should be familiar. As with any other governmental activity, public spending may not violate constitutional guarantees such as the right of equal protection. In addition, when local governments act in a proprietary capacity, they may not make contracts that bind their successors in office. A "proprietary" function is one undertaken outside normal governmental obligations and often is one committed to benefit the private sector or generate profit. Providing sewer services has been found to be a proprietary function [60].

One other important legal limitation on the spending power concerns debt limiations. Several state constitutions provide that the legislature may not create any debt or liability except for specified purposes and amounts. Other state constitutions declare a state may not incur a debt except for ordinary business or upon a vote of the people. The legislature may be prohibited from authorizing a debt unless provision is made for concurrent tax revenue to discharge the debt within a designated number of years [61].

States and localities sometimes successfully circumvent these debt ceilings. Legislatures have bypassed referendum approval of debt by the issuance of special revenue bonds. Cities have obtained special statutory exemptions, tied revenue bonds to construction of facilities that generate service fees to discharge the debt, and undertaken long term lease-purchase agreements rather than outright purchases [62]. In spite of these methods to inject flexibility into seemingly inflexible laws, an examination of potential limitations on energy expenditures remains a prerequisite before spending programs designed to save energy should be recommended.

NOTES TO APPENDIX I

1. The U.S. Supreme Court has, however, recently reviewed several land use cases. In Village of Belle Terre v. Boraas, 416 U.S. 1 (1974), the Court held that a local zoning ordinance could prohibit unrelated individuals from living together in a single family residential district. In Warth v. Seldin, 422 U.S. 490 (1975), the court focused on procedural issues rather than the substance of the land use policy itself and denied standing to developers and members of minority classes to challenge allegedly exclusionary zoning practices in a New Jersey community. In City of Eastlake v. Forest City Enterprises, Inc., 96 S.Ct. 2358 (1976), the court upheld a requirement of a mandatory referendum to veto or reaffirm zoning decisions of a city council in Eastlake, Ohio. And in Village of Arlington Heights v. Metropolitan Housing Development Corp., (January 11, 1977, No. 75–616), it found that the Village's refusal to rezone for low and moderate income housing was not racially motivated and thus did not violate the equal protection clause of the U.S. Constitution.

2. Of course, the U.S. Congress has actively influenced land use policies through enactment of air, water, and noise legislation.

3. For a fuller review of legal issues raised by implementation of land use programs, see Michael E. Gleeson et al., "Urban Growth Management Systems: Evaluation of Policy-Related Research", Planning Advisory Service Reports nos. 309, 310 (Chicago: American Society of Planning Officials, 1975); and David R. Godschalk et al., Constitutional Issues of Growth Management (Chicago: American Society of Planning Officials, 1977).

4. Thurlow v. Massachusetts, 46 U.S. 504, 582 (1847).

5. See Village of Euclid v. Ambler Realty Co., 272 U.S. 365, 386 (1926).

6. Village of Belle Terre v. Boraas, 416 U.S. 1, 9 (1974).

7. Before his appointment to the U.S. Supreme Court, Justice Louis D. Brandeis earned a reputation for his legal briefs that offered a barrage of social statistics and expert opinions supporting the rationality of federal legislation that was being challenged by opposing counsel.

8. New Mexico Energy Resources Act of 1975, N.M. Stat. Ann. §65–13–2 (Supp. 1975).

9. *See, e.g.*, Just v. Marinette County, 56 Wis.2d 7, 201 N.W.2d 761 (1972); Associated Home Builders v. City of Walnut Creek, 4 Cal.3d 633, 484 P.2d 606, 94 Cal. Rptr. 630 (1971); Aunt Hack Ridge Estates, Inc. v. Planning Commission, 160 Conn. 109, 273 A.2d 880 (1970). *But see* Baker v. Planning Board of Framingham, 353 Mass. 141, 228 N.E.2d 831 (1967).

10. *See* Golden v. Planning Board of the Town of Ramapo, 30 N.Y.2d 359, 285 N.E.2d 291, *appeal dismissed*, 409 U.S. 1003 (1972); and Construction Industry Ass'n of Sonoma County v. City of Petaluma, 522 F.2d 897 (9th Cir. 1975), *cert. denied*, 424 U.S. 934 (1976).

11. *See, e.g.*, Vernon Park Realty, Inc. v. City of Mount Vernon, 307 N.Y. 493, 121 N.E.2d 517 (1954); and Southern Burlington County NAACP v. Township of Mt. Laurel, 67 N.J. 151, 336 A.2d 713, *appeal dismissed*, 423 U.S. 808 (1975).

12. Fred P. Bosselman et al., *The Taking Issue*, prepared for the U.S. Council on Environmental Quality (Washington, D.C.: U.S. Government Printing Office, 1973); and Edward J. Sullivan, The Taking Issue, 5 *Environmental Law* 515 (1975).

13. Sullivan, *supra* note 12. Professor Donald G. Hagman is preparing a study for the U.S. Department of Housing and Urban Development on compensatory techniques that can help avoid the "windfalls and wipeouts" that landowners experience as a result of government regulation.

14. Just v. Marinette County, 56 Wis.2d 7, 201 N.W.2d 761 (1972).

15. One land use expert who holds this point of view is Professor Norman Williams, Jr. *See* Williams, *American Land Planning Law*, vol. 5, §162.06 (Chicago: Callaghan & Co., 1975), pp. 438–39, note 6.

16. *See* Euclid v. Ambler Realty, 272 U.S. 365 (1926); Hadacheck v. Sebastian, 239 U.S. 394 (1915); HFH, Ltd. v. Superior Ct. of Los Angeles Co., 15 Cal.3d 508, 542 P.2d 237, 125 Cal. Rptr. 365 (1975), *cert. denied*, 96 S.Ct. 1495 (1976); and Just v. Marinette Co., 56 Wis.2d 7, 201 N.W.2d 761 (1972).

17. *See* Williams, *supra* note 15 at vol. 5, §162.06, p. 438, for a list of states that do not follow the majority rule. Illinois is the chief example of a state that puts the legal burden on the public agency to show the public benefits from regulation of private property rights.

18. Robert M. Anderson, *American Law of Zoning*, vol. 1, §2.23, (Rochester, New York: Lawyer's Co-operative Publishing Co., 1968), p. 102.

19. Golden v. Planning Board of the Town of Ramapo, 30 N.Y.2d 359, 285 N.E.2d 291, *appeal dismissed*, 409 U.S. 1003 (1972). There were some exceptions to the contiguous growth goal since some kinds of development were exempt from the adequate public facilities requirements. *See* discussion, pp. 148–149, *supra*.

20. Just v. Marinette County, 56 Wisc.2d 7, 201 N.W.2d 761 (1972); Turner v. County of Del Norte, 24 Cal. App.3d 311, 101 Cal. Rptr. 93 (1972); *See generally* Gleeson, *supra* note 3 at 66.

21. *See* Gleeson, *supra* note 3 at 74, for a fuller discussion of inverse condemnation.

22. *See, e.g.*, Bydlon v. United States, 175 F.Supp. 891 (Ct. Cl. 1959) (*per curiam*).

23. J. Fulham and F. Scharf, Inverse Condemnation, 26 *Stan. L. Rev.* 1439, 1450 (June 1974).

24. HFH, Ltd. v. City of Cerritos, 15 Cal.3d 508, 542 P.2d 237, 125 Cal. Rptr. 365 (1975), *cert. denied*, 96 S.Ct. 1495 (1976).

25. *See* Randall W. Scott, ed., *Managment and Control of Growth*, vol. I, chs. 6, 7, *passim* (Washington, D.C.: The Urban Land Institute, 1975); and Herbert M. Franklin et al., *In-Zoning, A Guide For Policy-Makers on Inclusionary Land Use Programs* (Washington, D.C.: The Potomac Institute, 1974).

26. *See* Kennedy Park Homes Ass'n v. City of Lackawanna, 436 F.2d 108 (2d Cir. 1970), *cert. denied*, 401 U.S. 1010 (1971).

27. Nor is it intended to imply that only communities interested in promoting orderly growth will face exclusionary problems. Indeed, most wealth- and race-related exclusionary policies have been imposed in developing communities without growth management programs.

28. *See* Mahaley v. Cuyahoga Metropolitan Housing Authority, 500 F.2d 1087 (6th Cir. 1974); Ybarra v. City of Town of Los Altos Hills, 503 F.2d 250 (9th Cir. 1974).

29. *See* U.S. v. City of Black Jack, 508 F.2d 1179 (8th Cir. 1974), *cert. denied*, 422 U.S. 1042 (1975); Kennedy Park Homes Ass'n v. City of Lackawanna, 436 F.2d 108 (2d Cir. 1970), *cert. denied*, 401 U.S. 1010 (1971).

30. Southern Alameda Spanish Speaking Organization v. City of Union City, 424 F.2d 291 (9th Cir. 1970); United Farmworkers of Florida Housing Project, Inc. v. City of Delray Beach, 493 F.2d 799 (5th Cir. 1974); and Kennedy Park Homes Ass'n v. City of Lackawanna, 436 F.2d 108 (2d Cir. 1970), *cert. denied*, 401 U.S. 1010 (1971).

31. Village of Arlington Heights v. Metropolitan Housing Development Corp., _____ U.S. _____ (1977) (refusal to rezone for low and moderate cost housing); Washington v. Davis, 96 S.Ct. 2040 (1976).

32. In San Antonio School District v. Rodriguez, 411 U.S. 1, 20 (1973), the U.S. Supreme Court limited poverty as a suspect classification to situations in which poverty results in both an inability to pay for a desired benefit and an "absolute deprivation of a meaningful opportunity to enjoy that benefit."

33. Natl. Land and Investment Co. v. Easttown Township Board of Adjustment, 419 Pa. 504, 215 A.2d 597 (1965).

34. *Id. See also* In re Appeal of Kit-Mar Builders, Inc. 439 Pa. 466, 268 A.2d 765 (1970); and In re Appeal of Girsh, 437 Pa. 237, 263 A.2d 395 (1970). Note, however, that in a more recent case, a Pennsylvania lower court held that three acre zoning was not unreasonable per se. DeCaro v. Washington Township, 21 Pa. Cmwlth. 252, 344 A.2d 725 (1975).

35. Township of Williston v. Chesterdale Farms, 462 Pa. 445, 341 A.2d 466 (1975).

36. Molino v. Borough of Glassboro, 116 N.J. Super. 195, 204, 281 A.2d 401, 405 (1971).

37. Southern Burlington County NAACP v. Township of Mt. Laurel, 67 N.J. 151, 336 A.2d 713, *appeal dismissed*, 423 U.S. 808 (1975).

38. Another New Jersey decision, still on appeal at the time this book was written, found that the general welfare standard of the police power imposes a duty on a township to anticipate regional housing needs in its zoning practice. Oakwood at Madison, Inc. v. Township of Madison, 117 N.J. Super. 11, 283 A.2d 353 (L. Div. 1971), *on remand*, 128 N.J. Super. 438, 320 A.2d 223 (L. Div. 1974).

39. 38 N.Y.2d 102, 341 N.E.2d 236, 378 N.Y.S.2d 672 (1975).

40. See pp. 116–122, *supra.*

41. Montgomery Co., Md., Code, ch. 25A (Michie Supp. 1975); "Administrative Guidelines to the Moderately Priced Housing Law, Montgomery County, Maryland" (Montgomery County Government, Department of Community and Economic Development, Office of Housing, September 1975), pp. 9–10.

42. *See* Scott, *supra* note 25, "Introduction and Summary," p. 18.

43. As noted elsewhere, however, Vermont's state land use law makes energy conservation a condition for approval of certain development permits (Vermont Land Use and Development Law, Vt. Stat. Ann. tit. 10, § 6086 (a) (9) (F) (Supp. 1975)); and Oregon requires local zoning and subdivision ordinances to conform to the statewide goal of energy conservation (Or. Rev. Stat. § 197.175 (1975–76)).

44. U.S. Department of Commerce, The Standard State Zoning Enabling Act, § 3 (rev. ed. 1926).

45. U.S. Const. amend. V.; Philip Nichols, *The Law of Eminent Domain*, rev. 3d ed. § 1.3 (New York: Matthew Bender, 1976), pp. 1–79.

46. *See* Barry A. Currier, Exploring the Role of Taxation in the Land Use Planning Process, 51 *Indiana L. J.* 27 (1975); and Norman Williams, Jr., The Three Systems of Land Use Control, 25 *Rut. L. Rev.* 80 (1970).

47. *See* Regional Science Research Institute, *Untaxing Open Space/An Evaluation of the Effectiveness of Differential Assessment of Farms and Open Space*, prepared for the U.S. Council on Environmental Quality (Washington, D.C.: U.S. Government Printing Office, April 1976); and Gregory C. Gustafson and L.T. Wallace, "Differential Assessment as Land Use Policy: The California Case," *Journal of the American Institute of Planners* 41, no. 6 (November 1975): 379.

48. E. Grant Garrison and Joe W. Russell, *Tax Strategies: Alternatives to Regulation* (Cambridge, Massachusetts: Ballinger Publishing Co., 1977).

49. 292 U.S. 40 (1934).

50. *Id.* at 44–45.

51. Andrews v. Lathrop, 132 Vt. 256, 315 A.2d 860 (1974).

52. Gleeson, *supra* note 3 at 77, citing Nashville, Chattanooga & St. Louis Ry. v. Browning, 310 U.S. 362 (1940); Michigan Cent. R.R. v. Powers, 201 U.S. 245 (1945); and San Antonio School District v. Rodriguez, 411 U.S. 1, 40 (1972).

53. *See* Jerome R. Hellerstein, *State and Local Taxation: Cases and Materials*, 3d ed. (St. Paul, Minnesota: West 1969).

54. *See, e.g.*, Switz v. Kingsley, 37 N.J. 566, 182 A.2d 841 (1962), which held that the New Jersey constitutional uniformity requirement forbade preferential assessment of real property. A constitutional amendment was necessary to permit nonuniform taxation. N.J. Const. art. VIII, §1.

55. This is the case in South Carolina. *See* Holzwasser v. Brady, 205 S.E. 2d 701 (S.C. 1974).

56. *See* pp. 135–138, supra.

57. *See* pp. 164–172, supra.

58. *See* Ivan J. Tether, *Government Procurement and Operations* (Cambridge, Massachusetts: Ballinger Publishing Company, 1977), for a more complete discussion of the ways governments can use their spending power to promote energy conservation.

59. Or. Rev. Stat. §197.175 (2) (b) (1975–1976); Oregon Land Conservation and Development Commission, State-Wide Planning Goals and Guidelines, adopted December 27, 1974, Goal Number 13.

60. *See* Robinson v. City of Boulder, 547 P.2d 228 (Colo. 1976) *(en banc)*.

61. *See* 72 Am. Jur. 2d *States, Territories and Dependencies* §7.8 (1974); 1⁘ McQuillin, *Law of Municipal Corporations* §41.03, 3d ed. (1969).

62. G.T. Mitay, *State and Local Governments: Politics and Prophecies* (New York: Scribner, 1966), p. 606.

Selected Legislation

The following pages contain excerpts from adopted and proposed legislation that states and localities may use as references
when developing energy-efficient land use policies. The legislation is suggestive only; it should not be adopted wholesale.
Strengths and weaknesses of various provisions have been discussed elsewhere in the book.

ENERGY CONSERVATION AND TRANSPORTATION GOALS AND POLI-CIES ADOPTED BY THE LINCOLN, NEBRASKA, CITY COUNCIL AND THE LANCASTER COUNTY, NEBRASKA, BOARD OF COMMISSIONERS

Following are excerpts from the Energy Conservation and Transportation Goals and Policies which were adopted in January 1976 by the
Lincoln, Nebraska, City Council and the Lancaster County, Nebraska,
Board of Commissioners for use in the development of a comprehensive plan. The two resolutions are the product of an energy conservation workshop held in September 1975 and recommendations of
both a citizen-based Goals and Policies Committee and the local planning commission. The goals and policies are specifically applicable to
the Lincoln-Lancaster County area, but are included here because
many ideas contained in the resolutions may be suggestive for other
localities interested in promoting energy-efficient land development.
Some guidelines contained in the resolutions are discussed more fully
elsewhere in this book.

Energy Goals and Policies Adopted by the Lincoln City Council by Resolution A–62436 on January 26, 1976, and by the Lancaster County Board of Commissioners by Motion on January 27, 1976, After a Joint Public Hearing on January 26, 1976, in the City Council Chambers, County-City Building

Preface: All energy goals and policies should be weighed carefully against the goals and strategies developed to prevent a negative employment or economic effect as well as any adverse effects upon the community as a whole.

Energy

Implement the concept of stewardship and conservation regarding the utilization of exhaustible energy resources, including the improved efficiency of the development of land and supporting systems, and prepare for the conversion to new energy sources as technology and financial feasibility permit.

Energy Sub-Goal 1: Land Use

Regulate the use of land and encourage the use of urban design so as to minimize the demand for energy consumption and maximize the effectiveness of energy consumed.

Policies

1. Regulate the use of land so as to provide higher density residential facilities in proximity to the Lincoln Center and other major activity centers.

2. Encourage the development of fewer and more intense multi-purpose centers and their concentration as opposed to the scattering of such activities in order to provide opportunity to eliminate or substantially reduce auto travel.

3. Encourage people to live in proximity to activity centers and particularly their place of employment.

4. Emphasize the revitalization of the Lincoln Center and the rehabilitation or redevelopment of established neighborhoods near the Lincoln Center.

5. Encourage radial or concentric growth about the Lincoln Center with new development to north, west, and south. When the objectives establishing growth areas to the north, west, and south have been substantially developed, growth to the east into Stevens Creek watershed area may be pursued.

6. Encourage land use arrangements and densities that facilitate energy-efficient public transit systems.

7. Encourage existing and future industries to conserve energy and improve energy efficiency.

8. Encourage site planning and designs which reduce demand for artificial heating, cooling, ventilation, and lighting.

9. Encourage the investigation of energy conservation and improved energy efficiency possibilities of centralized heating and cooling facilities serving building complexes.

Energy Sub-Goal 2: Transportation
Plan, design, and manage a coordinated system of public and private transportation programs and facilities which maximize passenger and freight miles traveled per unit of energy consumed.

Policies
1. Provide the facilities and programs for increased utilization of public transit, carpooling, and bicycle and pedestrian systems.
2. Reduce the need for and utilization of the private automobile.
3. Continue to improve the effectiveness of existing and future roadways so as to minimize unnecessary energy consumption by improving circulation through engineering procedures and roadway improvements.

*   *   *

Energy Sub-Goal 3: Community Facilities
Exhibit governmental leadership and innovation related to the conservation and efficient utilization of energy for community facilities and services.

Policies
1. The location, design, and operation of community facilities such as schools, churches, libraries, recreational facilities, university facilities, and other public buildings should encourage energy conservation and efficient energy utilization by such means as multi-purpose or joint uses.

*   *   *

3. All public lighting systems should be designed and operated to efficiently utilize energy without sacrificing public safety.

*   *   *

Energy Sub-Goal 4: Building Design
Encourage the design and construction of buildings and building complexes so as to effectively utilize all energy sources.

Policies
1. Building design and orientation should strive to effectively utilize natural lighting and reduce the effects of exposure to extreme weather conditions, thereby reducing the need for mechanical heating, cooling, and ventilation.

*   *   *

4. Landscape materials should be utilized effectively to reduce the adverse effects of weather conditions.

*   *   *

6. Buildings should be designed and built to utilize waste heat to reduce the demand on public utilities.

**Transportation Goals and Policies Adopted by the
Lincoln City Council by Resolution A–62436 on
January 26, 1976, and by the Lancaster County Board
of Commissioners by Motion on January 27, 1976,
After a Joint Public Hearing on January 26, 1976,
in the City Council Chambers County-City Building**

Preface: All transportation goals and policies should be weighed carefully against the goals and strategies developed to prevent a negative employment or economic effect as well as any adverse effects upon the community as a whole.

Transportation

Plan, develop, and maintain a comprehensive, balanced, integrated, safe, and efficient transportation system, including both facilities and programs, to ensure mobility for all segments of the population, to ensure the social, economic, and environmental well being of the residents of the area, and to best effectuate the desired development pattern.

Transportation Sub-Goal 1

Provide and maintain a system of roads, streets, and highways relating to both present and anticipated land uses, that will allow the continued adequate multimodal movement of people and goods, while incurring the least social, economic, and environmental harm to residential neighborhoods, activities, and land uses.

Policies

1. Provide assistance, through public resources, for the extension of major streets and roads only to those areas where growth is desired, as shown in the Comprehensive Plan, and refuse assistance for possible development where growth is not desired without inhibiting necessary rural functions.

2. Assistance through public resources should not be provided in such a manner as to encourage the leap-frogging of large vacant areas in order to reach proposed areas of development.

*   *   *

Transportation Sub-Goal 2

Encourage arrangements of land uses that facilitate the expanded use of non-auto modes of travel, the increased occupancy of autos, or the use of energy-efficient forms of transport as an integral part of a transportation system which provides for the adequate movement of people and goods while maintaining the quality of the living and working environment.

Policies

1. Encourage the concentration of major employment and activity centers, particularly in relation and proximity with higher density residential areas, in order to facilitate shorter travel distances, the use of non-auto modes of travel,

and/or the increased occupancy of autos. Encourage people to live in proximity to such activity centers, particularly their place of employment.

2. Public investment should be directed toward encouraging projects that will effectuate the development of land use arrangements that contribute toward the multi-modal movement of people and goods, minimize auto trips, or promote the use of transit.

3. Compatible business and residential uses should be arranged and designated in multi-purpose regional centers so as to encourage walking, biking, or transit usage and to eliminate or reduce the need for vehicular travel between destinations.

4. De-emphasize vehicular movement on primary pedestrian streets in the Lincoln Center while improving amenities, safety, and environment for the pedestrian to the extent that consideration is given to the prohibition of auto travel on these and such other streets as necessary to constitute an auto-free pedestrian zone.

5. Encourage the development of long-term parking, served by public transit, in the perimeter of the Lincoln Center and discourage long-term parking within the core of the Lincoln Center.

6. Encourage development of parking near the perimeter of the urban area to serve the Lincoln Center with express buses.

*   *   *

Transportation Sub-Goal 5
A system of bikeways and walkways should be developed which would provide convenient and safe movement of non-motorized traffic.

Policies
1. Develop an overall system of trails and bikeways which would include bicycle lanes on specially marked streets as well as bicycle and hiking trails in linear parks.

2. Provide convenient and safe bicycle routes connecting the Lincoln Center and other major activity areas, particularly the University of Nebraska campus, with adequate provision for parking.

*   *   *

4. Provide a system of sidewalks to enable safe, direct, and convenient pedestrian access to all areas of the community.

5. Encourage an integrated system of skywalks in the Lincoln Center to reduce pedestrian-auto conflicts and to provide a convenient alternate level of pedestrian movement.

PROPOSED ENERGY POLICY FOR FLORIDA

WHEREAS, energy availability strongly impacts upon every aspect of human existence and is essential to the health, safety, and welfare of the people of this state and to the well-being of the state economy, and

WHEREAS, Florida is particularly dependent upon other states and nations to supply its energy needs, and

WHEREAS, the majority of Florida's energy requirements are obtained from petroleum and natural gas, and these fuels are in shortest supply, and

WHEREAS, Florida remains somewhat isolated electrically because of relatively weak inter-ties with other states, and

WHEREAS, wasteful, inefficient, uneconomic, and unnecessary use of energy will result in a serious depletion of energy resources and represents a potential threat to preserving the health, safety, and welfare of the people of Florida, and

WHEREAS, alternative sources of energy are years from being fully developed and there is a pressing need to accelerate research and development of these sources, and

WHEREAS, efficient utilization and management of energy resources represents a meaningful, immediate, and appropriate state response to the energy problem which will protect the health, safety, and welfare of the people of Florida by reducing the economic costs of energy usage, eliminating waste and inefficiency in energy use thereby increasing economic productivity, reducing the rate at which our domestic energy resources are depleted which in turn increases economic flexibility of the people of Florida, and decreasing the pressure to develop marginally efficient methods of energy production and thereby reduce the flow of capital from the nonenergy sections of the economy and avoiding serious impacts on our environment, NOW, THEREFORE,

Be It Resolved

It shall be the policy of the State of Florida to:

1. Energy Conservation
Promote and develop the effective use of energy in the state, and to discourage all forms of energy waste.

2. The Responsibility of State Government
Play a leading role in developing and instituting energy management programs aimed at promoting energy conservation; to include energy considerations in all planning; and to maintain efficient utilization and management of energy resources used within state agencies.

3. Support of Local Government
Encourage local governments to consider energy in all planning, and to support their work in promoting energy management programs.

4. Energy Supply
Consider in its decision making the energy needs of each economic sector: residential, industrial, commercial, agricultural and governmental.

5. Information and Education
Promote energy education and the public dissemination of information on energy and its environmental, economic and societal impacts.

6. Alternative Energy Sources

Encourage the research and development of alternative and renewable energy resources.

7. Resource Development

Give due consideration to the social, economic and environmental impacts of energy-related activities so that detrimental effects of these activities are understood and minimized.

8. Contingency Planning

Develop and maintain energy emergency preparedness plans to minimize the effects within Florida of an energy shortage.

(September 28, 1976)

SENATE BILL 100—OREGON LAND USE ACT OF 1973 (excerpts)

Comprehensive Planning Coordination

General Provisions

197.005 Legislative findings. The Legislative Assembly finds that:

(1) Uncoordinated use of lands within this state threaten the orderly development, the environment of this state and the health, safety, order, convenience, prosperity and welfare of the people of this state.

(2) To promote coordinated administration of land uses consistent with comprehensive plans adopted throughout the state, it is necessary to establish a process for the review of state agency, city, county and special district land conservation and development plans for compliance with state-wide planning goals and guidelines.

(3) Except as otherwise provided in subsection (4) of this section, cities and counties should remain as the agencies to consider, promote and manage the local aspects of land conservation and development for the best interests of the people within their jurisdictions.

(4) The promotion of coordinated state-wide land conservation and development requires the creation of a state-wide planning agency to prescribe planning goals and objectives to be applied by state agencies, cities, counties and special districts throughout the state.

(5) The impact of proposed development projects, constituting activities of state-wide significance upon the public health, safety and welfare, requires a system of permits reviewed by a state-wide agency to carry out state-wide planning goals and guidelines prescribed for application for activities of state-wide significance throughout this state.
[1973 c.80 §1]

197.010 Policy. The Legislative Assembly declares that, in order to assure the highest possible level of liveability in Oregon, it is necessary to provide for properly prepared and coordinated comprehensive plans for cities and counties, regional areas and the state as a whole. These comprehensive plans:

(1) Must be adopted by the appropriate governing body at the local and state levels;

(2) Are expressions of public policy in the form of policy statements, generalized maps and standards and guidelines;

(3) Shall be the basis for more specific rules, regulations and ordinances which implement the policies expressed through the comprehensive plans;

(4) Shall be prepared to assure that all public actions are consistent and coordinated with the policies expressed through the comprehensive plans; and

(5) Shall be regularly reviewed and, if necessary, revised to keep them consistent with the changing needs and desires of the public they are designed to serve. [1973 c.80 §2]

197.015 Definitions for ORS 197.005 to 197.430, 215.055, 215.510, 215.515, 215.535 and 453.345. As used in ORS 197.005 to 197.430, 215.055, 215.510, 215.515, 215.535 and 453.345, unless the context requires otherwise:

(1) "Activity of state-wide significance" means a land conservation and development activity designated pursuant to ORS 197.400.

(2) "Commission" means the Land Conservation and Development Commission.

(3) "Committee" means the Joint Legislative Committee on Land Use.

(4) "Comprehensive plan" means a generalized, coordinated land use map and policy statement of the governing body of a state agency, city, county or special district that interrelates all functional and natural systems and activities relating to the use of lands, including but not limited to sewer and water systems, transportation systems, educational systems, recreational facilities, and natural resources and air and water quality management programs. "Comprehensive" means all-inclusive, both in terms of the geographic area covered and functional and natural activities and systems occurring in the area covered by the plan. "General nature" means a summary of policies and proposals in broad categories and does not necessarily indicate specific locations of any area, activity or use. A plan is "coordinated" when the needs of all levels of governments, semipublic and private agencies and the citizens of Oregon have been considered and accommodated as much as possible. "Land" includes water, both surface and subsurface, and the air.

(5) "Department" means the Department of Land Conservation and Development.

(6) "Director" means the Director of the Department of Land Conservation and Development.

(7) "Special district" means any unit of local government, other than a city or county, authorized and regulated by statute and includes, but is not limited to: Water control districts, irrigation districts, port districts, regional air quality control authorities, fire districts, school districts, hospital districts, mass transit districts and sanitary districts.

(8) "Voluntary association of local governments" means a regional planning agency in this state officially designated by the Governor pursuant to the federal Office of Management and Budget Circular A−95 as a regional clearinghouse. [1973 c.80 §3]

Land Conservation and Development Commission

197.030 **Land Conservation and Development Commission; members, appointment, confirmation, term, vacancies.** (1) There is established a Land Conservation and Development Commission consisting of seven members appointed by the Governor, subject to confirmation by the Senate in the manner provided in ORS 171.560 and 171.570.

(2) In making appointments under subsection (1) of this section, the Governor shall select from residents of this state one member from each congressional district and the remaining members from the state at large. At least one and no more than two members shall be from Multnomah County.

(3) The term of office of each member of the commission is four years, but a member may be removed by the Governor for cause. Before the expiration of the term of a member, the Governor shall appoint a successor. No person shall serve more than two full terms as a member of the commission.

(4) If there is a vacancy for any cause, the Governor shall make an appointment to become immediately effective for the unexpired term.
[1973 c.80 §5]

197.035 **Commission officers, selection; quorum; compensation and expenses.** (1) The commission shall select one of its members as chairman and another member as vice chairman, for such terms and with duties and powers necessary for the performance of the functions of such offices as the commission determines. The vice chairman of the commission shall act as the chairman of the commission in the absence of the chairman.

(2) A majority of the members of the commission constitutes a quorum for the transaction of business.

(3) Members of the commission are entitled to compensation and expenses as provided in ORS 292.495.
[1973 c.80 §§7, 8]

197.040 **Duties of commission; generally.** (1) The commission shall:

(a) Direct the performance by the director and his staff of their functions under ORS 197.005 to 197.430, 215.055, 215.510, 215.515, 215.535 and 453.345.

(b) In accordance with the provisions of ORS chapter 183, promulgate rules that it considers necessary in carrying out ORS 197.005 to 197.430, 215.055, 215.510, 215.515, 215.535 and 453.345.

(c) Cooperate with the appropriate agencies of the United States, this state and its political subdivisions, any other state, any interstate agency, any person or groups of persons with respect to land conservation and development.

(d) Appoint advisory committees to aid it in carrying out ORS 197.005 to 197.430, 215.055, 215.510, 215.515, 215.535 and 453.345 and provide technical and other assistance, as it considers necessary, to each such committee.

(2) Pursuant to ORS 197.005 to 197.430, 215.055, 215.510, 215.515, 215.535 and 453.345, the commission shall:

(a) Establish state-wide planning goals consistent with regional, county and city concerns;

(b) Issue permits for activities of state-wide significance;

(c) Prepare inventories of land uses;

(d) Prepare state-wide planning guidelines;

(e) Review comprehensive plans for conformance with state-wide planning goals;

(f) Coordinate planning efforts of state agencies to assure conformance with state-wide planning goals and compatibility with city and county comprehensive plans;

(g) Insure widespread citizen involvement and input in all phases of the process;

(h) Prepare model zoning, subdivision and other ordinances and regulations to guide state agencies, cities, counties and special districts in implementing state-wide planning goals, particularly those for the areas listed in subsection (2) of ORS 197.230;

(i) Review and recommend to the Legislative Assembly the designation of areas of critical state concern;

(j) Report periodically to the Legislative Assembly and to the committee; and

(k) Perform other duties required by law.
[1973 c.80 §§9, 11]

197.045 Powers of commission. The commission may:

(1) Apply for and receive moneys from the Federal Government and from this state or any of its agencies or departments.

(2) Contract with any public agency for the performance of services or the exchange of employes or services by one to the other necessary in carrying out ORS 197.005 to 197.430, 215.055, 215.510, 215.515, 215.535 and 453.345.

(3) Contract for the services of and consultation with professional persons or organizations, not otherwise available through federal, state and local governmental agencies, in carrying out its duties under ORS 197.005 to 197.430, 215.055, 215.510, 215.515, 215.535 and 453.345.

(4) Perform other functions required to carry out ORS 197.005 to 197.430, 215.055, 215.510, 215.515, 215.535 and 453.345.
[1973 c.80 §10]

197.050 Interstate agreements and compacts; commission powers. If an interstate land conservation and development planning agency is created by an interstate agreement or compact entered into by this state, the commission shall perform the functions of this state with respect to the agreement or compact. If the functions of the interstate planning agency duplicate any of the functions of the commission under ORS 197.005 to 197.430, 215.055, 215.510, 215.515, 215.535 and 453.345, the commission may:

(1) Negotiate with the interstate agency in defining the areas of responsibility of the commission and the interstate planning agency; and

(2) Cooperate with the interstate planning agency in the performance of its functions.
[1973 c.80 §12]

197.055 Delegation of commission functions to Oregon Coastal Conservation and Development Commission, review, approval; staff and financial assistance. (1) The Land Conservation and Development Commission, by agreement with the Oregon Coastal Conservation and Development Commission created by ORS 191.120, may delegate to the Oregon Coastal Conservation and Development Commission any of the functions of the Land Conservation and Development Commission. However, the Land Conservation and Development Commission must review and grant approval prior to any action taken by the Oregon Coastal Conservation and Development Commission with respect to a delegated function.

(2) The Land Conservation and Development Commission may provide staff and financial assistance to the Oregon Coastal Conservation and Development Commission in carrying out duties under this section.
[1973 c.80 §16]

197.060 Biennial report; draft submission to committee; contents. (1) Prior to the end of each even-numbered year, the department shall prepare a written report for submission to the Legislative Assembly of the State of Oregon describing activities and accomplishments of the department, commission, state agencies, cities, counties and special districts in carrying out ORS 197.005 to 197.430, 215.055, 215.510, 215.515, 215.535 and 453.345.

(2) A draft of the report required by subsection (1) of this section shall be submitted to the committee for its review and comment at least 60 days prior to submission of the report to the Legislative Assembly. Comments of the committee shall be incorporated into the final report.

(3) Goals and guidelines adopted by the commission shall be included in the report to the Legislative Assembly submitted under subsection (1) of this section.
[1973 c.80 §56]

Land Conservation and Development Department

197.075 Department of Land Conservation and Development. The Department of Land Conservation and Development is established. The department shall consist of the Land Conservation and Development Commission, the director and their subordinate officers and employes.
[1973 c.80 §4]

197.080 Department monthly report required. The department shall report monthly to the committee in order to keep the committee informed on progress made by the department, commission, counties and other agencies in carrying out ORS 197.005 to 197.430, 215.055, 215.510, 215.515, 215.535 and 453.345.
[1973 c.80 §55]

Director

197.085 Director; appointment; compensation and expenses. (1) The commission shall appoint a person to serve as the Director of the Department of Land Conservation and Development. The director shall hold his office at the pleasure of the commission and his salary shall be fixed by the commission unless otherwise provided by law.

(2) In addition to his salary, the director shall be reimbursed, subject to any applicable law regulating travel and other expenses of state officers and employes, for actual and necessary expenses incurred by him in the performance of his official duties.
[1973 c.80 §13]

197.090 Duties of director. Subject to policies adopted by the commission, the director shall:

(1) Be the administrative head of the department.

(2) Coordinate the activities of the department in its land conservation and development functions with such functions of federal agencies, other state agencies, cities, counties and special districts.

(3) Appoint, reappoint, assign and reassign all subordinate officers and employes of the department, prescribe their duties and fix their compensation, subject to the State Merit System Law.

(4) Represent this state before any agency of this state, any other state or the United States with respect to land conservation and development within this state.
[1973 c.80 §14]

Land Conservation and Development Account

197.095 Land Conservation and Development Account; continuous appropriation; fees and other revenues to be deposited. (1) There is established in the General Fund in the State Treasury the Land Conservation and Development Account. Moneys in the account are continuously appropriated for the purpose of carrying out ORS 197.005 to 197.430, 215.055, 215.510, 215.515, 215.535 and 453.345.

(2) All fees, moneys and other revenue received by the department or the committee shall be deposited in the Land Conservation and Development Account.
[1973 c.80 §15]

Joint Legislative Committee on Land Use

197.125 Joint Legislative Committee on Land Use; executive secretary. The Joint Legislative Committee on Land Use is established as a joint committee of the Legislative Assembly. The committee shall select an executive secretary who shall serve at the pleasure of the committee and under its direction.
[1973 c.80 §22]

197.130 **Members; appointment; term; vacancies; expenses; majority vote required in actions.** (1) The Joint Legislative Committee on Land Use shall consist of four members of the House of Representatives appointed by the Speaker and three members of the Senate appointed by the President. No more than three House members of the committee shall be of the same political party. No more than two Senate members of the committee shall be of the same political party.

(2) The chairman of the House and Senate Environment and Land Use Committees of the Fifty-seventh Legislative Assembly of the State of Oregon shall be two of the members appointed under subsection (1) of this section for the period beginning with October 5, 1973.

(3) The committee has a continuing existence and may meet, act and conduct its business during sessions of the Legislative Assembly or any recess thereof, and in the interim period between sessions.

(4) The term of a member shall expire upon the convening of the Legislative Assembly in regular session next following the commencement of the member's term. When a vacancy occurs in the membership of the committee in the interim between sessions, until such vacancy is filled, the membership of the committee shall be deemed not to include the vacant position for the purpose of determining whether a quorum is present and a quorum is the majority of the remaining members.

(5) Members of the committee shall be reimbursed for actual and necessary expenses incurred or paid in the performance of their duties as members of the committee, such reimbursement to be made from funds appropriated for such purposes, after submission of approved voucher claims.

(6) The committee shall select a chairman. The chairman may, in addition to his other authorized duties, approve voucher claims.

(7) Action of the committee shall be taken only upon the affirmative vote of the majority of the members of the committee.
[1973 c.80 §23]

197.135 **Duties of committee, generally.** The committee shall:

(1) Advise the department on all matters under the jurisdiction of the department;

(2) Review and make recommendations to the Legislative Assembly on proposals for additions to or modifications of designations of activities of state-wide significance, and for designations of areas of critical state concern;

(3) Review and make recommendations to the Legislative Assembly on state-wide planning goals and guidelines approved by the commission;

(4) Study and make recommendations to the Legislative Assembly on the implementation of a program for compensation by the public to owners of lands within this state for the value of any loss of use of such lands resulting directly from the imposition of any zoning, subdivision or other ordinance or regulation regulating or restricting the use of such lands. Such recommendations shall include, but not be limited to, proposed methods for the valuation of such loss of use and proposed limits, if any, to be imposed upon the amount of compensation to be paid by the public for any such loss of use; and

(5) Make recommendations to the Legislative Assembly on any other matter relating to land use planning in Oregon.
[1973 c.80 §24]

Citizen Advisory Committees

197.160 State Citizen Involvement Advisory Committee; county citizen advisory committees. To assure widespread citizen involvement in all phases of the planning process:

(1) The commission shall appoint a State Citizen Involvement Advisory Committee, broadly representative of geographic areas of the state and of interests relating to land uses and land use decisions, to develop a program for the commission that promotes and enhances public participation in the development of state-wide planning goals and guidelines.

(2) Within 90 days after October 5, 1973, each county governing body shall submit to the commission a program for citizen involvement in preparing, adopting and revising comprehensive plans within the county. Such program shall at least contain provision for a citizen advisory committee or committees broadly representative of geographic areas and of interests relating to land uses and land use decisions.

(3) The state advisory committee appointed under subsection (1) of this section shall review the proposed programs submitted by each county and recommend to the commission whether or not the proposed program adequately provides for public involvement in the planning process.
[1973 c.80 §35]

Comprehensive Planning Responsibilities

197.175 Cities and counties planning responsibilities; compliance with state-wide goals and guidelines. (1) Cities and counties shall exercise their planning and zoning responsibilities in accordance with ORS 197.005 to 197.430, 215.055, 215.510, 215.515, 215.535 and 453.345 and the state-wide planning goals and guidelines approved under ORS 197.005 to 197.430, 215.055, 215.510, 215.515, 215.535 and 453.345.

(2) Pursuant to ORS 197.005 to 197.430, 215.055, 215.510, 215.515, 215.535 and 453.345, each city and county in this state shall:

(a) Prepare and adopt comprehensive plans consistent with state-wide planning goals and guidelines approved by the commission; and

(b) Enact zoning, subdivision and other ordinances or regulations to implement their comprehensive plans.
[1973 c.80 §§17, 18]

197.180 State agency planning responsibilities. State agencies shall carry out their planning duties, powers and responsibilities and take actions that are authorized by law with respect to programs affecting land use in accordance with state-wide planning goals and guidelines approved pursuant to ORS 197.005 to 197.430, 215.055, 215.510, 215.515, 215.535 and 453.345.
[1973 c.80 §21]

197.185 Special district planning responsibilities. Special districts shall exercise their planning duties, powers and responsibilities and take actions that are authorized by law with respect to programs affecting land use in accordance with state-wide planning goals and guidelines approved pursuant to ORS 197.005 to 197.430, 215.055, 215.510, 215.515, 215.535 and 453.345.
[1973 c.80 §20]

197.190 Regional coordination of planning activities; alternatives. (1) In addition to the responsibilities stated in ORS 197.175, each county, through its governing body, shall be responsible for coordinating all planning activities affecing land uses within the county, including those of the county, cities, special districts and state agencies, to assure an integrated comprehensive plan for the entire area of the county. For purposes of this subsection, the responsibility of the county described in this subsection shall not apply to cities having a population of 300,000 or more, and such cities shall exercise, within the incorporated limits thereof, the authority vested in counties by this subsection.

(2) For the purposes of carrying out ORS 197.005 to 197.430, 215.055, 215.510, 215.515, 215.535 and 453.345, counties may voluntarily join together with adjacent counties as authorized in ORS chapter 190.

(3) Whenever counties and cities representing 51 percent of the population in their area petition the commission for an election in their area to form a regional planning agency to exercise the authority of the counties under subsection (1) of this section in the area, the commission shall review the petition. If it finds that the area described in the petition forms a reasonable planning unit, it shall call an election in the area to form a regional planning agency. The election shall be conducted in the manner provided in ORS chapter 259. The county clerk shall be considered the election officer and the commission shall be considered the district election authority. The agency shall be considered established if the majority of votes favor the establishment.

(4) If a voluntary association of local governments adopts a resolution ratified by each participating county and a majority of the participating cities therein which authorizes the association to perform the review, advisory and coordination functions assigned to the counties under subsection (1) of this section, the association may perform such duties.
[1973 c.80 §19]

State-wide Goals and Guidelines

197.225 Preparation; adoption. Not later than January 1, 1975, the department shall prepare and the commission shall adopt state-wide planning goals and guidelines for use by state agencies, cities, counties and special districts in preparing, adopting, revising and implementing existing and future comprehensive plans.
[1973 c.80 §33]

197.230 Considerations; priorities. In preparing and adopting state-wide planning goals and guidelines, the department and the commission shall:

(1) Consider the existing comprehensive plans of state agencies, cities, counties and special districts in order to preserve functional and local aspects of land conservation and development.

(2) Give priority consideration to the following areas and activities:

(a) Those activities listed in ORS 197.400;

(b) Lands adjacent to freeway interchanges;

(c) Estuarine areas;

(d) Tide, marsh and wetland areas;

(e) Lakes and lakeshore areas;

(f) Wilderness, recreational and outstanding scenic areas;

(g) Beaches, dunes, coastal headlands and related areas;

(h) Wild and scenic rivers and related lands;

(i) Flood plains and areas of geologic hazard;

(j) Unique wildlife habitats; and

(k) Agricultural land.

[1973 c.80 §34]

197.235 Public hearings; notice; citizen involvement implementation; submission of proposals to commission. (1) In preparing the state-wide planning goals and guidelines, the department shall:

(a) Hold at least 10 public hearings throughout the state, causing notice of the time, place and purpose of each such hearing to be published in a newspaper of general circulation within the area where the hearing is to be conducted not later than 30 days prior to the date of the hearing.

(b) Implement any other provision for public involvement developed by the state advisory committee under subsection (1) of ORS 197.160 and approved by the commission.

(2) Upon completion of the preparation of the proposed state-wide planning goals and guidelines, the department shall submit them to the commission for approval.

[1973 c.80 §36]

197.240 Commission action; public hearing; notice; revision; adoption. Upon receipt of the proposed state-wide planning goals and guidelines prepared and submitted to it by the department, the commission shall:

(1) Hold at least one public hearing on the proposed state-wide planning goals and guidelines. The commission shall cause notice of the time, place and purpose of the hearings and the place where copies of the proposed goals and guidelines are available before the hearings with the cost thereof to be published in a newspaper of general circulation in the state not later than 30 days prior to the date of the hearing. The department shall supply a copy of its proposed state-wide planning goals and guidelines to the Governor, the committee, affected state agencies and special districts and to each city and county without charge. The department shall provide copies of such proposed goals and guidelines to other public agencies or persons upon request and payment of the cost of preparing the copies of the materials requested.

(2) Consider the recommendations and comments received from the public hearings conducted under subsection (1) of this section, make any revisions in the proposed state-wide planning goals and guidelines that it considers necessary and approve the proposed goals and guidelines as they may be revised by the commission.
[1973 c.80 §37]

197.245 **Commission revision.** The commission may periodically revise, update and expand the initial state-wide planning goals and guidelines adopted under ORS 197.240. Such revisions, updatings or expansions shall be made in the manner provided in ORS 197.235 and 197.240.
[1973 c.80 §38]

197.250 **Compliance with state-wide planning goals required.** All comprehensive plans and any zoning, subdivision and other ordinances and regulations adopted by a state agency, city, county or special district to carry out such plans shall be in conformity with the state-wide planning goals within one year from the date such goals are approved by the commission.
[1973 c.80 §32]

197.255 **County review of comprehensive plans required; compliance advice.** Following the approval by the commission of state-wide planning goals and guidelines, each county governing body shall review all comprehensive plans for land conservation and development within the county, both those adopted and those being prepared. The county governing body shall advise the state agency, city, county or special district preparing the comprehensive plans whether or not the comprehensive plans are in conformity with the state-wide planning goals.
[1973 c.80 §39]

197.260 **County reports on comprehensive planning compliance required annually.** Upon the expiration of one year after the date of the approval of state-wide planning goals and guidelines and annually thereafter, each county governing body shall report to the commission on the status of comprehensive plans within each county. Each such report shall include:

(1) Copies of comprehensive plans reviewed by the county governing body and copies of zoning and subdivision ordinances and regulations applied to those areas within the county listed in subsection (2) of ORS 197.230.

(2) For those areas or jurisdictions within the county without comprehensive plans, a statement and review of the progress made toward compliance with the state-wide planning goals.
[1973 c.80 §44]

Interim Comprehensive Planning

197.275 **Existing plans and regulations remain in effect until revised.** Comprehensive plans and zoning, subdivision, and other ordinances and regulations adopted prior to October 5, 1973, shall remain in effect until revised under ORS

197.005 to 197.430, 215.055, 215.510, 215.515, 215.535 and 453.345. It is intended that existing planning efforts and activities shall continue and that such efforts be utilized in achieving the purposes of ORS 197.005 to 197.430, 215.055, 215.510, 215.515, 215.535 and 453.345.
[1973 c.80 §40]

197.280 Interim comprehensive planning goals. Prior to approval by the commission of its state-wide planning goals and guidelines under ORS 197.240, the goals listed in ORS 215.515 shall be applied by state agencies, cities, counties and special districts in the preparation, revision, adoption or implementation of any comprehensive plan.
[1973 c.80 §41]

197.285 City and county interim comprehensive plans to comply with interim goals; state-wide planning goals and guidelines after approval. Each city or county shall prepare and the city council or the county governing body shall adopt the comprehensive plans required under ORS 197.005 to 197.430, 215. 055, 215.510, 215.515, 215.535 and 453.345 or by any other law in accordance with ORS 197.280 for those plans adopted prior to the expiration of one year following the date the commission approves its state-wide planning goals and guidelines under ORS 197.240. Plans adopted by cities and counties after the expiration of one year following the date of approval of such goals and guidelines by the commission shall be designed to comply with such goals and any subsequent amendments thereto.
[1973 c.80 §42]

Review of Comprehensive Plan Provisions, Ordinances and Regulations

197.300 Commission authorized to review plan provisions and ordinances and regulations; petition; standing; filing deadline. (1) In the manner provided in ORS 197.305 to 197.315, the commission shall review upon:

(a) Petition by a county governing body, a comprehensive plan provision or any zoning, subdivision or other ordinance or regulation adopted by a state agency, city, county or special district that the governing body considers to be in conflict with state-wide planning goals approved under ORS 197.240 or interim goals specified in ORS 215.515.

(b) Petition by a city or county governing body, a land conservation and development action taken by a state agency, city, county or special district that the governing body considers to be in conflict with state-wide planning goals approved under ORS 197.240 or interim goals specified in ORS 215.515.

(c) Petition by a state agency, city, county or special district, any county governing body action that the state agency, city, county or special district considers to be improperly taken or outside the scope of the governing body's authority under ORS 197.005 to 197.430, 215.055, 215.510, 215.515, 215.535 and 453.345.

(d) Petition by any person or group of persons whose interests are substantially affected, a comprehensive plan provision or any zoning, subdivision or other ordinance or regulation alleged to be in violation of state-wide planning goals approved under ORS 197.240 or interim goals specified in ORS 215.515.

(2) A petition filed with the commission pursuant to subsection (1) of this section must be filed not later than 60 days (excluding Saturdays and holidays) after the date of the final adoption or approval of the action or comprehensive plan upon which the petition is based.
[1973 c.80 §51]

197.305 Review proceedings based on administrative record; conduct; intervenors. (1) All review proceedings conducted by the commission pursuant to ORS 197.300 shall be based on the administrative record, if any, prepared with respect to the proceedings for the adoption or approval of the comprehensive plan provision or action that is the subject of the review proceeding.

(2) The commission shall adopt such rules, procedures and regulations for the conduct of review proceedings held pursuant to ORS 197.300, in accordance with the provisions of ORS 183.310 to 183.500 for hearings and notice in contested cases.

(3) A city, county, state agency, special district or any person or group of persons whose interests are substantially affected may intervene in and be made a party to any review proceeding conducted by the commission with the approval of the commission, upon the request of the hearings officer appointed to conduct such proceeding or upon the approval by the hearings officer of a request by such agency, person or group of persons for intervention in the review proceeding.
[1973 c.80 §52]

197.310 Hearings officers to conduct proceeding and make recommendation; commission review; orders; judicial review, enforcement. (1) In carrying out its duties under ORS 197.300, the chairman of the commission shall assign each petition to be reviewed by the commission to a hearings officer who shall conduct the review proceeding.

(2) A hearings officer shall conduct a review proceeding in accordance with the rules, procedures and regulations adopted by the commission. Upon the conclusion of a hearing, the hearings officer shall promptly determine the matter, prepare a recommendation for commission action upon the matter and submit a copy of his recommendation to the commission and to each party to the proceeding.

(3) The commission shall review the recommendation of the hearings officer and the record of the proceeding and issue its order with respect to the review proceeding within 60 days following the date of the filing of the petition upon which such review proceeding is based. The commission may adopt, reject or amend the recommendation of the hearings officer in any matter.

(4) No order of the commission issued under subsection (3) of this section is valid unless all members of the commission have received the recommendation

of the hearings officer in the matter and at least four members of the commission concur in its action in the matter.

(5) Any party to a review proceeding before the commission who is adversely affected or aggrieved by the order issued by the commission in the matter may appeal the order of the commission in the manner provided in ORS 183.480 for appeals from final orders in contested cases.

(6) The commission may enforce orders issued under subsection (3) of this section in appropriate judicial proceedings brought by the commission therefor. [1973 c.80 §53)

197.315 Referral to hearings officer for additional information or evidence; suspension of time period for commission action upon referral. (1) If, upon its review of the recommendation of a hearings officer and the record of the review proceeding prepared following a review proceeding before the commission, the commission is unable to reach a decision in the matter without further information or evidence not contained in the record of the proceeding, it may refer the matter back to the hearings officer and request that the additional information or evidence be acquired by him or that he correct any errors or deficiencies found by the commission to exist in his recommendation or record of the proceeding.

(2) In case of a referral of a matter back to the hearings officer pursuant to subsection (1) of this section, the 60-day period referred to in subsection (3) of ORS 197.310 is suspended for a reasonable interval not to exceed 60 days. [1973 c.80 §54]

Comprehensive Planning by Commission

197.325 Commission required to prescribe plans and regulations for non-complying lands; time extensions for plan completion; plans prescribed to comply with statewide planning goals. (1) Notwithstanding any other provision of law, after the expiration of one year after the date of the approval of the initial state-wide planning goals and guidelines under ORS 197.240, upon 90 days' notice to the affected governing body or bodies, and upon public hearings held within 30 days thereafter, the commission shall prescribe and may amend and administer comprehensive plans and zoning, subdivision or other ordinances and regulations necessary to develop and implement a comprehensive plan within the boundaries of a county, whether or not within the boundaries of a city, that do not comply with the state-wide planning goals approved under ORS 197.005 to 197.430, 215.055, 215.510, 215.515, 215.535 and 453.345 and any subsequent revisions or amendments thereof.

(2) If the city or county has under consideration a comprehensive plan or zoning, subdivision or other ordinances or regulations for lands described in subsection (1) of this section, and shows satisfactory progress toward the adoption of such comprehensive plan or such ordinances or regulations, the commission may grant a reasonable extension of time after the date set in this section for completion of such plan or such ordinances or regulations.

(3) Any comprehensive plan or zoning, subdivision or other ordinance or

regulation adopted by the commission under subsection (1) of this section shall comply with the state wide planning goals approved under ORS 197.005 to 197. 430, 215.055, 215.510, 215.515, 215.535 and 453.345 and all subsequent revisions or amendments thereof.
[1973 c.80 §45]

197.330 Cities and counties liable for costs of commission planning; statement of costs; collection; failure to pay, withholding state cigarette and liquor revenue share; appeal of cost determination. (1) Whenever the commission prescribes a comprehensive plan or zoning, subdivision or other ordinances or regulations for lands described in subsection (1) of ORS 197.325, the costs incurred by the commission and the department in the preparation and administration of such plan or ordinances or regulations shall be borne by the city or county for which the commission has proposed such plan or ordinances or regulations. Upon presentation by the commission to the governing body of the city or county of a certified, itemized statement of costs, the governing body shall order payment to the commission out of any available funds. With respect to a city or county, if no payment is made by the governing body within 30 days thereafter, the commission shall submit to the Secretary of State its certified, itemized statement of such costs and the commission shall be reimbursed upon the order of the Secretary of State to the State Treasurer, from the city's or county's share of the state's cigarette and liquor revenues.

(2) Within 10 days of receipt of the certified, itemized statement of costs under subsection (1) of this section, any city or county aggrieved by the statement may appeal to the Court of Appeals. The appeal shall be taken as from a contested case under ORS 183.480. Notice of the appeal shall operate as a stay in the commissioner's right to reimbursement under subsection (1) of this section until the decision is made on the appeal.
[1973 c.80 §50]

Activities of State-wide Significance

197.400 Activities of state-wide significance; designation; effect upon state agency responsibilities. (1) The following activities may be designated by the commission as activities of state-wide significance if the commission determines that by their nature or magnitude they should be so considered:

(a) The planning and siting of public transportation facilities.

(b) The planning and siting of public sewerage systems, water supply systems and solid waste disposal sites and facilities.

(c) The planning and siting of public schools.

(2) Nothing in ORS 197.005 to 197.430, 215.055, 215.510, 215.515, 215. 535 and 453.345 supersedes any duty, power or responsibility vested by statute in any state agency relating to its activities described in subsection (1) of this section; except that, a state agency may neither implement any such activity nor adopt any plan relating to such an activity without the prior review and comment of the commission.
[1973 c.80 §25]

197.405 Additional activities, designation; commission recommendation; committee review; submission to Legislative Assembly. (1) In addition to the activities of state-wide significance that are designated by the commission under ORS 197.400, the commission may recommend to the committee the designation of additional activities of state-wide significance. Each such recommendation shall specify the reasons for the proposed designation of the activity of state-wide significance, the dangers that would result from such activity being uncontrolled and the suggested state-wide planning goals and guidelines to be applied for the proposed activity.

(2) The commission may recommend to the committee the designation of areas of critical state concern. Each such recommendation shall specify the criteria developed and reasons for the proposed designation, the damages that would result from uncontrolled development within the area, the reasons for the implementation of state regulations for the proposed area and the suggested state regulations to be applied within the proposed area.

(3) The commission may act under subsections (1) and (2) of this section on its own motion or upon the recommendation of a state agency, city, county or special district. If the commission receives a recommendation from a state agency, city, county or special district and finds the proposed activity or area to be unsuitable for designation, it shall notify the state agency, city, county or special district of its decision and its reasons therefor.

(4) Immediately following its decision to favorably recommend to the Legislative Assembly the designation of an additional activity of state-wide significance or the designation of an area of critical state concern, the commission shall submit the proposed designation accompanied by the supporting materials described in subsections (1) and (2) of this section to the committee for its' review. [1973 c.80 §26]

197.410 Planning and siting permit required; enjoining violations. (1) No project constituting an activity of state-wide significance shall be undertaken without a planning and siting permit issued under ORS 197.415.

(2) Any person or agency acting in violation of subsection (1) of this section may be enjoined in civil proceedings brought in the name of the county or the State of Oregon. [1973 c.80 §30]

197.415 Planning and siting permits required; application; city, county, state agency review and recommendation; issuance; conditions; restrictions. (1) On and after the date the commission has approved state-wide planning goals and guidelines for activities of state-wide significance designated under ORS 197. 400, no proposed project constituting such an activity may be initiated by any person or public agency without a planning and siting permit issued by the commission therefor.

(2) Any person or public agency desiring to initiate a project constituting an activity of state-wide significance shall apply to the department for a planning and siting permit for such project. The application shall contain the plans for the

project and the manner in which such project has been designed to meet the goals and guidelines for activities of state-wide significance and the comprehensive plans for the county within which the project is proposed, and any other information required by the commission as prescribed by rule of the commission.

(3) The department shall transmit copies of the application to affected county and state agencies for their review and recommendation.

(4) The county governing body and the state agencies shall review an application transmitted to it under subsection (3) of this section and shall, within 30 days after the date of the receipt of the application, submit their recommendations on the application to the commission.

(5) If the commission finds after review of the application and the comments submitted by the county governing body and state agencies that the proposed project complies with the state-wide goals and guidelines for activities of state-wide significance and the comprehensive plans within the county, it shall approve the application and issue a planning and siting permit for the proposed project to the person or public agency applying therefor. Action shall be taken by the commission within 30 days of the receipt of the recommendation of the county and state agencies.

(6) The commission may prescribe and include in the planning and siting permit such conditions or restrictions that it considers necessary to assure that the proposed project complies with the state-wide goals and guidelines for activities of state-wide significance and the comprehensive plans within the county.
[1973 c.80 §27]

197.420 Joint application and permit where two or more permits required for activity. If the activity requiring a planning and siting permit under ORS 197.415 also requires any other permit from any state agency, the commission, with the cooperation and concurrence of the other agency, may provide a joint application form and permit to satisfy both the requirements of ORS 197.005 to 197.430, 215.055, 215.510, 215.515, 215.535 and 453.345 and any other requirements set by statute or by rule of the state agency.
[1973 c.80 §28]

197.425 Binding letter of interpretation by commission; committee consultation required; request form. (1) If any person or public agency is in doubt whether a proposed development project constitutes an activity of state-wide significance, the person or public agency may request a determination from the commission on the question. Within 60 days after the date of the receipt by it of such a request, the commission, with the advice of the committee and of the county governing body for the county in which such activity is proposed, shall issue a binding letter of interpretation with respect to the proposed project.

(2) Requests for determinations under this section shall be made to the commission in writing and in such form and contain such information as may be prescribed by the commission.
[1973 c.80 §29]

197.430   Enforcement powers. If the county governing body or the commission determines the existence of an alleged violation under ORS 197.410, it may:

(1) Investigate, hold hearings, enter orders and take action that it deems appropriate under ORS 197.005 to 197.430, 215.055, 215.510, 215.515, 215.535 and 453.345, as soon as possible.

(2) For the purpose of investigating conditions relating to the violation, through its members or its duly authorized representatives, enter at reasonable times upon any private or public property.

(3) Conduct public hearings.

(4) Publish its findings and recommendations as they are formulated relative to the violation.

(5) Give notice of any order relating to a particular violation of its state-wide goals, a particular violation of the terms or conditions of a planning and siting permit or a particular violation of ORS 197.005 to 197.430, 215.055, 215.510, 215.515, 215.535 and 453.345 by mailing notice to the person or public body conducting or proposing to conduct the project affected in the manner provided by ORS chapter 183.
[1973 c.80 §31]

OREGON LEGISLATION AND GUIDELINES ON REAL PROPERTY TAX APPRAISAL AS AFFECTED BY LAND USE PLANNING AND ZONING

308.235   Valuation of Land

Taxable real property shall be assessed by a method which takes into consideration the applicable land use plans, including current zoning and other governmental land use restrictions, the improvements on the land and in the surrounding country and also the use, earning power and usefulness of such improvements, and any rights or privileges attached thereto or connected therewith, the quality of the soil, and the natural resources in, on or connected with the land, its conveniences to transportation lines, public roads and other local advantage of a similar or different kind. Where land is situated within an irrigation, drainage, reclamation or other improvement district, the value of the land shall not be deemed to be increased until the construction and improvement of the district have been completed to the point that water may be delivered to or removed from the land, as the case may be.

Or. Rev. Stat. §308.235

I. Plan and Zone Are Consistent

Example A

PLAN: SINGLE FAMILY
        RESIDENTIAL

Zone:
  Single family
  residential

Vacant
land

a. The plan and zone designations are the same—single family residential.
b. Property should be classified as single family residential and appraised based on that use.
c. Comparable sales should be taken from a comparable single family residential area where the plan and the zone are the same.

Example B

PLAN: SINGLE FAMILY
        RESIDENTIAL

Zone:
  Single family
  residential

Single
family
house

Same as Example A except property should be classified as single family residential improvement.

I. Plan and Zone Are Consistent (cont'd.)

Example C

PLAN: COMMERCIAL

Zone:
Single
family
residential

Multifamily
units

a. The plan and zone are consistent—
   single family residential.
b. Property is presently developed to a
   preexisting nonconforming use (multifamily units) to both the plan and zoning.
c. It is presumed that the present use,
   although nonconforming, will be permitted so long as the present buildings
   are used on the land.
d. Property should be classified as multifamily residential improved and appraised based on that use.
e. Comparable sales should be taken
   from comparable multifamily residential property in an area with the same
   plan and zone restrictions. This is necessary to reflect the probable shorter
   term of the nonconforming use.

Example D

PLAN: SINGLE FAMILY
        RESIDENTIAL

Zone:
Commercial

Property
improved
with
house

a. The plan and zone are consistent—commercial.
b. Single family residential use is permissible under the plan as a permitted
   lower density use.
c. Property should be classified as commercial improved property.
d. Land should be valued as vacant and
   available for commercial use, using
   sales of comparable commercial land.
e. House should be valued recognizing
   economic obsolescence.

   NOTE: Under HB 2333, the land
          may qualify for deferral.

II. Plan Requires Lower Use Than Zone

Example A

PLAN: SINGLE FAMILY
     RESIDENTIAL

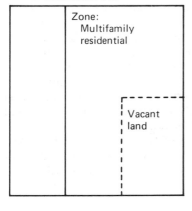

a. The plan and zone differ—single family residential for the plan and multifamily residential for the zone.
b. The plan sets the highest possible use.
c. It is presumed that a building permit would not be issued for other than single family residence.
d. Multifamily development of the land is not permitted (since it is a higher density use than permitted by the plan) and cannot be the basis for valuation.
e. Land should be classified single family residential and appraised based on that use.
f. Comparable sales should be taken from comparable single family residential property.

Example B

PLAN: SINGLE FAMILY
     RESIDENTIAL

Zone:
   Multifamily
   residential

Multifamily
units

a. The plan and zone differ—single family residential for the plan and multifamily residential for the zone.
b. Property is presently developed to a preexisting nonconforming use (multifamily units) to the controlling plan.
c. It is presumed that the present use, although nonconforming, will be permitted so long as the present buildings are used on the land.
d. Property should be classified as multifamily residential and appraised based on that use.
e. Comparable sales should be taken from comparable multifamily residential property in an area with the same plan and zone restrictions. This is necessary to reflect the probable shorter term of the nonconforming use.

III. Plan Permits Higher Use Than Zone

Example A

PLAN: COMMERCIAL

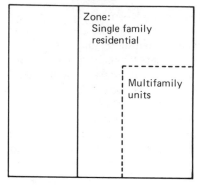

a. The plan and zone differ—commercial for the plan and single family residential for the zone.
b. The lower use zoning is permissible (unless the comprehensive plan specifies one particular use) and, on vacant land, will control unless rezoned.
c. Property should be classified as single family residential and appraised based on that use.
d. Comparable sales should be taken from a comparable single family residential area (see example III C).

Example B

PLAN: COMMERCIAL

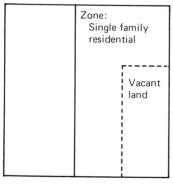

a. The plan and zone differ—commercial for the plan and single family residential for the zone.
b. Property is presently developed to a preexisting nonconforming use (multifamily units) to the zone but may be a permissible lower density use under the plan.
c. It is presumed that the present use, although nonconforming at least to the zone, will be permitted so long as the present buildings are used on the land.
d. Property should be classified as multifamily residential improved and appraised based on that use.
e. Comparable sales should be taken from comparable multifamily residential property.

NOTE: If plan does not permit a lesser use than commercial (commercial only), the land would be classified and appraised as commercial property, and the buildings appraised recognizing economic obsolescence (see example I D).

III. Plan Permits Higher Use Than Zone (cont'd.)

Example C

PLAN: COMMERCIAL

Zone:
  Single
  family
  residential
	Zone:
	  Commercial

B A C

a. Lots A, B, and C have a comprehensive planning designation of commercial use.
b. Subject property A, zoned single family residential, is to be appraised at market value with consideration for the comprehensive plan and zoning.
c. Lot C recently sold for $30,000 and is zoned commercial.
d. Lot B recently sold for $20,000 and is zoned single family residential.
e. Recent sales of lots with both the comprehensive plan and zoning designation of single family residential have been at $4,000.
f. Sale of Lot C cannot be used as a comparable for appraising lot A as the zoning allows a more intensive use. The rejection of this sale as a comparable is mandatory under the Martindale and Johnson decisions.
g. Sale of Lot B can be used as a comparable in appraising Lot A. This sale takes into consideration the land use plan and zoning of Lot A which is required under ORS 308.235.
h. The use of sales from an area in which the land use plans and zoning allows only single family residential use would not take into consideration the current land use plan of Lot A, and should not be used.

MONTGOMERY COUNTY, MARYLAND, ORDINANCE CREATING HIGH DENSITY, MIXED USE ZONES NEAR TRANSIT STATIONS

Ordinance

BE IT ORDAINED by the County Council for Montgomery County, Maryland, sitting as a District Council for that portion of the Maryland-Washington Regional District located within Montgomery County, Maryland, that the following language is hereby added:

Section 59—51.6 TS—R Zone
Transit Station—Residential Zone

a. *Intent and Purpose*

The TS—R Zone is intended only for those areas of the County which have been designated Transit Station Development Areas by approved and adopted master plan; however, it is not the intent that every area around a transit station shall be designated a Transit Station Development Area. These areas may be near Metro transit stations not found within central business districts or they may be areas adjacent to central business districts but within 1,500 feet of a transit station. Within these Transit Station Development Areas the TS—R Zone is intended for locations where multi-family residential development already exists or where such use is recommended by an approved and adopted master plan.

The TS—R Zone is designed to accomplish the following purposes:

Promote the effective use of the Transit Station Development Area and access thereto;

Provide multi-family residential densities for use in locations within walking distance of the transit station; and

Provide a range of densities that will afford planning choices to match the diverse characteristics of the several Transit Station Development Areas within the County.

It is further the purposes of this Zone to provide the maximum amount of freedom possible in the design of buildings and their grouping and layout within the areas classified in this Zone; to stimulate the coordinate, harmonious, and systematic development of the area within the Zone, of the area surrounding the Zone, and of the Regional District as a whole; to prevent detrimental effects to the use or development of adjacent properties of the surrounding neighborhood; to provide housing to persons of all economic levels; and to promote the health, safety, morals, and welfare of the present and future inhabitants of the Regional District and County as a whole.

In order to facilitate and encourage the innovative and creative design of uses and the development of land uses most compatible and desirable within the areas of each transit station, development shall be in accordance with a plan of development meeting the requirements of this section and processed in accordance with the provisions of this Zone and Ordinance. This section is not to be construed as implying or requiring that any proposed plan of development must be approved.

The fact that an application for TS—R zoning complies with any or all specific requirements and purposes set forth herein shall not be deemed to create a presumption that the resulting development would be compatible with surrounding land uses and in itself shall not be sufficient to require the granting of an application. The following regulations shall apply in the TS—R Zone:

b. *Development Standards. The Development Standards Governing This Zone Shall Be As Follows:*

(1) *Uses Permitted*

No building, structure, or land shall be used and no building or structure shall be hereafter erected, structurally altered, enlarged, or maintained, except for one or more of the following uses:

Residential

Dwellings, any type; except trailers, hotels and motels
Rental of guest rooms to not more than two roomers in any one single-
family dwelling unit

Institutional

Churches and other places of worship
Library, museums and similar institutions of a non-commercial nature
Housing and related facilities for elderly or handicapped persons

Retail Sales and Services subject to standards set forth in subsection (3) below
Retail Sales and Services such as:

Telegraph and messenger service
Newsstand or bookstore
Florist
Gift or jewelry store

Personel Service

Barber shop or beauty shop
Dry cleaning pick-up station (may include pressing)
Laundry, pick-up station
Laundry, self-service
Valet shop
Medical or dental offices

Signs

Public Services

Publicly owned and operated uses
Ambulance service or rescue squad
Parks, playgrounds and other recreational areas
Taxicab stand (but not including storage while not in use)

Accessory Buildings and Uses

(2) *Special Exceptions*

The following uses may be permitted as special exceptions in accordance with the provisions of Section 59—120.

Residential

Hotels and motels

Institutional

Child care home or center

Food and Drug Stores

Food or beverage store
Delicatessen and sandwich shops
Drug store
Restaurants (not including drive-ins)

(3) *Retail Sales and Consumer Service Establishments*

Any retail sales and consumer services establishments as set forth in (1) and (2) above shall be incidental to and may be located only within a multiple-family structure which is six (6) or more stories in height, in a development which contains one hundred and fifty (150) or more dwelling units provided:

(a) There shall be no entrances directly from the street to such establishments;

(b) No sign relating to such establishment shall be visible from outside of the building;

(c) Such establishments shall not be located above the ground level floor, except that a restaurant may be permitted on the top or penthouse floor thereof;

(d) No deliveries shall be made except to occupants within such structure or in the immediate development;

(e) Establishments shall be so located and constructed to protect tenants of the building from noise, traffic, odors and interference with privacy.

(4) *Density and Area Requirements*

(a) Lot size. The minimum lot size shall be 40,000 square feet.

(b) Density. The density of development permitted on any lot shall not exceed 150 dwelling units per acre, nor shall the maximum floor area ratio exceed 2.5.

(c) Lot Coverage, percentage of. Not more than 35 percent of the net lot area shall be covered by buildings or accessory uses.

(d) Green Area. Not less than 50% of the net lot area shall be devoted to green area as defined in Section 59—1. Not less than 50% of the green area shall be devoted to active and passive recreational purposes.

(5) *Street Access and Frontage*

Each tract in the TS—R Zone shall have frontage on a public street. The adequacy of the frontage shall be determined by the Planning Board. Points of access to public roads shall be subject to approval by the appropriate highway authority.

(6) *Building Height Limit*

The maximum height permitted for any building shall be determined in site plan review. In approving height limits, the Planning Board shall take into consideration the size of the lot or parcel, the relationship of the building or buildings to surrounding uses, the need to preserve light and air for the residents of the development and residents of surrounding properties, and any other factors relevant to height of the building.

(7) *Off-Street Parking*

Parking shall be provided in accordance with Section 59—79 and shall be so located as to have a minimal impact on any adjoining residential properties.

(8) *Roads*

Interior roads may be private or public but private roads shall have a minimum width of 20 feet for two-way traffic and 10 feet for one-way traffic, and shall be paved and maintained in good repair.

(9) *Public Facilities and Amenities*

A development shall conform substantially to the facilities recommended by the approved and adopted master plan, including the granting of such easements or making such dedications to the public as may be shown thereon or shall be deemed necessary by the Planning Board to insure the compatibility of the development with the surrounding area.

(10) *Procedures for Application and Approval*

(a) Application and approval of the TS—R Zone shall be in accordance with the provisions of Section 59—31.4.

(b) Detailed site plans shall be submitted and approved in accordance with the provisions of Section 59—31.5.

Section 59—51.7 TS—M Zone
Transit Station—Mixed Zone

a. *Intent and Purposes*

The TS—M Zone is intended only for those areas of the County which have been designated Transit Station Development Areas by approved and adopted Master Plans; however, it is not the intent that every area around a transit station shall be designated a Transit Station Development Area. These areas are near Metro transit stations not located within central business districts.

Within these Transit Station Development Areas the TS—M Zone is intended for locations where substantial commercial or office uses already exist or where such uses are recommended by an approved and adopted Master Plan.

The TS—M Zone is designed to accomplish the following purposes:

Promote the optimum use of the transit facilities by assuring the orderly development of land in Transit Station Development Areas and access, both vehicular and pedestrian, to Metro Stations;

Provide for the needs of the workers and residents of Transit Station Development Areas;

Provide for the incidental shopping needs of the transit facility riders at Metro Stations having parking facilities for large numbers of riders;

Minimize the necessity for automobile transportation by providing, in largely residential transit station areas, the retail commercial uses and professional services that contribute to the self-sufficiency of the community;

Obtain amenities for the residents and workers in transit station areas not ordinarily obtainable in conventional zoning classifications.

It is further the purpose of this Zone to prevent detrimental effects to the use or development of adjacent properties or the neighborhood and to promote the health, safety, morals, and welfare of the present and future inhabitants of the district and the County as a whole.

In order to encourage and facilitate desirable development of land uses, it is further the purpose of this Zone to eliminate some of the specific restrictions which regulate, in some other zoning categories, the height, bulk and arrangement of buildings and the location of the various land uses, and to substitute for these regulations the requirement that all development be in accordance with a plan of development meeting the requirements of this section.

This section is not to be construed as implying that any proposed plan of development must be approved. The fact that an application complies with all specific requirements and purposes set forth herein shall not be deemed to create a presumption that the application is, in fact, compatible with surrounding land uses and, in itself, shall not be sufficient to require the granting of any application.

b. *Development Standards. The Development Standards Governing This Zone Shall Be As Follows:*

(1) *Uses Permitted*

No building, structure, or land shall be used and no building or structure shall hereafter be erected, structurally altered, enlarged, or maintained, except for one or more of the following uses:

Residential

Dwelling unit, any type, except hotel or motel, trailers

Institutional

Churches and other places of worship
Library, museums and similar institutions of a non-commercial nature
Educational institutions, private

Recreational

Bowling alley
Health clubs or recreational
Theaters or cinemas, indoor
Private club

Retail Sales and Services

 Food and drug stores

Food or beverage store
Delicatessen and sandwich shops
Restaurant
Drug store

Personal service

Barber shop or beauty shop
Dry cleaning pick-up station (may include pressing)
Laundry, pick-up station
Laundry, self-service
Valet shop
Shoe or hat repair
Telegraph and messenger service
Stationery or office supplies
Bank or financial institutions
Variety store and dry goods store including department stores

 Miscellaneous Sales and Service

Radio and TV repair

Offices, Professional, Business, Clinical

Signs

Public Services

Public owned and operated uses
Ambulance service or rescue squad
Parks, playgrounds and other recreational areas
Taxicab stand (but not including storage while not in use)
Public utility buildings

(2) *Special Exceptions*

The following uses may be permitted as special exceptions in accordance with the provisions of Section 59–120:

Residential

Hotel or motel

Institutional

Child care home or center

Retail Sales and Service

Automobile filling stations and minor repairs
Automobile repair and service center for minor repairs and replacement
   placed underground or within an enclosed larger structure
Automobile rental

Miscellaneous Sales and Service

Pet shop
Radio and TV broadcasting studios
Medical and dental laboratories

(3) *Density and Area Requirements*

(a) Lot size. The minimum lot size shall be 40,000 square feet.

(b) Density. The density of development permitted on any lot shall not exceed a maximum floor area ratio of 3.0.

(c) Lot coverage, percentage of. No more than 60 percent of the net lot area shall be covered by buildings or accessory structures.

(4) *Parking*

Parking shall be provided in accordance with Section 59−79.

(5) *Public Facilities and Amenities*

(a) Not less than 10 percent of the net lot area shall be devoted to amenity space.

(b) A development shall conform substantially to the facilities and amenities recommended by the approved and adopted Master Plan, including the granting of such easements or making such dedications to the public as may be shown thereon or shall be deemed necessary by the Planning Board to insure the compatibility of the development with the surrounding area and to assure the ability of the area to accommodate the uses proposed by the application.

(6) *Procedures for Application and Approval*

(a) Application and approval of the TS−M Zone shall be in accordance with the provisions of Section 59−31.4.

(b) Detailed site plans shall be submitted and approved in accordance with the provisions of Section 59−31.5.

Section 59−31.4. General Regulations. Application and Approval of Transit Station Zones

a. *Application for Development Plan Approval*

In addition to requirements contained in Sections 59−195 through 59−209, an application for reclassification to the TS−M or TS−R Zone shall be accompanied by a development plan for the property sought to be reclassified, a copy of which shall be submitted to the Planning Board for its recommendations as consistent with the purpose and intent of the applicable zone in the event of such reclassification, and five copies of which shall be made available to civic associations in the area of the proposed rezoning and the general public. No such application shall be approved by the District Council until the development plan has been reviewed by the Planning Board.

b. *Submission Requirements for Development Plan*

The proposed development plan shall consist of a text, maps, and drawings and any other information which the applicant may deem necessary to support his application which shall clearly describe how the proposed development of the site will meet the standards and purposes of the applicable zone. Such text, maps, and drawings shall include the following information:

(1) The principal existing physical characteristics of the site, including but not limited to, a topographical analysis of slopes and subsoil conditions, the delineation of major vegetative growth, floodplains, significant water bodies, landfills, rock outcroppings, and areas of historic significance;

(2) An analysis of the relationship of the existing physical characteristics of the site to the surrounding neighborhood;

(3) A land use plan showing: the proposed location of structures and improvements on the site; the proposed gross floor area ratio and dwelling units of the total development; the type of dwelling units and number of bedrooms; the location of land for public use, such as streets, schools, or parks, identifying land to be dedicated to the public; heights and elevations of proposed buildings and structures including pedestrian circulation systems (interior and exterior) with identification of public and private areas and their dimensions; the locations of points of access to and from the site and to public transportation facilities where access to the same is provided, as well as street parking spaces; and, the location and dimensions of all off-street parking spaces;

(4) A detailed statement describing the manner in which the development conforms to the approved and adopted Sector Plan and the purposes of the applicable zone;

(5) A statement and analysis demonstrating the manner in which the proposed development will result in a more efficient and desirable development than could be accomplished by the use of the standard method of development;

(6) A staging program, including a schedule of development stating the sequence in which all structures, open and amenity spaces, pedestrian and vehicular circulation systems, and other amenities are to be constructed, indicating the relationship to, if any, and coordination with, the County's approved capital improvements program;

(7) Proposed restrictions, agreements or other documents indicating the manner in which any land intended for common, quasi-public or amenity space use, but not proposed to be in public ownership, will be held, owned, and maintained for the indicated purposes;

(8) Such other matters as the applicant may consider of importance in the evaluation of the development plan or as the Planning Board may require in order for it to evaluate compliance of the proposed development with the requirements and purposes of the applicable zone;

(9) A list by name and address of all adjacent property owners.

c. *Review and Recommendation by the Planning Board*

In considering an application for the TS—M or TS—R Zone, the Planning Board shall consider whether the application and the accompanying development plan fulfill the purposes and requirements of the applicable zone. The Planning Board shall make specific recommendations to the District Council concerning those matters which, under the provisions of subsection (f)(2) of this section, the District Council must consider in acting upon an application for the

TS—M or TS—R Zone. In addition, the Planning Board shall recommend approval, approval with recommended modifications, or disapproval of the development plan which accompanies the application; particularly considering, in regard to the development plan, those matters which, under the provisions of subsection (f)(2) of this section, the District Council must consider in acting upon an application for the TS—M or TS—R Zone. The Planning Board shall forward its written recommendation to the District Council and the applicant, together with the technical staff report thereon.

d. *Review and Recommendation by the Hearing Examiner*

In addition to the requirements of Sections 59—203, 59—204, and 59—206, the Hearing Examiner shall consider the development plan as a part of the application for purposes of conducting the required public hearing and preparing the required report and recommendation to the District Council.

e. *Amendment of a Development Plan Prior to Approval*

A development plan may be amended by the applicant up to 30 days prior to review and recommendation by the Planning Board.

f. *Review and Approval by the District Council*

(1) Approval of a TS—M or TS—R Zone by the District Council shall be deemed to constitute approval of the development plan, which is a part of the application for zoning reclassification.

(2) Basis for Approval. Before approving an application for the TS—M or TS—R Zone, the District Council shall consider whether the application fulfills the purposes and requirements set forth in the appropriate section. The fact that an application complies with all of the specific requirements and purposes set forth in the appropriate section shall not be deemed to create a presumption that the proposed development would carry out the purposes of the applicable zone, nor that the proposed development plan would result in a more efficient and desirable development than could be accomplished by the use of conventional zoning categories, nor that it would result in compatibility with surrounding development; nor shall such compliance, by itself, be sufficient to require the granting of the TS—M or TS—R Zone or the approval of the development plan submitted.

The District Council shall make the following specific findings, in addition to any other findings which may be found to be necessary and appropriate to the evaluation of the proposed reclassification:

(a) That the zone requested is in substantial accordance with the use and/or density indicated by the master plan, and that it does not conflict with the capital improvements program, the general plan, and other pertinent County plans and policies.

(b) That the proposed development complies with the purposes of the appropriate zone and provides for the safety, convenience, and amenity of the residents of the development and the neighboring area.

(c) That the proposed development complies with the general regulations for the appropriate zone.

(d) That the proposed development will be compatible with the surrounding neighborhood.

(e) That the proposed vehicular and pedestrian transportation systems are adequate and efficient.

(f) That any proposals, including restrictions, agreements, or other documents, which show the ownership and method of assuring perpetual maintenance of those areas which are intended to be used for recreational or other common or quasi-public purposes, are adequate and sufficient.

(g) That by its design, by minimizing grading and by other means, the proposed development would tend to prevent erosion of the soil and to preserve natural vegetation, existing topography, and other natural features of the site.

(h) Any other matters which the District Council finds to be necessary and appropriate to the evaluation of the proposed reclassification.

g. *Amendment of a Development Plan*

Any proposal for amendment to a development plan subsequent to approval by the District Council of a Transit Station zone shall be filed with the Planning Board. An amendment to a development plan shall not change the area zoned TS—M or TS—R. The Planning Board, after holding a public hearing, shall act to approve or disapprove of such amendment within sixty days of the filing of the application, unless the applicant grants a waiver of the time limitation. The Planning Board shall evaluate such amendment in accordance with the provisions of subsection (c) of this section. The Planning Board's written recommendation of approval or disapproval stating reasons therefor, together with the technical staff report, shall be forwarded to the District Council and the applicant. The District Council shall act to approve or disapprove of the recommendation of the Planning Board within forty-five days of the receipt by the District Council of the action of the Planning Board, unless the Council on its own motion extends the time period.

Section 59—31.5 General Regulations. Detailed Site Plan Review for Transit Station Zones

a. *Submission of Detailed Site Plan*

Detailed site plans for all or any part of a transit station zone development shall be filed with the Planning Board. Each detailed site plan shall:

(1) Be in accordance with the approved development plan.

(2) Include all of the information required for the submission of a preliminary subdivision plan, as set forth in Chapter 50 of this Code.

(3) Show the existing topography and proposed grading of the site at contour intervals of not more than two feet, including existing vegetation and other natural features, rock outcroppings, bodies of water and watercourses, fifty-year floodplains, existing tree and plantcover, by variety, and scenic views. Landfills and existing structures shall also be shown.

(4) Include a grading plan, showing water runoff drawings and calculations and plans for siltation and erosion control, both during and after construction.

(5) The location, height, ground coverage and use of all structures, and location and areas of open spaces, parking facilities and areas dedicated to public spaces. Calculations of building coverage, numbers of parking spaces and areas devoted to open spaces shall also be indicated.

(6) All utility service lines, and all easements and right-of-ways, existing or proposed.

(7) Adjacent highways and streets serving the site, noting centerlines, widths of paving, grades and median break points.

(8) The location, dimensions and grades of all roads, streets and driveways, parking facilities, loading areas, points of access to surrounding streets and pedestrian walks and pathways.

(9) For each residential structure, the number and type of dwelling units, classified by the number of bedrooms, and the total floor area, if any, to be used for commercial purposes.

(10) The floor areas of all non-residential buildings and the proposed uses for each structure.

(11) A landscaping and screening plan, showing all manmade features and the location, size and species of all planting materials.

(12) An exterior lighting plan, covering all parking areas, driveways and pedestrian ways, and including the height, number and type of fixtures to be installed and the computed average light intensity levels to be provided.

(13) The location of all public schools, parks and other community recreational facilities, indicating the location and use of all land to be dedicated to public use.

(14) Documents indicating in detail the manner in which any land intended for common or quasi-public use, but not proposed to be in public ownership, will be held, owned and maintained in perpetuity for the indicated purposes.

(15) If a detailed site plan is one of a number of detailed site plans within a transit station zone development, each detailed site plan shall show how it is related to and coordinated with other detailed site plans, either completed, under construction, or yet to be submitted.

(16) Any additional information which may be required by the Planning Board in order to enable it to evaluate the detailed site plan.

b. *Review and Approval by the Planning Board*

The Planning Board shall approve, approve subject to modifications or disapprove each detailed site plan. The Planning Board shall notify the applicant in writing of its action not later than sixty days after receipt by the Planning Board of the detailed site plan, unless the applicant consents in writing to an extension of this time limitation. In reaching its decision upon each detailed site plan, the Planning Board shall consider and determine:

(1) Whether the detailed site plan is substantially in accordance with the approved development plan.

(2) Whether the detailed site plan is in accordance with the applicable requirements and purposes of the applicable transit station zone.

(3) Whether the open spaces, including developed open space, are of such size and location as to serve as convenient areas for recreation, relaxation, and social activities for the residents and patrons of the development and are so planned, designed and situated as to function as necessary physical and aesthetic open areas among and between individual structures and groups of structures. In connection therewith, whether the setbacks, yards and related walkways are so located and of sufficient dimensions to provide for adequate light, air, pedestrian circulation, and necessary vehicular access.

(4) Whether the pedestrian circulation system is so located, designed and of sufficient size as to conveniently handle pedestrian traffic efficiently and without congestion; the extent to which the pedestrian circulation system is separated from vehicular roadways so as to be safe, pleasing and efficient for movement of pedestrians; and whether the pedestrian circulation system provides efficient, convenient and adequate linkages among residential areas, open spaces, recreational areas, commercial and employment areas, and public facilities.

(5) Whether the vehicular circulation system is so designed and located as to provide an efficient, safe, and convenient transportation network.

(6) Whether the detailed site plan is coordinated and compatible with other existing and proposed detailed site plans and with existing and proposed surrounding development.

(7) Whether each use is so located, of such size and so landscaped as to be compatible with the other uses on the detailed site plan as well as adjacent existing and proposed structures and uses.

(8) Whether the arrangements for the ownership and maintenance of open space land and facilities and adequate to provide for permanent preservation and maintenance of such facilities and land for their indicated uses.

(9) Whether the detailed site plan satisfies the requirements of Chapter 50 of this Code for approval of a preliminary subdivision plan.

c. *Effect of Detailed Site Plans*

Record Plats required by the Montgomery County Subdivision Regulations, Chapter 50 of the Montgomery County Code, (1972 Ed.), as amended, shall be approved only in accordance with Detailed Site Plans and Preliminary Subdivision Plans approved by the Planning Board. Building Permits and Use and Occupancy Permits shall be issued only in accordance with Detailed Site Plans approved by the Planning Board. Any failure to conform with approved Detailed Site Plans; Preliminary Subdivision Plans, and Record Plats shall be cause for denial of Building Permits and Use and Occupancy Permits. Any failure to conform with issued Building Permits and Use and Occupancy Permits shall be cause for revocation of such permits.

This Ordinance shall take effect immediately following its enactment.

SUGGESTED ORDINANCE DEREGULATING FENCE SETBACK AND CONSTRUCTION IN DAVIS, CALIFORNIA

**An Ordinance Deregulating Fence Setback
and Construction in Davis**

Section 1: Findings

A. The people of California face the likelihood of energy and resource short-falls as competition for scarce resources increases.

B. Regulation of personal property and behavior is becoming increasingly burdensome.

C. Fences can increase privacy to allow full use of south facing windows. Current fence setback requirements are excessive and will cause shading of south glass in many cases.

D. Fences also can increase security of personal property and allow further use of natural ventilation.

E. Fences encourage more intensive use of property and can increase the effective size of a lot, allowing use of smaller lots, thereby reducing sprawl and conversion of agricultural land. Protection of agricultural land is important for energy as well as environmental and human considerations.

F. Hedges provide other benefits in terms of cooling, infiltration, wind speed reduction, and wildlife habitat.

G. Fencing would reduce complaints over untidiness and would reduce interference of neighbor with neighbor and reduce city involvement in personal affairs.

H. Full inspection of fences and hedge installation and modification would be costly and complex and would produce few benefits to the public health, safety and welfare.

Section 2: Fences Deregulated

Therefore, the City Council of Davis does hereby amend:
Section 29−199:(c) to read

Fences, hedges, or walls not exceeding seven feet in height may occupy any portion of a side, rear, or front yard; provided, however, that any fence on a corner lot at an intersection without stop signs or signal controls shall be placed in a manner that will protect the public safety. In most cases this will require that a fence or hedge over three feet in height above the average crown of adjacent streets shall not be less than 20′ from the point of intersection of the street right of way line, or less than 10′ from the street right of way line at any point.

Reprinted from:
Living Systems, "Planning for Energy Conservation, Draft Report,"
Prepared for the City of Davis, California, pursuant to HUD Project
Grant No. B−75−51−06−001 (Winters, California, 1976).

FEDERAL STATUTE PROMOTING MIXED USE BUILDINGS
(Public Buildings Cooperative Use Act of 1976, Pub. L. No. 94–541)
(excerpt)

Be it enacted by the Senate and House of Representatives of the United States of America in Congress assembled,

TITLE I

Sec. 101. This title may be cited as the "Public Buildings Cooperative Use Act of 1976."

Sec. 102. (a) In order to carry out his duties under this title and under any other authority with respect to constructing, operating, maintaining, altering, and otherwise managing or acquiring space necessary for the accommodation of Federal agencies and to accomplish the purposes of this title, the Administrator shall—

(1) acquire and utilize space in suitable buildings of historic, architectural, or cultural significance, unless use of such space would not prove feasible and prudent compared with available alternatives;

(2) encourage the location of commercial, cultural, educational, and recreational facilities and activities within public buildings;

(3) provide and maintain space, facilities, and activities, to the extent practicable, which encourage public access to and stimulate public pedestrian traffic around, into, and through public buildings, permitting cooperative improvements to and uses of the area between the building and the street, so that such activities complement and supplement commercial, cultural, educational, and recreational resources in the neighborhood of public buildings; and

(4) encourage the public use of public buildings for cultural, educational, and recreational activities.

(b) In carrying out his duties under subsection (a) of this section, the Administrator shall consult with Governors, areawide agencies established pursuant to title II of the Demonstration Cities and Metropolitan Development Act of 1966 and title IV of the Intergovernmental Cooperation Act of 1968, and chief executive officers of those units of general local government in each area served by an existing or proposed public building, and shall solicit the comments of such other community leaders and members of the general public as he deems appropriate.

SUGGESTED RESOLUTION SUPPORTING INCREASED TREE SHADING IN EXISTING DEVELOPMENT IN DAVIS, CALIFORNIA

Whereas, the City Council recognizes the energy and economic benefits of shading streets and parking lots, and whereas, most existing streets and parking lots in Davis are undershaded and would benefit from further shading, and whereas, the City can set a positive example for the rest of the community by bringing existing streets and parking lots up to the new standard where existing planting will not meet the 50% requirement in 15 years.

Now, therefore, the City Council of the City of Davis does hereby resolve to support an increased planting program and directs the Parks and Recreation Department to identify areas in the City where supplemental street tree plantings should be made. A plan for such plantings and a cost estimate should also be prepared for each of the next three year's budget.

90° BASE TEMPERATURE

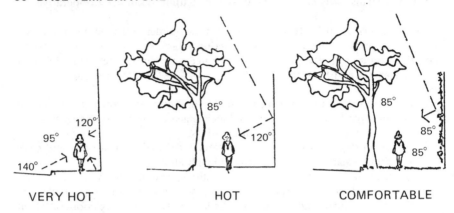

VERY HOT   HOT   COMFORTABLE

Reprinted from:
   Living Systems, "Planning for Energy Conservation, Draft Report,"
   Prepared for the City of Davis, California, pursuant to HUD Project
   Grant No. B–75–51–06–001 (Winters, California, 1976).

SUGGESTED ORDINANCE REQUIRING FUNCTIONAL LANDSCAPING IN NEW COMMERCIAL DEVELOPMENT IN DAVIS, CALIFORNIA

Section 1: Findings
A. Deciduous trees, vines and other landscaping can provide excellent cooling during the summer through evapotranspiration and shading of buildings (windows, walls or roofs), sidewalks and streets. This cooling reduces the heat load on buildings and reduces energy use.
B. Air temperature and radiation effect human comfort equally.
C. Walls and streets can reach very high surface temperatures (140°+) in the summer. These high temperatures make walking and bicycling very unpleasant and encourage use of the automobile.
D. Landscape can improve air quality, aesthetics, wildlife habitat, and noise control.
E. Current landscape is often chosen to minimize maintenance cost of landscape without consideration of potential benefits. These include savings in energy for cooling, improved human comfort, and increasing bicycle and pedestrian traffic.

Section 2: Requiring Functional Landscape Plans

Therefore, the City Council of the City of Davis does hereby amend section 29.831(c) regulating CN development and adds new sections for CC, CT, CS and CH to read.

Landscaping: Landscaping must cover a minimum of 10% of the site. A landscape plan with proposed planting and reasonable expected 15 year growth pattern (plan and elevation) must be submitted and approved before a building permit can be issued.

These plans must show the amount of shading provided on August 21 at 8 A.M., 12 noon, and 4 P.M. Plantings and mechanical shades must provide 50% shading of all exposed horizontal surfaces (excluding roof) and to provide similar shading for east, west, and south walls abutting sidewalks, paths, or walls within 15 years.

This percentage shall be calculated as follows: For all surfaces project the shadows of the planting for 8 A.M., 12 noon, and 4 P.M. (solar time, August 21), calculate the percentage area that is shaded at each of these times and calculate the average percentage as follows:

$$\% \text{ area} = \frac{(\% \text{ area (8am)} + \% \text{ area (12 noon)} + \% \text{ area (4pm)}}{3}$$

In addition, the Community Development may in some cases require a narrative text to accompany the landscape plan describing the materials used, their impact on the microclimate, water use and maintenance, effect on noise reduction, effect on wind, value for glare reduction, and value as wildlife habitat.

Reprinted from:
Living Systems, "Planning for Energy Conservation, Draft Report," Prepared for the City of Davis, California, pursuant to HUD Project Grant No. B−75−51−06−001 (Winters, California, 1976).

OREGON BICYCLE TRAILS AND FOOTPATHS LAW

366.514 Use of Highway Fund for Footpaths and Bicycle Trails

(1) Out of the funds received by the department or by any county or city from the State Highway Fund reasonable amounts shall be expended as necessary for the establishment of footpaths and bicycle trails. Footpaths and bicycle trails shall be established wherever a highway, road or street is being constructed, reconstructed or relocated. Funds received from the State Highway Fund may also be expended to maintain such footpaths and trails and to establish footpaths and trails along other highways, roads and streets and in parks and recreation areas.

(2) Footpaths and trails are not required to be established under subsection (1) of this section:

(a) Where the establishment of such paths and trails would be contrary to public safety;

(b) If the cost of establishing such paths and trails would be excessively disproportionate to the need or probable use; or

(c) Where sparsity of population, other available ways or other factors indicate an absence of any need for such paths and trails.

(3) The amount expended by the department or by a city or county as required or permitted by this section shall never in any one fiscal year be less than one percent of the total amount of the funds received from the highway funds. However:

(a) This subsection does not apply to a city in any year in which the one percent equals $250 or less, or to a county in any year in which the one percent equals $1,500 or less.

(b) A city or county in lieu of expending the funds each year may credit the funds to a financial reserve or special fund . . . to be held for not more than 10 years, and to be expended for the purposes required or permitted by this section.

(4) For the purposes of this chapter, the establishment of paths and trails and the expenditure of funds as authorized by this section are for highway, road and street purposes. The department shall, when requested, provide technical assistance and advice to cities and counties in carrying out the purpose of this section. The division shall recommend construction standards for footpaths and bicycle trails. The division shall . . . provide a uniform system of signing footpaths and bicycle trails which shall apply to paths and trails under the jurisdiction of the department and cities and counties. The department and cities and counties may restrict the use of footpaths and bicycle trails under their respective jurisdictions to pedestrians and nonmotorized vehicles.

(5) As used in this section, "bicycle trail" means a publicly owned and maintained lane or way designated and signed for use as a bicycle route.

Or. Rev. Stat. §366.514 (Supp. 1975)

CALIFORNIA BIKEWAYS ACT

2370. The Legislature hereby finds and declares that traffic congestion, air pollution, noise pollution, public health, energy shortages, consumer costs, and land-use considerations resulting from a primary reliance on the automobile for transportation are each sufficient reasons to provide for multimodal transportation systems.

2371. It is the intent of the Legislature in enacting this chapter to establish a bicycle transit system. It is the further intent of the Legislature that this transit system shall be designed and developed to achieve the functional commuting needs of the employee, student, businessman, and shopper as the foremost consideration in route selection, to have the physical safety of the bicyclist and bicyclist's property as a major planning component, and to have the capacity to accommodate bicyclists of all ages and skills.

2372. As used in this chapter, "bicycle" means a device upon which any person may ride, propelled exclusively by human power through a belt, chain, or gears, and having either two or three wheels in a tandem or tricycle arrangement.

2373. As used in this chapter, "bikeway" means all facilities that provide primarily for bicycle travel. For purposes of this chapter, bikeways shall be categorized as follows:

(a) Class I bikeways, which provide a completely separated right-of-way designated for the exclusive use of bicyles and pedestrians with crossflows by motorists minimized.

(b) Class II bikeways, which provide a restricted right-of-way designated for the exclusive or semiexclusive use of bicycles with through travel by motor vehicles or pedestrians prohibited, but with vehicle parking and crossflows by pedestrians and motorists permitted.

(c) Class III bikeways, which provide a right-of-way designated by signs or permanent markings and shared with pedestrians or motorists.

2374. The department shall establish recommended minimum general design criteria for the development, planning, and construction of bikeways, including, but not limited to, the design speed of the facility, the space requirements of the bicycle and bicyclist, minimum widths and clearances, grade, radius of curvature, bikeway surface, lighting, drainage, and general safety. In addition, the department, in cooperation with county and city governments, shall establish mandatory minimum safety design criteria for the construction of bikeways.

2375. The department shall establish uniform specifications and symbols for signs, markers, and traffic control devices to control bicycle traffic; to warn of dangerous conditions, obstacles, or hazards; to designate the right-of-way as between bicycles and vehicles; to state the nature and destination of the bikeway; to exclude unauthorized vehicles; and to warn pedestrians and motorists of the presence of bicycle traffic.

2376. All city, county, and regional departments of public works, parks and recreation, planning agencies, or departments, and other local agencies having authority over, or responsibility for the development of, bikeways shall utilize all minimum safety design criteria and uniform specifications and symbols for signs, markers, and traffic control devices established by the department pursuant to Sections 2374 and 2375.

2377. Any city or county may prepare and submit to the department for review and approval its bikeway plan. No plan shall be reviewed and approved which has not received the prior review and the comments of the appropriate transportation planning agency specified in Section 29532 of the Government Code. Such plan shall include, but not be limited to, the following elements:

(a) Route selection, which shall include, but not be limited to, the commuting needs of employees, businessmen, shoppers, and students.

(b) Land use and population density and settlement patterns.

(c) Transportation interface, which shall include, but not be limited to, coordination with other modes of transportation so that a bicyclist may employ multiple modes of transportation in reaching his destination.

(d) Citizen and community involvement in planning.

(e) Flexibility and coordination with long-range transportation planning.

(f) Local government involvement in planning.

(g) Provision for rest facilities, including, but not limited to, restrooms, drinking water, public telephones, and air for bicycle tires.

(h) Provision for parking facilities, including, but not limited to, bicycle parking with theft prevention devices located at, in, or near civic and public buildings, transit terminals, business districts, shopping centers, schools, parks and playgrounds, and other locations where people congregate.

2378. Any city or county which has received approval from the department for its bikeway plan may apply to the department for funds for bikeways and related facilities which will implement such plan. Such funds shall be granted to the applicant on a matching basis which provides for the applicant's furnishing of funding for 10 percent of the total cost of constructing the proposed bikeways and related facilities. Such funds may be used, where feasible, to apply for and match federal grants or loans.

2379. For purposes of providing for a coordinated network of bikeways, a board of supervisors, in cooperation with the cities in the county, may elect to distribute portions of county funds received pursuant to this chapter to cities within the county based on a formula devised by the board.

2380. The governing body of a city, county, or local agency may:

(a) Establish bikeways.

(b) Acquire, by gift, purchase, or condemnation, land, real property, easements, or rights-of-way to establish bikeways.

(c) Establish bikeways pursuant to Section 21207 of the Vehicle Code.

2381. Rights-of-way established for other purposes by cities, counties, or local agencies shall not be abandoned unless the governing body thereof determines that the rights-of-way or parts thereof are not useful as bikeways.

State highway rights-of-way shall not be abandoned until the department first consults with the local agencies having jurisdiction over the areas concerned to determine whether the rights-of-way or parts thereof could be developed as bikeways. If an affirmative determination is made, before abandoning such rights-of-way, the department shall first make such property available to local agencies for development as bikeways in accordance with the terms and procedures of Sections 104.15 and 156.8 of this code and Section 14012 of the Government Code.

2382. The Bicycle Lane Account is continued in existence in the State Transportation Fund, and moneys in the account are continuously appropriated to the department for expenditure for the purposes specified in this chapter. Unexpended moneys shall be retained in the account for use in subsequent fiscal years.

2383. The department shall allocate and disburse moneys from the Bicycle Lane Account according to the following priorities:

(a) To the department, such amounts as are necessary to administer the provisions of this chapter.

(b) To cities and counties, for bikeways and related facilities, in accordance with the priorities specified in Section 2386. To be eligible for funding, such bikeways shall be approximately parallel to state, county, or city roadways, where the separation of bicycle traffic from motor vehicle traffic will increase the traffic capacity of the roadway.

2384. The Legislature finds and declares that the construction of bikeways pursuant to Section 2383 constitutes a highway purpose under Article XXVI of the California Constitution and justifies the expenditure of highway funds therefor.

2385. The Bikeway Account is hereby created in the State Transportation Fund, and moneys in the account are hereby continuously appropriated to the department for expenditure for the purposes specified in this chapter. Unexpended moneys shall be retained in the account for use in subsequent fiscal years.

2386. The department shall allocate and disburse moneys from the Bikeway Account for projects accomplishing the following purposes, according to the following order of priority:

(a) Construction of class I bikeways in order to complete existing bikeways or bicycle routes that will serve the greatest volume of commuters, including, but not limited to, those routes which connect with existing or proposed mass transit terminals. For the purposes of this subdivision, the volume of commuters shall be calculated exclusive of recreational usage and shall include, but not be limited to, employees, businessmen, shoppers, and students.

(b) Construction of other class I bikeways for commuters that are contained in the city or county bikeway plan. Such bikeways shall serve the greatest volume of commuters, as calculated in subdivision (a).

(c) Elimination of hazards to bicyclists on existing bikeways or bicycle routes.

(d) Provision of bicycle parking facilities with theft prevention devices located at, in, or near civic or public buildings, transit terminals, business districts, shopping centers, and schools.

(e) Any other projects which in the judgment of the department will best implement the city or county bikeway plan and the intent of the Legislature expressed in this chapter.

2387. The department shall not finance projects with moneys in accounts created pursuant to this chapter which could be financed appropriately pursuant to the provisions of Article 3.5 (commencing with Section 156) of Chapter 1 of Division I, or fully financed with federal financial assistance.

2388. No funds received pursuant to this chapter shall be expended for the maintenance of any bikeway.

2389. If available funds are insufficient to finance completely any project whose eligibility is established pursuant to Section 2383 or 2386, such project shall retain its priority for allocations in subsequent fiscal years.

2390. No county or city shall receive more than 25 percent of the total of moneys appropriated to either the Bicycle Lane Account or the Bikeway Account in a single fiscal year.

2391. The department may enter into an agreement with any city or county concerning the handling and accounting of moneys disbursed pursuant in this chapter, including procedures to permit prompt payment for the work accomplished.

2392. The department, in cooperation with county and city governments, shall adopt and promulgate necessary rules and regulations for implementing the provisions of this chapter.

2393. The sum of nine million dollars ($9,000,000) is hereby appropriated annually, for each fiscal year, from the General Fund to the Bikeway Account in the State Transportation Fund.

2394. The Legislative Analyst shall review the implementation of this act for the purpose of evaluating to what extent the act's purposes have been effectuated and shall report thereon to the fiscal committees of the Legislature on January 1, 1979.

SEC. 7. Section 12804 of the Vehicle Code, as amended by Section 1 of Chapter 162 of the Statutes of 1975, is amended to read:

12804. (a) The examination shall include a test of the applicant's knowledge and understanding of the provisions of this code governing the operation of vehicles upon the highways, the ability to read and understand simple English used in highway traffic and directional signs, and his understanding of traffic signs and signals, including the bikeway signs, markers, and traffic control devices established by the Department of Transportation. The applicant shall be required to give an actual demonstration of his ability to exercise ordinary and reasonable control in operating a motor vehicle by driving the same under the supervision of an examining officer and submit to an examination appropriate to the type of motor vehicle or combination of vehicles he desires a license to drive, except that the department may waive the driving test part of the examination of an applicant who holds a valid license issued by another state, territory or possession of the United States, the District of Columbia, or the Commonwealth of Puerto Rico. The examination shall also include a test of the hearing and eyesight of the applicant and such other matters as may be necessary to determine the applicant's mental and physical fitness to operate a motor vehicle upon the highways and whether any ground exists for refusal of a license under this code. The examination for a class 1 or class 2 license under subdivision (b) of this section shall also include a report of a medical examination of the applicant given not more than two years prior to the date of the application by a physician licensed to practice medicine. The report shall be on a form approved by the department or by the Federal Highway Administration or the Federal Aviation Administration of the United States Department of Transportation. In establishing the requirements consideration may be given to the standards presently required of motor carrier drivers by the Federal Highway Administration of the United States Department of Transportation. Any physical defect of the applicant which in the opinion of the department is compensated to insure safe driving ability shall not prevent the issuance of a license to the applicant.

(b) In accordance with the following classifications any applicant for a driver's license shall be required to submit to an examination appropriate to the type of motor vehicle on combination of vehicles he desires a license to drive:

(1) Class 1. Any combination of vehicles and includes the operation of all vehicles under class 2 and class 3.

(2) Class 2. Any bus, any "farm labor truck," any single vehicle with three or more axles, any such vehicles towing another vehicle weighing less than 6,000 pounds gross, and all vehicles covered under class 3.

(3) Class 3. A three-axle housecar, any two-axle vehicle, and any such

housecar or vehicle towing another vehicle weighing less than 6,000 pounds gross, except a bus, two-wheel motorcycle, or "farm labor truck."

(4) Class 4. Any two-wheel motorcycle. Authority to operate vehicles included in a class 4 license may be granted by endorsement on a class 1, 2 or 3 license upon completion of appropriate examination.

(c) Class 1 and class 2 drivers' licenses shall be valid for operating class 1 or class 2 vehicles only when a medical certificate approved by the department or the Federal Highway Administration or the Federal Aviation Administration of the United States Department of Transportation is in the licensee's immediate possession which has been issued within two years of the date of the operation of such vehicle, otherwise the license shall be valid only for operating class 3 vehicles and class 4 vehicles if so endorsed. A person holding a valid class 1 or class 2 driver's license on May 3, 1972, may operate class 1 or class 2 vehicles without a medical certificate until such time as the license expires.

(d) The department may accept a certificate of driving experience in lieu of a driving test on class 1 or 2 applications when such certificate is issued by an employer of the applicant provided the applicant has first qualified for a class 3 license and also met the other examination requirements for the license for which he is applying. Such certificate may be submitted as evidence of the applicant's experience or training in the operation of the types of equipment covered by the license for which he is applying.

(e) The department may accept a certificate of competence in lieu of a driving test on class 4 applications when such certificate is issued by a law enforcement agency for its officers who operate class 4 vehicles in their duties provided the applicant has also met the other examination requirements for the license for which he is applying.

SEC. 7.5. Section 12804 of the Vehicle Code, as amended by Section 1 of Chapter 162 of the Statutes of 1975, is amended to read:

12804. (a) The examination shall include a test of the applicant's knowledge and understanding of the provisions of this code governing the operation of vehicles upon the highways, the ability to read and understand simple English used in highway traffic and directional signs, and his understanding of traffic signs and signals, including the bikeway signs, markers, and traffic control devices established by the Department of Transportation. The applicant shall be required to give an actual demonstration of his ability to exercise ordinary and reasonable control in operating a motor vehicle by driving the same under the supervision of an examining officer and submit to an examination appropriate to the type of motor vehicle or combination of vehicles he desires a license to drive, except that the department may waive the driving test part of the examination of an applicant who holds a valid license issued by another state, territory or possession of the United States, the District of Columbia, or the Commonwealth of Puerto Rico. The examination shall also include a test of the hearing and eyesight of the applicant and such other matters as may be necessary to determine the applicant's mental and physical fitness to operate a motor vehicle upon the highways and whether any ground exists for refusal of a license under this code. The examination for a class 1 or class 2 license under subdivision (b) of this section shall also include a report of a medical examination of the applicant given not more than two years prior to the date of the application by a physician licensed to practice medicine. The report shall be on a form approved by the de-department or by the Federal Highway Administration or the Federal Aviation Administration of the United States Department of Transportation. In establishing the requirements consideration may be given to the standards presently required of motor carrier drivers by the Federal Highway Administration of the United States Department of Transportation. Any physical defect of the applicant which in the opinion of the department is compensated to insure safe driving ability shall not prevent the issuance of a license to the applicant.

(b) In accordance with the following classifications any applicant for a driver's license shall be required to submit to an examination appropriate to the type of motor vehicle or combination of vehicles he desires a license to drive:

(1) Class 1. Any combination of vehicles and includes the operation of all vehicles under class 2 and class 3.

(2) Class 2. Any bus, any "farm labor truck," any single vehicle with three or more axles, any such vehicles towing another vehicle weighing less than 6,000 pounds gross, and all vehicles covered under class 3.

(3) Class 3. A three-axle housecar, any two-axle vehicle, and any such housecar or vehicle towing another vehicle weighing less than 6,000 pounds gross, except a bus, two-wheel motorcycle, motor-driven cycle, or "farm labor truck."

(4) Class 4. Any two-wheel motorcycle, any motor-driven cycle, or any motorized bicycle. Authority to operate vehicles included in a class 4 license may be granted by endorsement on a class 1, 2 or 3 license upon completion of appropriate examination.

(c) Class 1 and class 2 drivers' licenses shall be valid for operating class 1 or class 2 vehicles only when a medical certificate approved by the department or the Federal Highway Administration or the Federal Aviation Administration of the United States Department of Transportation is in the licensee's immediate possession which has been issued within two years of the date of the operation of such vehicle, otherwise the license shall be valid only for operating class 3 vehicles and class 4 vehicles if so endorsed. A person holding a valid class 1 or class 2 driver's license on May 3, 1972, may operate class 1 or class 2 vehicles without a medical certificate until such time as the license expires.

(d) The department may accept a certificate of driving experience in lieu of a driving test on class 1 or 2 applications when such certificate is issued by an employer of the applicant provided the applicant has first qualified for a class 3 license and also met the other examination requirements for the license for which he is applying. Such certificate may be submitted as evidence of the applicant's experience or training in the operation of the types of equipment covered by the license for which he is applying.

(e) The department may accept a certificate of competence in lieu of a driving test on class 4 applications when such certificate is issued by a law enforcement agency for its officers who operate class 4 vehicles in their duties provided the applicant has also met the other examination requirements for the license for which he is applying.

(f) Notwithstanding the provisions of subdivision (b), any person holding a valid California driver's license of any class may operate a motorized bicycle without taking any special examination for the operation of a motorized bicycle, and without having a class 4 endorsement on such license.

SEC. 8. Section 21207 of the Vehicle Code is amended to read:

21207. This chapter does not prevent local authorities from establishing, by ordinance or resolution, bicycle lanes separated from any vehicular lanes upon highways, other than state highways as defined in Section 24 of the Streets and Highways Code and county highways established pursuant to Article 5 (commencing with Section 1720) of Chapter 9 of Division 2 of the Streets and Highways Code, and from regulating the operation, and use of bicycles and vehicles with respect to such bicycle lanes.

Bicycle lanes established pursuant to this section shall be constructed in compliance with provisions pertaining to bikeways in Section 2376 of the Streets and Highways Code.

SEC. 8.5. Section 21207 of the Vehicle Code is amended to read:

21207. This chapter does not prevent local authorities from establishing, by ordinance or resolution, bicycle lanes separated from any vehicular lanes upon highways, other than state highways as defined in Section 24 of the Streets and Highways Code and county highways established pursuant to Article 5 (commencing with Section 1720) of Chapter 9 of Division 2 of the Streets and Highways Code, if such bicycle lanes installed after January 1, 1976, conform, as provided in Section 2376 of the Streets and Highways Code, to the minimum safety design criteria established by the Department of Transportation in cooperation with county and city governments and to the uniform specifications and symbols for signs, markers, and traffic control devices.

SEC. 9. It is the intent of the Legislature that the General Fund moneys appropriated by Section 2393 of the Streets and Highways Code shall be derived first from the revenues accruing to the General Fund by the repeal of Section 30102 of the Revenue and Taxation Code by this act.

SEC. 10. Notwithstanding Section 2231 of the Revenue and Taxation Code, there shall be no reimbursement pursuant to this section nor shall there be any appropriation made by this act because there are no state-mandated local costs in this act and any revenue loss implied herein is not reimbursable under Section 2231 of the Revenue and Taxation Code.

SEC. 11. It is the intent of the Legislature, if this bill and Senate Bill No. 671 are both chaptered and amend Section 12804 of the Vehicle Code, and this bill is chaptered after Senate Bill No. 671, that the amendments to Section 12804 proposed by both bills be given effect and incorporated in Section 12804 in the form set forth in Section 7.5 of this act. Therefore, Section 7.5 of this act shall become operative only if this bill and Senate Bill No. 671 are both chaptered, both amend Section 12804, and Senate Bill No. 671 is chaptered before this bill, in which case Section 7 of this act shall not become operative.

SEC. 12. It is the intent of the Legislature, if this bill and Senate Bill No. 939 are both chaptered and become effective January 1, 1976, both bills amend

Section 21207 of the Vehicle Code, and this bill is chaptered after Senate Bill No. 939, that the amendments to Section 21207 proposed by both bills be given effect and incorporated in Section 21207 in the form set forth in Section 8.5 of this act. Therefore, Section 8.5 of this act shall become operative only if this bill and Senate Bill No. 939 are both chaptered and become effective January 1, 1976, both amend Section 21207, and this bill is chaptered after Senate Bill No. 939, in which case Section 8 of this act shall not become operative.

SUGGESTED DAVIS, CALIFORNIA, RESOLUTION TO PREPARE PEDESTRIAN FACILITIES PLAN

Section I: Findings
A. The value of walking as an energy conserving, non-polluting form of transportation warrants further consideration of pedestrian planning in existing and future development.

B. Pedestrians require certain types of support facilities, walkways signals, benches, bathrooms, and microclimatic factors.

C. The Core Area is an ideal location for immediate retrofitting for pedestrians, and would serve as a demonstration for developers and neighborhood groups who wish to improve their pedestrian facilities.

Now, therefore, let it be resolved by the City Council of the City of Davis:

Section II: Pedestrian Plan to be Prepared
That the Community Development Department shall prepare (or have prepared) a pedestrian plan for presentation to the City Council by January 1, 1977. And that this plan shall include recommendations for routing, shading, easement acquisition, and other such facilities as deemed necessary along with a program and budget to develop these facilities in Davis. The Council hereby allots $10,000 for the preparation and printing of this plan.

Reprinted from:
Living Systems, "Planning for Energy Conservation, Draft Report,"
Prepared for the City of Davis, California, pursuant to HUD Project
Grant No. B-75-51-06-001 (Winters, California, 1976).

SUGGESTED RESOLUTION ADOPTING NEW STREET STANDARDS FOR DAVIS, CALIFORNIA

Whereas, the City Council of the City of Davis recognizes that the energy cost of wide streets is excessive, involving in part the energy cost of construction, the energy cost of converting prime agricultural land to streets, the adverse impact of wide streets on the microclimate, and the even more critical effects of resulting sprawl on energy use in transportation, and

Whereas, the adverse microclimate caused by wide streets discourages pedestrians and bicyclists and further increases energy use for transportation by encouraging people to use automobiles with air conditioners, and

Whereas, wider streets reduced perceived impedance and increase speed and reduce safety, and

Whereas, financial benefits of narrow streets are reflected in maintenance savings at a time when City revenues are decreasing,

Now, therefore, the City Council of the City of Davis decrees that it would be in the public interest to revise street standards to minimize energy use and financial cost and directs the Public Works Department to revise the street standards

Be it further resolved and ordered that these revised standards will take effect sixty days after the resolution is passed.

Reprinted from:
Living Systems, "Planning for Energy Conservation, Draft Report," Prepared for the City of Davis, California, pursuant to HUD Project Grant No. B–75–51–06–001 (Winters, California, 1976).

PROPOSED BILL ADDING ENERGY IMPACT STANDARDS TO SUBDIVISION REGULATIONS IN COLORADO

Be it enacted by the General Assembly of the State of Colorado:

SECTION 1. 30–28–133 (3), Colorado Revised Statutes 1973, as amended, is amended BY THE ADDITION OF A NEW PARAGRAPH to read:

30–28–133. *Subdivision regulations.* [Subdivision regulations . . . shall require subdividers to submit . . . the following items:]

(3) (e) Adequate evidence of the future availability of energy to support the proposed subdivision development. Such future supply shall be sufficient in terms of quantity and quality. Such evidence shall include, but not be limited to, the following:

(I) Evidence of utility capability to support adequately the proposed development;

(II) A statement of the type and source of energy to be supplied;

(III) A statement of rights-of-way and easements that may be required in order to serve the proposed development;

(IV) A statement of variances sought by or granted to any certified utility in conjunction with service facilities necessary for supplying the proposed development;

(V) A statement of the relationship of existing generating capacity to the estimated demand for service by the proposed development, which relationship shall be given in terms of the individual development and in the aggregate of all pending applications within the service territory of the certificated utility;

(VI) Evidence to show compliance by the developer with energy-conserving measures and standards to reduce the total demand and energy requirements of the proposed subdivision from what they would be otherwise. Such evidence shall include a complete statement and evaluation of the energy savings effected for the proposed subdivision.

SECTION 2. 30–28–133 (4), Colorado Revised Statutes 1973, is amended BY THE ADDITION OF A NEW PARAGRAPH to read:

30−28−133. *Subdivision regulations.* [Subdivision regulations . . . shall also include as a minimum, provisions governing the following matters:]

(4) (e) Standards and technical procedures applicable and necessary for efficient collection of solar energy. For purposes of this paragraph (e), collection of solar energy should be considered for the building as a whole, including proper climate and site orientation which in most cases should maximize collection of solar heat in the winter and minimize it in the summer, as well as for proper orientation for purposes of operating a solar energy device or system, either attached or detached from the building, for heating and cooling, hot water, or the generation of electrical power.

SECTION 3.   30−28−133 (6), Colorado Revised Statutes 1973, is amended BY THE ADDITION OF THE FOLLOWING NEW PARAGRAPHS to read:

30−28−133. *Subdivision   regulations.*   No   board . . . shall   approve   any preliminary plan or final plat for any subdivision . . . unless the subdivider has provided the following materials as part of the preliminary plan or final plat subdivision submission:

(6) (d) Evidence to establish that provision has been made in the platting, in the layout of roads, and in other site changes for the orientation of structures to receive substantial benefits from the natural energies afforded by the sun, the wind, and other energy-related characteristics as determined by evaluation of the microclimate details of the proposed subdivision site;

(e) Evidence to establish that long-term energy is available to support the subdivision without undue detrimental land use and environmental impacts and that energy-conserving measures have been incorporated in the preliminary plan or final plat subdivision submission.

SECTION 4.   *Effective date.*   This act shall take effect January 1, 1977.

SECTION 5.   *Safety clause.*   The general assembly hereby finds, determines, and declares that this act is necessary for the immediate preservation of the public peace, health, and safety.

(Colo. H.B. 1166, 2d Regular Sess., 50th Gen. Ass.)

RAMAPO, NEW YORK, ZONING AMENDMENT CONDITIONING DEVELOPMENT PERMITS ON ADEQUATE PUBLIC FACILITIES

1. Amend §46−3, Definitions, by adding after "Day Camp" and before "Dog Kennel" the following:

Development Use, Residential
The erection or construction of dwellings on any vacant plots, lots, or parcels of land. It shall not include the alteration, repair, demolition, or maintenance of existing dwellings or construction or erection of structures accessory to dwellings.

Any person acting in such manner as to come within the definition of development use, residential, shall be deemed to be engaged in residential development which shall be a separate use classification under this ordinance and subject to the requirement of obtaining a special permit from the Town Board.

Developer, Residential

Any person (a) who, having in interest in land, causes it directly or indirectly to be used for residential development, or (b) who directly or indirectly sells, leases, or develops or offers to sell, lease, or develop, or advertises for sale, lease, or development any lot, plot, parcel, site, unit, or interest for a residential development use, or (c) who engages directly or indirectly or through an agent in the business or occupation of selling, leasing, developing, or offering for sale, lease, or development, a residential development use or any lot, plot, parcel, site, unit, or interest for a residential development use, and (d) who is directly or indirectly controlled by, or under direction or indirect common control with, any of the foregoing shall be deemed to be engaged in development use, residential.

Development, Agent

Any person who represents, or acts for or on behalf of a residential developer, in selling, leasing, or developing, or offering to sell, lease, or develop any interest, lot, plot, parcel, site, or unit for residential development use, except an attorney at law whose representation of another person consists solely of rendering legal services.

2. Amend §46–3, Definitions, by adding after "Camp" and before "Cellar" the following:

Capital Budget

The capital improvement program adopted by the Town Board pursuant to §99-g of the General Municipal Law for a six year period of effectiveness for the development of the unincorporated area of the town in accord with the master plan and official map, establishing the order of priority for all capital projects as shown on the official map and master plan in order to provide for maximum orderly, adequate, and economical provision of transportation, water, sewerage, drainage, parks and recreation, schools, municipal facilities and structures, and other public requirements.

Capital Plan

The capital improvement program adopted by resolution of the Town Board for the seventh through eighteenth year period of effectiveness, for the development of the unincorporated area of the Town in accord with the master plan and official map, which shall establish two general orders of priority, the seventh through twelfth year, and the thirteenth through eighteenth year, for all capital projects as shown on the official map and master plan in order to provide for maximum orderly, adequate, and economical provision of transportation, water, sewerage, drainage, parks and recreation, schools, municipal facilities and structures, and other public requirements.

3. *Delete* from §46–9A, Table of General Use Regulations, RR–80 Col. 2 "Uses Permitted By Right," Nos. 1 and 12 thereof as follows:

"1. One-family detached residences with not more than one principal building on a plot," and

"12. Residences subject to §281 Town Law pursuant to provisions of density zoning resolution adopted by Town Board."

And change Nos. 2 through 11 respectively to Nos. 1 through 10 respectively.

4. *Delete* from §46–9A, Table of General Use Regulations, R–15 Col. 2 "Uses Permitted by Right," No. 2 thereof as follows:

"2. Two-family residences."

5. *Delete* from §46–9A, Table of General Use Regulations, PO Col. 2 "Uses Permitted by Right," No. 1 thereof as follows:

"1. Same as RR–80 Nos. 1, 4, 5, 6, 7, 8, 9, and 12" and

Add to §46–9A, Table of General Use Regulations, PO Col. 2 "Uses Permitted by Right," No. 1, as follows:

"1. Same as RR–80 Nos. 3, 4, 5, 6, 7, and 8."

6. Add to §46–9A, Table of General Use Regulations, RR–80, Col. 2A "Uses by Special Permit of the Town Board" the following:

"3. One-family detached residences with not more than one principal building on a plot. (subject to §46–13.1)

4. Residences subject to §281 Town Law pursuant to the provisions of the density zoning resolution adopted by the Town Board. (subject to §46–13.1)"

7. Add to §46–9A, Table of General Use Regulations, R–15 and HO, Col. 2A "Uses by Special Permit of the Town Board" the following:

The number "1" before the words "Same as RR/80"; and "2. Two-family residences. (subject to §46–13.1)"

8. Add a new §46–13.1 to read as follows:

§46–13.1. Special Permit Uses—Town Board
Residential Development Use

A. General Considerations
The Town of Ramapo has been experiencing unprecedented and rapid growth with respect to population, housing, economy, land development, and utilization of resources for the past decade. Transportation, water, sewerage, schools, parks and recreation, drainage, and other public facilities and requirements have been and are being constructed to meet the needs of the Town's growing population, but the Town has been unable to provide these services and facilities at a pace which will keep abreast of the ever-growing public need.

Faced with the physical, social, and fiscal problems caused by the rapid and unprecedented growth, the Town of Ramapo has adopted a comprehensive master plan to guide its future development and has adopted an official map and a capital program so as to provide for the maximum orderly, adequate, and economical development of its future residential, commercial, industrial, and public land uses and community facilities including transportation, water, sewerage, schools, parks and recreation, drainage, and other public facilities.

In order to insure that these comprehensive and coordinated plans are not frustrated by disorganized, unplanned, and uncoordinated development which would create an undue burden and hardship on the ability of the community to translate these plans into reality, the following objectives are established as policy determinations of zoning and planning for the Town of Ramapo:

1. To economize on the costs of municipal facilities and services to carefully phase residential development with efficient provision of public improvements;

2. To establish and maintain municipal control over the eventual character of development;

3. To establish and maintain a desirable degree of balance among the various uses of the land;

4. To establish and maintain essential quality of community services and facilities.

The Town, through its master plan, official map, zoning ordinance, subdivision regulations, capital program, and complementary planning programs, ordinances, laws, and regulations has mandated a program of continuing improvements which is designed to insure complete availability of public facilities and services so that all land in the Town is capable of development in accord with proper planning. The haphazard and uncoordinated development of land without the adequate provision of public services and facilities available will destroy the continuing implementation and successful adoption of the program. Residential development will be carefully phased so as to insure that all developable land will be accorded a present vested right to develop at such time as services and facilities are available. Residential land which has the necessary available municipal facilities and services will be granted approval. Residential land which lacks the available facilities and services will be granted approval for development at such time as the facilities and services have been made available by the ongoing public improvement program or in which the residential developer agrees to furnish such facility or improvement in advance of the scheduled program for improvement of the public sector.

These regulations are adopted pursuant to the authority of the Constitution of the State of New York, the Statute of Local Government, the Town Law, and the Municipal Home Rule Law of the State of New York by providing for comprehensive planning and zoning for the government, protection, order, conduct, safety, health, and well being of the persons and property in the Town and consistent with the purposes set forth in Article 16 of the Town Law in facilitating the adequate provision of transportation, water, sewerage, schools, parks, drainage, municipal facilities and structures, and other public requirements in order to encourage the most appropriate use of land throughout the Town as provided in the master plan, official map, capital program, laws, ordinances and regulations, and other comprehensive planning performed by the Town.

B. Special Permit Required for Residential Development Use

(1) Prior to the issuance of any building permit, special permit of the Board of Appeals, subdivision approval, or site plan approval of the Planning Board for residential development use, a residential developer or development agent shall be required to obtain a special permit from the Town Board.

(2) The provisions of this section shall not be applicable to subdivisions finally approved by the Planning Board and filed in the Rockland County Clerk's Office prior to the effective date of this section.

C. Procedure for Special Permit

(1) The residential developer or development agent shall be required to submit an application to the Administrative Assistant to the Boards and Commissions in such detail as shall be set forth in regulations established by the Town Board of the Town of Ramapo, including a map showing the location of all land holdings of the applicant in the same ownership in the immediate vicinity and the extent of the land proposed for development. Said Administrative Assistant shall review the application with respect to all of the standards set forth in §46-13.1D as to the availability of municipal services and facilities and projected improvements scheduled in the capital budget and capital plan of the Town. The Administrative Assistant may request reports from appropriate town, county, or municipal agencies, boards, or officials as may be required. Within forty-five (45) days of the submission of the application, the Administrative Assistant shall report his findings in writing to the Town Board and the Town Clerk shall proceed to notice the application for public hearing at the first regular meeting of the Town Board not less than two weeks after the submission of the written report.

(2) The Town Board shall within thirty (30) days after conclusion of the public hearing render its decision. In the event of approval of the application without conditions the Town Board shall also render its determination as to the number of residential dwellings that shall be permitted to be built pursuant to the requirements of §46-13.1E.

D. Standards for Issuance of Special Permit

No special permit shall be issued by the Town Board unless the residential development has available fifteen (15) development points on the following scale of values:

(1) *Sewers*
  (a) Public sewers available in RR−50, R−40, R−35, R−25, R−15, and R−15S districts . . . . 5 points
  (b) Package Sewer Plants . . . . 3 points
  (c) County approved septic system in an RR−80 district . . . 3 points
  (d) All others . . . . 0 points

(2) *Drainage*

Percentage of Required Drainage Capacity Available

    (a) 100% or more . . . . 5 points

    (b) 90% to 99.9% . . . . 4 points

    (c) 80% to 89.9% . . . . 3 points

    (d) 65% to 79.9% . . . . 2 points

    (e) 50% to 64.9% . . . . 1 point

    (f) Less than 50% . . . . 0 points

(3) *Improved Public Park or Recreation Facility Including Public School Site*

    (a) Within ¼ mile . . . . 5 points

    (b) Within ½ mile . . . . 3 points

    (c) Within 1 mile . . . . 1 point

    (d) Further than 1 mile . . . . 0 points

(4) *State, County, or Town Major, Secondary, or Collector Road(s) Improved with Curbs and Sidewalks*

    (a) Direct Access . . . . 5 points

    (b) Within ½ mile . . . . 3 points

    (c) Within 1 mile . . . . 1 point

    (d) Further than 1 mile . . . . 0 points

(5) *Fire House*

    (a) Within 1 mile . . . . 3 points

    (b) Within 2 miles . . . . 1 point

    (c) Further than 2 miles . . . . 0 points

All distances shall be computed from the proposed location of each separate lot or plot capable of being improved with a residential dwelling and not from the boundaries of the entire parcel. The Town Board shall issue the special permit specifying the number of dwelling units that meet the standards set forth herein.

E. Vested Approvals and Relief

(1) *Vested Approval of Special Permit*

(a) The Town Board shall issue an approval of the application for special permit vesting a present right for the residential developer to proceed with residential development use of the land for such year as the proposed development meets the required points as indicated in the scheduled completion dates of the capital budget and capital plan as amended or failing to meet such points then for the final year of the capital plan as amended. Any improvement scheduled in the capital budget for completion within one year from the date of application for the special permit shall be credited as though in existence on the date of application. Any improvement scheduled in the capital budget or capital plan more than one year from date of application shall be credited as though in existence as of the date of the scheduled completion.

(b) A developer may advance the date of authorization by agreeing to provide such improvements as will bring the development within the required number of points for earlier or immediate development. Such agreement shall be secured by either a cash deposit or surety bond sufficient to cover the cost of the proposed improvement, the form, sufficiency, and amount of which bond shall be determined by the Town Board.

(c) All approved special permits vesting a present right to future development shall be fully assignable without restriction.

(d) Nothing herein contained shall prevent such land from being immediately used for all other uses other than residential development use, as is authorized by the zoning ordinance.

(2) *Relief*

Any residential developer or development agent who has applied for a special permit from the Town Board pursuant to §46–13.1, shall be entitled as of right, to appeal within one year from the Town Board's determination granting the vested approval to the Development Easement Acquisition Commission, pursuant to Chapter 11 of the Code of the Town of Ramapo, for a determination pursuant to §11–4(B) of the Development Easement Acquisition Law as to the extent to which the temporary restriction on residential development use of the land shall affect the assessed valuation placed on such land for purposes of real estate taxation and such assessed valuation on such land shall be reduced as provided in the Development Easement Acquisition Law as compensation for the temporary restriction placed on the land.

F. Variances

(1) The Town Board shall have the power to vary or modify the application of any provision of §46–13.1 of this ordinance upon its determination in its legislative discretion, that such variance or modification is consistent with comprehensive planning for proper land use including the master plan, official map, capital budget, and capital plan upon which this ordinance is based and with the health, safety, and general welfare of the Town and its inhabitants.

(2) Upon receiving any application for such variance or modification, such application shall be referred to the Planning Board of the Town of Ramapo for a report and recommendation of said Planning Board with respect to the effect of the proposed variance or modification upon the comprehensive planning of the Town including the master plan, official map, capital budget and plan, existing ordinances, laws, and regulations and the health, safety, and general welfare of the Town and its inhabitants.

(3) All applications for variance or modification shall be filed with the Administrative Assistant to the Boards and Commissions who shall forward same within two weeks after receipt to the Planning Board for its report. Such report shall be made in writing and shall be returned by the Planning Board to the said Administrative Assistant within 30 days of such reference. The said Administrative Assistant shall forward said report to the Town Board and the Town Clerk shall proceed to notice the application for public hearing at the first regular meeting of the Town Board not less than two weeks after submission of the written report by the Planning Board. The Town Board shall render its determination within thirty (30) days after conclusion of the public hearing.

G. Fees

(1) The fee for each special permit application pursuant to §46–13.1(C) to the Town Board shall be Twenty-five Dollars ($25.00) plus Ten Dollars ($10.00) for each proposed dwelling unit, payable at the time of said application and are not refundable.

(2) The fee for each application for a variance pursuant to §46–13.1(F) to the Town Board shall be Twenty-five Dollars ($25.00) plus Ten Dollars ($10.00) for each proposed dwelling unit payable at the time of the application and are not refundable.

OREGON BOUNDARY COMMISSIONS STATUTE
(excerpts)

Local Government Boundary Commissions

Generally

199.410 Policy. (1) The Legislative Assembly finds that:

(a) A fragmented approach has developed to public services provided by local government and such an approach has limited the orderly development and growth of Oregon's urban areas for the maximum interest of all its citizens.

(b) The programs and growth of each unit of local government affect not only that particular unit but also the activities and programs of a variety of other units within each urban area.

(c) As local programs become increasingly intergovernmental, the state has a responsibility to insure orderly determination and adjustment of local government boundaries to best meet the needs of the people.

(2) The purpose of ORS 199.410 to 199.512 is to provide a method for guiding the creation and growth of cities and special service districts in Oregon in order to prevent illogical extensions of local government boundaries and to assure adequate quality and quantity of public services and the financial integrity of each unit of local government.
[1969 c.494 s.1]

Jurisdiction; General Procedure

199.460 Jurisdiction of boundary commission over boundary changes. (1) A boundary commission has jurisdiction of a proceeding to consider a boundary change if any part of the territory included or proposed to be included within the affected city or district is within the jurisdiction of the commission.

(2) If the territory subject to the proceeding is within the jurisdiction of two or more commissions, the highest assessed value commission shall have primary jurisdiction in the conduct of the proceeding under ORS 199.410 to 199.512, and all other commissions having jurisdiction of the territory shall cooperate in the conduct of the proceeding. On the call of the highest assessed value commission, the commissions shall meet as a joint commission to hold hearings and to adopt a final order in the proceeding. As used in this subsection, "highest

assessed value commission" means the commission having jurisdiction of the greatest portion of the taxable assessed valuation of the affected territory. [1969 c.494 s.10; 1971 c.462 s.6]

199.461 Study of proposed boundary change; hearing; authority over changes; notice to public officials. (1) When the boundary commission receives a petition in a boundary change proceeding, it shall:

(a) Cause a study to be made of the proposal offered by the petition.

(b) Conduct one or more public hearings on the proposal.

(2) After the study and hearings, the boundary commission may alter the boundaries set out in a petition for formation or a minor boundary change of a city or district or in a petition for consolidation of cities so as either to include or exclude territory. If the commission determines that any land has been improperly omitted from the proposal and that the owner of the land has not appeared at the hearing, in person or by his representative designated in writing, the commission shall continue the hearing on the petition and shall order notice given to the nonappearing owner requiring him to appear before the commission and show cause, if any, why his land should not be included in the proposal. Notice to nonappearing owners may be given by personal service or by letter sent by first-class mail, at least 10 days prior to the date to which the hearing has been continued. The required notice may be waived by the nonappearing owner.

(3) On the basis of the study and after hearing, the boundary commission shall approve the proposed boundary change as presented or as modified by the commission or disapprove the proposed change, by an order stating the reasons for the decision of the commission. Any person interested in a boundary change may, within 30 days after the date of a final order, appeal the order for review under ORS 34.010 to 34.100.

(4) Immediately after the effective date of a final order entered under subsection (3) of this section and a proclamation declaring a minor boundary change approved if any is entered under subsection (3) of ORS 199.505, the commission shall file a copy of the order and proclamation, if any, with the Secretary of State, the assessor and the county clerk of each county in which the affected territory, city or district is located, and the clerk of the affected city or district. If the commission disapproves a minor boundary change, it shall send a copy of the final order to the person who actually filed the petition and to the affected city or district.

[Formerly 199.475]

199.462 Standards for review of changes; territory which may not be included in certain changes. (1) In order to carry out the purposes described by ORS 199.410 when reviewing a petition for a boundary change, a boundary commission shall consider economic, demographic and sociological trends and projections pertinent to the proposal, and past and prospective physical development of land that would directly or indirectly be affected by the proposed boundary change.

(2) Subject to any provision to the contrary in the principal Act of the affected district or city and subject to the process of transfer of territory:

(a) Territory within a city may not be included within or annexed to a district without the consent of the city council;

(b) Territory within a city may not be included within or annexed to another city; and

(c) Territory within a district may not be included within or annexed to another district subject to the same principal Act.
[Formerly 199.515; 1975 c.361 s.2]

199.463 Notice; hearing. (1) Notice of a public hearing conducted by a boundary commission under ORS 199.461 shall be published by at least one insertion in a newspaper of general circulation in the affected city, district or territory not more than 25 days nor less than 15 days before the hearing. A second notice may be published either by a second insertion in a newspaper of general circulation in the affected city, district or territory or by letter sent first-class mail addressed to each owner of land in the affected territory not more than 15 days nor less than 8 days before the hearing. The commission may also cause the notice to be posted in not less than three public places within the affected city, district or territory at least 15 days before the hearing. The commission may provide for publication by broadcasting on radio or television stations.

(2) Notice of a hearing shall describe the proposed boundary change, state the time and place of the hearing and that any interested person may appear and shall be given a reasonable opportunity to be heard.

(3) A hearing may be adjourned or continued to another time, but not more than seven days later than the time stated in the notice of the hearing unless the notice of the hearing is revised and republished. Notice of the hearing shall be revised and republished if the hearing is adjourned to a place other than the place stated in the notice of the hearing.
[Formerly 199.520]

199.464 Commission approval for exercise of additional district function, to extraterritorially extend district or city sewer or water line or to establish privately owned community water system. (1) Approval or disapproval under this section shall be based on the policy stated in ORS 199.410 and the standards set forth in ORS 199.462. A commission shall take action on any matter referred to it under this section in the manner provided for action by the commission upon a petition for a minor boundary change initiated under subsection (3) of ORS 199.490. Any action taken by the commission under this section is subject to judicial review as provided in subsection (3) of ORS 199.461 for judicial review of final orders of the commission.

(2) Without the approval of a boundary commission, a district with territory in the jurisdiction of the commission may not initiate an additional function of the district. Any proposal by a district to initiate an additional function shall be referred immediately to the boundary commission that has jurisdiction of the

territory in which the district lies. The district shall take no further action on the proposal unless the commission approves the proposal as proposed or modified.

(3) Without the approval of a boundary commission, a city or district with territory in the jurisdiction of the commission shall not extend a water or sewer line extraterritorially to an extent not effected on October 5, 1973. Tentative plans for such extraterritorial extension shall be submitted to the boundary commission that has jurisdiction of the territory in which the extension is proposed. If the commission disapproves the plans, no further action may be taken.

(4) Except as provided in paragraphs (d) and (e) of subsection (5) of this section, within territory subject to the jurisdiction of a boundary commission, no person may establish a community water supply system or a privately owned sewerage system or privately owned disposal system or extend a water line or sewer line without commission approval. Tentative plans for such approval shall be submitted to the boundary commission that has jurisdiction of the territory for which the establishment or extension is proposed. However, extension by a city or district of water lines or sewer lines shall be governed by subsection (3) of this section and the requirements of this section shall not apply to establishment of a city-owned community water supply system within its boundaries.

(5) (a) A community water supply system within the territory subject to the jurisdiction of a commission may apply to the commission for allocation of service territory. If the territory is allocated to a community water supply system, no other community water supply system may serve within the territory without approval of the commission and the approval may not be given so long as the existing system is reliable and has an adequate quality and quantity of water.

(b) In condemning all or part of the properties and allocated service territory of a private community water supply system through eminent domain, the acquisition price shall be fair market value.

(c) No part of the acquisition price for all or part of a community water supply system acquired by eminent domain shall be specially assessed against the property within the acquired service territory, or its owners on a special benefit assessment basis.

(d) A community water supply system to which service territory has been allocated under this subsection may extend or establish water lines within the territory without further approval of the commission.

(e) Upon application filed on or before January 1, 1976, the Public Utility Commissioner shall allocate to a community water supply system that territory which it was serving adequately and exclusively on June 12, 1975, and that territory which previously had been allocated to it under this section by the Public Utility Commissioner prior to June 12, 1975. Such allocation shall be binding upon the commission.

(6) Action which under this section requires approval by a boundary commission but is taken without that approval may be enjoined, upon suit in a court of competent jurisdiction, by the boundary commission in whose territorial jurisdiction the action is taken.

(7) As used in this section:

(a) "Water line" includes every water line except a line connecting a community water supply system with the premises of the water user unless the line provides for extraterritorial extension of service.

(b) "Sewer line" includes every gravity sewer line that is eight inches or more in diameter and all force lines regardless of size, except a line connecting a sewer system with the premises of the user unless the line provides for extraterritorial extension of service.

(c) "Community water supply system" means a source of water and distribution system whether publicly or privately owned which serves more than three residences or other users where water is provided for public consumption including, but not limited to, a school, farm labor camp, an industrial establishment, a recreational facility, a restaurant, a motel, a mobile home park, or a group care home.

(d) "Sewerage system" is that system described by subsection (5) of ORS 468.700.

(e) "Disposal system" is that system described by subsection (1) of ORS 468.700, except for individual subsurface disposal systems.

(f) "Tentative plans" submitted to the boundary commission for approval shall include:

(A) For the establishment of a water system or extension of a water line:

(i) The source of the supply and quantity of water available.

(ii) The transmission, distribution and storage system size and location.

(iii) The proposed number of service connections, a map, and a legal description indicating the proposed service area.

(B) For the establishment of a sewer system or extension of a sewer line:

(i) The location of the treatment facility and outfall or other method of disposal.

(ii) The size and location of the collection system.

(iii) The proposed number of service connections, a map, and a legal description indicating the proposed service area.
[1973 c.684 s.2; 1975 c.330 s.1]

Boundary Change Procedure

199.465 When petition for major boundary change required; when economic feasibility statement required; effect of filing petition; effect of appeal. (1) When a major boundary change is initiated by a legally sufficient petition as provided by the principal Act, if the territory subject to the petition is within the jurisdiction of a boundary commission, the filing agency notwithstanding the principal Act, shall file, within 10 days after the petition is filed, a certified copy of the petition with the boundary commission having jurisdiction of the change. If the petition proposes formation of a city or district it shall be accompanied by an economic feasibility analysis. The analysis shall include among other items a description of the services or functions to be performed or provided by the new unit and an analysis of their relationship to other existing or needed government services.

(2) The proceeding under the principal Act shall be suspended from the date

the petition is filed with the filing agency until the date the commission files a certified copy of its final order with the filing agency. Suspension of the proceeding under this section shall not continue for more than 120 days after the date the commission receives the petition.

(3) If the decision of the commission on the petition is not filed with the filing agency within the 120 days, the petition shall be considered approved by the commission.

(4) Notwithstanding subsection (3) of this section, if a final order of a commission is appealed for review by the circuit court and a copy of the notice of appeal is filed with the filing agency prior to the expiration of the period of suspension provided by subsection (2) of this section, the suspension period shall be extended and continue until the appeal is determined and the results thereof certified to the filing agency.
[1969 c.494 s.11; 1971 c.462 s.10; 1973 c.433 s.1]

199.470 [1969 c.494 s.12; repealed by 1971 c.462 s.20]

199.475 [1969 c.494 s.13; 1971 c.462 s.7; renumbered 199.461]

199.480 Filing of major boundary change order; effect of filing. In a proceeding for a major boundary change, a certified copy of the final order of the boundary commission shall be filed with the filing agency from which the commission received the petition. If the copy is so filed within the 120 days prescribed by subsection (2) of ORS 199.465 and:

(1) If the commission approved the petition as presented or as modified, the proceeding shall continue as provided by the principal Act; except that when a commission considers and enters a final order on a petition:

(a) The city council or county or district board need not call or hold a hearing on the petition and shall not change boundaries as described by the final order of the commission.

(b) An election on the proposed change, if required under the principal Act, shall be held, on a date that may be fixed by the commission, within 120 days after the date of the final order; and all elections on one proposal shall be held on the same date.

(c) The final order, in a proceeding to merge or to consolidate districts or to dissolve a district and transfer its functions, assets and liabilities to a county service district, shall conclude the proceeding for all purposes; and the merger, consolidation or dissolution and transfer shall take effect 45 days after the date the commission adopts the final order in the proceeding.

(2) If the commission disapproved the petition, the proceeding shall terminate.
[1969 c.494 s.14; 1971 c.462 s.11; 1973 c.664 s.4]

199.485 Commission authority to initiate major change; resolution as petition; content and filing of resolution. (1) A boundary commission may initiate a proceeding for a major boundary change in territory subject to its jurisdiction by adopting and within 10 days thereafter filing with the proper filing agency a resolution proposing the change and by proceeding in accordance with the principal Act of the affected city or district, ORS 199.465, 199.480 and this section. When the resolution is filed with the filing agency, thereafter for all purposes the resolution shall be considered as if it were a petition filed in accordance with the principal Act.

(2) The resolution shall:

(a) Identify the affected city or district;

(b) State the kind of boundary change proposed;

(c) Contain a legal description of the boundaries of the affected territory;

(d) If the proposal concerns a district, designate the principal Act of the affected district;

(e) Have attached a map showing the location of the affected territory; and

(f) Include whatever additional information the principal Act of the affected city or district authorizes or requires petitioners to include in or with a petition for such a boundary change.

(3) In proceedings initiated under this section, the filing agency is not required to send a copy of the resolution to the boundary commission, but the commission shall, except in formation proceedings, file a certified copy of the resolution with the affected city or district within five days after the date the resolution is filed with the filing agency, unless the city or district is the filing agency.

[1969 c.494 s.15; 1971 c.462 s.12; 1973 c.664 s.5]

199.487 Commission authority to initiate minor change; nonapplicability of certain boundary change procedures; effect of commission action. (1) Within the jurisdiction of a boundary commission, a minor boundary change proceeding may be initiated as provided by ORS 199.490. In addition, a city annexation proceeding may be initiated as provided by ORS 222.170, 222.750 or 222.850 to 222.915. Minor boundary change proceedings shall be conducted as provided by this section, ORS 199.490, 199.495, 199.505 and 199.510.

(2) ORS 222.111 to 222.160 and the statutes of the state that govern annexation of territory to, or withdrawal of territory from, districts do not apply in territory subject to the jurisdiction of a boundary commission. However, a city annexation proposal initiated under ORS 199.490 may include a tax differential proposal authorized by subsection (2) of ORS 222.111. ORS 222.530 shall not apply in territory subject to the jurisdiction of a boundary commission unless the affected territory constitutes at least 60 percent of the area and 60 percent of the assessed value of the district.

(3) Notwithstanding any charter or statutory provision to the contrary except ORS 222.180, a final order or a proclamation of a boundary commission declaring a minor boundary change approved is effective to change the boundary of the city or district without the necessity of any further action by the voters or the governing body of the city or district.

[Formerly 199.540]

199.490 Procedure for minor boundary changes or transfers of territory. (1) A proceeding for a minor boundary change other than a transfer of territory may be initiated:

(a) By resolution of the governing body of the affected city or district;

(b) By petition signed by 10 percent of the registered voters residing in the affected territory;

(c) By petition signed by the owners of at least one-half the land area in the affected territory; or

(d) By resolution of a boundary commission having jurisdiction of the affected territory.

(2) A transfer of territory proceeding may be initiated:

(a) By joint resolution of the governing bodies of the affected districts or cities;

(b) By petition signed by 10 percent of the registered voters residing in the affected territory;

(c) By petition signed by the owners of at least one-half the land area in the affected territory; or

(d) By resolution of a boundary commission having jurisdiction of the affected territory.

(3) The petition or resolution shall:

(a) Name the affected city or district and state whether it is proposed to annex, withdraw or transfer territory;

(b) Describe the boundaries of the affected territory;

(c) If the proposal concerns a district, designate the applicable principal Act;

(d) Have attached a map showing the location of the affected territory; and

(e) Be filed with the boundary commission having jurisdiction of the affected territory.

(4) When a city annexation is initiated:

(a) As provided by ORS 222.170 or 222.750, the petition proposing the annexation shall be filed with the boundary commission having jurisdiction of the annexation.

(b) As provided by ORS 222.850 to 222.915, the findings adopted by the Administrator of the Health Division under ORS 222.880 shall be considered the initiatory action and a certified copy of the findings shall be filed with the boundary commission having jurisdiction of the annexation, at the same time a copy of the finding is filed with the affected city.

(5) Except when a boundary change is initiated by an affected city or district under subsection (1) or (2) of this section or by the Administrator of the Health Division as provided by paragraph (b) of subsection (4) of this section, the boundary commission shall notify the affected city or district that a petition has been filed or that the commission has adopted a resolution. If the petition complies with the requirements of the applicable statutes, the commission shall proceed as provided by ORS 199.460 to 199.463 and 199.490 to 199.512.

(6) Unless the parties appearing at a hearing for a minor boundary change agree to a postponement of the adoption of a final order, a final order approving or disapproving a minor boundary change must be adopted within 90 days after the date the petition or resolution is filed with the commission. If a final order approving or disapproving a minor boundary change is not adopted within 90 days after the petition or resolution is filed or within the period of postponement, the petition or resolution shall be considered approved by the commission.

A postponement shall not be for a period exceeding one year from the date the petition or resolution initiating the change is filed with the commission.
[1969 c.494 s.16; 1971 c.462 s.14; 1973 c.808 s.1; 1975 c.157 s.3; 1975 c.361 s.3]

199.495 Effect of ORS 199.490. In a proceeding initiated as provided by subsection (3) of ORS 199.490:

(1) If the proposed annexation is approved by the commission, the final order shall be effective at the time specified in the final order except that the effective date shall not be more than one year after the date the final order is adopted. If no effective date is specified in the final order, the order shall take effect on the date the order is adopted. The order shall not be subject to ORS 199.505.

* * * *

199.505 Effective date of minor changes; objection; election. (1) If the boundary commission by its final order approves a minor boundary change other than a transfer of territory, the change shall take effect at the time specified in the final order, but the effective date shall not be less than 45 days, nor more than one year, after the date the commission adopts the final order approving the change. If no effective date is specified in the final order, the order shall take effect 45 days after the commission adopts the final order approving the change. However, the change shall not take effect unless it is also approved by the qualified voters, if within 45 days after the date of the adoption of the order:

(a) Written objections to the change signed by not less than 20 percent of the qualified voters in the affected territory are filed with the commission; or

(b) A resolution objecting to the change adopted by the city council of the affected city or district board of the affected district is filed with the commission.

(2) If objections as required by this section are filed by a city council or district board, the council or board shall call and hold an election in the affected city or district on the boundary change as approved. If objections are filed by the qualified voters, the commission shall certify the fact of the objections to:

(a) The city council or district board of the affected city or district, if the change involves a withdrawal of territory, whereupon the council or board shall call an election in the city or district.

(b) The county board of the county where the territory is located, if the change involves an annexation, whereupon the board shall call an election in the territory. Where a minor boundary change has been initiated pursuant to paragraph (a) of subsection (1) of ORS 199.490, cost of an election required by this paragraph shall be paid by the city or district to which the territory is proposed to be annexed.

(3) An election required by subsection (2) of this section shall be held, on a date that may be fixed by the commission, within 120 days after the expiration of the time allowed for filing objections under subsection (1) of this section and shall be conducted in accordance with the principal Act. A city council or a

board that calls an election under this section shall certify the results of the election to the commission. If a majority of those voting on the proposition in each election approve the change approved by the commission, the commission thereupon shall proclaim the results of the election. Upon the adoption of the proclamation the change shall take effect.

[1969 c.494 s.17; 1971 c.288 s.1; 1971 c.462 s.16; 1975 c.157 s.2; 1975 c.361 s.4]

199.507 Effective date of transfer of territory; objections; election. (1) If the boundary commission by its final order approves a transfer of territory, the change shall take effect at the time specified in the final order, but the effective date shall not be less than 45 days, nor more than one year, after the date the commission adopts the final order approving the change. If no effective date is specified in the final order, the order shall take effect 45 days after the commission adopts the final order approving the change. However, the change shall not take effect unless it is also approved by the qualified voters if within 45 days after the date of the adoption of the order:

(a) Written objections to the change signed by not less than 20 percent of the qualified voters in the affected territory are filed with the commission; or

(b) A resolution objecting to the change adopted by the district board or city council of any affected city or district is filed with the commission.

(2) If an objection is filed by the board of a district or city council of a city which under the final order would lose territory, it shall call and hold an election within its boundaries on whether the territory designated for transfer should be withdrawn from the district or city.

(3) If an objection is filed by the board of a district or city council of a city which under the final order would acquire the territory, it shall call and hold an election within its boundaries on whether the territory designated for transfer should be annexed to the district or city.

(4) If objections are filed by the qualified voters, the commission shall certify the fact of the objections to the county board of the county where the territory is located whereupon the board shall call an election within the boundaries of the territory proposed for transfer on whether the territory should be transferred.

(5) An election required by this section shall be held, on a date that may be fixed by the commission, within 120 days after the expiration of the time allowed for filing objections under subsection (1) of this section and shall be conducted in accordance with the principal Act. The results of the election shall be certified to the commission. If a majority of those voting on a proposition in each and all elections approve the change approved by the commission, the commission thereupon shall proclaim the results of the election. Upon the adoption of the proclamation, the change shall take effect.

[1975 c.361 s.61]

(Or. Rev. Stat. §§199.410 et seq).

PROPOSED BILL AUTHORIZING TRANSFER OF DEVELOPMENT RIGHTS IN NEW YORK

The People of the State of New York, represented in Senate and Assembly, do enact as follows:

Section 1. Legislative declaration. It is the intent of the legislature in enacting this chapter to provide the means whereby any city, town or village may provide for transfer of development rights within a land use management program in order to protect natural, scenic, recreational and agricultural qualities of open lands including critical resource areas and enhance sites and areas of special character or special historical, cultural or aesthetic interest or value.

The legislature finds that the growth and spread of urban development is encroaching upon, or eliminating open and distinctive areas and spaces of varied size and character, including many having significant agricultural, ecological, scenic, historical or aesthetic values, which areas and spaces if preserved and maintained in their present state would constitute important physical, social, aesthetic or economic assets to existing or impending urban and metropolitan development.

The legislature hereby declares that the public welfare will be furthered by empowering any city, town or village to provide for transfer of development rights as part of a local land management program provided that transfer of development rights not be utilized to increase the overall maximum permissible density in a jurisdiction providing for such transfer.

§2. The general municipal law is hereby amended by adding thereto a new article, to be article twelve-G, to read as follows:

Article 12–G
Transfer of Development Rights

Section 239-z. Transfer of Development Rights;
Conditions; Procedures

§239-z. Transfer of development rights; conditions; procedures. Notwithstanding any other provision of law, the legislative body of any city, town or village is hereby empowered by resolution to provide in its zoning ordinance for transfer of development rights subject to the conditions hereinafter set forth. The purpose of providing for transfer of development rights may be to protect the natural, scenic or agricultural qualities of open lands including critical resource areas, to enhance sites and areas of special character or special historical, cultural or aesthetic interest or value and to enable and encourage flexibility of design and careful management of land in recognition of land as a basic and valuable natural resource. The conditions hereinabove referred to are as follows:

a. That transfer of development rights be authorized only

(i) where the transfer is from one lot to another within the same district provided the transfer does not result in exceeding the overall maximum permissible density for the district, and/or

(ii) where special districts are designated from which and to which transfer of development rights is authorized. The district from which transfer of development rights may be authorized shall include natural, scenic, recreational or agricultural qualities of open land or possess special character or sites of special historical, cultural or aesthetic values sought to be protected. The district to which transfer of development rights may be authorized shall be a district which the local governmental body has found after evaluating the effects of increased development that there exists adequate public facilities including adequate transportation, water supply, waste disposal and fire protection, there will be no environmentally damaging consequences and such increased development is compatible with the development otherwise permitted and will not significantly interfere with the enjoyment of other land in the vicinity.

b. That the procedure for transfer of development rights be administered by the planning board or commission and that such transfer be permitted only upon application for use of this procedure by a land owner to the planning board or commission which shall review the application in light of the provisions of the transfer of development rights ordinance and shall conduct a public hearing held on notice published at least twice in the official newspaper of the locality not more than twenty days and again not less than ten days prior to such hearing before granting or denying the application. A planning board or commission granting an application must specifically find the transfer furthers the purposes of the ordinance and meets all conditions of the ordinance. The local legislative body may provide that such determinations be subject to permissive referendum or review by the legislative body.

A legislative body of a city, town or village modifying its zoning ordinance to provide for transfer of development rights pursuant to this section shall follow the procedure for adopting and amending its zoning ordinance provided under its zoning enabling law in the general city, town or village laws as the case may be.

§3. This act shall take effect immediately.

(N.Y. Assembly Bill No. 8928, July 11, 1975).

BUCKINGHAM TOWNSHIP, PENNSYLVANIA, ZONING ORDINANCE WITH TRANSFER OF DEVELOPMENT RIGHTS PROVISIONS

Section 216   Development Rights
One of a series of rights inherent in fee simple ownership of land; others include air rights or mineral rights, which may be separated from the land.

(a) *Certificates of Development Rights:* A certificate entitling the owner to build a dwelling unit. The certificate is usable only as indicated in Article VI.

(b) *Transfer of Development Rights (TDR):* A procedure set forth in Article VI of this Ordinance, permitting owners of Agricultural land to be compensated for the restrictions imposed upon their land by selling Certificates of Development Rights.

Section 304 Statements of Purpose and Intent
for the Districts

A. Agricultural Districts: Districts whose purpose is the maintenance of the agricultural industry and preservation of farm land.

1. Agricultural (AG)—The Agricultural District is intended to preserve agriculture as the primary use in land outside the development district. The district permits limited residential uses as well as agricultural uses. The standards and densities are intended to provide a positive incentive for the preservation of large amounts of open space.

2. Agricultural Preservation District (AP)—The purpose of this district is to regulate permitted agricultural uses in areas permanently preserved for agricultural use under the provisions of Article VI. The zone is a "floating zone" which the Supervisors shall create only in the agricultural district upon the initiative of a landowner who wishes to transfer the development potential of his land to another site by selling his development rights. This district provides for the continuation of agriculture as a permanent use in the township.

B. Development Districts: The purpose of these districts is to provide for the orderly growth and development of residential, commercial, industrial and institutional uses to the year 1990. The area in total constitutes the development district defined in the comprehensive plan.

Section 502 Table of Performance Standards

The standards in this table shall apply to each district. All standards must be met. These standards may be less strict than other performance standards in this Article; the strictest standard shall always govern. The Minimum Site Area column refers to the number of acres which a developer must own to be able to qualify for this use. The minimum lot area column, on the other hand, refers to the minimum lot size for single-family, single-family cluster, or non-residential uses.

[table reprinted on pp. 312–313.]

District	Maximum Densities[b]		Maximum Densities[b]	
	DUs/AC Gross	wo/DR[b] Net	DUs/AC Gross	w/DR[b] Net
Agricultural				
Single-family	0.50	0.50	—	—
Single-family Cluster	0.30	3.0	—	—
Performance Subdivision	0.50	5.0	—	—
Agriculture	—	—	—	—
Other	—	—	—	—
Agricultural Preservation[d]				
Single-family	0.04	0.04	—	—
Performance Subdivision	0.04	2.0	—	—
Agriculture	—	—	—	—
Other	—	—	—	—
Country Residential				
Single-family	0.80	0.87	1.8	1.80
Single-family Cluster	0.80	1.33	1.9	3.16
Performance Subdivision	0.80	1.33	4.9	8.16
Other	—	—	—	—
Village Residential				
Single-family	0.80	0.87	1.8	1.80
Single-family Cluster	0.80	1.14	1.9	3.68
Performance Subdivision	2.5	3.57	5.5	7.86
Other	—	—	—	—
Village Center				
Single-family	2.3	2.30	3.2	3.20
Performance Subdivision	3.0	4.29	6.0	8.57
Other	—	—	—	—
Neighborhood Conservation				
Single-family	0.85	0.85	—	—
Other	—	—	—	—
Planned Industrial				
All Uses	—	—	—	—
Planned Commercial				
All Uses	—	—	—	—
Institutional				
All Uses	—	—	—	—

[a]DENSITY—WARNING   Gross density is included for the layman's convenience only. The net density is controlling, see Section 501. The capacity of any site, and number of development certificates is based on *Net Density* and differs from site to site, pursuant to the calculations in Section 501.

[b]DR, Development Rights, see Article VI.

Minimum Open Space Ratio	Maximum Impervious Surface Ratio	Minimum Site Area	Minimum Lot Size	Maximum Number of DUs
—	0.07	2 Ac	1 Ac	5
0.90	0.06	10 Ac	10,000	—
0.90	0.20	20 Ac	—	—
—	0.05	5 Ac	5 Ac	—
—	0.15	20 Ac	20 Ac	—
—	0.03	25 Ac	25 Ac	—
0.98	0.03	100 Ac	—	—
—	0.05	5 Ac	5 Ac	—
0.95	0.05	25 Ac	—	—
—^{c}	0.15	20,000	20,000	10
0.40	0.15	5 Ac	10,000	—
0.40	0.30	5 Ac	—	—
—	0.35	2 Ac	2 Ac	—
—	0.15	20,000	20,000	10
0.30	0.20	3 Ac	10,000	—
0.30	0.35	5 Ac	—	—
—	0.35	2 Ac	2 Ac	—
—	0.26	10,000	10,000	10
0.30	0.35	5 Ac	—	—
—	0.80	1 Ac	1 Ac	—
—^{c}	0.12	1 Ac	1 Ac	—
—^{c}	0.12	2 Ac	2 Ac	—
—^{c}	0.55^e	5 Ac	1 Ac	—
—^{c}	0.80	20,000	20,000	—
—^{c}	0.80	20,000	20,000	—

[c]No minimum required open space. See Section 501 for net buildable site area calculation.

[d]This district is created by transfer of development rights pursuant to Article VI.

[e]Impervious surface ratio may be increased to a maximum of .70 when development certificates are utilized. See Section 603(c).

Article VI Transfer of Development Rights

Section 600 Purpose

The purpose of this article is to permanently protect a vital natural resource: farmlands and agricultural soils. Recognizing that this cannot be accomplished using traditional large lot zoning techniques, without creating inequities in the valuation of land, Transfer of Development Rights (TDR) is authorized. TDR is a technique which recognizes the two conflicting views of the land which pose a dilemma to planning. The first view classifies land as a commodity, owned by an individual whose rights cannot be too severely limited by the township's police power. The second view is that of the public—that land is a resource, limited in quantity, some of which has unique characteristics which identify its highest and best use. Both views have merit. Rather than see how far one or the other might be extended, TDR recognizes both by providing an alternative method of realizing the land's development potential: the sale of development certificates rather than lots. The creation of a permanent agricultural district is accomplished pursuant to this article when a landowner voluntarily chooses to sell the certificates issued him pursuant to this article.

Section 601 Certificates of Development Rights

The Township of Buckingham, by the adoption of this Ordinance, creates Certificates of Development Rights.

Section 602 Distribution and Sale of Development Rights

Development Rights shall be held by the Township. These rights are available to all landowners (who are not governmental agencies) owning a tax parcel of ten (10) or more acres in the Agricultural (AG) District, which at the time of the adoption of this Ordinance is unimproved or in agricultural or single-family residential use. Each landowner owning a tax parcel of ten (10) or more acres shall be given notice by registered mail of the number of certificates available to him within six (6) months of the adoption of this Ordinance. The certificates shall be issued by the Township only when a landowner in the Agricultural District actually requests that his development certificates be transferred to a person, corporation, partnership, or other legal entity having an interest in a specific parcel of land in a Development District (see Section 304), who will immediately attach said certificates to said specific parcel of land in a Development District which will run with the land in perpetuity.

The number of certificates available to the aforementioned landowners is established by multiplying the number of acres shown on the tax record for the property by 1.0, subject to the following limitations:

(a) The amount of Development Certificates available to the landowner shall be reduced by one for every residential structure situated on the property at the time of the adoption of this Ordinance.

(b) Development Certificates are not available for any parcel of ground or portion thereof subject to an easement or restrictive covenant prohibiting or preventing development.

The number of certificates available represents an average of the number of dwelling units which could actually be built under the zoning in effect prior to the adoption of this Ordinance and shall be adequate compensation for the loss of the rights of development, in accordance with Section 605, theretofore permitted by this Ordinance.

The development certificates may be issued and sold to a person, corporation, partnership, or other legal entity in Buckingham Township so designated by the landowner pursuant to the following:

(c) The submission to the Township Zoning Officer of an agreement of sale for said certificates, duly executed by the parties, which shall be recorded with the Bucks County Recorder of Deeds.

(d) If the agreement of sale entails the issuance of the last remaining certificates available for the tax parcel, the following provisions shall apply:

(1) The landowner selling said development rights shall file with the Recorder of Deeds, a restrictive covenant running with the land, as set forth herein, effecting the parcel of land of said landowner from which the Development Rights have been transferred. The restrictive covenant shall be as follows:

"Under and Subject, nevertheless, that said premises described herein shall not be used, at any time, for those uses designated as not permitted ("N") in the Agricultural Preservation District as set forth in Article IV of the Buckingham Township Zoning Ordinance adopted on March 6, 1975; and further, construction and/or placement of buildings or facilities on said premises shall only be permitted if it is in accordance with the standards established in Section 502 relating to the Agricultural Preservation District of the Buckingham Zoning Ordinance adopted March 6, 1975; and not inconsistent with the permitted uses within the Agricultural Preservation District as provided for in said Ordinance adopted on March 6, 1975, provided, however, additional uses may be permitted and/or alternate standards established for said premises provided said uses and/or standards are authorized by an amendment to the Township Zoning Ordinance which is enacted following:

(i) the adoption by the Township Supervisors of a legally and constitutionally valid revision to the Township's Comprehensive Plan consistent with the provisions of Article I, §27 of the Commonwealth of Pennsylvania Constitution, and

(ii) said revision to the Comprehensive Plan is approved by a majority of the registered voters of the Township in a duly authorized and held referendum.

And the grantee, for himself, his heirs and assigns, by the acceptance of this indenture, agrees with the grantor, his heirs and assigns, that said restrictions and conditions shall be a covenant running with the land, and that in any deed of conveyance of said premises or any part thereof to any person or persons, said restrictions and conditions, when modified pursuant to the provisions contained herein, shall be incorporated by reference to this indenture and the record hereof or as fully as the same are contained herein."

(2) The parcel shall be designated Agricultural Preservation ("AP") and be subject to the limitations and restrictions imposed by said designation in this Zoning Ordinance as well as the limitations and restrictions imposed on said land by virtue of any restrictive covenants.

If any portion of a tax parcel is to be sold, transferred, or developed, the landowner shall comply with the requirements of Section 605.

Section 603   Marketability of Certificates
of Development Rights

The creation of a market for Certificates of Development Rights is essential if the transfer of such certificates is to be a real alternative to development. Such a market is provided by the following provisions:

(a) Within the Country Residential (CR) district, Village Residential (VR) district, Village Center (VC) district and Planned Industrial (PI) district, the net density permitted on a property may be increased as specified in Section 502.

(b) Development at the higher density specified in Section 502 shall be permitted, provided all other provisions of this Ordinance and the subdivision regulations are followed; and where the applicant owns certificates of development rights in an amount equal in number to the increase in dwelling units over that permitted without certificates.

(c) Within the Planned Industrial (PI) district the floor area ratio or impervious surface ratios may be increased through the purchase of development certificates. Because of the variety of uses permitted in this district, the increase in floor area will be used to determine the number of certificates that must be purchased. Since either floor or impervious surface may be the limiting factor, the developer shall show floor area with and without the bonus. An addition of floor area shall require .35 certificates per 1000 square feet.

(d) Development proposals consistent with the residential density requirements of Section 502 shall be approved without the purchase of development rights. Nothing in this Ordinance, other than the incentive to increase the density on one's property, shall require a landowner to purchase development certificates.

Section 604   Taxation

Certificates of development rights, when attached to a specific parcel of land located in the Township, shall be considered as real property, and may be transferred only to landowners within Buckingham Township. Upon being issued, pursuant to Section 602, certificates shall be recorded in the Bucks County Recorder of Deeds Office and notification must be given to the Bucks County Board of Assessors.

Section 605 Transfer of Property; Sale of Property; Development of Property

Prior to the subdivision, or development of a property, or transfer or sale of any portion thereof, eligible for development certificates, wherein the landowner has previously sold or cancelled any of the development certificates available to said property, said landowner must first designate, with an appropriate legal description, that portion of the property to be designated as AP and that portion to be designated as AG in accordance with the number of development certificates then available to the property. The landowner in determining which portion thereof shall be designated AP shall:

(a) Ascertain the area of the property to be designated AP. Said area shall be equal to the number of development certificates attached to said property, which were previously sold or cancelled; and

(b) Select that portion of the property, with the requisite number of acres to be designated as AP, in accordance with the following criteria:

　　(1) Shall be primarily composed of Class I, II and III agricultural soils, if such soils are present;

　　(2) Shall not be landlocked; and

　　(3) Shall be contiguous and be of a general configuration approved by the Planning Commission.

Upon the Township's approval of said designation by the landowner, the landowner shall subject said portion of the parcel to a restrictive covenant as set forth in Section 602(d) of this Ordinance.

Section 606 Appeal on Marketability

The Township, recognizing that marketability is essential to the fairness of the system of development rights transfer, will institute special appeal procedures for those whose development rights cannot be marketed under this system at fair market value. The Township believes that it has created a system in which sales between willing buyers and willing sellers will result in owners of development rights being fairly compensated. In order to protect landowners and to give the Township an opportunity to study in detail the impact and effectiveness of Transfer of Development Rights, the following appeal procedure is provided:

(a) A landowner who claims that his Development Rights are unmarketable, may appeal to the Supervisors. The landowner shall be required to submit evidence regarding asking price, length of sale period, and offers from buyers and their names to the Planning Commission.

(b) The Township Planning Commission shall introduce evidence of other land or certificate sales, the number of properties or certificates for sale, an appraisal of the certificates' value by a realtor, and an evaluation of the market conditions compared to the conventional land market for one-acre lots in adjoining municipalities.

(c) The Planning Commission shall hear all evidence and submit its recommendations to the Supervisors for action.

(d) The Supervisors, pursuant to a public hearing, upon receiving written recommendations from the Planning Commission, shall evaluate the marketability of the certificates. If it finds that the certificates are unmarketable, then the Supervisors shall:

(1) Purchase the certificates and/or the entirety at fair market value; or

(2) Make an exception for the individual property; or

(3) If the evidence clearly indicates a need, change the allocation of development certificates, or size of development area, or the bonus achieved by using the development certificates, or some combination thereof to make certificates marketable.

Section 607   Biennial Review

With any new concept being applied for the first time, it is to be expected that problems can arise. The Township believes that a biennial review is necessary to insure the workability of Transfer of Development Rights. The Planning Commission shall conduct a biennial review at an advertised public meeting. Such review shall consider: (a) Is the system functioning? (b) Is the concept of fair compensation being realized under the system; (c) Is the marketability still present as a result of developments in the past year? (d) Is the tax situation working against the goals of development rights? (e) Comments from the general public. Upon completion of said review, the Planning Commission shall submit recommendations to the Supervisors for action to correct any problem. The first review under this section shall be within one year of effective date of this Ordinance.

Section 608   Public Ownership
of Development Certificates

The Township may raise funds for the acquisition of development certificates or may accept certificates through conditional approval or gift. The Township may cancel such certificates or may sell them. Township sales shall meet the following conditions:

(a) The Township shall hold a public hearing.

(b) Evidence must show that there are no certificates available at fair market value, and the only way the developer has to purchase certificates at fair market value is from the Township.

(c) Two appraisals shall be required to establish fair market value.

(d) The purchaser shall submit evidence on his inability over a period of time to find a willing seller.

(e) All funds gained through resale of development rights shall be used for agricultural preservation.

Section 609   Cancellation of Development Certificates

The Township shall cancel development certificates:

(a) When a landowner requests cancellation;

(b) When Zoning Permit(s) is (are) issued in conjunction with development pursuant to the requirements of the AG District, wherein should the landowner realize the maximum allowable development on the site's net buildable site area, all development certificates shall be cancelled. Where the net buildable site area is partially developed, a proportionate amount of development certificates shall be cancelled.

(c) When a Zoning Permit is issued for construction of an A8 Farm Unit as described in Section 405, one development certificate shall be cancelled for each such use issued a Zoning Permit.

The landowner shall be given written notice of the balance of development certificates available to him whenever a full or partial cancellation is effected.

When a request for cancellation is made for any given property, the Township shall rezone said property to AP.

Buckingham Township, Pennsylvania, Zoning Ordinance, *as amended* March 18, 1976.

SUGGESTED LOCAL RESOLUTION REQUIRING ENERGY IMPACT STATEMENTS FOR NEW DEVELOPMENTS

Whereas, development within [name locality] has accelerated to such a degree as to generate concern as to its effects upon energy supply and demand, and

Whereas, it is necessary that the [local governing body] be provided with such sufficient information by developers and other applicants for subdivision or development approvals, permits, licenses, and certificates as to show the effect of such development on energy supply and demand, and

Whereas, [name of locality] is charged with the protection of the general health, safety, morals and welfare of the community,

Now, therefore, be it resolved, that as a prerequisite to all applications for subdivision or development approvals, permits, licenses or certificates before [appropriate governing or administrative body,] there shall be supplied to these [appropriate governing or administrative body] prior to the hearing date, [as part of the Environmental Impact Statement presently required by (§ ＿＿ of the City Code)], an "Energy Impact Statement," which shall contain information concerning the measurable effect of the intended development upon energy supply and demand in [name of locality] and mitigation measures taken to reduce energy demand by the intended development, and it is further

Resolved, that such a questionnaire shall be prepared by [appropriate agency] and submitted to the applicant for completion, at least two (2) weeks before the scheduled hearing date, and it is further

Resolved, that such, "Energy Impact Statement" shall require information in such depth, breadth and detail as to enable the [appropriate agency or governing body conducting hearings] to make a determination upon the application before it, and it is further

Resolved, that the responsibility for the completion and inclusion of all pertinent and relevant material shall be on the applicant and the application for subdivision or development approvals, permits, licenses, or certificates shall not be granted until the Energy Impact Statement has been completed by the applicant and reviewed by the [appropriate agency or governing body].

[Note that, alternatively, the resolution may provide for the local planning staff to prepare the energy impact statement based on information supplied by the applicant.]

(Adapted from a Penfield, New York, Resolution
requiring environmental impact statements)

SUGGESTED LOCAL ORDINANCE REQUIRING ENERGY IMPACT STATEMENTS FOR MAJOR DEVELOPMENTS

Construction of any major development project shall not be commenced until sixty (60) days subsequent to the filing of the energy impact statement. Within said 60 day period the [local governing body] shall hold a public hearing on the energy impact statement. Notice of the hearing shall be published in a newspaper of general circulation within the area no less than one week prior to the date of the hearing. The building inspector shall not issue any building permit or certificate of occupancy or compliance for any structure within a major development project except upon a finding by the [local governing body] that the requirements of this ordinance have been met. Nor shall any approval, permit, license, certificate, or filing provided for by any zoning ordinance, subdivision control ordinance, or other land use control be granted or allowed by the [local governing body], the building inspector, or any other public official or body except upon a finding by the [local governing body] that the requirements of this ordinance have been met.

(Adapted from an environmental impact
statement ordinance for Holden Beach,
North Carolina.)

Selected References

American Law Institute. *A Model Land Development Code*. Philadelphia, 1975.

Balshone, Bruce L. et al. *Bicycle Transit, Its Planning and Design*. New York: Praeger Publishers, 1975.

Bangs, Frank S. and Bagney, Conrad, eds. "Transferable Development Rights." Planning Advisory Service Report No. 304. Chicago: American Society of Planning Officials, 1975.

Bennett, Margaret M. "Transfer of Development Rights: Promising But Unproven New Approach to Land Use Regulation." Philadelphia: Pennsylvania Environmental Council, Inc., 1976.

Bosselman, Fred P. et al. *The Permit Explosion: Coordination of the Proliferation*. Washington, D.C.: The Urban Land Institute, 1976.

Bosselman, Fred P. et al. *The Taking Issue*. Prepared for the U.S. Council on Environmental Quality. Washington, D.C.: U.S. Government Printing Office, 1973.

Brooks, Mary. "Bonus Provisions in Central City Areas." Planning Advisory Service Report No. 257. Chicago: American Society of Planning Officials, 1970.

Burchell, Robert W. and Listokin, David, eds. *Future Land Use/Energy, Environmental, and Legal Constraints*. New Brunswick, New Jersey: Rutgers University Press, 1975.

Carroll, T. Owen et al. *Land Use and Energy Utilization, Interim Report*. Washington, D.C.: Office of Conservation and Environment of the Federal Energy Administration, 1975.

Christensen, Kathleen. *Social Impacts of Land Development*. Washington, D.C.: The Urban Institute, 1976.

Citizens' Advisory Committee on Environmental Quality. *Citizen Action Guide to Energy Conservation*. Washington, D.C.: U.S. Government Printing Office, 1973.

The Conservation Foundation. *Energy Conservation Training Institute*. Washington, D.C., n.d.

Council of State Governments. *State Growth Management.* Prepared for the Office of Community Planning and Development, U.S. Department of Housing and Urban Development. Washington, D.C.: U.S. Government Printing Office, 1976.

Darmstadter, Joel. *Conserving Energy/Prospects and Opportunities in the New York Region.* Baltimore: Johns Hopkins University Press, 1975.

Edwards, Jerry L. and Schofer, Joseph L. *Relationships Between Transportation Energy Consumption and Urban Structure: Results of Simulation Studies.* Evanston, Illinois: Northwestern University, 1975.

Ford Foundation, Energy Policy Project. *A Time to Choose: America's Energy Future.* Cambridge, Massachusetts: Ballinger Publishing Company, 1974.

Fraker, Harrison and Schorske, Elizabeth. "Energy Husbandry in Housing: An Analysis of the Development Process in a Residential Community." Center for Environmental Studies Report No. 5. Princeton, New Jersey: Princeton University, 1973.

Freilich, Robert H. and Ragsdale, John W., Jr. Timing and Sequential Controls—The Essential Basis for Effective Regional Planning: An Analysis of the New Directions for Land Use Control in the Minneapolis—St. Paul Metropolitan Region. 58 *Minn. L. Rev.* 1009 (1974).

Gerrard, Michael. "Disclosure of Hidden Energy Demands: A New Challenge for NEPA." *Environmental Affairs* 4, no. 4 (1975): 665–66.

Gil, Efraim. "Energy-Efficient Planning: An Annotated Bibliography." Planning Advisory Service Report No. 316, Chicago: American Society of Planning Officials. 1976.

Gleeson, Michael E. et al. "Urban Growth Management Systems: An Evaluation of Policy-Related Research." Planning Advisory Service Report Nos. 309, 310. Chicago: American Society of Planning Officials, 1975.

Goldberg, Philip. "Planning With Energy." Philadelphia: Rahenkamp, Sachs, Wells & Associates, Inc., 1975.

Hammond, Jonathan et al. "A Strategy for Energy Conservation: Proposed Energy Conservation and Solar Utilization Ordinance for the City of Davis, California. Davis, California, 1974.

Hayes, Denis. *Energy: The Case for Conservation.* Worldwatch Paper 4. Washington, D.C.: Worldwatch Institute, January 1976.

Hittman Associates. *Residential Energy Consumption/Single-Family Housing.* Washington, D.C.: U.S. Government Printing Office, 1973.

———. *Residential Energy Consumption/Multi-Family Housing, Final Report.* Washington, D.C.: U.S. Government Printing Office, 1974.

Keyes, Dale L. *Land Development and the Natural Environment: Estimating Impacts.* Washington, D.C.: The Urban Institute, 1976.

———. "Metropolitan Development and Air Quality." Land Use Center Working Paper No. 5049–16. Washington, D.C.: The Urban Institute, 1976.

Keyes, Dale L. and Peterson, George E. "Metropolitan Development and Energy Consumption." Land Use Center Working Paper. Washington, D.C.: The Urban Institute, 1976.

Knowles, Ralph L. *Energy and Form: An Ecological Approach to Urban Growth.* Cambridge, Massachusetts: MIT Press, 1974.

Living Systems. "Planning for Energy Conservation, Draft Report." Prepared for the City of Davis, California, pursuant to HUD project grant No. B−75−51−06−001. Winters, California, 1976.

Marcus, Norman and Groves, Marilyn W., eds. *The New Zoning: Legal, Administrative, and Economic Concepts and Techniques.* New York: Praeger Publishers, 1970.

Meshenberg, Michael J. "The Administration of Flexible Zoning Techniques." Planning Advisory Service Report No. 318. Chicago: American Society of Planning Officials, 1976.

Mosena, David et al. "Institutional Factors Influencing the Acceptance of Community Energy Systems and Energy-Efficient Community Design: Public Planning, Administration, and Regulation." Prepared for Energy and Environmental Systems Division of Argonne National Laboratory, Contract No. 31−109−38−3078. Chicago: American Society of Planning Officials, 1976.

Muller, Thomas. *Fiscal Impacts of Land Development.* Washington, D.C.: The Urban Institute, 1975.

_____. *Economic Impacts of Land Development: Employment, Housing, and Property Values.* Washington, D.C.: The Urban Institute, 1976.

Nationwide Personal Transportation Study. "Household Travel in the United States." Report no. 7. Washington, D.C.: U.S. Department of Transportation, Federal Highway Administration, 1972.

_____. "Home-to-Work Trips and Travel." Report no. 8. Washington, D.C.: U.S. Department of Transportation, Federal Highway Administration, 1973.

_____. "Mode of Transportation and Personal Characteristics of Tripmakers." Report no. 9. Washington, D.C.: U.S. Department of Transportation, Federal Highway Administration, 1973.

_____. "Purposes of Automobile Trips and Travel." Report no. 10. Washington, D.C.: U.S. Department of Transportation, Federal Highway Administration, 1974.

Olgyay, Victor. *Design With Climate: Bioclimatic Approach to Architectural Regionalism.* Princeton, New Jersey: Princeton University Press, 1963.

Pauker, Guy J. *Can Land Use Management Reduce Energy Consumption for Transportation?* Santa Monica, California: The Rand Corporation, 1974.

Priest, W. Curtiss et al. "An Overview and Critical Evaluation of the Relationship Between Land Use and Energy Conservation." Vol. I, Main Report. Cambridge, Massachusetts: Technology + Economics, Inc., March 2, 1976.

Real Estate Research Corporation. *The Costs of Sprawl, Detailed Cost Analysis* and *Literature Review and Bibliography.* Washington, D.C.: U.S. Government Printing Office, 1974.

Regional Plan Association, Inc. *Regional Energy Consumption.* New York: 1974.

Roberts, James S. *Energy, Land Use, and Growth Policy: Implications for Metropolitan Washington.* Washington, D.C.: Metropolitan Washington Council of Governments, 1975.

Rose, Jerome G., ed. *Transfer of Development Rights.* New Brunswick, New Jersey: Center for Urban Policy Research, Rutgers University, 1975.

Scott, Randall W., ed. *Management and Control of Growth, Vol. I—III.* Washington, D.C.: The Urban Land Institute, 1975.

Skidmore, Owings & Merrill, Study Group, and Portland Bureau of Planning, Policy Section. "City Working Paper on Land Use and Energy." Comprehensive Plan Working Paper No. 13. Portland, Oregon, Fall 1976.

So, Frank S.; David R. Mosena; and Frank Bangs. "Planned Unit Development Ordinances." Planning Advisory Service Report No. 291. Chicago: American Society of Planning Officials, 1973.

State Energy Office. *Data Collection and Policy Analysis Section, A Planner's Handbook on Energy (With Emphasis on Residential Uses).* Tallahassee, Florida: State of Florida, Department of Administration, 1975.

Tabors, Richard D. et al. *Land Use and the Pipe.* Lexington, Massachusetts: D.C. Heath and Co., 1976.

Toner, William. "Planning for Home Occupations." Planning Advisory Service Report No. 316. Chicago: American Society of Planning Officials, 1976.

Urban Systems Research & Engineering, Inc. *The Growth Shapers/The Land Use Impacts of Infrastructure Investments.* Prepared for the U.S. Council on Environmental Quality. Washington, D.C.: U.S. Government Printing Office, 1976.

Williams, Norman, Jr. *American Land Planning Law.* Vol. 1—5. Chicago: Callaghan & Co., 1975.

Williams, Robert H., ed. *The Energy Conservation Papers.* Cambridge, Massachusetts: Ballinger Publishing Company, 1975.

Witherspoon, Robert E. et al. *Mixed-Use Developments: New Ways of Land Use.* Washington, D.C.: Urban Land Institute. 1976.

Index

About the Author

Corbin Crews Harwood, project attorney at the Environmental Law Institute, is a graduate of Smith College and Columbia Law School. After practicing law with a private firm in Washington, D.C., she joined ELI in 1975 as a member of the Energy Conservation Project. In addition to her energy work, Ms. Harwood is assisting in the preparation of a wetlands protection guidebook.

GLASSBORO STATE COLLEGE